A Vision *for* Change

Speeches and Writings of AD Patel, 1929-1969

A Vision *for* Change

Speeches and Writings of AD Patel, 1929-1969

EDITED BY

BRIJ V LAL

ANU
THE AUSTRALIAN NATIONAL UNIVERSITY

E PRESS

ANU

E PRESS

Published by ANU E Press
The Australian National University
Canberra ACT 0200, Australia
Email: anuepress@anu.edu.au
This title is also available online at: http://epress.anu.edu.au/

National Library of Australia Cataloguing-in-Publication entry

Author: Lal, Brij V.

Title: A vision for change : speeches and writings of AD Patel, 1929-1969 / Brij V Lal.

ISBN: 9781921862328 (pbk.) 9781921862335 (ebook)

Subjects: Patel, A. D. (Ambalal Dahyabhai), 1905-1969.
            Fiji--Politics and government--20th century.
            Fiji--History.

Dewey Number: 320.099611

Cover design and layout by ANU E Press

Cover photograph by Robert Norton.

Printed by Griffin Press

Contents

Part II. Bitter Sweet: The Politics of the Fiji Sugar Industry, 1943-1969

Part III. Land and Livelihood

Part IV. Society and Culture

Acknowledgments

For their support and kindness over the years, I thank the family of AD Patel, in particular the late Mrs Leela Patel. The National Library of Australia helped me get access to Fiji newspapers and the Pacific Manuscripts Bureau provided additional assistance, thanks to Ewan Maidment and Kylie Moloney. The National Archives of Fiji has my deep gratitude for all the help they have given me over nearly thirty years. Bob Norton was, as always, generous in sharing his own research material and experience of working on Fiji since the 1960s. Kamal Iyer and Jagindar Singh have given unstinted support to my efforts to understand the complex dynamics of Indo-Fijian politics over the years. 'Bade Bhai' Harish Sharma read a draft of the manuscript, picked up typos and made many helpful suggestions, as did Jack Corbett of my own Department. Doug Munro and Robert Norton made many helpful suggestions for revising the Introduction. Maxine McArthur prepared the manuscript for publication with exemplary patience and care. Padma has been my indispensible Rock of Gibraltar for this project and for everything else I have done in my professional life. My Department of Pacific and Asian History has my gratitude for giving me the time and space to complete this work. I am eternally grateful to whatever quirk of fate which brought me to The Australian National University. For research and reflection, there is no other place in the world quite like it.

Brij V Lal
Canberra

Introduction

'Bliss was it in that dawn to be alive,' AD Patel quoted William Wordsworth's celebration of the French Revolution as he launched the 1966 election campaign at the Century Theatre in Suva, 'but to be young was very heaven.' He was unwell, an acute, insulin-dependent diabetic now also suffering from pneumonia. His mother's recent death in India would have added to his emotional woes. 'My voice has failed me today,' he told his anxious audience long concerned about his failing health. But he was undaunted. 'Mine is the fortune of being alive in this dawn. Mine is the misfortune that I won't be able to share the very heaven.' His premonition of impending mortality sadly proved accurate. Three years later, on 1 October 1969, he died of a massive heart attack at his home in Nadi, almost exactly a year before Fiji became independent from the United Kingdom after ninety-six years of colonial rule.

'AD was a fine man stubborn, sometimes too much so for comfort,' wrote QVL Weston on 24 October 1969, 'but it was through his stubbornness that he got his way, and I think when the tale is told by the historians, it will usually be accepted that his way was right.' Now the Chief Secretary of Nauru, he had been Commissioner Western based at Lautoka in the early 1960s, witnessing at first hand as the Government's chief civilian administrator in the sugar belt of Fiji, the first stirrings of political change as Fiji moved haphazardly towards internal self-government and eventually independence. 'Mixed societies such as Fiji contain a lot of inborn prejudices which get out of tune with the times,' he continued, 'and take a leader of the quality and convictions of AD to shift.' Forty years later, in 2009, business tycoon Mahendra Motibhai Patel wrote: 'The late AD Patel was a leader ahead of his time. His legacy and words of wisdom still resonate in the history of Fiji. His contributions in the Legislative Council are unmatched in content, delivery, eloquence and logic.' He was a breath of fresh air, Motibhai went on, changing metaphors, 'like a meteor shining brightly against the dark clouds of colonialism.' If Patel had lived another ten years instead of dying on the eve of independence in 1969, 'Fiji would have been a totally different place, but it was not to be.' What might have been had Patel lived on is a matter best left to conjecture, but the warm tribute was surprising. Motibhai was a key pillar of the Fiji establishment, a Commander of the British Empire no less, a luminary of the Alliance Party, and a close confidant of AD Patel's opponent, the Alliance Party leader and Prime Minister Ratu Sir Kamisese Mara.

This belated tribute to Patel's contribution to the public life of Fiji would not be news to a rapidly dwindling number in the passing generation who lived through those tumultuous years and shared his vision for a free, democratic and non-racial Fiji. But Patel is now among the forgotten figures of Fijian history, pilloried in officially authorized accounts for his unceasing commitment to the principles of democracy and racial equality. The official angle of vision even now excludes Patel, and other Indo-Fijian leaders, from their proper place among leaders who had a hand in shaping Fiji's destiny. This omission is not surprising. Patel championed independence for Fiji, but the fruits of his endeavours were to be enjoyed by those who opposed his vision (and indeed the advent of independence itself). Moreover, the edifice of postcolonial Fiji was built on the pillars of primordiality rather than the political ideology which Patel championed all his life. The passage of time has vindicated Patel's vision for Fiji. It is now widely recognized that the politics of racial representation and the exclusionary political culture it spawned has been the principal cause of Fiji's political difficulties, a powerful impediment to building a cohesive nation comprising different ethnicities under the overarching umbrella of a common citizenship. In a strange twist of irony, those celebrated as the founders of postcolonial Fiji, with its racially compartmentalized structure, also helped plant the seeds of its eventual destruction. The politics of race finally came to consume Fiji. Yesterday's heroes have become today's villains.

In 1997, I published my *A Vision for Change: AD Patel and the politics of Fiji*. The book was a study of Patel's public life and contributions to the political and economic life of Fiji from the late 1920s to the late 1960s. I had intended then to publish a companion volume of his speeches and writings, but the publishers baulked at the size of the project. For the record, the University of the South Pacific's Institute for Pacific Studies refused to have anything to do with the project at all because it was not written by, or was about, a Pacific Islander (according to their narrow ethnic definition). Twelve years later, fate intervened and I was drawn back to the unpublished volume. As post-coup Fiji struggled to find an appropriate constitutional framework for its multi-ethnic population, I re-visited Patel's political quest. It is a very strange irony indeed that Patel's vision for a non-racial political culture is now being championed by the military regime in power, although his name is expressly excised from the domain of public discourse. It must be discomforting for those presently in power to give authorship of their non-racial projects to a man long reviled as a villain, an enemy of the Fijian people, a would-be usurper of their rights and privileges. Patel's plea in the mid-1960s as the Member for Social Services for primary and secondary schools not be racially designated as 'Indian' or 'Fijian' is now being implemented two generations later. So, too, is his championship of a non-racial common electoral roll. His call since the mid-1950s for all Fiji citizens to be called 'Fijian,' and the native inhabitants to be designated as 'Taukei' is now materializing half a century later, though not in manner he, as a dedicated democrat, would have ever approved.

Ambalal Dahyabhai Patel was born on 13 March 1905 in a landed family in the Charotar tract of the Kheda District of Gujarat made famous by Mahatma Gandhi's satyagraha campaigns. As I wrote in my book, Patel 'came from a community that was politically powerful, socially prestigious, fiercely independent, land-based and in the forefront of Indian nationalist politics. His community and region had produced leaders who were attracting attention beyond the borders of their district.' After graduating with a Bachelor of Arts degree with honours, Patel was sent to London to prepare for the Indian Civil Service (ICS) examination. There was nothing more prestigious in the entire architecture of the British Empire than being an officer of the ICS. It was the preserve of the best and the brightest of Indian society.

But AD Patel changed his mind in London as he mixed with other nationalist-minded Indian students, many of whom would go on to nationally and internationally distinguished careers in the various professions. Patel opted for the law instead. London in the 1920s was the centre of activism for the rights of Indian communities settled in various parts of the world. Among the distinguished leaders of that cause was Henry S Polak, a Jewish émigré from South Africa who had worked with Mahatma Gandhi there. He was constantly on the look out for bright young men whom he could send to the far-flung colonies to work for the welfare of the Indian communities settled there. SB [Shiwabhai Bhailalbhai] Patel had been sent to Fiji on this mission in 1927. AD Patel arrived a year later, on 11 October 1928 and made Fiji his permanent home. The two men were not related, but worked cooperatively throughout. SB was a private person of reflective temperament whose preferred *modus operandi* in public life was quiet diplomacy as an intermediary.[1] AD, although no less reflective, was a charismatic leader who flourished on the public stage in the role of advocate.

AD, as he was popularly known to the public, was in the public eye from the moment he arrived in Fiji. He was elected president of the Lautoka branch of the Indian National Congress on 15 May 1929, different from an organization by the same name formed in Suva by Dr Hamilton Beattie a day earlier. Shortly afterwards, he was elected president of the Indian Association of Fiji, with the Arya Samaj leader Vishnu Deo as its secretary.[2] Patel was ineligible on residency grounds to context the 1929 elections but he was, as the papers here show, at the forefront of Indian political leadership in Fiji, leading deputations to

---

1   In the words of the late HM Lodhia, Nadi politician, SB Patel was 'versatile, well-read, rarely lost his head, and not emotional.' He arrived in Fiji on 12 December 1927.

2   Vishnu Deo OBE (1900–1968); member of Legislative Council, 1929–1959 when with failing eyesight he retired after a brief period in the Executive Council. He was a close colleague of AD Patel's but became a bitter foe later when disagreement developed between the two men about who was best suited to represent the Indian community in the Executive Council. For a brief biography, see Brij V Lal, 'Pandit Vishnu Deo: Indian Leader, Social Reformer,' in Stewart Firth and Daryl Tarte (eds.), *20th Century Fiji: People who shaped this nation* (Suva: University of the South Pacific, 2001), 73–74.

the Government House, drafting memoranda, and presiding at political rallies throughout the country. He finally entered the Legislative Council in 1944, after being narrowly defeated in the 1937 elections by local law clerk Chattur Chandrasenan Singh, and remained its member until 1950. After electoral defeats in 1950 and again in 1953, he retreated to his thriving law practice in Nadi. He was out of public office, but never out of the public eye. The colonial government appointed him to the Education Advisory Board and the Library Advisory Committee in 1957. He continued as the Legal Advisor to Sangam and as the General Manager of its schools. He regularly addressed social gatherings and conferences and wrote in the weekly he founded in 1949, *The Pacific Review*. Most of the short pieces included in this volume come from this period, but his once warmly-remembered speeches have now gone with the passing of the older generation.

I might add parenthetically that several old timers asked me if their favourite speeches were in the book. A retired primary school teacher recalled a speech from the 1950s, now lost forever, about 'The Five Most Abused Words in the English Language.' He could remember only three: Religion, Democracy and Communism. Jagindar Singh, a former president of the Federation Party, remembered Patel's response to those who said that as a passenger (rather than indentured) migrant, Patel had one foot in Fiji and one in India. This was a fairly common, if also misleading, characterization of the Gujaratis in Fiji. A very sick Patel replied prophetically to a hushed audience, 'The truth is, I have one foot in Fiji and one foot in the grave.' Harish Sharma, former NFP and Opposition Leader, recalled an emotional speech during the tense 1968 by-election. Contesting the nine Indian communal seats, Patel told a packed audience that they had to win only seven seats as two were already in the bag. People were puzzled. After a strategic pause as he surveyed the crowd, Patel remarked that one seat already won was MT Khan's. Khan had said in 1966, when he was a Federation candidate, '*Maut hi mujhe is party se juda karegi.*' Only death will make me part with the party. Since he had left the party and was contesting for the Alliance, he must be dead. The other was PK Bhindi. During the course of a Legislative Council debate, John Falvey had interjected that the only good Gujarati was a dead Gujarati. Patel said that since Bhindi was standing for the Alliance, he must be a 'good' Gujarati and, therefore, a dead one. The emotional impact of speeches like these is difficult to convey, especially in translation, but they are remembered across the decades by those who heard them. There was a time in Fiji when huge rallies were the order of the day as people travelled miles to listen to speeches by their leaders. Rallies were theatre as well as serious business. But they are now a thing of the past.

In 1960, Patel once again entered the political arena as the principal leader of the Federation of Cane Growers [formed in 1959] and a key figure in the strike of that year, appearing subsequently before the Eve Commission in 1961.[3] In 1963, he re-entered the Legislative Council and remained its dominant figure for the rest of the decade until his death in 1969. During this period, he was the founding president of the Federation Party[4] and the acknowledged leader of the Indo-Fijian community. The politics of the sugar industry and the gradual move towards internal self-government consumed him and this is reflected in his speeches and writings. This was also a time of great stress for him. Apart from diabetes, from which he suffered for decades, he also succumbed to pneumonia and heart problems which eventually claimed his life but which did not prevent him from pursuing his political vision with relentless energy. He was determined to remain in harness until the very end.

The entry of AD Patel (and in a different way that of SB Patel) changed the dynamics of the representational politics of the Indo-Fijian community. After the deportation of Manilal Maganlal Doctor in October 1920 for his leadership of a strike in Suva that year—he came to Fiji in 1912 at the request of Indo-Fijian leaders—the Indo-Fijian community lacked a single qualified barrister with the necessary linguistic and technical skills to engage the colonial officialdom with assurance and competence rather than simply as supplicants.[5] Patel performed that role with distinction. As the papers here show, he was a leader of deep, some might even say stubborn, conviction, consistent in his private utterances and public positions, and unafraid to take the path less trodden if he was convinced of its essential virtue. He was, as Chief Justice Sir Clifford Hammett once remarked, a born advocate of force and fluency, an instinctive leader of rare talent. His stubbornness, to which Quentin Weston alluded, provoked a sharp response from his political opponents, often leading them to adopt a position directly opposed to his own, no matter how persuasive the argument. But it also earned him their respect. Sir Robert Foster observed in his last dispatch before independence in 1970 that Patel was 'an intellectual, sincere and dedicated,' whose opponents 'respected some of his qualities no matter how bitterly they disliked his views.' Fair, non-racial political representation and equality of all voters irrespective of ethnicity was at the heart of Patel's political project, but what truly endeared him to his people was his pride in his own culture and philosophy in which he was deeply steeped: he was a fluent scholar of Sanskrit literature; and he tried to instill that pride among his people. All this meant much to a community emerging from the shadows of indenture, continuously

---

3 For the record, the key members of the Committee were Ajodhya Prasad, AD Patel, Bechu Prasad, K Ramaswamy Pillay, Pandit Ram Narayan, KS Reddy, Ram Newaj, SM Koya, Shiv Datta, Baijnath Prasad, Vijay R Singh, Girwar Prasad, and James Madhvan, the last three from Vanua Levu.

4 Formally launched in 1964 as a political party with a written constitution after a few years as the Citizens Federation under whose banner Patel had contested the 1963 elections.

5 See Hugh Tinker, 'Odd Man Out; The Loneliness of the Colonial Indian Politician, The Career of Manilal Maganlal Doctor,' *The Journal of Imperial and Commonwealth History* (October, 1973), and KL Gillion, *The Fiji Indians: Challenge to European Dominance, 1920-1946* (Canberra: ANU Press, 1977), 21–38.

reminded by the officialdom of its humble beginnings, and struggling to create a distinct cultural identity for itself in a colonial society prone to viewing them more often than not as alien beasts of burden, not much more.[6] The Indians of Fiji might be poor in body and material possession, Patel argued, but not poor in spirit or cultural heritage. He admired aspects of western culture,[7] but refused to accept that it was superior to his own.

Surprise is sometimes expressed about why a person of AD Patel's patrician background involved himself in soul-destroying politics of the remote and reactionary colonial society that Fiji was. He was, after all, a wealthy lawyer and landlord, and he was not born in Fiji. He was a Gujarati, while the majority of the Indians in Fiji were of North and South Indian stock, descendants of indentured labourers. This surprise reflects the ethnic preoccupations and stereotypes of our own times. AD Patel belonged to a generation of Indians who were deeply imbued with the Gandhian ideals of service to their fellow countrymen in far-flung corners of the world. Manilal Maganlal Doctor was among the early poliical activists, who fought the cause of social and political equality for the Indian community in Mauritius and in Fiji. Manilal Ambalal Desai was another, one of the leaders of the East African Indian National Congress in Nairobi in the 1920s.[8] They all believed deeply in the fundamental oneness of humanity and in the distinct possibility of a non-racial state founded on the principles of equality and justice. That vision, once so powerful and compelling, seems quaint and incongruous in our age of identity politics.

The volume is divided into four parts, each dealing with a subject or a theme to which AD Patel made a contribution. Part I deals with political and constitutional issues in Fiji from the late 1920s to the eve of Patel's death in 1969. The memoranda, speeches, letters, and reports of conference proceedings are organized chronologically and they are, for the most part, self-explanatory though I have provided additional information where the context demanded it. The fundamental points emphasized in them are the need for a common roll, a non-racial citizenship, political integration and towards the end, the importance of independence. In the last major political speech Patel made on radio on the eve of the 1968 by-elections, he urged immediate independence with a democratic constitution, Fiji to become a republic with an elected indigenous Fijian Head of State, the promotion of social equality and the provision of social security, security of tenure for farmers and the adoption of English, Fijian, Hindustani or Urdu as the common languages of Fiji.

---

6   The majority of Indians in Fiji were either Sanatanis (orthodox Hindus) or Arya Samaji. Patel was a believer in the philosophy of Swami Vivekananda, exemplified in Fiji by the Ramakrishna Mission.

7   Patel sent his children to private schools in England (Sherbourne School for Girls in Dorset and Millfield School) because he admired the discipline of English education.

8   See Mary N Varghese, 'The East Indian National Congress 1914-1939: A Study of Indian Political Activity in Kenya', PhD thesis, Dalhousie University, 1975.

Forty years later, there would seem to be nothing exceptionable in these demands. Indeed, they would be viewed as commonplace: but not in the 1960s. Fijians and Europeans opposed any suggestion of non-racial political integration. Race, Ratu Mara said repeatedly, was a fact of life, in fact the inexorable fact in the political governance of the country. He wanted the principle of Fijian paramountcy acknowledged and recognized, while Patel wanted equal partnership between the two major communities. The 1970 Independence Constitution, which was largely Ratu Mara's handiwork, enshrined race as the principal mode of political representation in parliament. Europeans refused to relinquish their uniquely privileged position in the body politic of Fiji, a stance in which they were supported by Fijian leaders for obvious political reasons: they always sided with the Fijians. Political independence, which Patel championed, was an anathema to these two groups, to be attained, if attained at all, on conditions determined by them, terms which in effect entrenched the established racially ordered political structure bequeathed by the departing British and with Fijian chiefs firmly in the saddle. No concerted effort was made to extend and strengthen the bonds of non-racial citizenship. Patel's speeches and writings provide glimpses of an alternative vision for Fiji whose essential correctness everyone acknowledged but whose feasibility many doubted in the hopelessly divided country that Fiji was.

Whether Fiji could have escaped the hurdles it encountered in its postcolonial journey had Patel's proposals been given a fair chance will remain one of those haunting questions of Fijian history. But what we do know, because it has been proved by subsequent events, is that the vision that the ruling Fijian and European elite championed, and had enshrined in Fiji's political system, eventually led to its demise. Race permeated the deepest sinews of the country's public institutions. Every issue of public policy, from appointments and promotions in the public service to the allocation of scholarships, affirmative action, and the distribution of development aid came to be viewed through the prism of race. Political activity was organized around race. And it came to be accepted by the ruling elite that the paraphernalia of elections notwithstanding, indigenous Fijians would always remain in power and Indo-Fijians in opposition or in government as a very junior partner. When that 'understanding' was overturned in the general elections of 1987, a military coup overthrew a democratically elected government to reinstate the established order of Fijian rule. Two decades later, in 2006, Commodore Frank Bainimarama led a coup which overthrew an indigenous Fijian-dominated government and, in the course of time, all the assumptions and understandings which underpinned the political order in Fiji, including the role of traditional institutions and practices in the body politic of the country.

Part II covers disputes in the sugar industry and AD Patel's role in them. These disputes had ramifications far beyond the industry itself, affecting political affiliations and race relations across the board. The early history of the Fiji sugar industry is covered comprehensively in Michael Moynagh's monograph, *Brown or White? A history of the Fiji sugar industry.*[9] Briefly, the (Australian) Colonial Sugar Refining Company came to Fiji in 1882 and remained there until 1973, three years after Fiji became independent. Initially, the CSR grew all its cane on its own plantations scattered around Viti Levu and Vanua Levu. By the early years of the 20th century, it began divesting itself of its plantations by selling or leasing them to its former officers. After the end of indenture in 1920, it started a new smallholder scheme of ten-acre farms which were leased to independent Indo-Fijian growers. Nonetheless, the Company maintained a tight grip on all aspects of sugar cane growing, from dictating the varieties of cane to be planted to determining the terms and conditions of milling. As AD Patel said, 'the relation between the Company and the growers was strongly reminiscent of the relationship of barons and serfs during the medieval ages. They had to take what was given to them and be thankful for the small mercies whether they liked it or not.' At the heart of Patel's project for the sugar industry was the demand for a full, properly regulated and enforceable partnership between the growers and the millers, conducted in a transparent manner and subject to independent scrutiny. The matter went beyond simple economics. For Patel, it touched on questions of fundamental human rights as far as the Indo-Fijian growers were concerned.

The first prolonged strike against the CSR took place in 1943.[10] It was led by AD Patel, with the assistance of Swami Rudrananda and SB Patel. He was also the leader of the 1960 strike. Patel's motives and modus operandi are subjects of continuing debate in Fiji. There are those who see him as a reckless opportunist fomenting discord in the sugar industry to gain political mileage for himself and economic benefit for the Gujarati business community (though precisely how the Gujarati merchants would benefit from the destruction of the colonial economy is not explained). Among those who made this claim was his arch foe Ajodhya Prasad, the leader of the rival Kisan Sangh.[11] Historian KL Gillion writes dismissively about the strike leaders such as AD Patel, saying that 'communalism, factionalism, pettiness and personal political ambition had triumphed over unity and statesmanship.'[12] This was also the official view, but the situation on the ground was much more complex. The contest between the Company and the Kisan was a contest between David and Goliath, and striking

---

9   *Canberra, ANU: Pacific Research Monograph No. 5, 1981.*

10   There was a strike in the sugar industry in 1921 but it was short-lived and not as disruptive.

11   Prasad published a two-volume history of the Kisan Sangh in Hindi, *Fiji Tapu Men Kisan Andolan, or, Kisan Sangh Ka Itihas* Rajkot, 1962).

12   KL Gillion, *The Fiji Indians: Challenge to European Dominance, 1920-1946* (Canberra: ANU Press, 1977), 172.

was never the first, reckless option. It was the protest of last resort. The papers included in this section contain many previously unpublished documents which throw a sharper beam of light on Patel's role and place in context some of the wilder allegations against him. The papers on the 1943 strike are drawn from a file on the dispute given to me by the late Swami Rudrananda. The sugar industry was once the backbone of Fiji's economy and the lifeblood of the Indo-Fijian community. The last decade (since the 1990s) has seen a sad decline in its fortune. It is now on its way out.[13]

Part III, 'Land and Livelihood,' deals with the perennial issues concerning land in Fiji. The issue was not so much the ownership of the land, which was settled soon after Cession in 1874, placing over eighty percent of all land in Fijian hands and which everyone accepted as a given fact of life. The fraught question was the terms and conditions upon which native land should be leased, principally to the landless agricultural community of Indo-Fijians. A variety of conflicting interests of the landowners on the one hand and tenants on the other had to be reconciled. The passage of the Landlord and Tenant Ordinance in the late 1960s was an important step in regularizing the terms and conditions of leasing the land and Patel supported the legislation with ambivalence because the solution, while welcome, was a short-term one. Some of Patel's political opponents argued, and some still do, that he was not keen on resolving the lease issue because he himself was a substantial landowner, forgetting that the new legislation imposed restrictions on the power of the landowners as no previous legislation had done and was, from the tenants' point view a better piece of legislation than its counterpart in the United Kingdom, as Trafford Smith of the Colonial Office writes. Nearly half a century later, the problem still remains unresolved, with untold consequences for the national economy, principally the future of the sugar industry, for which Indians were brought to Fiji in the first place. But with expiring leases not renewed and world competition for the sugar market stiffening, the heart has gone out of the sugar industry. Once the sole source of livelihood for the majority of the Indo-Fijian community, it is now for many a part-time activity, continued more as a matter of habit than with any realistic expectation of a sustainable income.

Part VI has Patel's speeches and papers on social and cultural issues facing the Indo-Fijian community and the Colony as a whole. These are mostly in the form of articles and editorials written by him for the weekly *Pacific Review*. Patel started this journal in 1949 to, among other things, 'break the narrow walls of isolation and make mutual contact and our contact with the outside world easy and beneficial,' 'to fight and resist imperialism, exploitary colonialism, racialism and such other natural enemies of the fundamental rights of human

---

13   See Padma N Lal, *Ganna: Portrait of the Fiji Sugar Industry* (Lautoka: Sugar Cane Commission of Fiji, 2008).

beings,' and to 'spread the light of knowledge and culture': fighting words in a small colonial society in a remote corner of the world untouched by the larger currents of thought. In its heyday in the 1950s, the *Pacific Review* would have to have been among the finest weeklies in the Pacific, including Australia and New Zealand. It published articles on cultural and philosophical themes and on politics and social issues by eminent writers and thinkers from around the world: on the great Indian short story writer Prem Chand, the Aboriginal artist Albert Namatajira, and reviews of books by scholars such as KL Gillion (*Fiji's Indian Migrants*), Marshall Sahlins (*Moala*) and JD Legge (*Britain in Fiji*). The weekly also afforded Patel the opportunity to present the reading public of Fiji with an alternative narrative of political and social developments in the colony. This was crucial at a time when Fiji was a closed world and the only daily in the Colony, the *Fiji Times*, was openly hostile to the Indo-Fijian interests and to any challenge to the established colonial order. The paper folded in the early 1970s. By then, independence having been achieved on terms acceptable to the Fijians and Europeans, the *Fiji Times* softened its hardline stance: it could now afford to be magnanimous to its critics. It helped, too, that a local-born editor, Vijendra Kumar, was at the helm, replacing the virulently anti-Federation editor and Alliance functionary Leonard Usher.

This volume comprises parliamentary speeches, transcriptions of public address, private correspondence, memoranda, and newspaper articles by and about Patel. Some of these are in the public domain but many are not. The speeches, including those given in the Legislative Council, often delivered without notes, full of allusion to events and issues now long forgotten, have had to be edited, sometimes quite severely, for coherence and clarity and to remove repetition and interjections and extraneous references. Care has been taken though to ensure that these excisions did not impair the flow of argument or the overarching theme of the occasion. Where a word or two had faded beyond legibility, I made the connections to ensure that the overall meaning remained. Minimal changes, if any, have been made to Patel's written memoranda and speeches preserved in the archives and in his own private papers. .

What the volume demonstrates amply is the enormous range of Patel's accomplishments at different levels and on a wide range of subjects. Patel's eloquence is evident in his speeches: the telling phrase, the mastery of the material at hand, its sequential, compelling exposition. Motibhai Patel's words quoted at the beginning of this essay capture a widely held view of Patel as a public speaker and debater. As Sir Robert Sanders, a senior civil servant in Fiji and close to the Fijian establishment, once said, 'From time to time I listened to him in Legco [Legislative Council] where he could unfold a complicated case with scarcely a note and in a quiet and mannered way. I particularly remember the way he would put his head on one side and adopt an air of guilelessness as he made a telling point.' Ratu William Toganivalu, one of the better orators on the Fijian side, said, 'there is magic in his delivery.' If Patel were to 'put up a case to say that this roof was painted black,' referring to the roof of the Legislative Council, 'they would believe him as I have often believed him.' Patel's strength derived not only from innate intelligence and an acute understanding of the Indian psychology but also from his wide reading. His house in Nadi had a well-stocked, but now depleted, library of books on subjects ranging from philosophy (existentialist philosopher Nicholas Berdyaev being a particular favourite but also Sarvapalli Radhakrishnan, Pierre Teilhard de Chardin and Jacque Barzun), Pacific and world history (Winston Churchill, Joseph C Grew, John Gunther, Sir Harry Luke, JD Legge, Deryck Scarr. CS Belshaw, Keith Sinclair, Cordell Hull), novels (Vladimir Nabokov, VS Naipaul, Charles Dickens, Rudyard Kipling, EM Foster, Thomas Hardy, DH Lawrence), and biographies and autobiographies (Nirad Chaudhry, HG Wells, Rabindranath Tagore, John F Kennedy, among others).

AD Patel belonged to a generation which listened religiously to the BBC and All India Radio, followed cricket on crackling transistors in pre-dawn hours, and read airmailed 'onion' editions of *The Times*; a generation for whom reading was an essential component of civilized life and writing the main means of long-distance communication. They took care with words and pride in the clarity of expression. They believed in the intrinsic liberating value of knowledge and in the broad Hindu view that knowledge set human beings free from untruth and ignorance, that truth ultimately triumphed over untruth, as the *Bhagvad Gita* says: *Satyame Vijayete*, Truth Ultimately Triumphs. It was out of this conviction that Patel started the *Pacific Review* and lent a generous helping hand in the founding of schools in the Indo-Fijian community. He was the manager of Sangam schools for many years and the principal founder of the Sri Vivekananda High School in Nadi, the Colony's first non-Christian, non-government high school. The opening of that school, against stiff official opposition concerned about potential lowering of educational standards and paucity of white collar jobs for school leavers, was an event of singular importance in the history of higher education for the Indo-Fijian community. Patel had in the early 1960s initiated discussions with the Government of India about establishing a university in Fiji when a clearly concerned colonial government of Fiji seized the initiative which led to the opening of the University of the South Pacific in 1968. For Patel and others like him, education was the key to intellectual liberation and social emancipation, leading to the fulfillment of the two most important goals of human life: personal enlightenment (*moksa*) and fruitful work (*artha*) through the selfless pursuit of duty (*dharma*).

This volume of papers is large as it is, but it constitutes only a fragment of the words AD Patel wrote and spoke during a public life spanning some forty years, from the late 1920s to the late 1960s. The words, now cold in print, do not capture the passion and urgency with which they were spoken or written. People understood Patel perfectly when he said that the question was not whether independence would come to Fiji, but whether it would come as Lakshmi, the goddess of wealth, or as Durga, the goddess of destruction. The cane growers understood precisely what Patel meant when he called the CSR Company a tyrannical mother-in-law of a very dutiful daughter-in-law that was the colonial government of Fiji. And everyone understood the hollowness of the 1965 electoral arrangements which had placed the Chinese on the European roll when Patel asked how was it possible that people who ate rat, bat and cat were with the Europeans when Indians had greater contact with and affinity for European culture. (He was understandably very unpopular with the Chinese community for a while). Some allusions to classical literature in Patel's speeches and writings will probably be beyond the cultural and intellectual experience of the present generation, references to King Canute and Kalidas and Don Quixote, to Alfred Lord Tennyson and William Wordsworth: reading for pleasure is no longer a favourite pastime in Fiji these days, and the narrowly focused school curriculum does not help, nor the constant turmoil in the public life of the country. Many in the post-religious generation may also not fully appreciate the underlying philosophical tone of some of the pieces with references to Hindu religion and ethics, to 'Ram Rajya' and 'Kalyug.' Patel's language of universalism may jar with readers brought up with the language of cultural and group rights and entitlements and other practitioners of identity politics. Times have changed.

The passage of time and changes in popular taste and temperament might make some words and phrases sound incongruous, archaic and downright anachronistic, such as the gendered nature of the language used, but they do convey clearly the main issues and concerns that dominated the life of one man and, indeed, the life of the community he represented. In the papers collected here, it will be possible to glimpse the outlines of another vision for Fiji, often articulated against great odds and staunch opposition. In the light of the subsequent history of Fiji, that vision stands vindicated. A preoccupation with primordiality as the principle of political organization has been a major cause of Fiji's postcolonial difficulties. Some might argue that Patel's militant insistence on a common roll was a strategic error in that it strengthened the political position of the chiefly establishment as they endeavoured to secure their political control in the electoral arena from 1963 onwards, and consolidated the Fijian-European alliance as both these groups feared Indian domination. Robert Norton has remarked: 'I cannot overstate the suspicious hostility of Fijians and Europeans to the common roll proposal of Patel and Co during the 1960s. It was viewed as *the* major threat to be combated and, for a little while, there was certainly fear in Fijian and European leaders that the British might impose such a change. The Federation Party leaders were absolutely uncompromising in this demand, and in that way played into the political hands of their opponents.' 'A wiser strategy,' he continues, 'might have been to argue for a power sharing arrangement that did not remove guaranteed ethnic representation.'[14]

Several things can be said in response. The Fijian-European alliance pre-dated the Indo-Fijians' demand for a common roll, though it might have helped consolidate it. Europeans championed the Fijian cause and sought Fijian alignment not out of altruism but to protect their privileged position. Assistant Colonial Secretary Ray Baker wrote to me to say that he found 'it a little strange that he [Patel] apparently made so little effort to get on good terms with leading Fijians and to persuade them of his good intentions—assuming they were good.'[15] As the documents here show, there was no lack of trying on Patel's part. The reality was that Fijian minds were already made up, and no amount of persuasive argument could change them. To the assertion that the common roll would inevitably lead to Indian domination, Patel argued how this could not happen because Indo-Fijians were concentrated in certain areas, principally in the sugar cane belt, while there were many areas where the Fijians dominated, such as in the maritime provinces. The single member constituencies which Patel proposed would lead to more wasted surplus votes than to Indian domination. In Patel's scheme, there would be seats reserved for the different groups but everyone would vote for the candidates. Political equality among voters via the common roll was at the heart of Patel's political project, leading hopefully to the dissolution of racial alignments. It is worth remembering in this context that Indian leaders first publicly articulated their demand for the common roll in 1929 when they were in a minority in Fiji. At the London conference, the Indian group put forward a proposal for very limited introduction of the common roll, but it was rejected by the European and Fijian delegations. Fijians insisted not only on guaranteed ethnic representation but also on European over-representation as a vehicle to achieve political paramountcy. The 1965 constitutional conference report specifically provided for the Governor to form a broad-based government: in effect a government of national unity. But Ratu Mara refused outright, to his belated regret. 'I regret to this day that I did not do that,' he said. 'AD Patel was an intelligent man. He would have worked along.'[16] And it is worth bearing in mind that consociationalism, favoured today as the preferred mode of political representation in ethnically divided societies today, was not a model in vogue in the British pattern of decolonization in the 1960s: the Westminster system was.

---

14 Private correspondence, 9 March 2011.
15 Ray Barker to Brij V Lal, 20 September 1990.
16 Kathleen Hancock, *Men of Mana: Portraits of three Pacific leaders: Ratu Sir Kamisese Mara, Afioga Va'ai Kolone, Sir Robert Rex* (Wellington: Steele Roberts, 2003), 34.

If there was a chink in Patel's political armour, it was in his confidence that 'world opinion,' as expressed in the United Nations' General Assembly, would put pressure on the United Kingdom to impose a broad-based, largely non-racial constitution on Fiji. By the late 1960s, that confidence was sorely tested. As a London-trained lawyer and an avowed admirer of many aspects of English culture, he had 'confidence and trust' in British institutions to play a fair, neutral role in negotiating a broadly acceptable political settlement for Fiji. But in this his faith was misplaced. The British were keen to leave Fiji with a constitution which had a veneer of representative democracy about it but which unmistakably put the Fijians in charge. Governor Sir Derek Jakeway's statement in January 1965 'that it was inconceivable that Britain would ever permit the Fijian people to be put under the heels of an immigrant community' was not an unfortunate choice of words, inflammatory in its implications; it was the articulation of explicit British policy in Fiji. Privately, many expatriate civil servants shared that view. Ray Barker has written that 'we were at that time pro-Fijian in the sense that we fell in sympathy with their perception of themselves as the taukei—the owners of most of the land but economically backward and overtaken in population by immigrant races.'[17] Combined Fijian and European rejection of the common roll and any power sharing arrangements in which Indo-Fijians might have a meaningful role to play, kept up the pressure. Postcolonial Fiji has paid an inordinately high price for the missteps and missed opportunities of the past.

Beyond what the documents in this volume say about AD Patel and his vision and struggles, they speak to the enormity of the task facing anti-colonial leaders who challenged the established order of things. Patel's relentless advocacy of democracy, human rights and racial equality challenged the very foundations of colonial rule in Fiji and the central tenets of British imperialism everywhere. And yet, despite the odds, Patel remained undaunted; he did not give up his struggle in despair nor compromise his deeply-held principles. That may have been his Achilles heel, as his critics often contended, but it was also his great strength which commands respect across the years. In some ways, Patel's fight against the CSR Company was even more fraught although, as Governor Sir Kenneth Maddocks wrote to me, 'there was no doubt that he had a case.'[18] CSR was a powerful monopoly with wide influence in the corridors of colonial power while the sugar cane growers were disorganized and divided. Patel was reviled for his role in leading the strikes in 1943 and 1960, but his determination to fight for justice and equity in the sugar industry never wavered, and in the end he triumphed, but not before suffering many personal and political setbacks and taunts along the way. Injustice had to be confronted, no matter what the price. As Patel was fond of saying, 'That which is unjust can really benefit no

---

17   Ray Baker to Brij V Lal, 20 September 1990.
18   Sir Kenneth Maddocks to Brij V Lal, 4 October 1989.

one; that which is just can harm no one.' To those who wanted him to tone down his rhetoric against the colonial establishment, his reply, quoting Teillhard de Chardin, was 'It does not matter if the water is cold or warm if you are going to have to wade through it anyway.' Truth triumphs in the end, says the *Bhagvad Gita*. In the case of AD Patel, the fundamental truth of his vision for Fiji was vindicated in the end, though long after he was gone.

Part I. Quest for Equality: The Political Struggle

1: Address to the 1965 London Constitutional Conference, 26 July 1965

I thank you [Secretary of State Anthony Greenwood] and the United Kingdom Government for the kind invitation and welcome extended us to this historic conference which is called to smelt the existing system of government in the Colony of Fiji and to forge and mould a new constitution which, I hope, will lead our country to complete independence in the not too distant future.

Political liberty, equality and fraternity rank foremost among the good things of life, and mankind all over the world cherishes and holds these ideals close to its heart. The people of Fiji are no exception. Without political freedom, no country can be economically, socially or spiritually free.

We in Fiji, as in many undeveloped countries of the world, are faced with the three most formidable enemies of mankind, namely, Poverty, Ignorance, and Disease. We need political freedom to confront these enemies and free our minds, bodies and souls from their clutches.

Needless to say, when I refer to political freedom, I mean democracy under the rule of law, the sort of freedom which the British people and the people of United States enjoy. We need freedom which will politically, economically and socially integrate the various communities living in Fiji and make out of them one nation deeply conscious of the responsibilities and tasks which lie ahead.

I call this conference important and historic because it is the first conference of its kind in the history of Fiji and it may very well prove the beginning of the end of a form of government which stands universally condemned in the modern world.

I have come to this conference with faith and trust in British people and their government which has set peoples of other colonies free and has led them on the path of economic and cultural development. After all, Fiji's problems are not as difficult or formidable as those which some of the colonies, which are now independent, have had to face and solve.

We, from our side, promise you full co-operation and serious consideration in the deliberations which lie ahead in this conference.

We have all got to guard ourselves against avoiding right decisions because they are unpleasant or run counter to our ingrained habits of preconditioned thought, or taking wrong decisions because they appear advantageous in the short run.

We must appreciate the fact that we owe great responsibility, not only to the people of the present generation but also of generations to come.

We have to resist the temptation of driving the boat on the shallow waters because of the fear that it will rock heavily if we steered it on the right course. Bearing all this in mind let us bend to the tasks before us.

In the end I pray to Almighty God who led the crown colonies like Australian and New Zealand to full independence, may He also lead us and our country to the same destination safely and in good heart.

Again, I most sincerely thank you, Sir, for your kind welcome.

2: Suva Town Hall Resolutions at a Public Meeting of Indians, 30 November, 1929

1. This public meeting of Indians loyally expresses its absolute concurrence with the just and timely Message No 18 of 1929 of His Excellency the Acting Governor[1] and unreservedly upholds the action proposed and taken by him in respect of Indian Education.

2. This public meeting of Indians expresses its full confidence in His Excellency the Acting Governor and in his Government.

3. This public meeting of Indians regrets and wholly condemns the action taken and the attitude adopted by the European Elected Members against the small increase of provision proposed by His Excellency the Acting Governor on the Draft Estimates of the Colony for the year 1930 for long expected development of a primary education, which has been neglected, and for the urgent improvement of existing system of education for Indian boys and girls.

4. This public meeting of Indians is strongly of [the] opinion that the ground of objection raised by the European Elected Members that the programme of the Director of Education is far beyond the financial capacity of the Colony is absolutely misleading and inconsistent with the considered opinion of the said members embodied in the Message No 11 of 1929 advocating immediate abolition of Income Tax of about 40,000 pounds a year, and that it was used with [the] intention to single out items proposed for Indian Education.

---

1   AW Seymour became the Acting Governor when Sir Eyre Hutson left Fiji in 1929. The Education Report was prepared by John Caughy, the first Director of Education in Fiji. He had held the same post in New Zealand.

5. This public meeting of Indians wholly disagrees with the misrepresentation made with the intent to prejudice the Right Honourable the Secretary of State for the Colonies by the European Elected Members that it is 'Not impossible in certain districts [that] Government schools intended for Indians of all creeds would meet boycott or non-co-operation' and respectfully assures the Government that the Indians have not and had not even dreamt of so doing.

6. This public meeting of Indians is of [the] opinion that the existing system of franchise which tends towards friction between the different races bearing allegiance to His Majesty the King Emperor is the cause of the present political upheaval in this Crown Colony and as the only satisfactory solution respectfully [requests] His Majesty's Government to consider the desirability of granting at an early date common franchise to all British subjects resident in Fiji.

7. This public meeting of Indians resolves that a copy of these resolutions be sent to His Excellency the Acting Governor with a request that he may be pleased to forward the same to the Right Honourable the Secretary of State for the Colonies.

Signed: AD Patel, et.al

3: Common Roll Conference with Sir Murchison Fletcher, 27 December 1929

His Excellency explained that the conference was convened on account of his desire that the Indian representatives should co-operate in the Legislative Council.[2] He explained the principles of a Crown Colony Government, and the way in which it differs from representative Self Government. He stated that the communal franchise had a special value when applied to a heterogeneous community in safeguarding the interests of the different groups, and it contained no suggestion of the inferiority of any group. It was, in fact, greatly desired in some places and His Excellency exemplified the instance of the Muslim community in Ceylon, who are strongly opposed to the common franchise. He expressed his disagreement with the action of the Indian ex-members in resigning from the Council when their motion on the franchise question was lost. He advised them that the proper procedure in this instance was to forward their protest by memorial through the Governor to the Right Honourable the Secretary of State for the Colonies, to co-operate in the Council, and to work in a constitutional manner for the achievement of their purpose.

---

2   Was Governor of Fiji from 22 November 1929 to 28 November 1936. During his tenure, as the several documents following show, Fletcher tried to have nomination replace election as the mode of representation in the Legislative Council, but without success. He also briefly floated the idea of more Chinese immigration to counter the influence of Indians, a proposal vetoed by the Colonial Office.

Mr. AD Patel said that he did not represent any section of the community,[3] but he was satisfied that the franchise on racial lines was unacceptable to the Indian community, and was likely to lead to ill-feeling upon racial lines. Acceptance of the present franchise was, in his opinion, impossible, and contrary to Indian interests and to those of the Colony. It was contrary, he said, to the principle of equal status for Indians with other races, both here and in other places,[4] and the acceptance of the communal franchise in Fiji must damage the cause of Indians in other colonies. He asked the Governor to recognise the fact of non-co-operation in Council, but assured His Excellency of the loyal co-operation of Indian political bodies, which were prepared to advise the Government upon questions affecting the welfare of Indians until a common franchise was granted.

Mr. John Grant[5] somewhat haltingly agreed with the views expressed by Mr. A.D. Patel. His Excellency interposed, disagreeing with an interpretation of the franchise which implied inequality, and expressed his inability to understand the boycott of the Council by the Indian members. He again explained the advantages of the communal franchise in dealing with a community composed of different races in their present stage of development, and the desirability of Indian members co-operating with the Government in the Legislative Council.

Mr. Sahodar Singh[6] expressed the opinion that the communal franchise implied an inferiority of the Indian community. Mr. S.B. Patel confined his remarks to the question of the principle involved, which, he said, implied the inferiority of the Indian community. He referred to the question of the position of Indians abroad, and to the effect on this question of acceptance of a communal franchise by Indians in Fiji. Mr. Abdul Kasim, speaking through an interpreter, said that a common franchise was the ideal franchise, and that a communal franchise does not give the Indian community sufficient representation.

His Excellency then thanked those present for attending, and requested them to give serious consideration to the matter, and to convey their decision to the Acting Secretary for Indian Affairs at an early date.

---

3   Patel, being a recent arrival, was ineligible to stand for the 1929 elections.

4   No doubt he had Kenya in mind where the battle for franchise was being actively fought. See Mary Varghese, 'The East African Indian National Congress, 1914-1939: A Study of Indian Political Activity in Kenya,' PhD thesis (Dalhousie University, 1975).

5   An Indian Christian who contested the 1929 election for the Southern Constituency and lost to Vishnu Deo (419) to 162. The first three elected Indian members in 1929 were Vishnu Deo, James Ramchandra Rao and Parmanand Singh.

6   Was a member of the Hindu Maha Sabha formed in 1926 and active in western Viti Levu.

4: Memorandum to Governor, 28 December 1929

We are grateful to Your Excellency for giving us an opportunity of airing our views on the franchise question. While deeply appreciating Your Excellency's desire and anxiousness for co-operation of the Indian members in the Council, we respectfully submit that we cannot see our way to accede to Your Excellency's wishes.

The claim for common franchise is a matter of principle to us and it is based upon a sincere and earnest desire of the Indian community to work in amity and harmony with other sister communities living in the Colony. We are of the opinion that the present franchise on communal basis is bad in principle and harmful in working and it tends to perpetuate the racial distinctions and bickering so much evident today in the Colony. Again, the present franchise denotes to our mind an inferiority of political status which is not consonant with the pledges and deliberations made on high and solemn authority regarding the equal political status, rights and privileges to Indian British subjects domiciled in various Crown colonies.[7] We are thankful to Your Excellency for your desire for co-operation but we regret we could not bring ourselves to co-operation under the present franchise which we do not believe in. We feel that working under the franchise would be not only doing a disservice to our community but also blocking the progress of the Colony as a whole.

We submit for Your Excellency's consideration that we do not ask for any manhood suffrage or any lower qualification for Indian voters, nor have we the slightest desire to look for Indian domination in the Council. We are prepared to accept the same qualification for voting as necessary for the electors of other communities. To us it is not a question of the number of our members in the Council. We only look for true recognition in practice of the principle of equal citizenship for Indians in the Colony.[8]

We have the honour to be,

Sir,

Your Excellency's obedient servants

Signed: SB Patel, AD Patel, John F Grant, Parmanand Singh, H. Sahodar Singh, V. Deo.

---

7   This is a reference to the Salisbury's Despatch of 1875 which in the end was not accepted by the Government of India but the promise of equality underpinned the broad principle of indentured emigration and reiterated subsequently.

8   The common roll demand was not pursued with any vigour after 1936 when CF Andrews visited Fiji and advised against it. Henry Polak wrote to Andrews on 30 April 1936: 'I am sure that you will agree that at the present time it would be extremely unwise to press for the common franchise. The question at the moment is not the common franchise versus the separate franchise, but the separate franchise versus nomination. I do not think that there is any likelihood of getting the common franchise so long as the Fijians are inarticulate and I think that the Colonial Office are not unreasonable in laying down that the matter should not be re-opened for the present until that aspect can be adequately dealt with. Will you, therefore, throw your whole weight into seeing that the common franchise question is not allowed to arise at the present time?'

5: Governor to Secretary of State, 2 January 1930

My Lord,

I have the honour to refer to Mr. Seymour's despatch No. 333 of the 13th November last, and to my telegram of the 2nd January, regarding the three Indian seats in the Legislative Council.

Writs in respect of the vacancies were only recently issued on the 25th November and the 16th December was appointed as the day for receiving nominations, but no candidates presented themselves. On the 27th December I summoned a conference, which was attended by seven leading members of the Indian community, Mr. [Alfred W] Seymour, Colonial Secretary, and Dr McGusty, Acting Secretary of Indian Affairs, being also present.

It was at once apparent that the Indians had come with their minds made up. They contented themselves with platitudes about brotherhood and equality, and they were not prepared to discuss the merits of their case. A common roll was the birthright of all Indians, and there was nothing more to be said. They countered with generalities the argument that in certain parts of the world the Muslim community was emphatic that a communal roll should be maintained. They stated, however, that it was not merely a question of local politics, and they hinted that they were acting under instructions from abroad. I am informed on good authority that these instructions come through Mr. HL Polak, resident in Dane's Inn in London.

On the 28th December, Dr McGusty brought to call upon me an Indian named Dr Sagayam,[9] who was formerly a member of the Indian Medical Service, and had three years' war service. Dr Sagayam expressed himself with complete candour. He said that ninety-eight per centum of the Indian community knew nothing and cared nothing about the relative merits of a common and a communal roll, or about Indian or Kenyan politics. They had sincerely appreciated the recent concessions of elected members, and they wanted representation in the Legislative Council. The Colony however was unable to produce more than the merest handful of men who were qualified to stand as candidates, and not one of them had the courage to run counter to dictation from India. The community was prosperous and contented, and the present deadlock was none of its seeking.

---

9   Dr A Deva Sagayam sought nomination to the Legislative Council in 1926 but missed out to the incumbent Badri Maharaj.

In the document dated the 28th December, six of the seven Indians who attended the conference have declared their inability to co-operate under the present franchise. Mr. Abdul Karim, representing the Muslim community, refused to append his signature.

I submit that no action is at present called for. If no candidates come forward, new writs will be issued, and in the meantime the better informed among the Indian community will, I think, be content to leave their interests in Government's safe-keeping.

6: Memorandum to the Governor, 5 March 1935

When we read the announcement of Your Excellency's short visit to England it made us naturally curious about the purpose of the visit. In view of the recent change in the constitution of the Municipal Councils of this Colony and in view of certain statements made by Your Excellency and the two Indian members in the Legislative Council, our minds rightly or wrongly associated Your Excellency's visit to England with the constitutional changes that Your Excellency suggested to the Secretary of State on your last visit home. If we are correct in our surmise, we would respectfully ask Your Excellency to bear patience with us if we place our point of view at some length and to convey it—if possible—verbatim to the Secretary of State for his full consideration.

We would like to take Your Excellency's mind back to the 28th of March 1934 when Sir Maynard Hedstrom[10] brought a motion to change the constitution of municipalities in Fiji. Speaking on this motion Mr. Munswamy Mudaliar[11] said: 'Your Excellency, the Indian opinion on this matter is divided, but it is very difficult to form any unanimous opinions. However, there is a large section of the community in my Division which is prepared to accept any constitution having equality for all the three communities.'

We also refer Your Excellency to the budget debates of October 1934 when Mr. K. B. Singh stated: 'A petition signed by 106 Indians was submitted through Your Excellency to the Secretary of State for the Colonies asking him to leave things as they are in connection with the municipal constitution. After a few days, another petition signed by 86 Indians was also submitted to the Secretary of State ...in favour of the motion introduced by the Senior elected member, that is in favour of Government control. [T]he petition, Sir, was endorsed by about 400 persons of the Northern and Western divisions. They further pointed out that they would advocate a system of nomination in the Legislative Council as well, if the Government would give an equal number of seats.

---

10   Born in Fiji in 1872, head of Morris Hedstrom Ltd, and member of the Executive Council.
11   Member of Legislative Council, 1932-1937 from North West Indian constituency.

Upon being interrupted by Your Excellency: 'Who advocated that? Who are 'they' who suggested nomination to the Legislative Council?,' Mr. K.B. Singh[12] said: 'The petition was signed by about 400 persons of the Northern and Western Divisions, Sir. I might be wrong, but as far as I can remember—I think I am 90 per cent right—they supported the system of nomination in the Legislative Council as well.' Then Your Excellency asked: 'Does the honourable member suggest that 90 per cent of all Indians support nomination for the Legislative Council?' To which Mr. K.B. Singh replied, 'Two or three petitions were submitted to the Government—the first, signed by 106 Indians, is in favour of keeping things as they are. The second and third petitions, signed by 86 and 400 respectively, were in favour of the Government control in the municipality. The second petition was endorsed by about 400 Indians who supported the system of nomination in the Legislative Council. Under such circumstances, Sir, I think it would be advisable to bring in constitutional changes which would keep all sections of the community in one constitution and would remove such dissensions.'

In summing up the debate Your Excellency said: 'I was interested to hear his (Mr. K.B. Singh's) remarks on the common roll. If I understand him alright, he says on behalf of his constituents that they would wish, if a common roll is not now attainable, to have an equal number of seats for each race, those seats to be subject to nomination. Is that a correct interpretation?' To this Mr. K. B. Singh replied: 'There are some people who prefer the elective system, but there is a number of leading Indians who advocate the nominative system with an equal number of seats in the Legislative Council, provided the Government is prepared to take one of the Indians on the Executive Council.'

Your Excellency may be aware that long before these statements were made by the two Indian members, they have ceased to retain the confidence of their constituents. Their constituents have time and often denounced them and their policy. In making the statements referred to, they have not consulted their constituents and deliberately with a set purpose have elected to grossly misrepresent the views of their constituents in order to serve their own personal ends. The term of the present Legislature is now about to expire. It is a foregone conclusion that they will not be returned to the Council at the next election. The introduction of a system of nomination is their only hope of ensuring their seats in the Council.

From the statements above quoted, we gather the impression that Your Excellency is prone to entertain those views of the two Indian members seriously as the views of a large and leading section of the community. If it is so, we respectfully

---

12 Kunwar Bachint Singh arrived in Fiji as a teacher for the Arya Samaj in 1927, entering the Legislative Council in 1932; was nominated member from 1937 to 1947.

beg to submit that Your Excellency will be making a grave mistake in accepting those statements at their face value. We would remind Your Excellency of the report of the Secretary for Indian Affairs Council paper No. l l laid on the table on the 14th day of July 1933 which states in reference of the two members that: 'The two Indian members who were finally returned were not drawn from the class that has hitherto played a part in political leadership.[13] To that we may confidently add that they are not drawn from the class that will play a part in political leadership in future under the system of franchise.

Prompted by a strong desire to ensure harmony and peace between different communities in this Colony and their welfare, we have undertaken this very important mission. We would be failing in our duty to our community and to this Colony if we did not point out the great patience, moderation and reasonableness which our community has shown in their demands. We do not grudge the other communities the privileges and rights that they have the good fortune of enjoying in this Colony. We do not desire that their rights and privileges should be curtailed in any way. What we desire and what we ask for is that we should be granted the same rights and privileges. That the rights and privileges of other communities are curtailed and encroached upon to place us all on a common level by depriving them of their franchise, is a sad thought which neither satisfies nor meets with our approval.

The right of having a voice in the Legislative and Executive affairs of the State is the most valued and highly cherished right of every citizen irrespective of whatever creed or race he belongs, and we may well be pardoned if we are not prepared to relinquish it in favour of a system of nomination which means a complete denial of that most valuable right.

The change suggested by Your Excellency in our opinion is not in the best interest of our community. It has been the sad experience of the community that the interest and welfare of Indians in this Colony has been the last concern of the Government of Fiji. Our experience and knowledge of the type of Indians nominated by the Government to fill the positions in different local bodies, and in the Legislative Council of this Colony in the past, give us strong reasons to believe that the people nominated by the Government will be on the whole the people who will be acquiescent to Legislative and Executive measures irrespective of whether they will be in the interest or against the interest of the community.

It must be remembered that the Indian community here is progressing rapidly in their way of life and is day by day taking keener and more intelligent interest in their own development and in the development of this Colony. We have reached

---

13   The two were KB Singh and Munswamy Mudaliar.

a stage in this Colony where the introduction of a system of nomination will be like filling new wine in old bottles. Such an anti-democratic and retrogressive step will have strong reaction from an overwhelming majority of the community which will result in our opinion in endangering peace and harmony that at present exist between different races and creeds in this Colony.

We must also emphasise the importance of the new constitution that India is about to receive and the effect it will have upon our people here. The new Indian Reform Bill is based upon fundamentally democratic principles. The innovation that Your Excellency suggests is antidemocratic and of such a nature that it must necessarily take away the most fundamental right of the taxpayer and place it absolutely and unreservedly in the hands of the Governor.

Let it not be misunderstood when we instance the new Indian Reform Bill that our community demands or even aspires to attain self government in Fiji. What we say and what we aspire to is that we shall have a right to criticize, a right to advise, a right to express our aspirations and our needs through the representatives elected by us in the governance of this Colony. If the present constitution has failed to bring about harmony and goodwill between different communities, it has done so because it is not liberal enough to bridge the gulf that exists at present between different races.

A further narrowing of the present constitution and taking it a few decades behind will not conduce to harmony and progress of the peoples of this Colony. If the Government thinks that a change in the constitution of the Legislative Council is absolutely imperative at this stage, it must be such as would be an advance on the present constitution and not a retrogression therefrom.

In conclusion, in view of the election that will shortly be held for the next Legislative Council we strongly urge that the question of any change to the present constitution be postponed until the new Legislative Council meets after the elections and that the existing constitution be continued for the present. The wishes of the community should be ascertained through the polls at the coming elections when our community has decided to make the question of franchise and nomination the main issue of the campaign. Knowing as we do the mind of our community, we have no doubt that an overwhelming majority of voters favour a system of franchise. Six months or a year more is but a moment in the history of any country. There is no urgency to effect any change in haste. 'Haste is waste' may be a common saying but it contains nuggets of wisdom which are not unworthy of being carefully considered.

(AD Patel, Vishnu Deo and others).

NB: The Indian Association, of which AD Patel was the President and Vishnu Deo the Secretary, sent a telegram to HLS Polak:

The majority of Europeans and Indians strongly oppose the motion adopted by Fiji Legislature advocating immediate change from elective to nominated representation without mandate from community. Two discredited Indian members and three Europeans for and three Europeans against motion telegraphed to Colonial Office by Acting Governor with request for instruction to extend life of Council expiring next month. Fijians neutral, Indian community beseech you take effective steps immediately to retain franchise.

7: A Delegation to the Governor, May 1935

Mr. [AD] Patel acted as leader of the deputation and Mr. Vishnu Deo as interpreter. Mr. Patel read a lengthy memorandum setting out the arguments against nomination.

His Excellency stated that he had listened with much interest to the memorandum. Before coming to the details, he desired to correct two erroneous suppositions, the one connecting his forthcoming visit to England with proposed changes in the constitution; the other attributing to himself or the Government the initiative in prompting the proposed alteration. His Excellency stated that his visit to England had no connection with the changes in the constitution; that neither he nor the Government would take the initiative in any proposed change, and that if an amendment is desired it would have to come as a result of some action in the Legislative Council by unofficial members and without any participation of the officials.

His Excellency analysed the political situation from the date of his first arrival as Governor of the Colony in November 1929, immediately after the three first Indian elected members led by Mr. Vishnu Deo had resigned from the Council on the defeat of their common roll motion. He understood that the desire of the Indian community was for equality, but in his opinion under a common roll the politically-minded Indians would swamp European interests by weight of numbers, and Fijian interests because Fijians are not politically-minded. A common roll could not be expected to secure racial political equality in the circumstances of Fiji, but would be likely, on the other hand, to perpetrate and accentuate racial differences. Nor, assuming the interests of the three races to be roughly equal, does the present form of the constitution provide equality of representation. Under the Crown Colony system of government, the official members were in the majority and under the special circumstances of Fiji there was no prospect of the introduction of a system of representative Government, although the unofficial members play an important part as leaders within and without the Legislative Council.

How then was equality to be attained? Unofficial representation of each of the races by four members would give a reasonable settlement of the Colony's present political difficulties, and the question was to choose between election and nomination. Under most circumstances election was preferable, but it presupposed common aims and interests which even in the Indian community, as was instanced in the case of the Muslims and other minorities, did not exist. Again the natives, the largest single unit in the population, are strongly opposed to the elective principle. Therefore the acceptance by all races of the nominative principle appears to be the only means of securing lasting political peace for the present. His Excellency was unable to make any pronouncement as to the attitude of the European community which returned the greatest number in any of the three races of unofficial members under the present constitution, but he thought it not unlikely that the Europeans might be willing to make a sacrifice in the interests of the attainment of a lasting solution.

As regards the statement in the memorandum that common roll representation is successful elsewhere, His Excellency said that this was certainly the case where common interests, race homogeneity, and ability to exercise the franchise existed, and he instanced its advantages in a country such as Australia. On the other hand, the strong demand for separate representation from minority interests had forced the inclusion of the communal principle in the new Indian constitution, and the same thing applied in Fiji not only with respect to the essential differences between the three main races, but with respect also to the differences within the Indian community itself.

His Excellency then stated that as he was not clear about the exact wishes of the deputation he would put certain questions to be answered by Mr. Patel or any other member. The questions were as follows, the answers having been given by Mr. Patel:

Q. Is it the desire of those who have signed the memorandum that there should be a common electoral roll?

A: The common roll principle is adhered to but the suggestion is that the wish of the people be ascertained from their representatives after the next general election.

Q: Is it desired by the deputation that the common roll principle should be applied at once?

A: If a common roll is not attainable at present, the matter will not be pressed.

Q: On the assumption that the common roll principle at present is unattainable, would you regard the present distribution of seats as equitable?

A: No.

Q: How far do you subscribe to my contention that the principle of equality between the three races should be attained by an equal distribution of seats between the three races?

A: While common roll is unattainable, we would regard this as satisfactory.

Q: In view of the opposition to the elective principle of the Fijians and of Indian minorities, do you regard the elective or the nominative system as the better suited to the conditions in the Colony?

A: It is admitted that the Indian community is not homogenous, but we ask that the elective principle should be retained.

Q: At an election what likelihood is there of a Muslim candidate being returned?[14]

A: A Muslim candidate would have an equal chance with a candidate derived from any other Indian section or community. (Mr. Patel here made the very doubtful statement that Muslims and Hindus live together on peaceful terms in Fiji, and that the remedy was for Muslims to put forward a candidate and to complain if he was not returned).

Mr. Patel expressed the appreciation of the members of the deputation for the patient hearing which they had received from His Excellency, and referred to the fact that while several misunderstandings had been removed by His Excellency, he hoped that the discussion and the memorandum had been of assistance also to His Excellency and the Government.

---

14 The Fiji Muslim League President Diljan and Secretary Hasan Raza wrote to the Governor on 4 March 1935 saying that the elective principle was 'neither desirable nor practicable,' and that under the existing arrangements, 'no Muslim candidate has a chance of being returned to the Council.' In a separate letter (dated 16 May 1935) one Walli who had signed the original election petition, retracted his support and advocated nomination.

8: Opposition to Nomination over Election, 19 May 1935[15]

The humble petition of Indian voters and other Indian residents in the district of Nadi in the Colony of Fiji sheweth:

1. That your humble petitioners are greatly surprised to hear that petitions have been prepared and presented to the Government requesting constitutional changes from the present system of elective representation to that of nomination.

2. That your humble petitioners are aware that the Indian community has never authorized the preparation and presentation of any petition advocating or supporting the introduction of a system of nominated representation in the Legislative Council of Fiji, or in the Municipal Councils of Suva and Levuka.

3. That your humble petitioners are shocked to learn that Mr. K.B. Singh supported by Mr. Munswamy Mudaliar[16] did on the 16th day of May 1935 introduce into the Legislative Council of Fiji a motion advocating that the European and Indian members be nominated and not elected and that the said motion was carried by 5 to 3 unofficial votes.

4. That your humble petitioners had not nor had the Indian community authorized either Mr. K.B Singh or Mr. Munswamy Mudaliar to introduce or to support such a motion.

5. That your humble petitioners strongly oppose the said motion and the introduction of a system of nomination in the Legislative Council of Fiji.

6. That your humble petitioners respectfully submit that the suggested reversion to the nominated system of representation is not in the best interest of the Colony and the various races resident therein and that it would be a direct negation of British democratic ideals.

7. That your humble petitioners are and have always been in favour of a system of franchise and respectfully urge that the present system of election be continued.

8. That your humble petitioners request that this petition be transmitted to the Right Honourable the Secretary of State for the Colonies for his kind consideration.

Your humble petitioners will ever pray.

(Sgd) A.D. Patel, K.N. Singh, K.K. Naiker & supporters & residents.

---

15 A similar petition was sent from several districts.
16 Both members of the Legislative Council.

Editor's Note: In the end, the government did not proceed with nomination, which was also opposed by the Government of India. The Letters Patent of 1937 provided that only two of the five Indian members of the Legislative Council would be nominated. The demand for common roll was also dropped after advice from CF Andrews who visited Fiji during the course of his visit to Australia and New Zealand.

9: Conundrums of Colonial Legislature, 21 December 1945

A letter from one of my constituents described the Legislative Council as an impotent legislature which only involved a waste of expenditure and was an unnecessary burden on the general revenue of the Colony. I would first like to analyse the position of this legislature and to examine how far that assertion is correct. We have here a legislature composed not only of an official majority but a majority which is under the direction of the Governor as far as voting is concerned, which means 16 members of Council are here just for the purpose of voting when the official Whip requires the votes, plus any explanations that the Government might have to make in regard to the questions that may be raised by the unofficial side. It is a very artificial and hollow position. It would also be very trying on those Official Members who are sitting in this Council who now and then have to just sink their personal views and express themselves as they are directed. What is more, it means only one thing, that they have to leave their official work, come to this Council to sit here day after day listening to perhaps boring and uninteresting dissertations from the unofficial side, knowing full well that the unofficial side cannot influence their minds in any way because they have no minds of their own to be influenced. There is only one mind in this Legislature, and that is the mind of the Governor. Perhaps a lot of time and expenditure could be saved if, in these circumstances, the Official Members as the heads of departments remained in their offices and attended to their official duties.

The position is equally hollow on the unofficial side. There are in this Council the so-called six Elected Members. I say 'so-called' because how many people in this Colony do they represent? There are three Indian Elected Members here and the total roll of voters who elect them in this Colony hardly amounts to 5,000, about 2,500 in my constituency [Northwest Viti Levu], a little less than that from Mr. Vishnu Deo's constituency [Southern], and merely 700 from Mr. [Badri Maharaj] Gyaneshwar's constituency [Northern]. Those are the numbers of voters from a community which is as large as the Fijian community in Fiji and would come to more than 100,000 souls. The position is the same with the European Elected Members. As far as the pure Europeans are concerned, probably most of them are voters, at least the male population, but as far as that section of the community which is frequently referred to as part-European is concerned, only a small percentage are voters and that is also again the male population.

As far as the Fijians are concerned, their own people, the common people, have no say whatever in their selection to this Council, so as far as the composition of the Council is concerned, whether it is the Official side or the Unofficial side, whether it is the elected members or the nominated members, the position is very, very hollow and artificial. If we are going to have a genuine Council where the public opinion can be genuinely and properly reflected, the first condition is the widening of the franchise. Every adult member of the population, whatever race he belongs to, must have a vote; it must be a question of universal suffrage. Doubts have been cast here about the fitness of the Fijian to elect his own representatives to this Council. I am personally quite convinced that the Fijian—the common Fijian—knows his mind just as well as we know ours. Perhaps some may be thinking of what I may call the pre-war Fijian mind. We must take one very important factor into consideration. The Fijian during the war came into contact with soldiers of other democratic countries like America and New Zealand. He [has] also got certain democratic ideas, political viewpoints, ambitions and aspirations as regards his political rights, and we cannot pour new wine into old bottles: we must make sufficient provision for them.

It has been said by some that it [the question of Fijian representation] should be left either to Government or to the Fijian Affairs Department. I would go a step further and suggest that it should be left to the Fijians themselves. A referendum can be taken and public opinion amongst the Fijians ascertained as regards their political aspirations. Someone mentioned that the Fijian is politically backward and the Indian is politically far in advance of him. The Indian belongs to one of the oldest civilizations in the world and consequently there is nothing surprising if his philosophical or political ideologies come to the same level as those of other civilized countries in the world. In comparison in terms of civilization our Fijian brethren in this Colony are in an adolescent stage. I do not see why it should be the responsibility only of the Fijian and the European that their interests should be safeguarded. I feel that it is the duty of the Indian as well.

In 1944 after the elections, when the unofficial side met, it decided that we would always try to stick together, take proper view of things and make a national stand on matters that affected us nationally. I would ask the Unofficial Members here in the Council to consider whether the Indian side of the Council has kept that pledge or not. We are not here to dominate over them, and I would like my European colleagues only to consider one thing, not only in the interests of the Colony but in the interests of their own community and its future. Let us examine the situation. This is a Colony in which nearly 96 percent of the population consists of what we call 'brown men' and 4 percent white men or Europeans, as you may choose to call them, and out of this 4 percent probably 2 percent are part-Europeans. The European community here has got brains, wealth and influence. The Europeans have to consider whether they are going to exercise these advantages in the interests of this Colony and in trying to make themselves the leaders of the Colony, or whether they are going to keep themselves into a narrow circle, always thinking in the terms of their own small community and trying to look upon themselves as the opponents of other communities.

The Europeans now have a fine chance of leadership if they but take a wider view and outlook. They can easily become not only the leaders of the European community but, if they get all these unnecessary suspicions out of their minds, the leaders of the Indian and Fijian communities as well. I would not mind being represented in this Council by Mr. Aime Ragg, although I am an Indian. It is just a question of mutual trust and confidence. Are we going to do something ourselves to foster amongst all these various communities that trust and confidence or are we just going to raise these bugbears one against the other and keep this Colony eternally divided into racial compartments? I know that in this Colony there is a certain type of European mind—not in all cases because I know there are many who understand and appreciate it—to whom the very mention of this word 'common roll' or 'common franchise' is a bugbear. One thing they overlook—if it is a question of common roll or franchise, it will not be thrust upon any community, I assure you. I personally believe that it will be only by voluntary consent. There is no question of dominating or forcing one's views on another, but I would seriously ask my European colleagues to consider this and consider it seriously.

Probably fifty years hence, as the population increases, Europeans will not be even one percent of the population, and one day there will come a time when other communities might raise the question as to how this came about, that one percent of the population has got the same number of representatives in the Council as, say, other communities who have about fifty percent of the total population of the Colony. Would it not be better then if there was a common roll and if right from the beginning, to allay suspicions and fears, the 18 allocated seats asked for in this Council were allocated to 18 constituencies and reserved on these lines, that certain constituencies were for the Europeans only and certain for the Fijians only and certain for Indians only; and in all the constituencies the voters, irrespective of whether they are European, Fijian or Indian, could only vote for the candidates in those reserved constituencies. Would not that give in the future the assurance and security to everyone in this Colony that even when those six European members sit in this Council they are not going there as the sole representatives of a small microscopic minority but they re going there as the representatives of the people in their constituencies. Won't there be a better guarantee of retaining the same position as they are enjoying now?

You might raise this bugbear of Indian domination temporarily but will it last forever? Should we not make allowance for the progress that these two communities, the Fijian and the Indian, will be making in the years to come, and in view of that ensure the European leadership for this Colony, and do not members see that that will be the best way to ensure it? The European community will then remain the leaders and the true leaders of the people of Fiji. There will be one further advantage—a common denominator of political outlook will be developed in this Colony. As it is we are all thinking in narrow terms, of our racial interests, but if we take that bold step forward, we would all be thinking in general terms, the interests of the people of this Colony. Would not that be an ideal worthwhile striving for?

I hold the view that the 18 Elected Members of this Council should be genuinely elected representatives and they can only be genuinely elected representatives of the people of this Colony if there is a wider franchise. I hope that better counsel will prevail. I hope that mutual suspicions will be done away with and we shall try to understand and accept one another's bona fides and if not immediately then in the near future we will come to realize that, after all, the best representation in this legislature would be that which ensures harmony and a common political outlook for the Colony. That can only be done by having a common franchise. Let us hope that the time will come when the demand for a common franchise will be looked upon and characterized not as an Indian demand but will become truly and genuinely the demand of all races, the European as well as the Fijian.

10: Deed of Cession Debate, 16 July 1946

In this debate[17] I am labouring under three disadvantages. First I have not got the genius of rushing in where angels fear to tread. Second, being a poor benighted heathen, I have not got the heart to hate any human being, whatever race they belong to, and thirdly, I cannot talk Irish. When I read this motion I thought that the words 'non-Fijian inhabitants' meant really 'non-Fijian inhabitants' and I thought that it was really a sportsmanlike act on the part of the mover of the

---

17   On the motion moved by AA Ragg 'That in the opinion of this Council the time has arrived in view of the general increase in the non-Fijian inhabitants and its consequential political developments to emphasise the terms of the Deed of Cession to assure that the interests of the Fijian race are safeguarded and a guarantee given that Fiji is to be preserved and kept as a Fijian country for all time.'

motion (being one of the non-Fijian inhabitants of the Colony) to move this motion in the interests of the Fijians, but my eyes were opened when [AA Ragg] interpreted these words as meaning 'Indians' and levelling his whole quantum of criticism against that particular community.

This motion has, to my mind, three implications. One implication is that for some reason or another, the Government of this Colony has either forgotten or overlooked the terms of the Deed of Cession and there is an urgent need for a reminder. Another implication is that the time has come when we have got to look to the Deed of Cession in order to safeguard Fijian interests; and the third implication is that, on account of the natural increase of the non-Fijian inhabitants of this Colony, it has been found necessary to again reiterate and emphasize the terms of the Deed of Cession. I was wondering all the time when Members supporting the motion spoke on this point as to what particular terms of the Deed of Cession they wished to emphasize.

I have been sitting here all day, but I am sorry to say that I have not so far heard which one, or how many of them, they want to be emphasized. The preamble shows the intention as to why the leaders of the Fijian community ceded this Colony to the British. There was a desire on their part to secure the promotion of Civilization and Christianity, and of increasing trade and industry within these islands. The second desire was that there should be order and good Government established in this Colony. Prompted by these two desires the ancestors of my honourable Fijian colleagues placed the sovereignty of these islands into British hands, and this sovereignty was tendered, as the preamble says, unconditionally. We might go back into the history of over 70 years' British rule in this Colony and examine whether these desires of the Fijian people have been fulfilled.

 Nobody in this Council has alleged that Christianity was not promoted or is being in any way driven out of this Colony. Nobody says that the Government and the non-Fijian inhabitants of this Colony have tried to drive civilization out of this country and reduce the people of this Colony to an abject state of barbarity. Nor can anyone say that vigorous steps have not been taken right throughout and are not being taken now for the promotion of trade and industry. I am glad to say that nobody in this Council ever questioned that order and good government was not established in this Colony and is not prevailing even now. So as far as the desires of the people who ceded this country to the British are concerned those desires are scrupulously fulfilled.

Now going into the covenants of this Deed: As regards the first covenant, it merely hands over the sovereignty and possession of these islands to Queen Victoria, her heirs and successors. As regards the second covenant, it gives full and unlimited powers to the British Government or to Queen Victoria and her heirs and her successors—if I may follow the language of the Deed—that the form and constitution of government, the means of the maintenance thereof and the laws and regulations to be administered within the said islands, shall be such as Her Majesty shall prescribe and determine. Nobody can so far say that there has been any departure on the part of the Government or on the part of the non-Fijian inhabitants from covenant two of this Deed.

Let us come to covenant three. That only provides for a temporary and provisional government pending the establishment of the British Administration in Fiji. That is a dead letter now; it has been already fulfilled and finished. Then we come to the fourth covenant. That provides for the vesting of all the surplus lands of the Colony into the British Crown. That has been already fulfilled. Those lands that were not already alienated to Europeans and others in this Colony and those lands which were not actually in possession or occupation of the native owners or those lands which were not of any use to them were under the covenant vested in the British Crown. Has there been any reason to complain on that ground? Let us come to covenant five. That gives the Crown the power to take and acquire, on payment of compensation, any land from the owners if required for public purposes. Surely the natural increase of the population has not affected that covenant in any way. I have not heard any complaints so far either from the Fijian Members or from the mover or the seconder of this motion, or from the Unofficial Members on this score.

I come to covenant six. That merely transfers the public buildings, stores, articles and all that to the British Crown. That is already fulfilled and done. It is a matter of the past. Covenant seven. Under this the Crown gives three promises. Promise No.1: 'The rights and interests of the said Tui Viti and other high Chiefs, the Ceding parties hereto, shall be recognized so far as is consistent with British sovereignty, and colonial form of government.' It has not been suggested in this Council that this promise has not been fulfilled. We come to the second promise: 'That all questions of financial liabilities and engagements shall be scrutinised, and dealt with upon principles of justice and sound public policy.' That is a matter of the past. It has not been alleged in this Council that this promise has not been kept. The third promise: 'That all claims to titles of land, by whomsoever preferred, and all claims to pensions or allowances, whether on the part of the said Tui Viti and other High Chiefs or of persons now holding office under them or any of them, shall in due course be fully investigated and equitably adjusted.' They have already been fully investigated and equitably adjusted; that promise has already been fulfilled.

So what in God's name is left in this Deed of Cession that the mover of this motion wants to be specially emphasized under this motion? He may throw dust in the eyes of others but I refuse to be blinded by any emotion or feeling, or allow my reason to be carried away by prejudice. That is the Deed of Cession that has been the subject of all this mud-slinging and hot air in this Council.

I am glad to have received this opportunity of hearing what members of other communities think about us. It always does us good and discarding all those harsh and insulting remarks made for what they are worth, I am highly gratified that there was nothing seriously wrong with my people in this Colony. When the opponents have got to resort to such criticism that we are a bad lot because though we had a shortage of women we did not mix with the Fijians and assimilate with them, or that because we are paying high rents and more money to the Fijians, the Fijians in those areas have become more immoral, or that because we have increased in numbers and have been prolific we have become a menace to Fijian interests—if this is the worst that our adversaries can say about us, thank God we have acquitted ourselves well in this Colony.

I would remind the Members here that this Deed of Cession was executed in the year 1874. The promise[18] was made to Indians soon after that Deed, that they will be treated as the citizens of this Colony, that they will be allowed an opportunity of settling here and becoming citizens and they will get the same rights as any other inhabitants of this Colony; and these promises were made, mark you, when all the signatories of the Deed were alive, and if anybody knew what they intended when they handed over this Colony to the British for government, certainly King Cakobau and his Chiefs who executed this Deed must have known; and can any Members here tell me or show me that any of these Chiefs or King Cakobau protested or alleged at the time when they were bringing Indians to this Colony that they were breaking the covenants of this Deed, or were committing a breach of faith with those who handed over this Colony into their hands?

Well, it was well understood and well appreciated then that we were coming here to play our part in turning this country into a paradise. Indians came here under that promise. They worked here for those people who gobbled up half a million acres of freehold land from the Fijian owners and we came and undertook to work under a system which, thank God, saved the Fijian race from the infamy of coming under—my community worked under that semi-servile state. As a matter of fact, if anything, the coming of my people to this country gave the Fijians their honour, their prestige, nay indeed their very soul. Otherwise I have no hesitation in saying that the Fijians of this Colony would have met with the same fate that some other indigenous races in parts of Africa met. I would ask my colleagues to consider that aspect of it before they condemn my people.

---

18   Patel is referring to the Salisbury's Despatch of 1875 which read: 'Above all things we must confidently expect, as an indispensable condition of the proposed arrangement, that the colonial laws and their administration will be such that the Indian settlers who have completed their terms of service to which they agreed, as the return for the expense of bringing them to the Colony, will be in all respects free men, with privileges no whit inferior to those of other class of Her Majesty's subjects resident in the Colonies.' The 'proposed arrangements' were declined by the Government of India but the spirit of fair and equitable treatment of the immigrants continued to underpin official policy.

They fear on the score that we are increasing in numbers. Well, they may think to themselves how was it that their numbers were depleted in this Colony: Indians certainly did not bring the measles and as Mr. Vishnu Deo pointed out, if the Fijians had looked upon the cow as their mother, as we do, and always thought of her milk more than her meat, the mortality rate in their community would not have been so high. Is that the fault of the Indians? Just consider one more point. In this Colony the Fijians are lucky enough to have child welfare activities going on amongst them for a number of years. There have been Fijian mid-wives and nurses already trained and working in their villages and doing splendid work while we, on the other hand, have to expose our women folk in the settlements to the quackery of untrained mid-wives and nurses and place the lives of the mothers and children into their incompetent hands; and still because of our keen care of our children if we increase in numbers, can you lay the blame at our door?

I would ask the Fijian Members also to consider this: socially we have not lived in this country as if we were a garrison in an alien country. We have lived with you and mixed with you, hob-nobbed with you all the time. We have never looked upon the Fijians as our inferiors because they are Fijians. In the time of difficulty or stress they have always gone to an Indian and they always found assistance from him. I was highly gratified to hear in this Council that all sides at least concede one thing—that they all had Indian friends. Well, I only beg of my opponents that they reciprocate that friendship. Socially we have not done you any harm.

Now let us consider the economic aspect. We developed this Colony and as the Commissioner of Labour pointed out, our people are the very sinews of the economic life of the Colony. Not only have we been paying higher and higher rents into your own hands but we are producing the wealth of this Colony, and directly or indirectly all races share in it and benefit by it and the Fijians are no exception, and let me point out that the money that they make from the Indians is mostly spent in European or Chinese concerns. Can they blame us for that?

Let me go a step further, politically: We had penal labour laws in this Colony, we did not have any provision for trade union laws in this Colony, we did not have any laws regarding compensation to workmen; as far as the brown men of the Colony were concerned, life and limbs of the Indians and Fijians had no value at all. Who fought for them? Those of my colleagues who claim to be the trustees of the Fijian race, or we who have been made out, or an attempt has been made to make us out, to be the menace of the Fijian race? We have fought that common battle. Who has been fighting the obnoxious and odious racial discrimination that prevails in Government Service? Have my colleagues who have taken upon themselves the white man's burden of being their trustees, have they taken up the cudgels for the Fijians or is it the Indians? And who have been prominently fighting for the political rights not only of the Indians but the Fijians as well? I again say 'The Indians.'

So even politically we have not been in any way your opponents or your adversaries. A promise was given to the Indians when they came to this Colony that land would be available to them and, as was pointed out by the Acting Secretary for Fijian Affairs went to India, persuaded Indians and brought a shipload of them to this Colony to settle down here.[19] Have my Fijian colleagues ever heard in this Colony or outside that since we were promised land, we should be given freehold land?[20] We have elected to be satisfied with occupying the position of the tenant of the Fijian in this Colony and all that we have been asking for is security of tenure. Indians have never stated that we must take away the lands from the Fijians. We ourselves have advocated the principle that the interests of the Fijians must always remain paramount in this Colony, that where those interests come into conflict with our interests, we readily agree to make our interests subservient to theirs.

Thank goodness our hands are clean, they are not stained with the blood of any race. Thank God our hearts are clean, we have worked hard and earned our bread by the sweat of the brow and from that bread we have always been ready and willing through our frugality to pass a portion to anyone else who cared to accept our hospitality or ask for our help. I would remind the Members of this Council that those who try to cry the Indians down may remember that in their hour of stress, although their own fellow compatriots were not prepared to help them, some Indian friend from some corner or another has readily and willingly come forward to help and has not accepted anything, not even thanks, into the bargain, and when such criticism comes one naturally feels like screaming out 'Et tu, Brute!'

The European Member for the Eastern Division wanted some sort of declaration from us that could allay the fears and suspicions of the Fijian community. Well, the assurance I am prepared to give on behalf of my people to our Fijian neighbours in this Colony is that we have all these years lived in this country,

---

19   Here Patel is referring to a 'mission' delegation from Fiji which went to India on 30 December 1919 to try and re-open emigration to Fiji. The planters were hoping for five thousand migrants a year. The delegation comprised of RSD Rankin, Receiver-General and TC Twitchell, Bishop of Polynesia, who represented the Planters Association of Fiji. The delegation assured the Government of India that the government of Fiji undertook to ensure that the economic and political rights of the Indians resident in Fiji would 'not be altered in any way to the detriment of Indians as compared with other residents.'

20   The delegation stated that the Land Settlement Ordinance of 1915 would be activated to enable the Fiji government to acquire land compulsorily, if necessary, for Indian settlement, with an initial sum of one hundred thousand pounds set aside for that purpose: 'Land Settlement is one of the most important features of the Fiji Scheme, as the Government of Fiji is anxious not merely to introduce labourers who will remain for a comparatively short period, but to secure further permanent population, which is one of the greatest needs of the Colony.'

as sugar in milk, and we shall always live just the same as we have done in the past. It has never been our desire to dominate over anybody, but let it be remembered that we will not tolerate any domination from others as well. As our previous Governor mentioned in this Council, 'In God's eyes all men are equal.' We sincerely believe in it: we shall live up to that maxim and we shall make every endeavour to make others live up to it, too. It is the only assurance that I can give, and I hope that you will accept it with the same sincerity with which it is being given this evening.[21]

11: In Defense of Democracy, 2 September 1948

Words are dangerous weapons if they are not used carefully. Fashionable phrases, however high sounding, if divorced from realities or exaggerated, only succeed in putting up the backs of those who are affected by them. This motion could have been debated in a spirit of moderation and friendliness. Unfortunately the mover of the motion got carried away with enthusiasm and overlooked the fact that words sometimes hit harder than bullets, and on account of that I notice a reaction in the extreme on the other side which I would not have expected in ordinary circumstances.

One of the phrases that the Member used was 'Palestine in Fiji'. Not only did that phrase have mischievous implications but it was unfair, definitely unfair, to the three great communities who have lived amicably side by side for over 70 years, and it has been used in utter disregard of history. In Palestine, the Arabs were the indigenous community and when the other community wanted to come in it was not, right from the beginning, received with open arms. But let us examine the history of Fiji. The Fijian community could not develop this country and, in order to establish a good and stable government and to develop the industrial and commercial potentialities of this territory and to promote Christian culture amongst them, they unconditionally but voluntarily surrendered this country to the British Crown, and one of the hopes expressed was that this country would be economically developed. Economic development needed capital, industrial and technical skill, coupled with man-power: England had capital, England had the necessary skill and organizational ability, but England was not in a position to fulfill the hope under which the surrender was made because England lacked cheap man-power; and for that purpose, to give effect to the Deed of Cession, with the consent of the Fijian people, the British Government approached India.

---

21   The motion passed read: 'That in the opinion of this Council, the Government and the non-Fijian inhabitants of the Colony stand by the terms of the Deed of Cession and shall consider that document as the Charter of the Fijian people.' The Government of India representative to Ceylon, to whom Patel had sent a copy of his speech, wrote on 10 December 1946: 'The motion was only a cloak for a diatribe against the Indian residents of Fiji. It was mainly due to the opposition so ably expressed by yourself and your other Indian colleagues that the original motion was amended in such a way as to make it comparatively harmless.'

They say it is an ill wind that blows nobody any good: grinding poverty has been the curse of India but that poverty provided Fiji with the cheap man-power that she was looking for. If the European community came here as a result of a voluntary contract contained in the Deed of Cession, my people also came here under a similar contract and a similar promise and that promise was given by the Imperial Government with the consent of the Fijian people, that those Indians who came here would have rights no whit inferior to those enjoyed by other subjects of His Majesty. Thus three races were thrown together by destiny and by the logic of history. It stands to the credit of all the three races that all of them so far have worked and co-operated and made this paradise of the Pacific that is Fiji. Why raise an unnecessary bogey that will suddenly make us start flying at each other's throats and turn these islands into an Armageddon?

I wish my European friends to realize that we are not intruders: we also have come and settled down here and played our important part in the destiny of this country. When the Deed of Cession is emphasized, please do not overlook the fact that we were also brought here under a similar contractual obligation. Even after the system of indenture was abolished, a high official and one of the heads of the Christian churches here was sent to India to persuade the Government and the people of India to send more people to come and settle in Fiji, telling them that they would get lands, that they would get the same privileges and the same treatment as other peoples resident here; the people who had fulfilled their contracts under the indenture were given similar promises and were encouraged to settle down here, and an overwhelming number of the present Indian community are the descendants of those people to whom those promises have been made.

The European Member for the Southern Division stated that the Government has violated the Deed of Cession because the people—referring to my community—that are brought into this Colony hold Asiatic religious concepts. When he used that phrase, he seemed to have forgotten geography: Christianity is also an Asiatic religious concept; Jesus Christ was born, lived and died on the soil of Asia, and never in his life visited Europe. Well, I happen to be one of those whose whole being is affected by an Asiatic religious concept. I believe in the principle of live and let live; I look upon envy and hate as evils which, if one cannot eradicate altogether from one's nature, one must at least learn to suppress. Is Christianity going to preach any ideal which is contrary to that? I believe, though I am a heathen, in the fatherhood of God and brotherhood of mankind. Is Christianity going to preach anything other than that? My religious education has taught me one thing: tolerance towards one another. It emphasizes that as all rivers flow into the same ocean, all religions lead to the same truth. Has Christianity got to quarrel with that? Is there anything in our life here or in the way we socially and culturally mix with our neighbours belonging to the other two great communities, is there anything in which you can say that we have done any harm to the Christian principles of life? Such irrational, unfounded allegations lead nowhere. We all realize that we are all here and we shall all be here always, and it will be in the mutual interest of all of us to live happily and harmoniously together.

Fear has been expressed in this Council that because the Indian community has made rapid progress and because the community rapidly increases in numbers, we have somehow become a menace to the interests of the other two communities. There may have been some sort of justification if we had ever attempted to try domination over the other two racial groups; such a fear would then have been well-founded but we realize and we have never made a secret of it that the Fijian interest in this Colony must always remain paramount. We also realize and we assume the responsibility with the other majority communities that the rights and privileges of the minorities ought not to be and must not be an iota less than the rights and privileges enjoyed by the majority. But at the same time, is it not incumbent on the minorities also to appreciate and realize the fact that they cannot expect or hope for privileges and rights in excess of those enjoyed by the majority? Harmonious relationship can only be brought about if we realize these factors. Let me make it plain again as I did previously in this Council, that the day we ask for a common franchise will be the day when we will be fortunate enough to win the confidence and trust of the other two communities, when they themselves will freely and voluntarily come and say, 'The time has arrived when we are all one; we are not afraid of you because you are predominant in numbers and we can willingly come together under a common franchise.' I hope and pray that all the three communities will live and work for such an ideal.

Opinion has been expressed in this Council that democracy is something that is horrible and terrible and that one should not touch it even with a barge pole. That only shows one thing: we are afraid of our own fellow beings. We have not got sufficient faith and trust in them; but the world is Marching on; however much we might like it to stop here, it is not going to stop or give us any consideration. There are many of us in this Council whose personal interests have been sacrificed, or may be sacrificed, in the near future at the altar of democracy, but that does not mean that democracy is an evil. We find in this Colony a new spirit: it is due to various factors, due to the impact of outside forces during the last war, due to Fiji being now on the map as a station on the international air routes. There are multiple causes that have created that spirit and it is for us to see that we provided new bottles for new wine. Of course, we should give consideration to the factors that may lead us, if we are not careful, to ultimate disaster.

From all the speeches that I have heard, there seems to be fear and mutual mistrust in all the four groups. The Europeans and the Fijians mistrust us and fear us because we are increasing in numbers. We fear that the Europeans and Fijians might combine against us and might trample upon our legitimate interests. The Government fears that any two racial groups might combine together to the detriment of the remaining racial group; and some of the Members on the Unofficial side fear that the Official group may dominate not only with the assistance or support of any one of the three racial groups but in spite of the concerted opposition of the three groups. Your Excellency mentioned that such an eventuality has not happened. Quite right. It has not happened because, unfortunately, so far, (even though I sincerely wish and desire to see this being achieved in the near future) the Unofficial side has not been able to combine together and offer a united front. The test might come when such an eventuality arises, but whether right or wrong, whether there is any foundation for it or not, the fear does exist and we should take notice of it.

Even if we take all these factors into consideration and face the realities, is there not still scope for improvement and expansion of our present political rights? As far as the Fijian community is concerned, the present system has created an admirable type of cultured and level-headed leadership and produced a leader, a great leader, like the Secretary for Fijian Affairs,[22] who in any community anywhere would be an ornament. But would not my Fijian colleagues realize that the time has come when they should produce not only great chiefs but [also] great commoners. I have found that feeling amongst some of the Fijian commoners who have become politically conscious on account of the impact of outside influences that took place during war-time. Can their aspirations not be conveniently accommodated without prejudice to the interests of the high chiefs and the interests of the Fijian community as a whole? I feel that they can. Amongst my own community, I have heard complaints that the franchise is too narrow, that we, in fact, do not come to the Council returned by the Indian population as a whole but by the comparatively well-to-do literate classes. I have always conscientiously tried to reflect the views and opinions not only of the voters who have sent me to this Council but of the masses that I am supposed to serve; but still that feeling is there and the feeling is genuine. Cannot their aspirations be accommodated? It is just a question of enlarging the size of this Council so that there may be a larger number of seats and a wider franchise so that we will be in a position to get a wider cross-section of opinion from each community which would further the interests of the Colony as a whole. I feel that there is a similar feeling amongst the Europeans also. All this can be done advantageously without bringing any bitterness in our deliberations.

The First Indian Nominated Member expressed his fears that the Muslims as a minority were in need of protection and safeguarding. In this general atmosphere

---

22   Ratu Lalabalavu Sukuna, later Ratu Sir Lala Sukuna. See Deryck Scarr, Ratu Sukuna: *Soldier, Statesman, Man of Two Worlds* (London: Macmillan, 1980).

of mutual fear and mistrust I do not blame him or his community if they also are suffering from similar maladies. But when he tried to make out—quoting his predecessor in this Council, Mr. Said Hasan—that the Muslims tried twice previously as candidates for election but failed on account of their smallness of numbers, I would like to read the reply given by the then European Member for the Eastern Division because, as it happens, both these Muslims had at one time or another stood for election in that Division. This is what Mr. [Harold] Gibson had to say in reply to Mr. Hasan's complaint:

> I am very sorry that this red herring of Muslims versus Hindus has been drawn across the track, and I hope it will not affect the ultimate result. There is no need for special protection of Muslims in Fiji, and indeed our friend the Senior Indian Nominated Member has told us that he is here to request the Muslim interests. We presume that most of the motions he has moved in this Council have been made in the interests of Muslims and, if we reflect, it is wonderful to see how the Hindus have almost always to a man supported him. Indeed one spectator said to me: 'Those Hindu Members always back up the Senior Hindu Member,' I said: 'He is not a Hindu: he is a Muslim.' But if you go back through the records you will see that the Indians always vote together. It was mentioned that Muslims had stood in Labasa on two occasions and had not got in. I told one of them myself that if he stood as an Indian and not as a Muslim he would have a better chance of getting in.

One has also got to remember that one of these Muslim candidates opposed a Christian candidate, and it was the Christian candidate who defeated him. As it happened, the Christian candidate belonged to a still small minority even among the Christians: he was a Roman Catholic. In spite of that he defeated his Muslim rival, and with the votes of the majority of Indian constituents he entered this Council. It was not a case of a candidate belonging to the majority community, namely, the Hindus, defeating a member of the minority community. There is also another convincing example before us in the person of the Indian Member for the Eastern Division who, as he himself told us yesterday, belongs to the Christian minority. The candidate who stood against him at the last election was a member of the majority community, namely, a Hindu, who belonged to one of the most influential Indian families in the Colony; culturally and educationally, he was a member of the Middle Temple; and as far as experience goes, he had served his term of three years in this Council with credit and distinction. If a candidate belonging to a minority community can defeat a candidate with all those advantages and can be elected to this Council I do not see where the fears of my Muslim friends and colleagues come in. I would like to appeal to my Muslim friends that if they like, let the proper type of candidates come out from their communities and work amongst the people, looking upon themselves as Indians first and Muslims afterwards, and then seek election. I feel certain that they will come to this Council without any difficulty.

Unfortunately, I notice a tendency amongst some of my European friends to encourage that type of separatist feeling amongst the Indians of this Colony. The mover of the motion accused the Government of following the 'divide and rule' policy, but I would like to ask some of my European colleagues that when they try to take up cudgels for our minorities, aren't they prompted by the same policy? If they are sincere and genuine and if they look upon Muslims as a community separate and apart from the Indians, it logically follows that we have got not three communities in Fiji but four, namely, Fijians, Europeans, Indians and Muslims. While the Indians, who are about the same in number as the Fijians, will be content to take the same number of seats as the Fijians themselves would ask for, the Europeans also should realize that if they get the same number of seats while they are 6,000 in numbers, they should allow a similar number of seats to the Muslim minority who are 16,000 in numbers. If my European colleagues are prepared to consider that suggestion and give the Muslim minority also the same representation as they themselves enjoy, as I say, the Indians will be content with what the Fijians ask and remain at parity with them; I have no objection, I would willingly support it.

But I would like to point out one thing before I finish this point. The very gentleman who expressed those fears in 1943 and who thought it fit that he should lodge a caveat, only seven days ago, on Thursday, September 16th, had his views expressed in a local paper. Said Mr. Said Hasan, President of the Fiji Muslim League: 'Hindus and Muslims in Fiji have too much in common to let a war interfere with their relationship.' He is further reported to have said that in the true sense of the term there are neither Hindus nor Muslims here and that Fiji Indians had much more in common than the two races in India. Well, I would recommend that the views expressed by this gentleman a week ago should be accepted in preference to the fears expressed by him in 1943, and the credit for the removal of such fears should be given to the majority Hindu community. I would like the Hon. Unofficial Members not to be carried away by the bitterness and heat that was brought into this debate but to consider the amendment dispassionately and in an objective manner. We have got to consider the possibilities of constitutional changes having due regard to all problems and difficulties that the presence of three racial groups in this Colony entails; we have got to face these problems and we have got to seek a solution, and a debate is hardly the way in which we can iron out our differences.

If anything, a debate actually accentuates them. The proper place to iron out such differences would be the conference table. If the Members vote for the [constitutional] amendment, it does not necessarily mean that at the conference table they are bound to vote for the change in the present constitution; but at least it will give us an opportunity to come together, to put our heads together and to try in all sincerity to find a solution of the present problems.

The Mover of the motion concluded his speech by quoting Mr. Winston Churchill. I should also like to conclude mine by quoting his famous words. 'Let us all go forward together.'

12: On Separate Representation for Muslims, 9 December 1949

The Indian community in Fiji has now entered the third generation and, as the saying goes, it is an ill wind that blows nobody any good: the indenture system contributed at least one good thing to the Indian community and that was the social fusion and breaking down of the caste system among the Indians even to the extent of breaking down the religious barriers. Where in India marriages between castes—inter-caste marriages—would have been thought something inconceivable and for which reformers had to sacrifice their lives and yet could not achieve their object, the indenture system by one sweeping blow, shattered the caste system and [made] inter-caste marriages the rule of the day. Inter-marriage was not limited to the various castes of the orthodox Hindus as the word 'Hindu' may be used in the religious sense, but it became the rule of the day amongst all Indians in the Colony, whether Muslims, Hindus or Sikhs. I know many prominent Hindus who are the sons of Muslim mothers, and therefore I say that the question of dividing Hindu and Muslim as two separate communities does not arise in Fiji, because not only has there been social intercourse, but there has also been a free mingling of blood and the whole Indian community here has been welded into one racial unit. Socially, too, all these years that I have been in Fiji, I have noticed Hindus participating in Tazia festivals when they were in vogue in Fiji, and Muslims participating in Ramlila festivals. If the Tazia festivals were discontinued in Fiji, they were discontinued at the instance of the Muslims.[23] To bring a parallel from thousands of miles away, from India, [which] has reached a critical and transitory stage in her historical development, is like the Roman Catholics and Protestants of this Colony going back into British history, back to the days of the Reformation, and saying that because the Roman Catholics burned the Protestants and the

---

23 Sunni Muslims as Tazia or Mohurram was a Shia festival commemorating the slaying of Hasan and Hussein, grandsons of Prophet Mohammed.

Protestants burned the Catholics, they are two separate units, and after all these years they should be classed as two separate communities, even in Fiji. We have got to be realistic. There may be certain sections and even among particular sections certain individuals who can only be regarded as fanatical. You find that in every religious group and in every social group. Because of the fanaticism of a few individuals the groups should not be permanently and perpetually segregated.

Complaint has been made about conversion of Muslims, which is called *Shuddhi*. I may say that I have been in this Colony for 20 years and the only instance of *Shuddhi* I came across was in Samabula where one Mohammedan was converted to Arya Samaj. The Hindu religion does not permit proselytizing. A man can only be born a Hindu; he cannot be made a Hindu. So there is no question of a Hindu trying to proselytize either a Christian or a Muslim or a follower of any other religion to Hinduism. And if one instance like that from the Muslim side, of conversion into the Arya Samajist group, makes the Muslim community feel bitter against the Hindu community, who are an innocent third party, then I must say that there is no justice in this world. In this very Colony I know so many Muslims who have been converted to the Christian faith, and yet I have not heard a murmur from the leaders of the Muslim community against the Christians. If the Muslims choose to beat the Hindu community with a big stick whether they are at fault or not, they may do so; but I must say that it does not contribute to the fellow-feeling and good neighbourliness that the mover referred to.

All these years, even now, not only socially and politically but even culturally, we have worked together. We have got the cultural organization here known as the Sangam in which all the people from the South [India] work together in furtherance of their common culture, and I am proud to say that in that organization the Muslims of Southern India work with as much sincerity and enthusiasm as the Hindus, and in that organization, I am proud to say, that my colleague and myself, I as a representative of the Hindus and he as a representative of the Muslims, have never seen any complaint on either side. Well, if we can carry on happily in one organization, why cannot we carry on like that in all organizations, including the political organization of the Colony, which is this Council? After all, every community and every little group have their own pet ideas and idiosyncrasies, but when we are looking at the national aspect, we have to forget them or subordinate them to the larger interests of the community as a whole.

All these years have proved that as far as economic and political interests of the Indian community in Fiji are concerned, there is no question of any conflicting interests between the Muslim and the non-Muslim. Economically we are all subjected to the same conditions, politically also we live under the same conditions. We are subjected to the same conditions in every respect; we have fought together for progress, shoulder to shoulder, and it has in no way resulted in any disadvantage to the Muslim community. I have not so far heard a complaint either publicly or in private from any member of the Muslim League that the trust and confidence they reposed in their elected Member has been in any way betrayed. If we are going to adopt the principle of separate representation for separate religious groups we must consider the claims of Sikhs and Christians in this Council; and if we follow the reasoning of my friend, even amongst the Christians we will have to make separate provision for the Roman Catholics and the Protestants.

The Imperial Government as early as 1926 or 1927 defined their objective as to the nature of representation in the Colonies in a Paper that was laid on the Table in the House of Commons—that a common franchise and a common roll is an ideal to be desired, to be aimed at and to be achieved. In this Colony some of the racial groups considered that it was not practicable in the present circumstances, however nice, desirable and attractive the idea might be, and we agreed *pro tem* that the three major communities of Fiji should have separate representation on separate rolls until such time as mutual misunderstanding and mistrust was removed and all the communities agreed to come together. To create yet another group in this Council is straying further away from the ideal instead of coming nearer and, as I pointed out, without any particular reason to justify it.

Still, if it is the feeling of the House that the interests of the Colony can be best served by having four groups in this Council instead of three, and if the Muslims are to be looked upon as a group separate and apart from the Indians, which would consist of Hindus, Christians, Sikhs, Jains, Parsis and others, then I have only one thing to say. The non-Muslim Indians in Fiji are about the same in number as the Fijians. If they are to be treated as a separate group from the Muslims, they will be satisfied with the same number of Members is this Council as may be given to the Fijians. That is only fair and just. We cannot be expected to take anything less than that. We are not asking for anything more. If the Council thinks that the Muslims should be a separate group and a separate community from the non-Muslim Indians, then, as they are equal in numbers to the Europeans, they should be given the same number of seats as the Europeans. That is the position in short. I am personally convinced that the interests of the Muslims in this Colony have been safeguarded and protected by the Indian Members in this Council right throughout. History has proved that they have no reason for any fear, and yet, if this small community, supported by some of my European colleagues, feel that they should have separate representation, by all means treat them as a separate community. Give them the same number of seats in this Council as are given to the European Members and let the non-Muslim Members have the same [number of seats] as the Fijians. We will be quite satisfied.

13: Wanted: A Common Electoral Roll, 16 August 1956

In any democratic country, the general election is both a means for the political education of the public as well as a good test for the political progress attained by the general public. An opportunity is provided by the election for different parties to place before the general electorate their own plans for the progress of the country in the different spheres of activity. And in the election campaign the different points of view are brought home to the public. The wisdom of the choice made by the public in the actual election will be a test of the maturity of outlook and the extent of enlightenment which the people have attained.

But this healthy function of an election will be possible only if certain fundamental pre-requisites of the system itself are present. The first and foremost of these is a common electoral roll in which the name of all adults, irrespective of race, sex or religion, are entered. This has been the system obtaining not merely in the United Kingdom but also in all modern democracies. For, all citizens have the same stake, the same rights and privileges and the same duties and responsibilities by his State of which he is a citizen. His religion or colour of skin or the country from which his ancestors originally came, had no relevance whatever to the right discharge of the duties of citizenship.

A common electoral roll is the most effective means of fostering a common outlook of loyalty and citizenship in a country. And that is evidently the reason why that system has been introduced, as the Secretary of State for Colonies stated recently in the House of Commons, in twenty two British colonies and territories. For territorial elections in Nyasaland and Northern Rhodesia, European and Asian electors are registered in a common roll. And the Governor of Tanganyika has announced his Government's intention to introduce direct elections on a common roll. So, too, is the case with Uganda and British Guiana. We find it hard to explain why the Common Electoral Roll has not yet been introduced here. And we feign hope that the Secretary of State will, before the next elections in Fiji, be able to include our Colony in the large group of colonies where a Common Roll is in force.

We need not mention here that means can be easily found for giving the representation that the present racial set-up provides for the Europeans, Fijians and Indians in the Legislative Council. But providing for the accommodation of more groups in the Council certainly cannot be in the interests of the Colony. Provision may and can easily be made for the reservation of five seats each in the Council for the Europeans, Fijians and Indians, so that the present distribution of membership in the Council is not disturbed as between the different races.

But the need for the candidates standing for election to approach all the citizens of the Colony will oblige them to consider the interests of the Colony as being more important than the petty interests of his community.

The Fijians would, according to this, have their rightful share in deciding not merely their own representatives in the Council but also the representatives of other races as well. In the early stages, it may be advisable to place before the electorate the panel of Fijian representatives which the Council of Chiefs is at present selecting for the final decision of the Governor. The chiefs will still retain their power in making up the panel. But the Fijian commoner will have some voice in the selection of his representatives. But only the members of the panel can stand as candidates in the general election.

Fiji, we submit to the attention of the British Government, deserves the Common Electoral Roll, at least for the next elections. What is good for Aden and twenty-one other colonies could certainly be useful, nay essential, for our Colony, which we claim to be as progressive and developed as any one of these twenty-two.

14: Last But Not Long!, 1 February 1960

The winds of political change are blowing all over the colonial territories and Fiji cannot hope to remain unaffected. People of Fiji hear about these radical changes on the radio, read about them in newspapers and discuss them in private conversation. People of Fiji compare their lot with that of the people of Hawaii and do not fail to observe the vast contrast. When Fiji is compared with Samoa, which stands on the threshold of independence, the contrast becomes still more glaring.

In the present age of fast world communications, it would be foolish to expect people of Fiji to become Rip Van Winkles and notice nothing. Some of the representatives of big vested interests in Fiji are carrying a concerted propaganda in Great Britain, Australia and New Zealand and in the Legislative Council of Fiji, that no real political change is wanted in Fiji; people only ask for more money; they don't ask for more votes. Such a propaganda in the latter half of the 20th century, even in the eyes of diehard imperialists abroad, must appear too good to be true.

There are at least three political groups in Fiji at the present moment. The group which advocates no change in the present political set up is the smallest, but most closely knit, and racially, politically and economically the strongest. This group represents the big European interests. Another group consists of the trade unions under extremist leaders who advocate and ask for complete political independence—here and now. It should not be forgotten, that a few days before the disturbances,[24] there was a mammoth meeting at Albert Park under the very shadow of the Secretariat building in Suva, when the demand for independence was raised. One of the members of the Legislative Council was the convener of the meeting.[25] It is true that the size of this group in the Colony is not very large at present, it should not be overlooked that it is larger than the diehard group of no-changers and with this important difference that while the number of no-changers remain the same, the number of the extremists is increasing from day to day.

In between this two opposing groups is the big mass of citizens from all races—Indians, Fijians and Europeans—who consider that political reforms are overdue that there should be substantial changes in the constitution of the Legislature providing for an unofficial majority, that the Executive should be made truly responsible to the Legislative Council and that local self-government should be introduced not only in the city of Suva and town of Lautoka but in all the townships and rural areas of Fiji. The constitutional changes should be such as would lead the country gradually and harmoniously to complete independence within a certain number of years. This large group at present is not so closely knit as the diehard group, nor is it so organized as the extremist group. Just now, numerically it is the largest group, represents all the races resident in the Colony, and is anxious to preserve racial harmony in the course of vast political changes which are inevitable. Unless this group organises itself and takes active steps, it will find itself gradually dwindling in numbers while the numbers of the extremists will keep on increasing until the time comes when there will be only two groups standing face to face—the diehards and the extremists.

Those who are in responsible positions should not bury their heads in sand ostrich-fashion, and pretend that people of Fiji want no political changes. It is often said that Fiji will be the last Colony to go out of Britain's colonial empire. That may be so. But it may not be very long before she does.

15: An Astounding Statement, 3 March 1960

People are astonished at the statement reported to have been made by the Governor, Sir Kenneth Maddocks, in Auckland to the effect 'that strife was largely between the two major racial groups, Fijians and Indians'. One wonders how a person holding such a high rank of responsibility can make an assertion so manifestly incorrect. It may not have occurred to His Excellency that such a tendentious statement is likely to cause lot of harm.

---

24   This refers to the strike in the oil industry in Suva in 1959.
25   BD Lakshman.

Luckily in this Colony, there is no strife between any races, and least of all between Fijians and Indians. Whenever occasions have arisen, these two great races have demonstrated their sense of solidarity and unity unmistakably. The strife in the Colony, if it can be so called, is really between the gigantic industrial and commercial concerns of the Colony and their underpaid workers who generally come from Fijian, Indian and other under-privileged races resident in the Colony. The struggle between them is going on since 1943 and as the workers get more united and better organized, the conflict is getting keener with the chances of success for the workers improving every day.

In 1943, the Colonial Sugar Refining Company's workers demonstrated complete unity which led to the rise in wages, improvement in living quarters and increase in concessions. More than that, the 1943 strike made the Colonial Sugar Refining Company realize the value and necessity of good relations with its employees. The Public Works Department, which unfortunately goes hand in hand with these big concerns, was the next to realize the impact of workers' solidarity. The 1958 strike in the C.S.R's mills made it abundantly clear that any attempt to divide workers on racial lines, caused resistance and resulted in welding them more solidly together. The Part- European workers joined Indians and Fijians and all of them made themselves stronger in the bargaining sphere. The 1959 strike in the oil trade further forged this unity into a strong unbreakable chain, and if there is any further industrial trouble, which we hope not, it is almost certain that workers of all races and ranks will join together with even greater unity than ever before to face such trouble.

The vested interests and the Government are trying to divert the attention of the people here and abroad from the real issues of low wages and poor living conditions of the working class by raising a bogey of Indian over-population calculated to bring about, if not actual hostility, at least apprehensiveness among other races and especially the Fijians. The propaganda may have some little effect in the beginning, but the way it is carried on persistently and ad nauseam in time and out of time, has flogged it into a dead horse, which now cannot be revived and made to serve their purpose. The rank and file of Fijians and Indians do and will always stick together in spite of any such propaganda to divide them. They will move forward together to attain their goal, but even in their March, they will extend their hands in friendship to other races in the Colony. Fijians and Indians realize that harmony and friendliness among all races is a *sine quo non* for a bright and happy future.

16: A Constitutional Mirage, 13 April 1961

Constitutional reforms are long overdue in Fiji. While some of the territories, the peoples of which are not as advanced as those of Fiji, have already received self-government, Fiji's Constitution still stands where it was 25 years ago. The European vested interests who oppose the change lay an over-emphasis on the multi-racial composition of the Colony's population. Almost all the colonies which have attained self-government are multi-racial and it has not so proved a serious obstacle in their case. There is no reason why it should prove an insurmountable obstacle in the constitutional progress of Fiji. If Fiji is going to be a self-governing country in future, it is essential that a political consciousness of nationhood should be established and fostered among all races. This can be brought about only by bringing all people of the Colony politically together irrespective of their race or creed or sex.

A universal adult suffrage based on a common electoral roll is the *sine qua non* of any real constitutional change. A common electoral roll is opposed by the European community on the ground that the Indians and Fijians being in a majority, the Europeans will be swamped and will have no chance of being elected to the Legislative Council. To allay their fears a provision should be made for reservation of certain seats for Fijian, Indian and European members based on a common roll. The present constitution is highly biased in favour of the Europeans and against the Indians and Fijians. This should be immediately rectified by providing for six Fijian, six Indian and three European members. There should be no nominated members on the unofficial side and there should be an unofficial majority in the Council.

The Government proposal of inviting the unofficial members of the Executive Council to undertake supervisory duties over government departments on condition that they will have to accept the majority decision of the Executive Council in which the official members will be in a majority and will have to either support the government or resign from the Executive Council, in effect compels an unofficial member of the Executive Council to fall into line with the Colonial Government. Instead of being responsible to the people, the 'members' or ministers will be responsible to the colonial bureaucracy. As long as they support the colonial rule, they will be considered 'responsible.' As soon as they choose to stand by their own constituents and oppose colonial rule, they will be considered irresponsible and thrown out of the Executive Council. The use of the phrase 'ministerial responsibility' in the Government's proposal is the greatest abuse of the phrase we have so far come across in the constitutional terminology. The heads of government departments or a colonial government have been trained in and are used to autocratic rule.

Colonial rule is the very antithesis of a responsible government and before claiming to teach ministerial responsibility to the elected representatives of the people, the heads of the departments have to learn to give up the authoritarian methods to which they have been used and to learn to respect and abide by the opinions and judgments of the people as reflected through their elected representatives in the legislature. It is sheer waste of time and money to adopt the government's proposal about training members in the Executive Council for the so-called ministerial responsibility. It presupposes that the members and ministers who have stuck to the government will become chosen ministers of the people when Fiji attains self-government, when it is quite obvious that they will become stooges of a colonial bureaucracy in the eyes of the people and as soon as the transfer of power takes place such stooges will most likely be swept out in the very first elections. This has happened in other colonies and it is sure to happen in Fiji.

There is no reason why the Fijians should not have equal political rights with the members of other races. The Government's proposal for Fijian representation partly by direct election and partly by election from the Council of Chiefs places the Fijian in an inferior political position. This should not be allowed. It will only create a political inferiority complex among the Fijians. The provision for allowing Fijian civil servants to stand for election can only result in there being in fact no real Fijian representative to look after Fijian interests. Being paid Government servants their first loyalty and complete obedience will be and ought to be to the government. Fijian interests can be best safeguarded by independent representatives. They should be placed on the same footing as Europeans and Indians in the election of their representatives. The Legislative Council under its present composition does not represent the people of Fiji. Even the unofficial side which consists of three Europeans and three Indians elected on a restricted electoral roll while the other nine unofficial members are either the nominees of the Governor or the Council of Chiefs, are far from being the real representatives or the people. The Government's proposals, in fact, deform the present Constitution instead of reforming it. Whatever the Legislative Council may say upon the subject when it comes before it, it is definite that it does not meet the approval of a large majority of the people of Fiji

17: Welcome to Sir Derek Jakeway, 24 February 1964

Your Excellency

We the Indian people assembled here today on behalf of the Indian Community extend to you and Lady Jakeway a hearty welcome.

Fiji is indeed most fortunate to have a person of your ability, experience and understanding as our Governor at a time which is crucial, if not critical, in its political evolution towards a self-governing state. We feel confident that the important part which you must have played in the course of your service in other colonies in their political and economic development will prove to be of great help and benefit to the people of Fiji at this juncture. Though Fiji is a multi-racial and multi-religious country, we are proud to say that all the races and religions live side by side in harmony and peace to a degree which is rarely found in other parts of the world. In our humble opinion, this is a good asset to start with in the building of a nation, and in that most urgent and important task, we pledge you our full co-operation and support.

Under the present and past constitutions, the three important races of the Colony viz the Indians, the Fijians, and the Europeans, are kept politically separate and apart in their representation in the legislative and municipal councils. A vast majority of Indians live on their farms, Fijians mostly live in their villages and the Europeans are largely concentrated in urban and industrial centres. The social contact between the three races, therefore, is not as much as one would desire. Our community will co-operate and participate in any measures which may be devised to promote social and political integration and understanding between all races residing in the Colony.

Your Excellency's arrival in the Colony coincides with the inauguration of the 1964–68 Development Plan in which the emphasis is rightly placed on the increase in the agricultural production. Our community is engaged mainly in agriculture and is well known for its thrift, industry, capacity for sustained effort and skill. If Indian farmers are provided with sufficient land and facilities for marketing the produce at economic price, they can play a very important role in the economic development and in raising the standard of living of the people of this Colony. We hope and trust that our people will be given adequate opportunities to undertake and fulfill their responsibilities in this all-important sector of economic progress.

All civilized countries of the world are at present engaged in eradicating poverty, ignorance and disease from their midst. Fiji is also trying to do it in a modest way. To win peace, prosperity and happiness for the people of Fiji, it is necessary to wage a war on these three great enemies of mankind. We hope and trust that measures will be taken and efforts will be intensified to eradicate them from our midst as far as possible. Fiji, like other countries, naturally has its own problems, but, we believe, they are capable of solution by mutual good will and understanding and by a spirit of give and take.

Though the duties which you may be called upon to perform during your Governorship may prove to be difficult and onerous, we feel sure that with the ability, experience and energy which you possess in an abundant measure will help you in discharging them for the benefit and welfare of the people of Fiji.

In the end we pray to Almighty God that your Excellency, Lady Jakeway and your children be pleased with good health, happiness, prosperity and long lives. May He make your and Lady Jakeway's stay amongst us enjoyable and happy.

With this prayer, I again extend to you and Lady Jakeway a very hearty welcome.

On behalf of the Indian Community,

AD Patel

Churchill Park, Lautoka

18: Protest Letter to Sir Derek Jakeway, 24 January 1965

Your Excellency

We strongly protest against Your Excellency's statement which you made about the Indian community of Fiji in Australia during your recent visit there. In particular, we take strong exception to two statements made by you, namely, 'that it was inconceivable that Britain would ever permit the Fijian people to be placed politically under the heels of an immigrant community.' So far as the placing the native communities under the heels of immigrant communities is concerned, British history has consistently followed this practice in many countries, the outstanding examples being South Africa, Australia, New Zealand, Canada and Singapore. It is, therefore, historically conceivable as far as British policy is concerned. Even in the case of Fiji at present, both the Indian and the Fijian communities are placed under the heels of a very small immigrant community, namely the Europeans. Your statement therefore is historically incorrect. The Indians have always taken sincere interest in the progress, prosperity and welfare of the Fijians and have looked upon them as fellow countrymen. Never has the Indian community harboured any intention to place the Fijians under their heels. The statement is, therefore, mischievous and creates a totally false impression both abroad and in Fiji that the Indians are out to politically dominate the Fijians and the Colonial Office is trying to prevent it. The statement in this respect is grossly untrue and mischievous. Besides, it tends to create mistrust in the minds of the Fijians against the Indians at a time when it is absolutely necessary to establish mutual trust and confidence between the two races. As the Head of the Government of Fiji, in our humble opinion, the obligation to see that there is harmony and confidence between the two races rests on your shoulders.

As to the question of self-government, we have made it abundantly clear that Fiji should have full internal self-government immediately. It is therefore misleading to say that 'Indians do not want self-government because they fear racial strife.' This statement naturally worries the Indian community. Mr. Nigel Fisher[26] when he visited Fiji in 1963 announced that the British Government will honour the Deed and the [Salisbury] Despatch equally and that Indians will also have the same right as others.

We do not know if the change of Government in Britain caused any change in that policy. We would therefore be very grateful if you will forward this letter to the Right Honourable the Secretary of State for the Colonies in order to find out whether there has been any change in the policy.

We regret to say that these statements have rudely shaken the confidence and trust the Indian community had in Your Excellency's impartiality which is so essential at this critical stage in the history of this Colony. It has also caused suspicion in our minds as to the bon fides and sincerity of the British Government.

We believe that the preservation and promotion of harmony and confidence between Indians and Fijians are of utmost importance and the Government has an obligation to work positively towards that end. We from our side conscientiously and faithfully try to work towards that goal and refrain from saying anything which will give offence to the other side. Unfortunately some elements among the Europeans and the 'Fiji Times' are resorting to methods designed to ignite ill-feeling between the two races and to fan the fire. We are grieved to find that the Fiji Broadcasting Commission for whose activities the Government is responsible, is also joining forces with these reactionary elements to refer to the activities of the Federation Party, to which the Fijian Association had taken strong exception. This was evidently done to inflame the people of the Federation Party against the Fijian Association and thereby drive a wedge between these two most important political organizations in the country and at the same time pouring out his malice towards the Federation Party by using such an abusive and insulting language. What is more, when the Federation Party approached the management through its legal advisor, it admitted the use of this abusive and insulting word[27] and tried to justify its use. We should like to know what steps the Government proposes to take in this matter and so to ensure that the radio is used to promote good will and understanding between the two races and not to pull them apart and be at loggerheads with each other.

---

26 Parliamentary Under-Secretary for the Colonies (July 1962–October 1963).
27 The word was 'Badmaash', meaning 'Hooligan'.

We deeply regret that we have to take up this matter with Your Excellency, highly unpleasant as it is, because we consider that harmonious race relations are vital in this country at all times and more especially at the moment.

19: Public Notice (Undated, 1965)

As the people of Fiji are aware, it is likely that a Conference to consider the new constitution for Fiji will be held in the near future.

The Indian members of the Legislative Council invite representations or suggestions on the question of future constitution for Fiji from Indian organizations, groups and individuals.

The subject matter of the representations or suggestions should cover, among other things, the following:

(1) The extent of self-government.

(2) Whether there should be a link between the Crown and Fiji and if so, the nature of such relationship.

(3) Composition of the legislature and method of election.

(4) Composition of the Executive and its power.

(5) Necessary safeguards for the rights of individuals and communities and how they should be preserved.

Such representations or suggestions may be sent to any Indian Member of the Legislative council or to the office of the Member for Social Services in Suva, at any time before the 9th January, 1965.

AD Patel

AIN Deoki

CA Shah

CP Singh

J Madhavan

SM Koya

20: Memorandum to Sir Derek Jakeway, 26 January 1965[28]

May it please Your Excellency

With due respect, we very much regret to inform you that we strongly resent the remarks made by you in the Conference of the Unofficial Members of the Legislative Council this morning to the effect that the selection of the Indian Delegates to the proposed London Constitutional Conference (which was based on a majority decision) was unreasonable and quite unacceptable to you.

We must place on record that at the December Conference we gathered the impression that each racial group would be entitled to select its delegates for the London Constitutional Conference to enable the Right Honourable the Secretary of State for the Colonies to issue invitations. At no time we were told that such selection should be made by unanimous vote and we venture to say that such a suggestion, if made, would have been bitterly opposed by our side. In the proceedings of the Legislative Council and other matters connected therewith, the democratic form of taking decision by majority is followed without exception, and we fail to see why you should require an unanimous decision on the part of the Indian members on this matter.

We also resent the interference of any member of another racial group in the selection of the delegates from our group. This morning's incident has given us a strong impression that this is being done to introduce discord and disunity on the Indian side at the London Constitutional Conference thereby placing the Indian Community at a disadvantage vis a vis the Fijians and Europeans. For the conference to succeed in its undertaking, it is imperative that the delegates of each racial group are able to speak with one voice and have the confidence, trust and the backing of the community they represent.

We would like to point out that the organization of the Federation Party is an attempt to introduce party system in the legislature but it does not mean that we only represent the people belonging to that party. As a matter of fact, we enjoy the confidence and trust of a vast majority of the Indians. There is no sectional or minority interest in the Indian Community represented by the Honourable C.P. Singh which is not represented by us and further we represent many such interests which neither of them do.

---

28 The petition was signed by SM Koya, CA Shah and James Madhavan, when AD Patel was Member for Social Services.

Furthermore, during the 1963 election, one of the platforms of the three elected members (who are signatories to this letter), was that representations should be made to bring about constitutional changes to give Fiji internal self-government, and we claim that a specific mandate was given to us on this subject.

In order to obtain invitation to the London Constitutional Conference it appears that Messrs. Deoki and Singh got busy to magnify existing differences in the Indian community and tried to create artificial minority interests. This tends to create sheer mischief and further discord and disunity at a time when unity is most essential. In our view, it is important that the United Kingdom Government should know at the London Constitutional Conference what the Indians as a whole want and not the individuals or splinter groups.

In the circumstances, we would request that this letter be forwarded to the Right Honourable the Secretary of State for the Colonies.

21: Resolutions passed at the AGM of the Federation Party at Lautoka, 25 April 1965

Resolution No.1

THAT this Annual General Meeting of the Federation Party

DECLARES

a) that certain vested interests and organizations in Fiji and in particular, the *Fiji Times*, the Public Relations Office and the Fiji Broadcasting Commission, have in the past, deliberately published distorted news concerning the proposed constitutional changes for Fiji, concerning inter-racial harmony in Fiji and concerning the political rights and views of the Indians in Fiji;

b) that they have transmitted such distorted news overseas with the sole object of creating animosity, misunderstanding and disharmony between the different racial communities living in Fiji; and

c) that they have created an atmosphere of mistrust and misunderstanding among the people of Fiji on matters aforementioned at a time when Fiji is going through its critical stage of political development, and

IT ASSERTS

That in the light of the facts stated above, it is inconceivable that any good purpose would be served by holding further discussions in Fiji between the Honourable Members of the Legislative Council on constitutional matters and,

IT DIRECTS

Its members, Messrs. A.D. Patel, S.M. Koya, C.A. Shah and J. Madhavan, not to hold any such discussions in Fiji with other Honourable Members of the Legislative Council but to present their views and opinions at the proposed Constitutional Conference to be held in London in the month of July, 1965.

Resolution No.2

That this Annual General Meeting of the Federation Party hereby expresses its fullest confidence in the four Honourable Members of the Legislative Council namely, Messrs. A.D. Patel, C.A. Shah, J. Madhavan and S.M. Koya in their respective ability and integrity to present the Indian Community's case at the forthcoming Constitutional Conference to be held in London in the month of July, 1965 and it empowers them to make all such representations and submissions which they may think fit and proper in their absolute discretion on all matters to be discussed at the said Conference with a view to obtaining fair, just and equitable rights for the Indians in Fiji and with the view to making a nation out of the several communities who live in and belong to Fiji.

Resolution No.3

That this Annual General Meeting of the Federation Party requests the Government of Fiji, the Native Land Trust Board, the Legislative Council of Fiji and all parties concerned to take all appropriate steps as soon as practicable to bring about a satisfactory solution concerning the problems affecting the security of tenure of leased lands, renewability of leases and compensation in cases of termination of leases and recognises that these problems exercise the minds of tenants of all races and that a satisfactory solution to these problems is of vital importance to the economic life of the Colony.

Resolution No.4

That this Annual General Meeting of the Federation Party deplores the action of the staff of the Public Relations Office, Suva, when they intentionally and deliberately distorted and incorrectly translated the *Jagriti* version of the address given by the party's President, the Honourable Mr. A.D. Patel, at a meeting of the Party held on Sunday the 4th April, 1965, at the Century Theatre, Suva, which said translation has been published in Fiji and abroad and it declares that it has no confidence in the staff of the said Office.

22: Letter to Sir Derek Jakeway, 30 April, 1965

I beg to acknowledge receipt of your letter dated 27th April, 1965.[29] In reply, I wish to draw your attention to the statement of the previous Governor in the Legislative Council in 1961 [Sir Kenneth Maddocks] on the proposed Membership System, in which he stated: 'On appointment members would be required to give an undertaking to accept collective responsibility; *that means that when policy matters are considered in Executive Council all members both official and unofficial would as at present be free to advise and express their views according to their conscience. Once a decision has been taken in Executive Council, however, then all would be bound by it whether it represents their personal view or not, or resign.'*

This was the extent of collective responsibility when the Portfolio of Social Services was offered to me and I agreed and accepted it.[30]

When you informed me by letter dated 29th June, 1964 that I shall be designated the Member for Social Services from 1st July, 1964 you sent me notes for the guidance of the members of the Executive Council under the membership system with the said letter:

> Executive Council will continue to be advisory to His Excellency the Governor as at present and all important matters of policy will continue to be decided by the Governor-in-Council. There will be, however, one very important change in that there will in future be collective responsibility of members of the Executive Council in the formulation and implementation of Government Policy. If any member disagrees with any policy decided in Executive Council to the extent that he is not prepared to bear his share of collective responsibility for that decision then the proper course for him is to resign.

In paragraph 7 under the same heading reads as follows:

---

29 The letter was written to Patel after the annual general meeting of the Federation Party in April 1965 had criticized the Fiji Broadcasting Commission for broadcasting misleading and at times inaccurate news about the activities of the party, expressing 'no confidence' in the FBC. Jakeway wrote: 'I must ask you to say, explicitly and immediately, whether you associate yourself with these statements in so far as they affect the Public Relations Office, which is a Government Department. You will realise that anything other than a public disassociation from these attacks on the Public Relations Office must bring into question your continued membership of the Executive Council.'

30 The Membership System was introduced on 1 July 1964. Ratu Kamisese Mara was Member for Natural Resources, JN Falvey Member for Communications and Works and AD Patel Member for Social Services. Patel's portfolio included cultural activities, education, health, prisons, social welfare and 'societies.' Heads of Departments retained full internal control of their departments, and were directly responsible to the Colonial Secretary in all matters relating to the civil service, to the Member in all matters relating to functional operations, and to the Financial Secretary in matters of financial administration.

In view of the doctrine of collective responsibility all unofficial members of the Executive Council will be required fully to support and defend *Government policy* in Legislative Council and in public.

I have supported the decisions taken in the Executive Council and shared responsibility both in the Legislative Council and in public. When I accepted the office I accepted responsibility only to the extent mentioned in the notes and no further.

Considering that under the Membership System I am supposed to undertake collective responsibility as stated above without any power or authority whatsoever, I am not prepared to agree to the extension of the responsibility to defend the actions of civil servants or to defend them against public criticism.

I found it difficult to carry on as a Member when all that I can do is to persuade the Heads of Departments one the one hand and you on the other. Sometimes I have succeeded, at other times I have failed. But I have continued, in the face of difficulties, to give such a one-sided system a fair trial and you must admit that I have faithfully carried out responsibilities in the formulation and implementation of government policies.

Some time ago, Mr. SM Koya, Mr. J Madhavan, Mr. CA Shah and myself complained to you about the Fiji Broadcasting Commission calling the members of the Federation Party 'Badmash' in its Hindi broadcast, which term is grossly abusive, insulting and provocative. Your reply was that you did not know the meaning of the word and Government had no control over the Fiji Broadcasting Commission as it was a self-financing body. You can hardly expect me to say that the Fiji Broadcasting Commission was impartial in applying that epithet to me and my colleagues.

As regards the Public Relations Office, if it wants to translate what appears in the Hindi periodicals and disseminate translations in English within the Colony and abroad, it is the duty of the office to ensure that the translations are correct and accurate.

Any translation of a Hindi article into English must of necessity be a deliberate and intentional act on the part of the translator. How can it be said that the translation of the 'Jagriti'[31] version of my speech by the Public Relations Office was not deliberate and intentional? I know Hindi and English languages very well and therefore I personally know that the translation is wrong, misleading and mischievous, while you and Mr. Hackett,[32] neither of whom possess any knowledge of the Hindi language and who have therefore to depend upon hearsay opinions, wish me to uphold the action of the Public Relations Office on its translations!

---

31   The name of the Hindi weekly which was an organ of the Federation Party. The name means 'New Age.'
32   EJF Hackett was Fiji's Public Relations Officer.

I assert that my view of the translation is correct and I am entitled to ask you, what steps you have taken against the person who translated that article.

In the end, I wish to emphasise that I have joined the Government to serve my people—not to forsake them; and I am not prepared to sell my soul for a mess of potage.

I am prepared to resign if you or the Secretary of State so wish.

23: Sir Derek Jakeway to Patel, 6 May 1965

Dear Mr. Patel

Thank you for your letter of 30th April.[33] The Governor-in-Council is the supreme executive authority in this Colony. The Civil Service is its agent for the execution of policy. Members of the Executive Council, whether with or without portfolio, are by convention expected to refrain from public criticism of the organization which serves them. No one is called upon to 'defend the wrong acts of Civil Servants or defend them from criticism.'

If members of Executive Council have cause to be dissatisfied with the actions of a Government department or officers thereof, the correct procedure is to report to the Colonial Secretary. In this particular instance, I am quite sure that the Colonial Secretary will carefully investigate any complaints made to him. If a prima facie case of negligence or misconduct is established, disciplinary proceedings as prescribed in Colonial Regulations will be instituted.

As regards the Fiji Broadcasting Commission, it is correct to say that I have no administrative control over the organization. Nevertheless, the Commission is by statute required to maintain a broadcasting service 'as a means of information, education, and entertainment and to develop its service to the best advantage and interests of the Colony.' By virtue of my power of appointment to the Commission, I have a responsibility for ensuring that the statutory duties of the Commission are faithfully carried out. The offensive reference which you quote in your letter was mentioned to me in the course of a discussion with you and other members of the Federation Party but I did not construe it to be in the nature of a complaint that I should take up. The correct procedure, if you wish

---

33   At first the Governor was inclined to take a hard-line against Patel but soon realized the folly of this course of action. He needed Patel in the Executive Council.Trafford Smith of the Colonial Office wrote to him on 17 May 1965: 'I feel sure that your decision that the balance of advantage lies in giving Patel the opportunity of remaining in the Government is the wise and right one. Let us hope that he does so and that the whole incident has not so seriously undermined the confidence of the other communities in the Indians as to make progress between now and the conference impossible.'

to pursue this, or any other instance of bias on the part of the Fiji Broadcasting Commission, should be to make representations direct to the Fiji Broadcasting Commission or to the Colonial Secretary.

Membership of the Executive Council involves participation in the Government. It does not stifle criticism of the Government, its officers or statutory bodies but it does imply direction of such criticism through different channels. A member cannot enjoy the advantage of operating from the inside and retain all the freedom of being on the outside. He cannot have it both ways.

I value your membership of the Executive Council and believe it to be in the national interest that you should continue to be a member and to retain your portfolio. I realize that this from time to time presents you with a conflict of loyalties, and I have hitherto much admired the way in which you have reconciled that conflict. At this juncture, in particular, it would be setback to the ideal of national unity for which we are both striving if the leader of the majority Indian party withdrew from the Government. If you share this view I hope you will refrain from active association with words or deeds which make it impossible to reconcile your continuation in the Government with the principle of collective responsibility and the conventions which surround that principle.

Yours sincerely

Derek Jakeway.

24: Memorandum to Unofficial Members of the Legislative Council, April 1965

Gentlemen,

I beg to thank you all for responding to my invitation and attending this meeting.

You will remember that when the idea was first mooted that unofficial members of the Legislative Council should hold meetings in Fiji among and between themselves on the proposed constitutional changes, it was generally agreed that the sole purpose of such meetings would be to ascertain and determine the areas of agreement and disagreement on the subjects under discussion. We have had three (3) such meetings under the chairmanship of His Excellency the Governor and an additional meeting under the chairmanship of the Honourable Ratu Edward Cakobau. On a close analysis of the matters already discussed at these meetings and those which appear on the Paper circulated to the Honourable Members by His Excellency the Governor, it is abundantly clear that we have now reached the stage that nearly all the remaining subjects for discussion are controversial and on which it is very unlikely any agreement would be reached in Fiji.

Bearing these points in mind, I have, nonetheless, decided to give an outline of my views and those of my colleagues why we advocate Common Roll and oppose Communal Roll in Fiji. I appreciate that some of you gentlemen would not agree with the views I now express but I assure you that they are being put forward so that you may seriously consider them before going to London.

Our case for Common Roll as against Communal Roll is as follows:

a). It is only through making one nation out of Fiji that we can achieve the sort of future we want for everybody. This goal can only be achieved if we accept Common Roll system of election.

b). Common Roll has been successful in a plural society. Examples are the former East and West African Colonies.

c). Common Roll will encourage the citizens to organise political parties along national lines and in the long run compel everyone else to think in terms of his country rather than a particular race, community or religion.

d). Communal Roll stands for divided loyalties, it inhibits national consciousness among the people; it is generally identified with religious fanaticism or racial separatism or economic or social privilege.

e). Communal Roll can be a serious obstacle to the successful operation of parliamentary democracy. The elected representatives of a racial or religious sub-community cannot afford to subordinate the interests of their people to those of larger community. Whether elected as independents, members of a communal party, or even as members of a party professing to transcend communal lines, they will not accept party discipline in a way to offend the group upon whose support their political future depends. It will inhibit the formation of secular parties. Success in politics will depend upon reflecting exactly the communal interests and prejudices. Compromise will be rendered difficult and relative party strength may be frozen for long periods because a party can grow only with an increase in the size of the community upon which it is based. In such a case government formed by one, or a coalition of two or more of these communal parties may not be able to meet the challenge of urgent social problems and a breakdown of representative government may occur, because the legislators and executives are prevented by communal loyalties from attacking the problems in a common sense fashion.f

f). Communal Roll tends to magnify communal differences and new communities discover themselves as further claims to separate representation are lodged.

g). Communal Roll, to the best of my knowledge, has been abandoned (with a few exceptions) by all the countries of the world.

I do take into account and appreciate the reasons why some of you gentlemen find it difficult to accept Common Roll at this stage. On the other hand, it is pleasing to note that generally speaking a number of us have accepted Common Roll in principle but they only wish to postpone its application till some future time.

I sincerely believe that our salvation lies in making one nation out of Fiji and for this and this reason alone, my colleagues and I commend our proposal for a Common Roll to you for your serious and earnest consideration.

AD Patel

25: Member of Social Services Office Notes, Pre-1965 constitutional conference

The Constitution should empower the local government to conclude trade agreements with other countries and provide for further delegations of authority to be made by British government.

1. Should there be independence with a special treaty vesting foreign affairs and defense in Britain as in case of Western Samoa?

2. Should there be only internal self-government?

3. What would be the extent of self-government?

4. Should the field of self-government be inviolable?

5. Would the British Government explicitly agree that it would be improper to encroach upon it?

6. Should the Crown retain full power of Constitutional amendment?

7. Should it retain unlimited legislative powers, exercisable by Governor-in-Council?

8. In whom should responsibility for external affairs be vested?

9. Should Fiji have power to conclude trade agreements with other countries?

10. Should Constitution provide for further delegation of authority in external affairs by the British Government?

11. *Should responsibility for defense be with the British Government?*

12. Should there be power vested in the Governor to stifle Bills and to refuse the royal assent to Bills excepting his responsibilities for defense and external affairs?

13. Should power be vested in the Crown to disallow Bills on similar grounds?

14. Should power of disallowance be limited only to acts prejudicially affecting the interests of the [illegible] of colonial government's [illegible]

15. Governor should not summon, preside at, or attend cabinet meetings.

16. Ex-Officio members of the present Executive Council should be withdrawn.

17. Should cabinet meeting come under the full control of Prime Minister?

18. The Prime Minister must be under constitutional duty to keep the Governor fully informed on all relevant matters of government.

19. How should the Prime Minister be appointed?

20. How should other ministers be appointed?

21. If the Prime Minster vacates, should the offices of ministers automatically become vacant?

22. Ministers will be individually and collectively responsible to the legislative.

23. The Executive should follow Westminster model of responsible government.

24. If a new appointment to the office of Governor becomes necessary, it should be made after consultation with local government.

25. Should be one house legislature.

26. There should be no Ex-Officio members.

27. There should be no nominated members—official or unofficial.

28. There should be no communal members elected on communal rolls.

29. There should be no communal and non-communal members elected on separate, non-communal mathematically weighted rolls.

30. No communal and non-communal members elected by the Legislative Council [?] itself.

31. No specially elected and nationally elected members.

32. No multi-member constituencies.

33. Should there be proportional representation?

34. Should be one man, one vote, one value.

35. There should be universal suffrage.

36. There should be single member constituencies, and the first-past-the-post system.

37. The Legislative Assembly should be wholly elected.

38. The Speaker should be elected by the Assembly from among its own members.

39. In fixing dates of sessions and proceedings of the Legislative Council, the Governor will act on advice of the Cabinet.

40. The Governor will exercise powers of dissolution in accordance with rules similar to the conventions obtaining in the United Kingdom.

41. The royal power of disallowance will probably cover only acts prejudicial to the interests of colonial stock holding.

42. Delimitation of electoral constituencies should be kept to the independent Electoral Commission.

43. The government should have the right to hire and fire and control of all government servants.

44. There should be a Public Service Commission which will be merely an advisory board

45. A Police Service Commission will also be an advisory board.

46. There should be Judicial Service Commission comprising a majority of judges among its members with the Chief Justice as its chairman.

47. There must be legislative authority for any public expenditure.

48. Provide for votes on estimates, the appropriation of supply, and unforeseen contingencies.

26: Opening Address to the 1965 Constitutional Conference, 26 July 1965

I thank you [Secretary of State] and the United Kingdom Government for the kind invitation and welcome extended us to this historic Conference which is called to smelt the existing system of government in the Colony of Fiji and to forge and mould a new Constitution which, I hope, will lead our country to complete independence in the not too distant future.

Political liberty, equality and fraternity rank foremost among the good things of life, and mankind all over the world cherishes and holds these ideals close to its heart. The people of Fiji are no exception. Without political freedom, no country can be economically, socially or spiritually free.

We in Fiji, as in many undeveloped countries of the world, are faced with the three most formidable enemies of mankind, namely, Poverty, Ignorance, and Disease. We need political freedom to confront these enemies and free our minds, bodies and souls from their clutches.

Needless to say, when I refer to political freedom I mean democracy under the rule of law, the sort of freedom which the British people and the people of United States enjoy. We need freedom which will politically, economically and socially integrate the various communities living in Fiji and make out of them one nation deeply conscious of the responsibilities and tasks which lie ahead.

I call this Conference important and historic because it is the first Conference of its kind in the history of Fiji and it may very well prove the beginning of the end of a form of government which stands universally condemned in the modern world.

I have come to this Conference with faith and trust in British people and their government which has set peoples of other colonies free and has led them on the path of economic and cultural development. After all, Fiji's problems are not as difficult or formidable as those which some of the colonies, which are now independent, have had to face and solve.

We, from our side, promise you full co-operation and serious consideration in the deliberations which lie ahead in this Conference.

We have all got to guard ourselves against avoiding right decisions because they are unpleasant or run counter to our ingrained habits of preconditioned thought, or taking wrong decisions because they appear advantageous in the short run.

We must appreciate the fact that we owe great responsibility, not only to the people of the present generation but also of generations to come.

We have to resist the temptation of driving the boat on the shallow waters because of the fear that it will rock heavily if we steered it on the right course. Bearing all this in mind let us bend to the tasks before us.

In the end I pray to Almighty God who led the crown colonies like Australian and New Zealand to full independence, may He also lead us and our country to the same destination safely and in good heart.

Again, I most sincerely thank you, Sir, for your kind welcome.

27: Interview with Malcolm Billings, BBC, 31 July, 1965

Malcolm Billings asked AD Patel about the 'consternation' his opening address at the conference caused, and if he had expected this reaction.

Patel: No. As a matter of fact this consternation arose from some misconception about the words self-government and independence. We have right from the start advocated that Fiji should have full internal self-government. But at present we are not asking for complete independence. What I said in my speech was that we should be in a position to attain complete independence in the not too distant future on the same lines as Australia and New Zealand.

Billings: This seemed to suggest though that you were hoping that independence would be put on the agenda.

Patel, Uh, no, at this stage we are not going to discuss anything about what form complete independence should take.

Billings: When do you think Fiji will be ready for internal self-government?

Patel: I believe that Fiji is already ready for internal self-government. Comparing conditions in Fiji with, say, conditions in Western Samoa, Tonga, Cook Islands—we are far ahead of them and I believe we can manage our own internal affairs as those countries.

Billings: Your critics say that if electoral changes are brought about, and internal self-government comes, there would be racial friction because of fears of racial domination by the Indians.

Patel: That is a mere fiction. As a matter of fact, to start with, Indians stand to lose. I would ask those people who are afraid of domination just to go through the figures of how many Indians are above the age of twenty who will be eligible for a vote. As a matter of fact, though we are in a majority, many of our people are more or less under 21.

Billings: But your majority is going to increase with the years because you are multiplying at a faster rate than the Fijians.

Patel: Even then we are spread out in such a way that our surplus votes are not going to get us surplus seats in the Council, as it happens in many countries, including Great Britain. Labour would be in a majority but their votes are concentrated in the industrial areas, so those votes are lost as far as the properties of winning seats are concerned. And I would not be surprised if there are more Fijians returned to the Legislative Council from the vote than Indians, in spite of our numerical superiority, because our votes will be wasted.

Billings: In the future could you ever see Fiji independence along the lines of Indian independence?

Patel: If by Indian independence you mean severing the connections with the Crown and establishing a republic, I say no.

Billings: When do you think Fiji could stand on its own two feet independent of any other nation?

Patel: I think it will take a long time before she can do that, but there is a good prospect of very interesting political developments arising out of Fiji's position in the Pacific region. Time might come when all the various territories in the South Pacific might think of coming together in a sort of loose confederation.

28: The Indian Delegation's Press Conference, 10 August 1965

Mr. AD Patel presided. With him were Messers Koya, Madhavan, Shah and Deoki. Mr. Singh did not attend.[34] Seventeen reporters attended. Mr. Patel asked the reporters to publish the statement of the delegation in full and requested that they should not merely use 'bits' which might be misleading and misrepresent the statement.

Mr. Koya, who read the statement on behalf of the delegation, introduced it by saying that the Indian delegates present at the Press Conference had all been bitterly disappointed by the outcome of the Conference and had resolved not to say anything either collectively or individually until a prepared statement was available. The statement said:

The Indian delegation has been bitterly disappointed with the unwillingness of the United Kingdom delegation to persuade the Fijian and European delegations of the desirability of introducing an electoral procedure as a first step towards attaining a democratic form of self-government in Fiji by which at least some members of the legislature should be eligible for election regardless of race, under a common franchise.

The Indians are bitterly disappointed by the recommendations of the United Kingdom delegation for an electoral plan which is calculated not only to disturb the present parity between the Fijian and Indian communities but also to place the Indians in a special discriminatory and inferior position of further isolation from other communities.[35]

---

34   Chandra Pal Singh was a nominated member of the Legislative Council, 1963–1966, and in the anti-Patel group. His political career ended with the 1966 elections.

35   Under the 1965 constitution, Fijians had 14 representatives in the Legislative Council, Indians 12 and Europeans 10. Chinese were placed on the European roll and Pacific Islanders on the Fijian roll, while no other ethnic group was put on the Indian roll. Until then, Fijians and Indians had ethnic parity in political representation.

The Indian delegation is bitterly disappointed by the recommendation by the United Kingdom delegation that a communal roll principle of election should be extended by the artificial equation of Chinese to Europeans and Rotumans and other Pacific Islanders to Fijians.

The Indian delegation is bitterly disappointed by the proposals made by the United Kingdom delegation which are calculated—intentionally or otherwise—to encourage the Europeans and Fijians to believe that the rejection by them of constitutional proposals put forward in a reasonable manner for the betterment of the Indian community, would be accepted by Great Britain without regard to the requirements of fair play and justice to all communities. It must be pointed out that the basis of the Indian delegation's complaint is that their community were at all times led to believe that by becoming settlers and adopting Fiji as their permanent home, they would enjoy rights and privileges no whit inferior to those of other races residing in Fiji.[36] The proposals relating to the composition of the legislature and the method of election are unjust, unfair, impracticable, and undemocratic. They will widen the existing racial divisions and make political integration of the different communities in Fiji, which is vital and necessary for the building of a homogenous democratic nation, extremely difficult, if not impossible.

Despite the fact that the Indian delegation asked for the immediate introduction of full internal self-government based on a common roll, they submitted an alternative proposal which would have catered for communal, cross-communal and common roll methods of election. The United Kingdom delegation made no serious effort to impress the Fijian and European delegations with the efficacy and practicability of this proposal nor of the need to reach a compromise which would have accommodated the views of all the delegations and thereby, in some measure, satisfy the demands of all races.

This should have been done in our opinion if the United Kingdom delegation was prepared to spend more time in the negotiations with the various groups both separately and collectively. The purpose of the Conference was to bring constitutional changes in Fiji as a step towards self-government. The proposals in the report have moved the Colony further away from that goal instead of taking a step towards it. The proposals are not, in our view, in keeping with the United Kingdom's declared policy of leading her Colonies towards democracy and political independence.

---

36   This is a reference to the words of the Salisbury's Despatch, 1875. The intention of equality was reiterated by the imperial government on several subsequent occasions.

A reporter: What will the Indian reaction be now?

Patel: I feel that all three delegations will have to go back to Fiji to consult their constituents and then each group will have to decide both their attitudes to these proposed changes and what steps they should take— either we accept them or reject them or accept them under protest but unless and until the groups have consulted their constituents at home they cannot make any final decisions.

A reporter: Do you think the Indian community might reject these proposals?

Mr. Patel: Certainly.

A reporter: What would then follow?

Mr. Deoki: It is better to jump the fence when we come to them. It is very difficult to say now.

A reporter: We understand that the Indian community are not entirely in support of your attitude on the common roll—that the Indians in Fiji are not unanimous on this.

Mr. Patel: If you mean by unanimous one hundred per cent, then of course it is not unanimous, but if you consider that eighty per cent or over eighty per cent is unanimous, then the Indian community is unanimous in their support of our policy. There are also quite considerable groups in the European and Fijian communities who are also of the same opinion as we are and who are in favour of a common roll, although they are a minority in their communities. If in any country you find eighty per cent of a community giving support to a policy, I think you can call that unanimous.

A reporter: How would common roll help the Indian community?

Mr. Patel: It would not help us but it would help to encourage in Fiji a national feeling. It has been said that we want common roll so that we can dominate the other races but that is not so. We believe that a common roll would eliminate the racial feeling which is doing so much harm. Every representative in the Legislative Council at present takes it that he is representing there the interests of his own racial group and all the time lays emphasis on his own racial group. We want to take out the racial element and introduce a national element.

A reporter: We are told that the possibility of two rolls could be considered—one part of the election on common roll and one on communal roll. Was that brought up at the Conference?

Mr. Patel: No. The United Kingdom delegation put forward its own proposals and these included cross-voting besides retaining communal voting. The United Kingdom delegation said that our compromise proposal was too late and instead of discussing it with the groups separately and then collectively, they stood aloof and left the three groups to talk about it alone. They knew full well that if they left the discussion on this compromise to the two groups, there was no prospect of any agreement at all. The United Kingdom delegation said that if the groups accepted it they would accept it but their attitude was one of indifference. They knew that no agreement could be reached if it was left to the three groups. They gave us the strong impression that because they were preoccupied with more important problems, we were not receiving as much attention as we should otherwise have received. I believe they would have been inclined to spend more time with us than they did if they had not been so preoccupied. I fear Aden put us in the background.[37]

A reporter: Is it possible that the system of cross-voting can be progressively intended to reduce the number of communal seats and increase the number of cross-voting seats? Would that not begin to meet your problem?

Mr. Patel: If the step we are taking is going to make the step to follow easier, then it is all right, but if the very first step is likely to make a further step more difficult, then it is wrong and that is what is going to happen with this. It is not the step but the manner in which they wish to make it. In effect, each voter will have four votes—one for his own race and the other three for each of the three communities. The idea uppermost in the voter's mind when he considers the candidates of the other races is which one is likely to help his racial group most so that instead of erasing the racial outlook it will intensify it. Every race will be looking for the stooge or puppet from other communities who is likely to help their race. What we want is a constitution which will encourage the formation of political parties on national lines.

A reporter: Has the Indian in Fiji full rights or is he a second-class citizen?

---

37 After the loss of the Suez Canal in 1956, Aden became the main base in the region for the British. An insurgency erupted there insurgency against British forces, lasting from December 1963 to November 1967.

Mr. Patel: Up to now, we have had racial parity in Legislative Council, irrespective of our numbers, but as long ago as 1929, when we were in a minority numerically, we protested that we wanted a common roll and did not want to be divided on racial lines.

A reporter: Was there any discussion inside or outside the conference on the land question?

Mr. Patel: Never as a problem in itself.

A reporter: Was there any discussion about he relationship with the Council of Chiefs?

Mr. Patel: No, except in connection with the two seats on the Legislative Council which will go to Fijians on the vote of the Council of Chiefs.

Mr. Deoki interpolated: We opposed unanimously that the Fijians should not have two extra seats but we did agree that if the chiefs wanted two Council of Chiefs members as such, we would have no objection to it provided that the number of Fijian seats was not increased. We had parity of representation in Legislative Council since 1929 when there were three Fijians, three Indians and three Europeans. When the Legislative Council elected membership was increased, it was five, five, and five; and when it was increased again it was six, six and six. We wish that parity of representation had been retained.

A reporter: How do you find the working of the Legislature? How do members vote?

Mr. Deoki: Voting is not on racial lines as a rule but on fundamental matters Europeans and Fijians tend to combine.

A reporter: Is it proposed that the Legislature should work out the land question? Is that the main question?

Mr. Patel: It is the main stumbling block.

Mr. Deoki: It is matter for discussion. We have a Landlord and Tenant report which will no doubt be discussed by all communities and the Council of Chiefs. That pertains to the land matter.

Mr. Patel: The land problem is mainly a question of security of tenure and tenants. The ownership of land is not questioned at all. Over eighty per cent of the land area belongs to the Fijians.

Mr. Deoki: We are seeking the right to renewal of long term leases and for compensation for improvements planned. At present there is no right of renewal of a lease and there is no compensation for improvements on land. The difficulty in Fiji is that some people have fears of what may happen if there are changes. Such fears should be catered for by way of safeguards provided in the constitution. We could give the safeguards and then we could move together along democratic lines.

29: Letter to Anthony Greenwood, Secretary of State for the Colonies, 12 August 1965

We must point out that the basis of the Indian Delegation's complaint is that their community were at all times led to believe that by becoming settlers and adopting Fiji as their permanent home, they would enjoy rights and privileges no whit inferior to those of other races residing in Fiji. In this connection, we beg to remind Her Majesty's Government that such a guarantee and undertaking was given in Lord Salisbury's Despatch in March 1875. The undertaking given in this Despatch has never been withdrawn or contradicted. Indeed it was accepted and confirmed by the Crewe Commission in 1910. This Despatch was a subject matter of public discussion in 1963 on the eve of the arrival in Fiji on Mr. Nigel Fisher, the then Parliamentary Under-Secretary of State for the Colonies. At the conclusion of Mr. Fisher's tour and on the eve of his departure, he made a public statement in which he categorically said that Her Majesty's Government considered that this Despatch was binding on her. He further said that the Indians rightly regarded that the Despatch conferred on them rights and privileges as the Fijians regarded the Deed of Cession in respect of their rights and privileges. In Mr. Fisher's view, the Indians could not be regarded as second-class citizens and that he considered that their rights and privileges were equal to those of other communities in Fiji. May we say without hesitation that the proposal to give two extra seats to the Fijians constitutes, in our view, a clear breach of Lord Salisbury's Despatch on the part of Her Majesty's Government.

We sincerely believe that political integration of the different communities living in Fiji is vital and necessary to the building of a politically homogeneous democratic nation. We assume that Her Majesty's Government accepts this view. However, the United Kingdom Delegation's proposals relating to the composition of the Legislature and the method of election are so unjust, unfair, impracticable and undemocratic that they will harden the existing racial divisions and make political integration extremely difficult, if not impossible.

You will note that at the outset, the Indian Delegation asked for the immediate introduction of full internal self-government based on the Common Roll system of election at the Conference. Nonetheless, our Delegation, for the sake of peace and harmony and to avoid a deadlock, submitted an alternative proposal. The substance of this proposal was that there should be part-communal, part cross-communal and part common roll method of election.[38] This proposal would have accommodated the views of the United Kingdom Delegation and that of the Fijian Delegation as a whole and thereby satisfying the demands of all races. Unfortunately, the United Kingdom Delegation made no serious effort to impress the Fijian and European Delegations of the efficacy, practicability and the need to reach a compromise. Such a compromise was, in our view, highly probable if only the United Kingdom Delegation had not committed themselves at the outset on its proposal for cross-communal system of voting and had cared to spend more time in the negotiation with various groups separately and collectively at the conference.

We are more than alarmed to note that along with the Bills concerning special subjects which would require more than two-thirds of the votes of the Legislative before they may be passed, it is in contemplation that the existing laws relating to Native Lands, namely, the Native Land Trust Board Ordinance, would be included in this category. We venture to say that in spite of the agreement reached between all the delegates in Fiji in April 1965, the United Kingdom Delegation indirectly brought the question of ownership of land and other allied matters for discussion before the Conference. The agreement was to the effect that the question of land should not form part of the agenda of the London Constitutional Conference, that the ownership of land, be it native or otherwise, would not be challenged, and that as the solution to the problems concerning the security of tenure, renewability of leases was vital from the viewpoint of the economic life of all the communities in Fiji, these matters should be discussed freely in Fiji and agreed upon.

The substance of this agreement was, in our opinion, brought to the notice of Her Majesty's Government through His Excellency the Governor, and yet land was discussed at the Conference. We cannot, for one moment, accept the proposition that the existing Native Land Trust Board Ordinance ought not to be changed. On the question of Native land, we cannot help saying that neither the Government of Fiji nor the architects of the relevant Bill in 1940 have honoured their undertakings which were given to the Legislative Council. In addition, this Ordinance contains unjust and iniquitous provisions and its operation has not helped the country, let alone the Fijian owners and Indian tenants. If Her Majesty's Government proceeds with this aspect of the proposal as contained in the Final Report of the Conference, we can see nothing but ruination for Fiji. For this reason, we feel we must advise Her Majesty's Government that the question of the ownership of Native land may well have to be raised again.

---

38   This proposal was put forward by Andrew Inder Narayan Deoki.

We note that the purpose of the Conference was to bring constitutional changes in Fiji towards internal self-government. These proposals, in our view, move the Colony away from that goal and they are not in keeping with the United Kingdom's declared policy of leading her Colonies towards democracy and political independence.

Since the conclusion of the Conference, we have given serious and anxious consideration to the proposals and after long deliberation we have come to the view that we must reject them.

It is our intention to oppose these proposals by peaceful and constitutional means. The implementation of these proposals, in our view, would create a grave racial disharmony leading to undesirable results. In this process an irreparable harm would be done to the country as a whole and we fear that goodwill, harmony and understanding, which has existed among all the races in Fiji over the last 90 years, would disappear for ever. The responsibility for any course of events arising out of the implementation of these proposals would rest, in our view, on Her Majesty's Government.

In the circumstances, we make this plea: that Her Majesty's Government take necessary steps to amend these proposals in consultation with the remainder of the Delegation and make an earnest effort so that a solution may be reached acceptable to all concerned.

30: Post-1965 Constitutional Conference: Century Theatre, August 1965

Ladies and Gentlemen, before discussing what was discussed at the London Conference, let us look into the history of Fiji.

Before the advent of British colonial rule in Fiji, settlers from Australia and New Zealand came and settled here. The early planters did their best to persuade the Fijians to cede Fiji either to the United States or to the United Kingdom. Finally, they were successful in persuading Ratu Cakobau to cede Fiji to the United Kingdom. At first the offer was refused. But when missionaries raised questions about the evils of black-birding, Great Britain was compelled to take over Fiji to bring stable government here, to prevent Fijians from being exploited by the Europeans. This was done under the Deed of Cession, without any conditions attached. To save the Fijians from the European settlers, the first Governor, Sir Arthur Gordon, brought Indian indentured labourers [to work on plantations here]. Gordon had been in Mauritius and he knew about the working of the indenture system, he knew how well the Indians worked and how they lived peacefully.

We Indians came to Fiji to save the Fijians from the clutches of the white settlers. We came here; we settled down here; and we were able to turn the virgin forest into agricultural land. And when you look back at the past ninety years of Fiji's history, we are proud to say that for all this time, we have never quarrelled with any other race. We lived happily among the other races—Fijians, Europeans, Chinese and others, like sugar in milk. We have always remained loyal to the British Crown. Look back at our history. Have we ever disrupted the peace of this Colony? We ourselves have suffered, but we have not allowed anyone else to suffer for us or through us. We have always thought of giving peace to other people.

And when we were brought to Fiji we were given certain promises. One promise was that if you become citizens of Fiji, you will have equal rights with other races, that your rights will not be one whit inferior to the rights enjoyed by other races. But I tell you, for the last ninety years, Britain has disregarded that undertaking. Even today they are trying to deceive us about the consequences of common roll, for example. Common roll cannot result in Indian domination, because we can't send any more representatives to the Legislative Council than any other race. We are in greater numbers in the Western division and perhaps Labasa, but there are other areas where other races dominate. Therefore, I see no reason why anyone should think that Indians will dominate. This is not the first time that Indians have raised the issue of common roll. This question was first raised in 1929. At that time, Indians were a minority community in Fiji. We could not have dominated anyone.

I have been trying to make this point very clear. We are asking for common roll so that every citizen lives happily with one another in this Colony as one nation, one people, one country. But what happens? The European and Fijian members are not prepared even to discuss the issue. Therefore the Federation Party decided that there was no point in discussing this matter in Fiji [before going to the London conference in July 1965]. Some people said that we should socialize with the Europeans and Fijians which might lead to an amicable resolution of the issue. But I tell you that we had members like Mr. CP Singh and Mr. [Andrew] Deoki who have been socializing with them but were still unable to reach any satisfactory resolution. What can one do when people shut their minds, put a padlock on their minds, and refuse to listen. To a blind man you can explain things. You can tell him not to go along a certain road. But what do you do when people with perfect eyesight prefer to go in blind alleys?

Let me tell you what happened at the London conference. At the opening of the conference, the Secretary of State in his speech said that this conference had been called to determine the future path of self-government in Fiji.[39] Before we

---

[39]   For more details, see Brij V Lal (ed.), *Fiji: British Documents on the End of Empire* (London: The Stationery Office, 2006), 238-252.

reached London, before the Conference, newspapers published what was going to be decided in the Conference. I quickly realised that the United Kingdom had decided in advance what the outcome was going to be and that we were called to rubber stamp its decision. I was prepared to give them the benefit of the doubt. The Conference was to show to the world that the people of Fiji were contented with British rule and that they wanted to leave the matters as they were. The United Kingdom government would be content to make a few minor improvements in the existing arrangements.

The speeches made at the Conference made things very clear. Mr. Falvey said that we are very happy in Fiji and that there was no need for any changes yet. Ratu Mara said that since his ancestors had ceded Fiji to the United Kingdom, we do not want to sever our links to the Crown. They thought I might echo their sentiments. But, of course, I could not do this. I had to tell the truth, and I told the truth. I must call a spade a spade. Now, is there any person in the world who does not want freedom to live as free human beings, with dignity and human rights? Slaves can be slaves forever, but we want freedom and we want to obtain it peacefully.

People in the United Kingdom were not as worried about our demands as people in Australia were. People in Australia were more upset than people in England. Why was Australia so upset? Because from the political and economic point of view, while people from the United Kingdom may be in higher position in government departments, it is Australia which rules Fiji. I have said many times that the colonial government of Fiji is the daughter-in-law of Australia. We have here the CSR Company, the Emperor Gold Mines, the Bank of New South Wales, Carpenters and Burns Philp. If you take this into account, the economy of the Colony is in the hands of these people. Copra industry is in the hands of Carpenters. The sugar industry is in the hands of the SPSM [South Pacific Sugar Mills Limited] the true name of which is the CSR Company. The gold mines are in the hands of the Emperor Gold Mines. And, of course, the banking sector is controlled by Bank of New South Wales. Bank of New Zealand and Bank of Baroda are small banks and they came much later. Therefore, whatever I say goes to Australia very quickly. It has been said that we are against the Government of Australia, or we are working against the people of Australia. We are not working against them. We are working against people who make us weak. We do not hate any particular race. But we are against laws which do not allow us to make any progress.

In the Conference, there were many matters upon which we could easily agree. The main point of difference was the composition of the Legislative Council. We want equality, equal rights for everyone. No one disagreed with this view. People in England agreed. No one disagreed. In the Conference, when the question about the system of election was raised, we were divided into three

65

sections to meet with the UK delegation separately as Indians, Europeans and Fijians. When the UK delegates met the Indian representatives, we placed our case before them. Mrs Eirene White said in her own words that 'We congratulate you for the very lucid and convincing manner in which you have placed your proposal before us.' She said she agreed with everything we had raised; there was no point of disagreement. We told her that if she agreed with our proposal than she should communicate this to the other delegates. But that did not happen. The UK delegation began to meet separately with the Fijians and the Europeans. This went on for two days. At one stage the Fijian members said that they did not wish to be separated from the Europeans and that they preferred to discuss things together. But Mrs Eirene White did not agree to this.

Before the Conference started, we were asked to sit anywhere we wished to in the Conference Hall. Europeans and Fijians sat together and the five Indian members sat together. But after a while, one member began to sit apart from us just to show to the other side that he did not agree with the rest of us. This conveyed the impression that the Indian delegates were divided, and there might be the possibility of a break in their ranks at some point. It was decided to expand the three categories (Indians, Fijians, Europeans) to include other groups not represented at the Conference. It was decided that with the Fijians should go the Micronesians, the Melanesians, Tongans, Rotumans, Samoans, Banabans, and other Pacific island groups and should be classed as Fijians. What surprised me most was the inclusion in the Fijian category of Banabans who came here only yesterday, they had their own Council, their own way of managing their land, have nothing whatsoever to do with the Native Land Trust Board. These Banaban people who came here only yesterday could be grouped with Fijians, but not Indians who have lived here for ninety years! They could be politically integrated with the Fijians but not us.

And the Europeans and the Chinese were put together in the same group. Now you will agree that Europeans have become rich because of the Indians. Indians have been living together with the Europeans for the past ninety years, working for the Europeans, but they cannot be politically integrated with them. If a black comes here from South Africa, he will be put on the European roll. It is the same thing with a Maori from New Zealand, a Malayan from Malaya, a Chinese from Malaya, and a Singhalese from Ceylon. If some one comes from Aden, he will be classed as a European too. Only the Indians are being isolated [Tape ends].

31: Response from Anthony Greenwood, 9 September 1965

My dear Mr. Patel

Since I returned to the office I have given very careful consideration to the letter of the 12th August addressed to me by you and your colleagues about the proposals contained in the Final Report of the Fiji Constitutional Conference 1965.

I fully appreciate your disappointment at the failure of the conference to reach agreement on proposals which might quickly lead to the introduction of full internal self-government based on the common roll. It is not, however, possible for the British Government in all the circumstances to impose an <u>apriori</u> solution of this type. The political facts of the situation must be taken into account. In Fiji these must necessarily include the views not only of the Indians but also of the Fijians and to a lesser extent those of the Europeans and other minority communities. The British Government took considerable pains before and during the conference to ascertain the views of all groups and communities in Fiji and the proposals put forward by the British Government and eventually accepted by a majority of the delegates at the conference constituted an attempt to make progress towards the general objective in a way which took into account the interests of all concerned.

I find it difficult to accept some of the comments in your letter on the probable effect of the proposals and believe that, at this stage. In the political evolution of Fiji, these proposals form a basis for constructive advance.

I note that you and your colleagues reject the conclusions set out in the Final Report and intend to oppose them by all constitutional means. The decision whether to take such action must of course rest with you. I would, however, ask you to bear the consequences of outright opposition in mind. In my view, it is far more likely to increase the suspicions of the other communities, particularly the Fijians, than to win them over to support your point of view, which must surely be your objective. I believe that a much more fruitful course of action and one which would be far more likely to lead to the political integration and racial harmony which we all want to see achieved, would be to co-operate fully in the introduction of the new constitution and, by showing that the measure of inter-racial voting which it will introduce does not adversely affect the interests of any race, to pave the way to further constitutional progress.

With best regards

Yours sincerely

Anthony Greenwood

32: Debate on London Constitutional Conference, 15 December 1965

I rise to oppose the motion. The motion says,

> That in the opinion of this Council, the views of delegates to the Fiji Constitutional Conference as adopted by Her Majesty's Government in a White Paper published in October, 1965 form a satisfactory basis for future political progress in Fiji along constitutional lines.

I am of the opinion that some of the provisions do not form a satisfactory basis for future political progress in Fiji. The most important and outstanding one is the composition and method of election to the Legislature. The constitutional proposals propose that a certain number of seats will be on the basis of communal representation, a certain number of seats will be on the basis of cross-community voting, and two seats will be reserved for the Council of Chiefs. I and four of my colleagues are of the view that if this country is ever going to undertake the responsibility of self-government, it is important and urgent that all these communities in this country are integrated into one nation, and the only way I see of political integration is by having a system of voting which does not separate people on the grounds of race or birth. It should be based on universal suffrage on the principle of one man one vote. It has been suggested that cross-community voting is a step towards such common franchise. I personally do not agree with that view. In my opinion, it further accentuates division amongst races. We in this country have been working under communal franchise since 1929 and, perhaps, even before that. If voting on separate communal roll were to bring about political integration after the lapse of all these years, we would have been ready for such integration. If some of us argue that we are still not ready for such integration, that clearly shows that communal franchise, or another garbled form of such a franchise which is called cross-community voting, is certainly not going to integrate us. Cross-communal voting impedes the formation or extension of parties on national lines.

What is happening at present in this country is that some racial groups are coming together just for the purposes of elections without in any way being willing to give up their racial identity or their racial interest. There are only two political organizations in this country to my knowledge who do not profess to be on racial lines and whose membership is open to people of all races in Fiji: one is the Federation Party to which I belong. The aim and object of the Party is to integrate the people of this Colony in one nation. It believes in the principle of unity in diversity, which means that diversity of views and requirements due to diverse cultural, racial, religious and economic background, should be taken into consideration to form one synthetic, acceptable view which will meet the requirements of the people as a whole in this country. This is the largest political party existing in Fiji and it has been working as a properly organized and disciplined party within this House. The only other party which I know of which is non-racial is the Labour Party which has been formed recently and is small. Apart from these two parties, I do not know of any single party which is non-racial or national.[40]

I thought, after the London Conference arriving at this conclusion, that cross-voting would lead people to political integration, that those who believed in such a course would dissolve racial organizations and begin to form political parties on non-racial national lines, but so far, I have not come across any evidence of that nature. His Excellency, in his address, mentioned the hope and the probability that there would be political alliances formed within various racial groups. Now, such alliances based on race and community in themselves perpetuate divisions on racial lines. They just come together to serve certain purposes and nothing more, and it comes in the way of forming political parties which would function in a self-governing country or in an independent country on what is called party lines. Permutations and combinations of various racial or religious groups can never forge the unity of a people; they are just loose units brought together to give the appearance of a united whole without, in fact, being a solid entity.

My other objection to cross-community voting is that it gives an equal number of seats to communities regardless of their size. On cross-community voting, Europeans have one seat, Fijians have one seat and Indians have one seat. Some members will probably say that Fijians are no longer Fijians in the sense that they include other Pacific Islanders. I know very well that Rotumans, Banabans and other Pacific Islanders are now included in the Fijian group but that is still predominantly a Fijian group. I know that the Chinese are included [in the European group] and it would also include Afghans, Malayans and Singhalese if they are here, or even the Negroes from Africa if they are here, but still that group which will be designated as 'Others' is predominantly European. The relative number of these groups is: Indians will be somewhere in the vicinity of 230,000, Fijians will be somewhere in the vicinity of 190,000 and this other group will be somewhere in the vicinity of 20,000 to 30,000. To have an equal number of seats for 30,000 or 190,000 or 230,000 does not really mean equality. It might appear to be equality as far as the seats are concerned, but is not equality as far as the value of the vote is concerned.

Another disagreeable feature of this cross-community voting is that a voter must vote for all the three candidates. Under a single member system, a voter is free

---

40   The membership of the Alliance Party had to be through membership of the Fijian Association (for Fijians), Indian Alliance (Indians) and General Electors (Europeans and others). There was no direct membership.

to vote for any candidate he likes and, if he does not approve of any of the candidates to be fit to represent his interests in the Council, he can refrain from voting altogether. But, as far as cross-community voting is concerned, he must vote for all three or none. If a voter, for instance, likes one or two candidates amongst those who have stood in the cross-community constituency, but he does not like or approve of one candidate, he is faced with a choice not to vote for any of them at all, which means that though he wants to vote for two candidates out of the candidates who have stood, he has got to vote for all the three, knowing fully well that he does not want to vote for one candidate who may, as a matter of fact, stand against his own interest. That means that when these candidates are elected, they are not truly elected by the electorate voting voluntarily and out of free will. There is a certain amount of compulsion, that whether you like it or not, you must cast one vote for each of the candidates of each of the three groups and, therefore, it cannot be called free democratic voting.

Communal voting prolongs or perpetuates division of people on racial lines and prevents them from integration into one nation. If communal franchise, as I have previously said, was a suitable mode of voting to bring the races together, then by now we should have been free for common franchise and common roll, by now we should all be on one and the same roll, and racial representations would be completely unnecessary. On the other hand, if it is argued, after all these years of communal separatism, that we are still not ready for political integration, then I say that communal franchise has been the real impediment. We had common roll in the municipality of Suva in 1929. Voters of all races who were eligible for a vote were voting for European candidates and nobody that I know of had ever raised any complaint that other races did not receive any representation in the Council. As a matter of fact, in this very House, it was pointed out many times in 1929, and afterwards, that common franchise worked very well in the Suva Town Council. One would have expected that the system that had worked in the municipal council would have been extended and given a trial in the central legislature of the Colony. But the United Kingdom Government abolished the common franchise in the Town Council and a system of nomination was introduced. No trial was given in this Council to a system which had worked well in a municipal council.

Another reason why I am opposed to this communal form of voting as proposed in the White Paper is that it is unfair to all communities except the European and the Chiefs. The Council of Chiefs is a small body of men who, under the proposed constitution as they do now, get two seats. The ordinary Fijian people get nine seats as do Indians though they are the two largest communities. Europeans, even with a few thousand Chinese thrown in, will be the smallest political unit in Fiji and they get seven members which is beyond all proportion to their numerical strength in the country. When worked out in detail it would probably amount to having 1,200 to 1,500 voters in the European constituency which will be called 'Others,' about 8,000 to 9,000 voters in the Fijian constituencies, about 10,000 to 12,000 voters in the Indian constituencies, which means that 1,200 to 1,500 voters will have a right to elect one member; about 8,000 to 9,000 Fijians will have the right to elect one member and 10,000 to 12,000 Indians will have the right to elect one member. This roughly means that the European vote is equivalent, as far as the representation in this House is concerned, to roughly about 8 or 9 Fijian votes to 10 Indian votes. What could be more unfair than that? How can anybody call that equality of status for all the racial groups in Fiji?

The system which is recommended in the new constitutional proposal swamps the majority community in Fiji in this Council. Indian community, if we are to count representation racially, comprises 50 percent to 51 percent of the population of the Colony and 50 percent to 51 percent of the Colony will have in this House 12 representatives. Fijians who comprise 43 percent of the population of this Colony will have 14 seats and Europeans and other who form about 6 to 7 percent of the population of this Colony will have 10 seats in the Council. Even the Fijian community with its fourteen seats in the Council cannot form a Government on their own; nor can the Indian community. The only community in this House which will hold the balance of power will be the European community. If they side with the Fijians, the Fijians can form the government. If they do not like the views of the Fijians or their actions are not considered in their best interests, they can change sides and side with the Indians and Indians will form the government. One cannot escape from the fact that the real centre of power under this Constitution is vested in the European group.

As I said before, the method of election by universal suffrage on the principle of one man one vote is the only right and proper democratic way of representation in this House. It is the only genuine method of democratic representation. It is the only way to bring about political integration and change a multi-racial society into one nation. It should precede and not follow racial integration. Some people say that we have not got integration in schools, that socially we have not integrated by marriage and intermingled our blood. I say that neither integration in schools nor racial miscegenation are necessary for political integration. Many countries have achieved it without any such steps. The Untied Kingdom itself is the hotch-potch of all races. There are many more races residing in the United Kingdom than there are in Fiji, yet their system of representation which is based on common franchise has worked well right throughout the ages and is working well even today. The Scots and the Welsh fight for home rule but I have never heard any Member of Parliament, whether from Scotland or from Wales, asking for separate racial representations.

There are Jews in England, there are Roman Catholics in England. They belong to different religions and, as far as the history of all these religions in England is concerned, it has not always been a peaceful one. The relations of Protestants and Roman Catholics, Jews and Christians, on many occasions, right throughout British history, have not always been cordial yet nobody has thought of separate representation there on religious grounds. Even under the proposed Constitution, one stroke of the pen brings about political integration between Rotumans, Banabans, Solomon Islanders, Polynesians and other Pacific Islanders. Rotumans and Fijians have all this time maintained separate racial and social identities. Banabans are living on their own in Rabi Island as a separate unit. The Polynesians and other Pacific Islanders are in no way socially or politically integrated with the Fijian race here, yet there was no difficulty. They are all put together on a common roll with a common franchise. Since the publication of the White Paper I have not heard a single protest coming either from the Fijians, Rotumans, Banabans or any other Pacific Islanders. As far as they are all concerned, common franchise and common roll is accepted.

Coming to the Europeans, the Chinese with their totally different social backgrounds, [have] no integration in schools, no racial miscegenation. There are still Chinese, Fijian, European and Indian schools, and I am trying my best to get their doors thrown open an to have all the schools integrated. But if that small amount of integration of a Chinese girl and my honourable friend's daughter going to the same school can be sufficient to bring the Chinese and European communities together on the common roll, I do not see why Indians and Europeans do not also come on the same common roll because my daughters also attend the school [Suva Grammar] where other European girls are attending. What I say is that this evidently proves how hollow the argument is that we have not got integration in schools and we have not got any racial mixture of blood and that is why it is not proper that all the races should be brought together and integrated into one political unit. As a matter of fact, almost all countries in the world have got many races and many religions, and they all follow their own religions; they even follow their own cultures, customs and traditions and yet politically they are a united nation. The outstanding examples are our neighbouring dominions, New Zealand and Australia, and also the United States of America. If these countries can politically integrate with immigrants who come to their countries and if they can integrate as soon as they set foot in that country and can be accepted as Australians and New Zealanders, even when they do not know a word of English, I do not see any difficulties when three races who have lived together in this country for nearly 90 years being brought together politically.

I have been questioned about India and Pakistan. That division in itself is a warning to us. If, in 1909, Minto-Morley reforms of communal franchise and representation had not been imposed upon the people of India against their wishes, there would not have been all the troubles and tribulations that the sub-continent is undergoing now. That is why of all the people, Indians are bitterly against communal representation because they have seen its painful results in course of time. It may not appear very serious now, but as time goes on, once people get used to the idea of a racial separation, racial attitudes harden and people start thinking in racial terms and racial interests which leads not to one nation but, in the course of political development, it leads to claims for several nations. That is what communal franchise did in India; that is what communal franchise is doing with Cyprus.

The demand for common roll or common franchise is neither unusual nor is it peculiar to the Indian community in Fiji, or to me, as has been sometimes attributed. Some people say that I originated the idea of the demand for common roll. As a matter of fact, in the polity of the world this has been one of the most ancient ideas. The British Parliament was probably the first. If any organization gets a credit for this system of representation, I think that should go to the Mother of Parliaments. That system of representation has now become more or less the universal mode of representation in democracy.

It is said that Indians want common franchise, but other races are opposed to it. I consider that a sweeping generalization. There are many men and women of all races who consider common roll in the best interests of the country. Even when my honourable colleague on my left had called a meeting in Suva before he went to London and where the predominant voice was the voice in favour of the communal roll, the supporters of common roll were not wanting. I am now reading from the *Fiji Times*. This issue is dated 2nd July 1965, and it is reported on page 7, under the heading 'Disagreement':

> Dr D.J. Lancaster said he did not agree with all that had been said, 'I think I speak for some others in this hall,' he declared, adding, 'We claim we are a democracy and I hope you will hear me.' He said he could not understand why the Europeans could claim an equal vote simply because they were Europeans. They numbered 20,000 in the Colony; they were a minority group, and he classed himself a member of one. 'How far are we going to go on this ethnic-racial demarcation and representation?' he asked.

Some of the leaders of the Methodist Church, before our going to London, also expressed their view in favour of common franchise. I know many educated Fijians, both here and some whom I met in London, also agree with the view that political integration of all races in Fiji as soon as possible is the only salvation for this country. So it is not as if asking for common franchise is merely an Indian demand, though Indians of course are large in numbers and are in support of that demand. But that has been right throughout because the Indians in this Colony, I am glad to say, have always fought against racialism and racial isolationism. The very first time they were given the opportunity of representation in this Council they opposed it on the grounds that it was dividing the races. Even when I am trying to bring about racial integration in schools, I have not met with any Indian committee opposing it. They have all been glad to throw their doors open to children of other races who, for all practical purposes in rural areas, are Fijian children. There has not been any opposition whatsoever. If I have come across any opposition, it is from some Fijian committees, some Fijian and some European schools. I am glad to say that the Indian community, though it was backward in education, took the sane, responsible and liberal view as far as racial issues were concerned. They have always made it a point to get on well with other races, to avoid friction, to avoid trouble as far as others were concerned. They felt honoured to invite people of other races to their homes; they considered it not only a sort of duty. As far as race relations in this Colony is concerned, this Colony has a proud record. Show me any other country in the world where three or more races have lived together over a period of about 90 years without any trouble [as we have here in this Colony].

We do not keep racial harmony by remaining separate and apart. We try to maintain harmony by drawing others closer to us. This racial separatism, as far as public institutions and this Council are concerned, was imposed upon Indians. The Indians accepted it, but not altogether willingly. They have to put up with it because of the conditions prevailing here; as they have been submerged in this Council all along; as it is designed that they should be submerged in the future Council under the new Constitution. Many Indians give up all hope, they lose heart and they bow to the inevitable, but in their heart of hearts, they have never been satisfied and they have never accepted this racial separation as being in the best interest either of the Indians, or the other races, or of the Colony. As a matter of fact, as far as the economic interest of this country is concerned, the employers and the employees cut across all racial barriers. There are employers belonging to all races in Fiji; there are European employers, Indian employers, Fijian and Chinese employers. There are workers belonging to all races; and as far as the interests of the employers and the employees are concerned, really they are non-racial.. There are farmers belonging to all races, and as far as their interests are concerned they are non-racial. Transport—buses, boats and taxis— are owned by Europeans, Indians, Fijians and the passengers who travel on them also belong to all races. Professional men—there are Indians, Europeans, Fijians. Civil Servants—all of them belong to all races. So as far as economic relationship is concerned, there is in fact an economic solidarity between various groups which comprise this Colony. One would like to see politics developing in this country more on the lines of economic interests rather than racial denominations. So much for the mode of representation in the Council.

Some people argue that if there was common franchise Indians will dominate, and all the other races will be subjugated to their domination. It starts on a wrong premise that if there is common franchise, all will necessarily vote on racial lines. If that were so, then there would not be any meaning in forming alliances under the cross-voting system because you would expect every voter to vote with his racial interest in mind and not with common interest, so the result will be that the majority will rule, and majority should rule and majority must rule. That is the democratic form of government. It may be asked, 'What happens to the minorities?' Under a democratic form of government, the minority today may be the majority and a government after another election. Under a democratic form of representation, there are no permanent minorities and permanent majorities, they fluctuate. A party system of government is formed and one party goes in opposition, another in government, but not necessarily the party which is governing will always govern. As regards their cultural or religious rights, or rights of individual freedom and liberty are concerned, they are usually safeguarded in a Bill of Rights, and the Bill of Rights should provide adequate safeguards for minority rights, the smallest minority being the individual. If individual rights are adequately safeguarded, minority rights are automatically safeguarded because minorities are composed of individuals. Nobody can claim to be entitled to special privilege in a democracy by reason of race, colour, creed, birth or sex.

In the foreword to the White Paper in paragraph 3, it is stated that 'on the 26th April, the Federation Party led by Mr. AD Patel decided to withdraw from these discussions,' referring to the discussions which were held in Fiji between the unofficial members of the Legislative Council. I would like to explain why the Federation Party had to discontinue their discussions. When the Federation Party decided to discontinue discussions, only those issues which referred to the composition of the Legislative Council and the method of election were left. As far as the Federation Party, and I would say the Indian community was concerned, it has been well known in this Colony since 1929 that the Indian community stands for common franchise and common roll. The European representatives and the Fijian representatives, led by European members, were strongly opposed to the common franchise and they were insisting that they were not prepared to budge an inch and they stuck to communal roll... The position was that the discussions were supposed to be confidential but, unfortunately, confidences were not kept. They came out in garbled form in the press, and it appeared to the Federation Party and to me, that as far as the question of the method of representation was concerned, there was no probable chance of a compromise. By the way things were appearing in the press, I could see that the only aim behind such publications was to create racial tension in the Colony. My colleagues and I were anxious to avoid any tension. We were of the opinion that perhaps this question which was so difficult to compromise on here may be solved in London through the kind offices of the United Kingdom delegation.

It is significant that after my colleagues and I discontinued discussions, there were still two Indian members who were ready and willing to carry on with the discussions and, in fact, they did join in those discussions. If there was any chance of a compromise, if there was any desire on the part of the Fijian and European members to reach a compromise on this important issue, they had a golden opportunity. I thought they would take that opportunity if for nothing else at least to discredit me and my Party and show to Fiji and to the outside world that there was a hope of compromise, that, in fact, they did reach a compromise and we were foolish in discontinuing the discussions. But no such thing happened. Even in London I and my colleagues had the feeling that the United Kingdom delegation did not try seriously to arrive at a compromise which would be acceptable to all parties.

Even when the Indian delegation put forward a compromise proposal by Mr. Andrew Deoki, and which proposal was agreed to by the Federation Party for the sake of compromise, it received a short shrift. The United Kingdom delegation, if I remember right, complained that the compromise proposal came too late. To this day, I do not understand 'too late for what?' In an important conference like that, if there is a serious and sincere desire to reach a solution which will be acceptable to all, it can never be too late. A few more days can be spent on it and an effort made to see if it is acceptable to all. I go further and say that even if that proposal was not acceptable to all, even then it was the duty of the United Kingdom Government to find some solution that would have been acceptable to all the three communities and not merely rest content with the proposals which were accepted by only two. I say that it is not too late even now. The United Kingdom Government can still make a serious effort to bring about a compromise which would be acceptable to all. The Indian community is, after all, the majority community in Fiji and it is as important to have its consensus to any proposals as it is to have of other communities. To ignore that fact is to be unfair to the majority community in Fiji. I said that even now it is not too late and the United Kingdom Government can still reconsider these proposals with a view to finding some solution which may be acceptable to all. If one conference has failed to arrive at a satisfactory compromise, conferences can be called again. It has happened with other countries; it can happen with Fiji. There is nothing extraordinary in that.

After the White Paper was published, I find that the racial attitudes in Fiji are hardening rather than softening. The latest evidence that I came across is the coat of arms placed on our Civic Centre, the picture of which is published in the *Fiji Times* in the issue dated Tuesday, the 14th December. In the Coat of Arms a

Fijian and a European are depicted holding a shield with an inscription at the bottom *Valataka Na Dina* which is translated by the *Fiji Times* as 'Fight for the Right.' I would like to know that in a city where 80 percent of the citizens are neither Fijian nor European, in a city of which 75 percent of the population is Indian, what is the reason behind choosing a coat of arms which depicts Fijians and Europeans with the words 'Fight for the Right'? Fight against whom? Well, this sort of thing has been smoldering secretly in this Colony for a long time, I am aware, but it has come to light now. This Coat of Arms, to say the least, is a provocation and a challenge to people belonging to other races both in Suva and outside Suva. Is this the indication of an attempt to bring political integration of all races in this Colony?

As far as these [constitutional] proposals are concerned, I say that the chiefs are given a seat in the Pullman car in this constitutional train. The Europeans are given a seat in the first class, the Fijian people are given a seat in the second class and the Indians are given a seat in the third class. The Governor, in his speech at the opening of this Council, referred to the constitutional proposals and said, 'No constitution is perfect and this is not the end of the road.' Consoling words, I agree, but this constitution is not merely imperfect. This constitution, in my opinion, is unfair and a constitution, however, imperfect it may be, must aim at one most important thing and that is to be fair to all citizens in the country. Not only is this constitution not fair, it is taking a wrong direction and it makes the journey prolonged and difficult.

I, for one, believe that Fiji is fit for complete independence. When we compare Fiji with countries like Samoa, Cook Islands and other territories, no one can say that we are in any way backward to those countries. If they can shoulder their responsibilities well, I do not see any reason why Fiji should not. I and the other members of the Indian delegation agree, and are still of the opinion, that two things should be maintained: one, a permanent link with the British Crown; and, two, full internal self-government. These were the two issues on which there was unanimity of agreement but the constitutional proposals put forward run far short of the target of full internal self-government. Many people have either misunderstood me or misconstrued my words consciously to create mischief. Complete independence does not mean severance from the British Crown; it does not mean getting out of the British Commonwealth. I made it plain in my speech at the opening of the Conference in London that complete independence that I am advocating is the sort of independence that countries like New Zealand and Australia are enjoying at present. Those countries are completely independent, they both have a permanent link with the British Crown, the Queen is the Head of the Government in both countries and both are members of the British Commonwealth.

The proposals that we put forward on the method of representation at the London Conference are fair, just and right proposals for the constitutional development of this country. It is highly gratifying to find that the proposals put forward by the Indian delegation are considered the proper proposals and supported by an overwhelming majority of votes in the United Nations. Eighty percent of the members of the United Nations voted for and hold that the constitution should be based on an unqualified system of democratic representation based on the principle of one man one vote. That is what we have been asking for at the Conference. That is what we have been asking for in Fiji all these years since 1929. Of the three countries which opposed it, one acted as a judge in its own case; one had a pecuniary interest in the country, and one has colonies in this part of the world. So at least we get endorsement from world opinion.

The motion says that this constitution forms a satisfactory basis for future political progress. On the grounds I have already mentioned, I say that these proposals do not form a satisfactory basis for future political progress in Fiji on constitutional lines and I urge the United Kingdom Government to negotiate further and try sincerely and seriously to bring about constitutional changes which will establish an unqualified system of democratic representation based on the principle of one man one vote. It is not too late yet.

33: Federation Party Letter to A.D. Patel[41], 6 August, 1966

Dear Sir

Today we are here in the Party's Working Committee to consider the selection of candidates for the Legislative Council and recommend their names to the general meeting later in the evening. This is the time to take stock of the record of the Party's Legco members without fear or favour.

You, Mr. President, in spite of your age and diabetes, have fully acquitted yourself of your responsibilities as leader of the Party's Legco wing and I as your colleague in the Party place on record my personal and also the Party's

41   Written by Madho Tikaram, President of the Suva branch of the Federation Party. In a secret memorandum that came my way as I was preparing this volume, an Australian official wrote: 'It is known that in 1965 he was seriously considering leading a left-wing group out of the party. The group was to be much more militant than the Federation Party and Koya wanted to name it Subhas Party after Subhas Chandra Bose who led certain Indian forces against Britain during World war II.' Koya was described as 'a gangster-lawyer, dangerous, rabid and unstable. Certainly he has a strong personality and a political history of excitability and outspokenness.' This assessment was by an Australian official, but similar views are expressed in official British documents at the Public Records Office, Kew Gardens.

appreciation of all the work that you have done for the Party and the people. Time is coming fast, if not already come, that your responsibilities should be shared by others and relieve you from overwork.

Mr. Madhavan deserves the Party's appreciation and gratitude for the unflinching work and loyalty that he has given to the Party to the best of his ability. Mr. Chirag Ali's is a special case. He arrived in the Party's LegCo wing through Government nomination. Though not highly educated, he brought sound common sense in his work, and though he spoke very little, he spoke to the point whenever he spoke. His loyalty to the Party has been well proved by him and he also deserves the gratitude and appreciation.

How I wish I could have said similar things for Mr. Koya. Unfortunately his record as a responsible and leading member of the Party and LegCo Member is not untarnished. Even at the risk of incurring his displeasure, I think, I as one of the Vice-Presidents of the Party, owe it to the Party, its principles and the people of Fiji, that I should record his shortcomings, not in a spirit of destructive criticism but in a spirit of comradeship as between people engaged in a common task and I hope he will appreciate the same. Real friends and comrades must criticize each other's faults with a view to remove such faults.

Mr. Koya has had a fairly good record in his performance in the Legco debates and to that extent he deserves the appreciation and gratitude of the Party. On the other hand, his interview and statement to the Daily Telegraph soon after the London Conference gave a very misleading picture of Indians in Fiji without consulting or even telling his colleagues, was a great embarrassment to his colleagues and the Party at large, and to the Indian community. His talks in Fiji with the Party members between his return from London and your return to the effect that we had lost all and that there should be left-wing and right-wing in the Party had a very demoralising effect on the Party workers and members. His rudeness to his colleagues and party workers and some others has by now become proverbial in the Party and his insulting behaviour to some good workers of the Party has had demoralising effect on the sincere workers of the Party. His tendency to get excited, to lend his ears to those who flatter him, ignore those in charge of actual facts and collecting facts from only those whom he considered his personal friends, has created a fear in the minds of some of the Party members that he is developing a tendency to indulge in clickwork [clique work], which if not checked now, may make it difficult to justify his name to the voters and create a danger of the Party falling in the hands of a click [clique]. His impulsive action in misleading the President that the work of registration of voters in Ba District had been very poor and asking the President to get extension of time has resulted in demoralising the Ba workers and cost the Indian community the loss of a lead of 10,000 voters over the Fijians.

Unless he assures the Working Committee that he accepts his mistakes and that in future he will show more respect and consideration for the feelings and views of the Party colleagues and workers and will work with more deliberation and consultation with his colleagues, I am of the opinion that he should not only be not selected as a candidate but should be asked to resign his post as Assistant Secretary and we should elect somebody with better temper and judgment to take his place, though he may continue on the working committee. If the Party aims at setting correct standards of public life in Fiji, as I believe it does, then we owe it to the Party's good name, to set an example to the people that the Party workers are courteous, selfless and determined workers for a cause without fear or favour.

34: The Secretariat to AD Patel, 23 September 1966

Dear Sir

You called at my office on the 19th September, 1966, to discuss the organization and procedures at polling stations for the forthcoming elections. I undertook to examine the points which you raised, and I now write to let you know the position.

You suggested that an elector on arrival at the polling station, should not be handed all his ballot papers simultaneously, but should be allowed to take one at a time, mark it and put it in the ballot box, before taking a second paper, or a third. The purpose of this would be to avoid confusion in the mind of a less well-educated elector as to which ballot paper related to a particular constituency, and to prevent marked ballot papers being placed in the wrong ballot boxes.

Before dealing with the mechanics of this suggestion, may I draw attention to the fact that, as an aid to voters, the ballot papers for the various constituencies will be in different colours, e.g. the Indian communal ballot papers will be yellow, while the Indian cross-voting papers will be pink. Thus the easiest way for an elector to distinguish one constituency from another is to remember these colours. I do not think it would be any easier, and it might indeed be more difficult, for an elector to try to remember (say) that the first paper which he receives is the Indian communal one, while the second is the Fijian cross-voting one, etc. There thus appears to be little to be gained, from the point of view of informing the voter which paper relates to which constituency, from issuing the papers singly and in a fixed sequence. One should also bear in mind that the candidates or their agents who may of course be present in the polling stations, will not be able to speak to electors therein, and will therefore not be able to give them any guidance on the question of which paper is which. Candidates or their agents will, however, have the opportunity before polling begins, and right up to the moment the elector enters the polling station, to impress upon him that the communal ballot paper (for example) is yellow and (if the voter is illiterate in English) that he should vote for (say) the second candidate on the yellow paper. Alternatively, if this is too much for the elector to remember, he has of course the option of asking the presiding officer to mark his papers for him.

Notwithstanding the aids to voting mentioned above, I have examined carefully the possibility of implementing your suggestion about the issue of ballot papers individually in succession. I regret, however, that it would not be practicable to implement it, because of the delay which it would inevitably impose on the processes of voting. For example, it would mean each voter having to address himself separately to three or four different clerks, and, more important, make three or four separate journeys into the polling booths and back, thus occupying a booth or booths for a length of time which, in the aggregate, would inevitably be greater than if he marked all his papers in one booth at one time.

It will, however, generally be possible for each elector to be handed his communal ballot paper separately from and shortly before he receives his cross-voting [ballot paper], although he will be required to take both types of paper (or such as he desires to use) before going into a polling booth to mark them. This will serve to re-emphasise the different nature of the types of paper.

Before leaving the question of ballot papers, I might add that arrangements have already been made for specimen ballot papers, in the appropriate colours, to be displayed in all polling stations. I am also arranging for posters to be issued, for display outside polling stations and elsewhere, showing the actual colours on which the various ballot papers are printed. Further publicity will also be given to this subject through the medium of the Fijian Broadcasting Commission.

You also asked whether I was satisfied that sufficient clerks etc. would be on hand at polling stations to deal with the number of voters expected. I have now made inquiries, and I can give you an assurance that this is so, always assuming that electors cooperate reasonably by not all leaving their voting until the last moment. At the bigger polling stations, two or more streams of voters will be dealt with simultaneously, by arranging for voters to be dealt with according to the initial letter of the name under which they are in one stream, and L to Z in another.

Regarding the question of voters who are in the queue at the time that voting closes, Regulation 40(2) of the Electoral Regulations, 1965, as amended by the discretion on presiding officers to extend the time of voting at any particular polling station, for a further period not exceeding two hours, if it is necessary to do so. This discretion will normally be exercised in favour of any voters who have reached the polling station by the appointed closing time, but not (save perhaps in exceptional circumstances) to permit voting by electors who fail to arrive until after the appointed closing time. It is therefore in the interests of all concerned for voters to arrive at polling stations as early as possible.

I trust that this explanation will have cleared up any remaining doubts which you may have had.

Yours sincerely

(sgd) Ian Thomson

(JS Thomson)

35: Launch of the 1966 Election campaign, Century Theatre, July 1966[42]

I hope you will excuse me if I fail to make myself audible to you on this most momentous occasion. My voice has failed me today.

As you all know, the longest journey always begins with a single step. We are taking the longest journey in the history of Fiji. We are taking this journey to meet our destiny, and I hope and pray to God that that destiny is full of promise of good things of life, to this country and to the people of this country: we who are living now and those who will follow us hereafter.

Wordsworth was inspired to say about the French Revolution: 'Bliss was it in that dawn to be alive, But to be young was very heaven.' In our history, I also feel and share the same sentiment. Mine is the fortune of being alive in this dawn. Mine is the misfortune that I won't be able to share that very heaven. But that should not deter me, or deter you, from our path of duty.

As you very well know, the most overriding objective of the Federation Party is to weld all the peoples of this country into one nation. We are subjected to a form of government which stands universally condemned in this world today. That form of government separated brother from brother merely on the basis of the pigmentation of their skin.

---

42   Recorded by Robert Norton during his fieldwork for his doctorate in Fiji. The doctoral thesis was eventually published as *Race and Politics in Fiji* (St. Lucia: University of Queensland Press, 1977).

Christians went on preaching in the churches, Muslims went on preaching in their mosques, Hindus went on preaching in their temples, that we are all children of the same Father. And yet, we betrayed our Father and we betrayed ourselves. We left the preaching of our great teachers and sages within the walls of the churches, mosques and temples, and when we came out, we debased and lowered ourselves more than even animals.

You find white cows and you find black cows and you find brown and red cows. The black cow never hates the white cow, or the white cow doesn't hate the red cow because of its skin colour. We claim to be the most intelligent creatures on the earth, but our intellect has not changed us or helped us, as it has helped the lower animal kingdom.

What mischief has been done over ninety years I know and you know cannot be undone in a day. It will take time. We will have to unlearn many things which we were taught—not for our own good but for the good of those who wanted to rule over us. We will have to unlearn that.

Ninety years of rule has entered our very vitals—our soul—and I can tell you that you can get rid of what comes from the outside easily, but it is difficult to get rid of what has become a part of your mental and spiritual makeup. All this while in Fiji I have felt proud that we live more harmoniously, more amicably, and in a more brotherly fashion, than people in many parts of the world—people who call themselves at the pinnacle of culture and civilisation: that is one thing which has always made me proud. And I was sorry to hear from the lips of a youngster in the Phoenix Theatre that there is racial disharmony in Fiji, and that we are all sitting on top of a volcano. A grosser lie cannot be uttered about Fiji, a grosser insult cannot be offered to the people of Fiji. And my heart grieved.

Anyhow, as I say, let us forget our past and let's face the future bravely and courageously. And look straight into the eye of things that are to come. A poet has said, 'The old order changeth, yielding place to new. And God fulfils himself in many ways.' We of this generation in Fiji have got to become instruments in His hands. We mortals cannot judge who is in the right and who is in the wrong.

Our opponents have spared no time, effort and energy to misrepresent us as a party: that we create racial disharmony, that we create racial hatred. They don't even stop to think that we are not so stupid as all that to think that we can build a nation, weld all the people together by hatred. Only the cement of love and understanding and sympathy can achieve that difficult task.

And we are conscious both of our responsibilities and our difficulties. We have many obstacles to surmount. Those who have don't give up easily. Those who have not have to strive hard to get what is rightly theirs. And that is what we are doing. When we criticise and expose racial discrimination in this Colony, they say that we are racists. But how can you eliminate an evil unless you lay your finger on that evil and try to eradicate it? You cannot remove that evil by just closing your eyes to it, and patiently suffering under it. It will only perpetuate the evil.

Let me tell you one thing. My whole spiritual and intellectual makeup has a culture and civilisation which is, in fact, the oldest, or at least one of the oldest cultures and civilisations in the world. Long before Jesus Christ came in this world and taught people that if anybody smites you on one cheek, offer the other, long before that, Lord Buddha taught the doctrine of non-violence, non-killing: don't hurt any living creature, let alone man, don't do anything that causes pain or suffering to others.

Our whole outlook in life and philosophy was summarized in one verse, and of that verse only one line: 'That is virtue which makes others happy; that is sin which makes others unhappy.' We have learned that. It has become the flesh of our flesh. You cannot get rid of it.

When I went to America last year, some prominent members of the Congress told me: 'Do you know what is wrong with you Indians?' I said 'No, I would be glad to know it from you.' They said, 'You are not sufficiently aggressive for the world. The world belongs to those who are aggressive. You people, through your culture, are too mild to cope with the problems of the world.' I told him that 'you may be right, but God gave us a man the like of whom comes on this earth once in thousands of years, and that is Mahatma Gandhi. We have pinned our faith on him. He has reminded us of our culture. He has reminded us of our religion. He has reminded us of our code of behaviour. And in all sincerity, we try to follow him.'

One party in a pamphlet circulated amongst its members said that the Federation Party is a very efficient political organization and if people return that party in a majority, and if Federation forms the government of Fiji, there will be chaos and bloodshed. I can assure you one thing: Federation Party believes in non-violence, Federation Party believes in love, Federation Party believes in bringing all people together and welding them into one nation. So, if chaos is going to come, it can only come from the opponents of this party. If we are returned to the Legislative Council through the ballot box, and if we are returned with a large majority, it only expresses the true opinion and feeling of the people towards us, and if people send us in a majority, who is going to take up sword against us? Those who are defeated?

I have taken all this time and elaborated this point because I know that too much misunderstanding has been created and is being created against our party, and especially against me. Some people say that I am trying to be a dictator. Some people say that I am ambitious and that I want to be the Prime Minister of Fiji. Let me make it clear once and for all: I seek no power because I know that all power corrupts. All that I seek for myself and my comrades, and my party and my people and my country which I consider in my hearts of hearts to be my own, I only aspire for one thing: that I may be of some service to them all. I am seeking service, the opportunity to serve, not to rule, not to dominate. And the band of candidates who have been selected and whose names will be announced, will take an oath before you to serve your party and to serve this country.

Now, let me come to the question of what is our party. You know, all over the world, the pattern of colonialism is just the same. In every sphere of life, the ruling race dominates: in politics, in the field of commerce, in the field of industry, in social life, and if I may be permitted to say it without giving offence to anybody, even in the field of religion, in the spiritual field. The aim and object of this party is to change the power structure. We don't want to usurp anything which rightly belongs to someone else. You know very well that our religion teaches us 'Don't covert what belongs to another. Whatever you want in this life, earn it yourself, and enjoy it after dedicating it to God.'

But it is quite natural. Those who hold power in this field are reluctant to share it with others. I feel they are fighting a rearguard action to hold on, to cling on to that power as long as they can. I can understand that too. If I was one of those 'haves' probably I might have done the same thing. I don't know. But as political and economic 'have-nots,' it is our duty to assert ourselves and to get our rightful share in the power structure. We don't want anything more. We won't be satisfied with anything less.

Some people spread the rumour that I am anti-European, and that I want to drive the Europeans out of this country. It is a wicked lie. How can this country run without capital, without know-how? They have been luckier than us. God has given them both these advantages over us. All that I wish to seek is that their know-how, their ability, their knowledge, their education, is put to the service of everybody in this Colony.

The aim of the Federation Party is to see that even the poorest, even the weakest citizen of this Colony, feels proud that he is a Fijian, feels proud that he is a human being, and regains that dignity which is by right his, and through force of circumstance he has lost. I want, and the Federation Party wants, to re-instill that dignity, that self-respect, and that pride in all our people. These are the spiritual values for which the Party stands.

Now let me come to the political side. I believe, and all my comrades believe, and all the thousands of members of the Federation Party believe, in the equality of man, equality before the law. There should be no special privileges by reason of race, religion, birth or sex. We want to change that. We don't want, and we are not seeking, that if a particular community is more in numbers, that community should dominate other communities. Nor can we tolerate the position that a minority should dominate a majority. We are in a majority, because we are kept apart, and we think on racial lines, which I hate. If Fiji becomes a nation, the majorities and minorities will not be permanent. They will change from time to time. Majorities and minorities will be decided by political exigencies and ideologies of the time. Who, for instance, in America can say that the Republicans are a permanent majority and the Democrats are a permanent minority? Who in Great Britain can say that Labour is a permanent majority, or the Tories are a permanent minority? Once we wipe out these racial barriers, there is no question of any race dominating another.

It has always been said that 'Oh, Federation Party is only paying lip-service to this, but it has got some devilish scheme in its heart.' How can we convince them of our *bona fides* until we are given an opportunity to prove our sincerity? How can we do it? Even our own small, tiny history, in its own way, proves what we are. I will give you the instance of Suva City Council. Go through its minutes, go through its records. You will always find one race voting in a block, especially when the time for election of the mayor and the deputy mayor comes. Indians as a race have never voted as a block. And some people say that that is because Indians are disunited. They don't give us the credit that Indians are not racial-minded. That is as far as the political side is concerned.

Let me come to the most important side of our life, and that is the economic side. Man cannot live by bread alone. Bread is only a means of life, bread is not life. And so, what makes life ennobling, enlightened and worth living? Living in a way that a Christian believes that at the end of the life, they will get salvation, the Muslims believe that they would find paradise, while the Hindus believe that they will find their ultimate merging in the Absolute. That is the aim of life. You find that in the heart of a small child, you find that in the heart of the biggest criminal. It is secretly lurking there. I have defended many murderers. I won't call them murderers, because most of them were acquitted. But I say that even in their hearts, there was that desire, that spiritual urge. For we are all living for that ultimate objective. That can be provided by three ways. [One is] continuous study. From the time you are born, you start learning. A baby starts learning without any teacher, without any school, without any equipment. In a human being's life, that is the time when he or she learns independently through God's blessing, without anybody's aid. So education is a most important and vital thing for us. And that education should be the type of education which liberates us, liberates man politically, socially, economically and spiritually.

Some people argue that we must have compulsory education first, and unless and until every child in this country gets elementary education—how to read, write and calculate— it is idle to think of a university. Let me remind them of one thing. The oldest university in recorded history that I know of, was the University of Dakshila in India, which was flourishing in 600BC—600 years before Christ was born. That university created great minds who wrote great books in the Sanskrit language. Those are the classics of Indian literature and today we all study them with pride. The most outstanding product of that university was the great genius in political science and in diplomacy and economics: Chanakya. If you have not read it, you must have heard of that classic on economics by Chanakya called *Chanakya Niti*.

Now, if India had waited for compulsory education before making a start for higher education and establishing a university, India could not have even one university now because there is so much illiteracy [in the country]. If that criterion was to be followed, there would be no university even now in the whole of Asia, Africa and Latin America. Let me remind you that when Oxford and Cambridge came into existence, hardly five percent of the population of England was literate. Those were the days when even kings and queens couldn't read and write, and signed their names with difficulty on official documents.

Remember this: our store of knowledge comes from the university. If we are all to limit ourselves to compulsory education, how poorer could we all be, how poorer the world would be, if we only knew how to read, write and calculate? It is the university which intellectually, morally and spiritually raises us from the level of animals. We need a university in Fiji even if we can't have compulsory education immediately. It is not the job of the university only to teach. The job of the university is to think, to discover, to invent and to impart the results of that thought, the discoveries and the inventions to the world. That is the aim and object of the Federation Party in the field of education.

Education, as I mentioned, needs study, but study alone is not enough. Education needs thinking. And may I take the liberty of telling you that, though there is so much of illiteracy in India, you will be surprised at the power of thinking that many of these illiterate in India possess. An illiterate labourer when he thinks and talks about philosophy, a professor of philosophy from the western world would be astounded. So thinking is also very important, and that also comes from university training. That is why we want university in Fiji urgently. There are difficulties in the way, I know, but with God's blessing I expect that we will be able to make a start in two or three years time.

We all talk of social services. We all talk of natural resources. We consider economics as something separate and apart from health and education. Here in Fiji, amongst certain circles, there is an impression that education and medical facilities are luxuries that we can do without and we can curtail. And they think that the only thing that matters is production, only thing that matters is pounds, shillings and pence. I know we need to raise and increase our production. But to increase production, we need education and health. This is not social service. It is not a luxury. It's a part of the economic development of the Colony. And the Federation Party does not wish to make that distinction and divide these two important essentials of development.

There is a tendency to think and a habit to say that we cannot do without outside capital. We should be guarded in our speech so that foreign investors may not be frightened off. It has become a fashion to say that capital is very, very shy and you have always got to be careful not to offend it. Federation Party believes in one thing: capital after all is a result of the sweat of men. They worked for it. We may be poor in Fiji: we are poor in Fiji. But if we made a determination that out of every pound we earn, at the most we will spend nineteen shillings, but one shilling will be saved. That one shilling is the capital. And those who have saved and who have become capitalists of the world, most of them were not born with a silver spoon in their mouths. They created capital with their sweat. We have got to do the same thing in Fiji. Self-help is the best help. Let us start it from our homes and our country.

Foreign capital, when it comes into the country, only invests in what we call expatriate industries. They will go in for mining, they will go in for logging, they will go in for copra and sugar. It is all taken out as a natural resource and taken abroad. Not one comes here with a manufacturing enterprise, to make things which can be made in this country, to make things which can save our natural resources and use those resources carefully and parsimoniously for ourselves and for our generations to come. For those manufacturing industries, we will have to depend on our own capital which we will have to create ourselves. And Federation Party believes in it, so that every encouragement will be given to people to save and form capital to establish manufacturing industries which will be helping them and helping the country. And the government will be taking an active part in trying to finance them, [providing] a certain portion of the finance; if they don't have the know-how, help them in providing the know-how; if they have no managerial ability, to help them with some sort of managerial ability, until their private enterprise can stand on its own feet.

A poor country has got to solve the problem of increase in the population, and providing employment for that population. In such a country, you can do it by establishing mills, you can use machinery, you can use many things. Even automation doesn't disturb that employment problem. But as far as we are concerned, we have got to see that the machine doesn't take the place of man. We have got to see that the machine doesn't deprive a man and his family of his livelihood. If we can employ ten men without the aid of machines, and if we employ a machine and take ten men out of jobs, Federation Party will give preference to those ten men's livelihoods before the employment of machines.

That does not mean we are against the employment of machinery. Machinery should be employed, then man's tasks can become easier, more comfortable, less strenuous, and can provide him with more leisure, which he can profitably enjoy what we call life in abundance: family life, home life, life with his children and his wife, life with friends, life with his fellow men, life on the sports field, life in the club, life in the cultural centres, and life in places of worship. This is the real, proper use of machines. If the machine can't do that, then machine is not a blessing; machine is a curse, at least to a country and people like us, at this stage of our development.

Socially, as I have already said, we should all be one: equal, nobody great and nobody small. I am trying always to see that in my life I can mix and talk with the humblest of citizens in Fiji on equal terms. I am doing it. So far, I am successful. Many people criticise me just because of that. I have heard people say that a Member for Social Services should not go into the market to buy vegetables. I go into the market not to buy vegetables—buying vegetables is merely an excuse. My servant can go and buy it and bring it home, but it gives me the opportunity of mixing with my own people on equal terms, easily. They only remember me as a fellow human being, which they can't if they come into that office in Government Buildings. I mix with people in my home and outside in the same way. And I can tell you that you can get more satisfaction in life through keeping your ego down and allowing the natural springs of love which are in your heart. I want all my comrades, I want all the members of the Federation Party, I want all the sympathisers and supporters of the Federation Party to take that: you should have self-respect within you and confidence enough to sit with and enjoy the company on equal terms with the greatest of the world as well as with the humblest.

I have taken a lot of your time, more time than I should have taken because unfortunately due to my ill-health, at this critical time, I was not able to prepare a speech. I only decided that I will tell you what came to my mind, and I have told you.

In the end, I wish to tell you one thing, one precept, from a holy book. 'Where there are stronger, take the side of the weaker, and by taking the side of the weaker, you will always be in the right.' That is my motto in life. I hope that will be the motto of the Federation Party. With love towards all and malice towards none, we will keep on working with courage and determination. And I want you to realise one thing: History demands sacrifice. We have made an appointment with our destiny, and we have got to keep that appointment. May God give us all the strength to fulfill that appointment. Thank You.

36: Political Address, Sigatoka Valley, 25 September 1966[43]

I have been hearing that people are being misled about the Federation Party. I wish to tell you about the Federation Party today, its objectives and what it is trying to do. Federation stands for 'union,' 'unity in diversity'. Flowers have different colours. They look different, they smell different. But if they are put together in a garland, they give a unique fragrance, as they grace the neck of humans or the feet of gods. The aim of the Federation Party is the same: to see that everyone unites and sticks together like flowers in a garland. I have been advocating that all Indians should unite. We are fifty one percent of the total population. It is important that we unite and show others what unity is. I am pleased to state that there are members of various races in the Federation Party. There are thousands of Fijians in the Party, along with some Chinese and some educated Europeans. These people fully understand the objectives of the Party.

In the 19th century, there was great stress on imperialism. England claimed that upon the entire realm of Great Britain the sun never set. That has changed today. After the Second World War, people of the world began to think about independence, that all countries should be free and that governments of free countries should be formed by the people themselves. The people of Fiji were also thinking along similar lines. People in the United Nations, too, have been saying that independence should be given to Fiji as soon as possible. Those people spreading rumours about the Federation Party asking for independence do not understand fully the objectives of the Federation Party. They do not understand what will happen in the future, and they are trying to forget the past. Those who have the power and the money do not want to part with their privileges. Such is the case throughout the world.

People of Britain have been ruling Fiji for a very long time. These people have been drawing big salaries. They have been getting inducement and other allowances. We do get employment but we are accused of not working properly, of being incapable and therefore not getting higher pay. The time has come for us to look after our own affairs. We have to therefore take the reins of government into our own hands and look after the people ourselves. We are a very proud species. We know that among the animals that God has created, we are the best. We have attributes not found in other animals.

---

43 The speech in Hindi recorded by Robert Norton and translated by Mr Pathik of the Nasinu Teachers' Training College.

But I wish to tell you one thing. There are black cows and red cows and brown cows. Have you ever found them quarrelling among themselves? Quarrelling and saying that since you are black or since you are brown, I am not going to graze with you? But what of humans, who claim a high degree of civilization for themselves? They are the ones who have created distinctions based on colour. This colour distinction among human beings does not allow people to have cross-cultural friendships. Where humans should understand each other's heart, they look at each other's face, look at each other's colour.

What does religion teach us? It teaches us that since we are all children of God, we should not discriminate against one another. If we are His children, why should we quarrel, what is the struggle for? Why should we then say to one another that you are a Fijian, or an Indian, or a European? Why can't we say that we all belong to one nation: the nation of Fiji? Some people say if independence came to Fiji, Indians will swamp the Fijians. And some people say that if independence comes to Fiji that Fijians will swamp the Indians. Both conclusions are wrong. We can get independence in Fiji only if we get together and make Fiji a nation.

The objective of colonialism is well known throughout the world: the policy of divide and rule. Why have they divided us, put Fijians in their villages and Indians in the fields [settlements]. Why have the Europeans built their bungalows on hills or have lived in towns? Who is responsible for this? Who made these [segregation] laws? Who made the law that requires a Fijian to seek the permission of the *turaga ni koro* [village headman] to leave his village? Fijians were forced to live in their villages like prisoners. These laws were made by the Fijian Affairs Board.

Everyone in the world wants to be free, to live wherever he likes; provided he abides by the laws he can live freely and do his own business and live peacefully. When I first came to Fiji, there was curfew in Suva, and I wondered why one was not allowed to go out of his dwelling after ten o' clock. No one was allowed even to go to a hotel after ten o'clock. I saw the Commissioner of Police and put to him that this was a strange law, that if one visits his friend and is delayed and happens to return to his hotel after ten, he can be apprehended by the police and put in a cell overnight. The Commissioner of Police laughed and explained 'Mr. Patel, this law was not intended to be enforced on you; you can go wherever you like, even after ten; the police will not arrest you.' Although I was not arrested, many Indians and Fijians were arrested and put in the cell. There was only one race [Europeans] who could move about freely, even after curfew hours.

When I went to Ba, I found a very good stream. I was very pleased at this. I went to my place, put on my bathing costume, brought a towel and dived in. No sooner was I in the water than a few Europeans arrived and when they saw me bathing in the water, they went away. The following day, being a Sunday, I had Mr. SB Patel, Mr. MT Khan and a few other visitors from Lautoka. I told them about the stream near the race course and how we could have a swim in it. We went to the stream and began to bathe.

As soon as we began to bathe, the Europeans who were there before us got into their cars and left. I could not understand this, the Europeans leaving just because we were bathing in the stream. The following day, Mr. Ragg arrived at my office and said that we were not allowed to bathe in the stream. I told Mr. Ragg that according to the law, the pool does not belong to you, but if I find out that it belongs to the public I will try and gather as many Indians and Fijians as I can and take them to the pool to bathe in it. The next day, I went to see the plan at the District Officer's office. The District Officer was Mr. Judd. When Mr. Judd saw that I was looking at the plan, he came to me and said that I could come to his residence which had a private pool and that I could come there at any time I liked, have tea at his place and swim in the pool. I said to Mr. Judd that I was very thankful for his offer, but I would still prefer to see the location of the pool and to see who owns it…There was a time in Fiji when there were separate public bathing places for Indians and Fijians and Europeans. The Fijians were able to understand fully that they and the Indians were looked down upon by the Europeans.

But it is quite different now. I am telling you that Indians and Fijians together make up ninety four per cent of the Colony's population. If the two groups are united, we could have heaven on earth here. The Fiji Visitor's Bureau advertises that 'Fiji is Paradise.' But is there not unhappiness here? Isn't there poverty and illiteracy? If there is, then this is not a paradise. As Member for Social Services, I have seen Indian and Fijian schools, and I have seen children at school and the syllabuses taught there. What is the state of facilities in the schools? How many government secondary schools are there? And yet they call this paradise?

When I was in India in 1962, I met Pandit Jawaharlal Nehru. I spoke to him about the possibility of having a university in Fiji. He fully supported my views and said the Government of India would fully support this scheme. When this was published in the newspapers, the *Fiji Times* said this was Patel's political stunt. When I returned to Fiji, everyone mocked me. This was in 1962. It was only two years later that the same AD Patel became Member for Social Services, and the portfolio for building a university in Fiji came into his hands. It was his good fortune that no sooner had he suggested this idea of a university in Fiji, the Government of Fiji hastily wrote to the Government of Great Britain to have a university in Fiji before Government of India got involved. The Government of Great Britain appointed a Commission chaired by Sir Charles Morris, and at the same time the Government of New Zealand announced that they would be leaving Fiji, their buildings and facilities becoming vacant. I have every confidence that by 1968, a university will be opened in Fiji. So it will be possible for those Indian and Fijian students who for financial reasons are not able to go overseas for further education will be able to become university graduates in Fiji.

It is being said to the Fijians that if the Federation Party comes to power, they will suppress the Fijians. When I speak, I speak from my heart and not from my lips only. I have lived in Fiji for the last thirty eight years, and during this time, if a Fijian has brought a case to me, I have fought his case without any fee. I will give an example of this issue. During the war years, when American soldiers were stationed in Nadi, an American soldier went to a village and probably asked for a girl. The Fijians got very annoyed and chased him from the village. They followed him and just near the Nadi Theatre, they gave him so much hiding that the poor chap bled. The American soldiers got very annoyed and they threatened to shoot the villagers and burn Fijian villages in the Nadi area. The same night, the Fijians came to my house at Nadi and they brought a Tabua with them. The Fijians then presented the Tabua to me. I said to them that I would give them all the help they needed and that they were to go back to the village and stay there without any fear.

I immediately wrote to the commandant of the army and asked him for an explanation of the matter. He said that the villagers need not be afraid of anything, and that it was a matter for the Fiji Government to investigate. Seven Fijians were arrested. At that time [1943] there was a strike and I was under house arrest. I wrote a letter to the Governor of Fiji and requested that I be allowed to represent the seven Fijians in the Lautoka Supreme Court. At that time, I was a prisoner of the Government of Fiji. I was allowed to travel to Lautoka, and for three weeks I fought this case. All were set free except one who was imprisoned for seven years. Now who can say that I am not a friend of the Fijians, or that I am their enemy? Those Europeans who advocate equality will only allow Fijians to enter their houses through the back door. But if a Fijian comes to my house, he enters through the front door and he sits side by side with me on the same sofa. When a Fijian visits the office of the Member for Natural Resources [Ratu Mara], he bends down on his knee and goes to his office. But when he visits my office as the Member for Social Services and when he tries to bend down, I hold him up by the arm and say to him: 'You sit beside me and talk to me face-to-face, and if you have any complaints, I will listen to it very carefully and I will try my best to help you.'

I will give you one or two examples of this. Two Fijians from Lau who were imprisoned in Suva were about to return to their villages in Lau at the finish of their term. But the Superintendent of Prisons said that they were to travel as deck passengers as soon as deck passage was available. These people wondered how they would fend for themselves during this time; they had no money. Someone suggested they should see the Member for Social Services, Mr. AD Patel. These two Fijians came to me and told me that they were unable to get passage to their village, and that it was not possible for them to live in Suva for a month because they had no money. I immediately asked my secretary to ring the shipping company and find out if any deck passages were available. The reply was in the negative. I asked him to ring again to see if there was any saloon passage available. He told me that one or two saloon passages were available. I at once asked him to send the two men by saloon passage. If any one from Lau had ever travelled from Suva to Lau in saloon passage, it was these two prisoners.

When I look at our schools, I find that all children are alike whether they are Indian, Fijian, European or Chinese. To me everyone is alike. We must work together for the good of the Colony. The Federation Party is thinking of the same, and working along these lines and will work along these lines in the future. There are people who always write against me in the papers. According to a Hindi saying, if I say mangoes, they will say tamarind. And people who read this in overseas newspapers express surprise when they finally meet me. 'Mr. Patel, we were thinking you might be some sort of a monster, but when we meet you, we find you are not that at all. You are not saying anything that should not be said.' The same thing happened at the London conference. The United Kingdom delegation said the same thing to us. Mrs Irene White said to me; 'Mr. Patel you have put your case very lucidly and convincingly before us, and there is not a single word in it with which I disagree.'

We know that if we have to bring peace in this country and that we have to be independent, and all that, we have to live peacefully together. We cannot fight and still live together. We have to cooperate and live together. We have to bring everyone together and the only way to do that is by means of common roll. We can no longer think along the lines that we are Fijians, we are Indians, we are Europeans or Chinese. We must think of ourselves as citizens of Fiji, that we are nationals of Fiji. We have to have a government in place which will bring peace and prosperity and deal with the three enemies of mankind: poverty, illiteracy and sickness. The Federation Party thinks that we are all alike in the eyes of God. We want equal rights and we dislike those people who create discrimination amongst us. We do not threaten anyone, nor would we tolerate threats from anyone.

I advocate that in our schools in Fiji, our three principal languages should all be taught, English, Fijian and Hindustani. It is not difficult to learn the three languages. My son, who is in England, learns five languages, including Spanish, French and Latin. If he can learn five languages (besides studying mathematics and political science), it should not be difficult for a child to learn only three languages. In England, every child has to learn three languages: French, Latin and English, which is his mother tongue. Now if he has to learn three languages, there is no reason why in our schools in Fiji, a child cannot learn three languages. When we learn each other's languages, we will be able to understand each other well, we learn about each other's culture and therefore living together will not be so difficult. When I called a conference in Suva to tell people that all schools should accept children of all races, Fijian managers, incited by others, refused to accept children of other races into their schools. They knew full well that standards in European schools were better than in their schools, that Indian schools came second and that Fijian schools were the weakest. But they refused to accept this offer. Now they want all schools to accept children of different races. Now the Suva Grammar School accepts children from all races. But this was not possible before. This is a time to think, and if we do not unite together, the consequence especially for the poor people will be bad. The decision is in our hands. We can decide. If we can unite, we can achieve this aim.

You, men and women who are voters, know that according to the new constitution, twelve Indian votes are equal to one European vote. Do you think this is justice? Can we have peace through this injustice? Can there be any peace if we know that this injustice is being done to us? The greatest enemy of human beings is fear. If a person lives in fear, he lives in slavery throughout his life, and when he dies, he dies a dog's death. On the other hand, those people who do not fear, or the person who does not fear, lives like a king because he has no one to fear except God. When people with no fear die, they die as brave people and people have respect for them. Take the example of Bapuji. Mahatma Gandhi worked for his country all his life. When independence came, there were communal riots, and he went from village to village, and wherever he went, peace came to the minds of the people. When he passed away, he passed away as a brave man. They said bad things about him when he was alive, but they worship him now. Take Lord Jesus Christ. Jesus Christ had only twelve disciples in the beginning. But after his death, the world worshipped him. People did not realise who he truly was.

I have great pleasure in telling you that the membership of the Federation Party now stands at seven thousand. This number has never been equalled by any union or Sangh in the history of Fiji. I may tell you one more thing, that in the Fijian Association, the membership is open only to Fijians. Similarly, in the General Voters Union, they can take membership of other people, but say if the

Member for Natural Resources wishes to become a member, his membership will be refused. I do not wish to say much about the Alliance because the Alliance says it 'Stands for All.' But I say if the Alliance is for all, then why do you oppose common roll? If you say you stand for all, then why do you have separate Indian, Fijian and European memberships? Why don't you unite and then you will be able to say that Alliance stands for all. Alliance also follows the policy of divide and rule. Federation Party is a political party. Alliance is not a political party but only a group of people. They themselves say that the Alliance was formed to oppose and defeat the Federation Party. What will happen after the election campaign when they have defeated the Federation Party? I don't know what will happen to the Indian members of the party if they disagree with the party leaders? They will be booted out of the Alliance or they will have to work as slaves for them.[44] And who will benefit in this? Only Mr. John Falvey, and of course he is the brains behind the Alliance.

It is my misfortune that after filing my nomination, I became the victim of pneumonia and I had to lie in bed for about a month. It therefore became impossible for me to come and see you. You must have heard that the Secretary of State for the Colonies, Mr. Fred Lee, was in Fiji and I toured with him to places in Suva. I went to the [Derrick] Technical Institute, Laucala Bay, the [Colonial War Memorial] Hospital and the Fiji School of Medicine Building. And when I was going down the steps, I suddenly collapsed. Dr [Charles] Gurd who was accompanying me and who knew I was very ill, got hold of me and guided me down the steps like a child, counting each step for me. I asked Mr. Fred Lee if he was tired. He said to me, 'To be very frank with you Mr. Patel, I say I am really tired.' I suggested he take a rest. When he was returning, he learnt that I was down with pneumonia. He wrote a personal note to me from the Nadi Airport saying that he was praying for my speedy recovery because 'Fiji needs you.' Now, we are fighting Great Britain. We are fighting Mr. Fred Lee. And yet it is Fred Lee who says that 'Fiji needs you Mr. Patel.' But I hear that people here don't want me, when I am not fighting with anyone in Fiji. Everyone in Fiji— Fijians, Indians, Europeans—are all alike to me.

If we want to bring peace, we have to bring prosperity and we have to be united and go forward together. We are one of the world's ancient people. Our civilization is the oldest in the world. Our religion is Sanatan [eternal]. It teaches us to speak the truth irrespective of the consequences. Our religion also teaches non-violence. We do not issue threats to anyone. You have the free right to vote. You think hard before you cast your vote. No one is supposed to demand your vote by personal threat or by showing violence or by bribery. I hear that it is

---

44   By the late 1970s, nearly all the founding members of the Indian Alliance had left the party and joined the National Federation Party, including Sir Vijay R Singh and James Shankar Singh, former Alliance cabinet ministers and presidents of the Indian Alliance.

being threatened that those who do not vote for the Alliance will be pushed out of their land by Mr. MacFarlane.[45] This is not true. I know this is not true. If Mr. MacFarlane is trying to give this threat, I am prepared to take up a case against him. But I know he will not do this because he is a lawyer and he knows the regulations full well. No one has to fear about land because unless there are two renewals of ten years' each, no one can be pushed out. The Fijian people are being incited that if the Federation Party comes to power, they will snatch their lands from them. I am trying to tell people that they should not have fear of anyone. The common Fijian people are being incited against me because the chiefs think that if they get common roll, they will lose their special privileges. I'd like to see the day when common roll comes to Fiji so that everyone works together for the good of Fiji irrespective of their race.

I have taken a lot of your time, and I thank you for listening to me patiently. I know that I have come to you very late. There are two reasons for this. I have already told you about my illness and then, since I am the leader of the Federation Party, I had to attend various meetings throughout Fiji to campaign for our candidates. I have come very late to my own constituency because I know that people understand that I am trying to work for the good of everyone, for the good of Fiji.

37: Call for a new Constitutional Conference, 1 September 1967

I beg to move:

> Undemocratic, iniquitous and unjust provisions characterize the existing Constitution and electoral laws of Fiji and their operation have caused alarm in the minds of right thinking people and have hampered the political advancement of Fiji along democratic lines and this House therefore is of the opinion that Her Majesty's Government of the United Kingdom should call a Constitutional Conference immediately to ensure that a new Constitution is worked out based on true democratic principles without any bias or distinction on the grounds of colour, race, religion or place of origin or vested interest either political, economic, social or other so that Fiji may attain self-government and become a nation with honour, dignity and responsibility as soon as possible.

The House is well aware, and it is also a matter of public knowledge, that the present Constitution was imposed upon the Indian community against the

---

45   DM MacFarlane was the Legal Advisor to the Native Land Trust Board.

expressed wishes of its elected representatives at the Conference. There was only one Indian delegate [CP Singh], who happened to be the Governor's nominee, who sided with the European and the Fijian delegations and showed his consent partly to the proposed Constitution. The Indian community opposed this Constitution and still opposes it because it is undemocratic, because it is iniquitous and because it is unjust. It is a serious obstacle in welding various communities residing in this country into a nation. It seriously hampers the political progress of this Colony towards independence by bringing into existence a reactionary Government. As is evident from the racial composition of the members sitting here, the Indian community, though it is the majority community in Fiji, [has only] twelve of us in this House. The European community, though it is a very small minority consisting of about 20,000 people including the Chinese, [has] 14 members sitting in this House. The Fijians, who are the second biggest community in Fiji, have only 14 Fijian members sitting in this House, which means that a small minority of 20,000 has gained [over] representation in this House which enables 14 Europeans to sit in this Council and take part in its deliberations.[46] This is obviously undemocratic as can be seen from the nature of the composition of this House. Under a colonial form of government, the population can be divided into two classes or two categories: one, those who benefit from colonialism and the other, those who suffer from colonialism.

If one analyses the composition of this House one can evidently see that the Government benches consist of those who have done well from a colonial form of government and still are doing well. The Opposition represents the voice of those who are the victims of colonialism and who happen to be the largest percentage of the total population of this Colony. Those who benefit from a colonial form of government are a small number of Europeans who enjoy political, economic and social supremacy in this country and amongst the Fijians, those who belong to the chiefly order.

You might find a few people in every section of the community who will gain benefit from colonialism through the governments they pick at the official table. Apart from that, the rest are under the stultifying influence of a system of government which stands universally condemned in the present world. When we expressed our opposition to this Constitution, the then the Secretary of State, Mr. Arthur Greenwood, called the members of the Indian delegation and told them that he understood our feelings but he wanted us to consider that, after all, this was not the last Constitutional Conference; there would be many more in the future. And even if the Indian members considered that this is a very undesirable form of Constitution which they would not like to accept, he would like us to consider, provided goodwill is brought to bear, even a bad

---

46   Patel here means the ten European members plus four Official Members.

Constitution could be made to work to mutual advantage and he requested us to give this Constitution a try, which we did. We accepted this Constitution under protest, we stood for election and we have worked in this Council in the spirit and hope of making a bad Constitution work to the benefit of the masses of the people, not [only] the privileged classes who enjoy the benefits of a colonial system of government. I do not know, probably the official side may complain that we in this Council did not sincerely make an attempt, as so many members from the opposite side have the habit, now and then, of insinuating that whenever we have expressed any opinion on any point straight away our sincerity is challenged. So I say, if you still feel that we have not sincerely given a trial to this Constitution which we should have, then I must say that this is the limit of our sincerity. We cannot go any further.

As is well known, even the electoral laws were not satisfactory even though they provided that there should be a secret ballot, the arrangement which was made for the method of casting votes by illiterate voters was far from voting by secret ballot. The largest numbers of illiterate voters amounting to several thousand were Indian voters. As far as literacy qualifications are concerned the Fijian and the European communities are in a very fortunate position. They enjoy almost universal literacy. When we proposed that some method should be adopted so that even an illiterate voter could identify the candidate for whom he wanted to vote by printing a picture, or a symbol on the ballot paper, the Colonial Secretary who was in charge of the election, did not agree even though the returning officer gave the opinion that it was quite practicable and was being done in other countries in the Commonwealth. The Government Printer also gave his opinion that it was practicable as far as the printing of the ballot papers was concerned as it would not create any complications or difficulties. What is more, we were told that to enable Indian illiterate voters to vote English numerical numbers would be put against the names of the candidates which would also be printed in the English language. If a man was illiterate how was he expected to be able to read even letters or numbers in a foreign language?

Our representations were summarily dismissed by informing us that of course even an illiterate person could read numbers in the English language, which is not true. Then to soothe us, an arrangement was made that those voters who could not understand how to vote would have the help and assistance of the polling officers. A voter had to give the name of the candidate for whom he or she wanted to vote and the polling officer would tick the ballot paper on his or her behalf. These polling officers were in the main Government men and most of them had votes as every voter in this Colony had and in their heart of hearts they had sides to take. When it was pointed out as to how anyone could find out, especially an illiterate voter, whether the polling officer had carried out his instructions faithfully and voted for the right candidate or not, we were told that nothing else could be done but that the Government suggested that we should send some detectives, that is literate voters, who would pretend to be illiterate, and ask the polling officer to vote for them so that such polling officers could be caught and they would be immediately removed. In fact several polling officers were caught and were immediately removed and I thank two Government officers—one Mr. Thomson, who was the Acting Colonial Secretary then, and the other, Mr. Strick, who was the District Commissioner Southern. I do not know what happened in other parts of this Colony, but I do know what happened in the Southern Division and the Western Division. Of course, we do not know what happened in the case of those who were not caught.

Another difficulty experienced by the voter in the elections was the choice of colours of various ballot papers. Instead of having contrasting colours, the colours were more or less harmonising and within the polling station I myself experienced difficulty of distinguishing between yellow and buff and I pointed it out to the polling officer and he agreed that he was also confused, so one can just understand how much these colours confuse illiterate voters. Even when a voter had to give one vote he would find difficulty in these circumstances but each voter had four votes to cast and when it was suggested that each voter should receive one ballot paper at a time, fill it out, cast it and then return for another it was pointed out that this would take a lot of time, so in order to save time each voter was given four ballot papers at a time, which confused him still further. I heard remarks from educated European voters outside the polling stations when they came out how complicated that system was and they themselves were confused. The simple Indian and Fijian voters who did not have much experience in casting votes were subjected to this with the result that we have got the form of government which consists of the beneficiaries of colonialism—a reactionary government which says on behalf of all the people of this country that they are in favour of status quo that the people of this country do not want freedom and that the people of this country would like to go on under the present form of Government and they openly praise the colonial form of government.

Time has come when in the interests of democratic freedom we have called for a halt. If this continues any longer attitudes will harden, difficulties will be created, the real aspirations and wishes of the overwhelming number of people in this country will be misrepresented abroad and, as is happening now, everybody who comes from outside will be told that we in Fiji like colonialism, we do not want freedom, nobody wants freedom. Racial attitudes will stiffen, the divisions will become still more rigid and defined and when the real time comes, people of this Colony will find it almost impossible to break all these rigid barriers in order to unite the various communities of this country lead them to nationhood. We have therefore decided to put forward this motion before the Council, and though I very well know that this motion, of course, will not be acceptable to the Government benches, in the name of the people of this country and in the name of democratic freedom I commend this motion to the House.

38: Federation Party Convention, Ba, 28-29 June, 1968

Much water has flowed under the bridge and many developments have taken place since we met in May last year in Suva.

At the conclusion of the Constitutional Conference in London, Mr. Anthony Greenwood called Indian delegates at Marlborough House and told them that he understood how keenly disappointed they were; he sympathised with them and admitted that the proposed Constitution was by no means satisfactory, that he appealed to the Indian leaders to give it a trial and promised that there will be another Constitutional Conference in two years. Putting trust in his words the Federation Party decided to give the Constitution a trial under protest.

Our first disillusionment came in the General Election which was rigged. The complicated system of voting was devised to confuse voters. The colours selected for the ballot papers were hard to distinguish in the polling booths. The provision for a secret ballot was turned into a mockery by postal ballot and appointing officers at the polling booths who were themselves voters and many of them openly hostile to our Party to tick the ballot papers and put them into relevant boxes for those who were ignorant or who did not know how to vote. The electoral regulations provide legal sanctions against candidates and voters who violated the regulations, but no legal sanctions are provided against any malpractice on the part of returning or polling officers or their assistants. Thus they were left to vote for any candidate they pleased with impunity in contravention to the requests of the voter. The government refused to provide pictorial symbols on ballot paper to enable illiterate voters to identify candidates by asserting that even illiterate voters ought to know English numerals. To cap it all polling booths in a large number of places were established on privately owned properties controlled by the owners and in many cases in Fijian villages, in homes of the chiefs. Most of the Alliance Fijian candidates occupied positions of power and influence in government service and were allowed to contest election while exercising their official powers and functions.

No wonder that such an election threw up a big majority consisting of diehard colonialist supremacists, Fijian civil servants, and their Indian hangers-on who are openly hated by the Indian community for the white colonialists-dominated Alliance Party. Though it was agreed at the constitutional conference that the existing convention will be followed in the setting up of the Executive Council, the Governor in violation of the agreement invited the Alliance to nominate un-official members to the Executive Council and to distribute un-official portfolios amongst its own members.[47]

As you all know, I was acknowledged as the Leader of the Opposition, and the Federation Party in the Legislative Council was declared to be the official opposition. We appealed to the Secretary of State against the action of the Governor which was in violation of the agreement reached at the Constitutional Conference. But the Secretary of State paid no heed to our protest and supported the Governor.

For 300 days we worked in the Legislative Council discharging faithfully our responsibilities as the guardians of the rights and interests of the people against the encroachments of those rights and interests by a government of despotic and greedy colonialists. Afraid to face us squarely in the debate, the Colonial Alliance Government made a practice of hastily using the guillotine.

The Government thus deprived us of the basic and most important privilege of a legislator, namely, the right of free and unfettered speech. Intoxicated with the power derived from a docile brute majority of yes men in the Legislative Council, the government did not even bother to consult the Opposition on any important issue of bipartisan national interest. The Governor, who enjoys ultimate absolute power under the Constitution, ignored the Opposition completely even in such important matters as the introduction of the ministerial system. Without consulting or even mentioning to the Opposition, the Governor decided to set up a Council of Ministers on the 1st of September, 1967 which consisted of seven Europeans, two Fijians chiefs and one Indian in a colony where Fijians and Indians form 94% of the population and Europeans barely 6% and the majority of whom are temporarily resident in the Colony in course of their employment in the colonial government and foreign European concerns.

Our cup of disillusionment was filled to the brim. The design of the British to establish a European colonialist-dominated government in Fiji was unmasked. We realized that the British through devices concealed in a cunningly devised constitution and by resorting to devious methods were imposing the rule of the colonial vested interests on the people of Fiji. To achieve independence and establish a truly democratic government of the people by the people for the people, it is imperative that the constitution be immediately revised and changed.

---

47 See *Report of theFiji Constitution Conference*, Command Paper 2783, House of Commons. Ratu Mara regretted not taking up the power-sharing offer made in the report. 'I regret to this day that I do did not do that,' he told a writer. 'AD Patel was an intelligent man. He would have worked along.' See Kathleen Hancock, *Men of Mana: Portraits of three Pacific leaders: Ratu Sir Kamisese Mara, Afioga Va'ai Kolone, Sir Robert Rex* (Wellington: Steele Roberts, 2003), 34.

The Opposition, therefore, decided to introduce a motion asking for a new democratic constitution based on one man one vote one constituency, and upon rejection of that motion to walk out from the Legislative Council, and to remain absent from the Council and vacate the seats in order to force a by-election if the British Government did not meanwhile make a favourable response.

We have now vacated our seats and are waiting for the by-election. The Governor whose duty is to issue a Writ of Election and hold by-elections upon the seats becoming vacant, has not even after a lapse of three months, issued the Writ of Election, providing yet another example of British Government's insincerity. The true nature of the present government has become apparent to the people through its legislative and administrative measures. People are already convinced that it rules for the benefit of one particular section to the detriment of workers, growers and small traders. Its favouritism and extravagance have become notorious and need no exposition.

I now state what our Party stands for and what tasks face us to avert the impending calamity. As I stated before, Fijians and Indians together form 94% of the total population. They are permanent residents of this country. Over 90% of Indians are born in Fiji and most of them represent third, fourth and even fifth generation of Indians in Fiji. Even those who are born in India have become permanent residents and citizens of Fiji. During ninety years of its rule in Fiji, the British have kept Fijians, Indians and other races apart by legislative measures and executive policy.

In spite of this division and segregation, the Indian and Fijian communities socially and economically are closer to each other than to any other community. They have lived together in friendliness, harmony and peace for about 90 years and have provided a good example of harmonious race relations to the world. Indians and Fijians are easily approachable to each other, and in the hour of need the Fijians turn to Indians for help. The third community, namely the Europeans, remain unapproachable and aloof from the two major communities.

 As communities of workers, cultivators and subordinates Fijians and Indians have common interest economically, socially and politically. Both communities are under the heel of the third community. In their common interests, Fijians and Indians should see that they don't allow the third party to drive a wedge between them. It should be appreciated by everyone that Indian and Fijian solidarity is vital for the happiness, peace and prosperity of all the inhabitants of this Colony. Anyone who tries to break that solidarity is not only an enemy of Fijians and Indians, he is equally an enemy of his own people whoever they may be. The Federation Party looks upon the preservation and promotions of Fijian and Indian solidarity and unity as one of its most important tasks.

I am glad to inform you that our Fijian brethren understand and appreciate us and are supporting and joining our Party in large numbers. Two scions of Fijian aristocracy have resigned from high positions in the government and joined our Party. They have set an example of patriotism and sacrifice before our young men and women. They are Ratu Julian Toganivalu and Ro Mosese Veresikete. [48] Ratu Julian Toganivalu has undertaken the difficult work of the Organising Secretary of our Party and Ratu Mosese Veresikete has accepted the responsible position of the editor of Pacific Review. I hope many more will follow their example and join us in bending to the all-important task of nation building.

For the information of our friends who have not yet become members of our Party, I wish to point out that the membership of our Party is open to any citizen of Fiji above the age of 18 years, irrespective of race, religion, origin or sex who accepts the aims, objectives, policy, programme and discipline of the Party and pays an annual fee of two shillings.

The Party aims to create a national consciousness among the citizens of Fiji irrespective of race, religion, origin or sex and to make Fiji a democratic nation in which all citizens will be equal in the eyes of law, in which all citizens will enjoy equal political rights, in which all citizens will have equal opportunities to advance according to their abilities. To accomplish this end, while actively working to unite the people, we must vigilantly guard against being duped by the notorious colonial policy of divide and rule. We shall also have to resort to necessary action for the removal of all constitutional and legal barriers which divide the races and keep them separate and apart and have a new constitution which will bring all citizens together in one man, one vote, one value constituencies.

This Party's aim is to work for immediate independence and to set up a democratic republic with a parliamentary government within the British Commonwealth. In order to maintain a link with the past, a person who is ethnically a Fijian will be elected as the Head of the State by a plebiscite based on adult suffrage at five yearly intervals. To preserve connection with Great Britain, independent Fiji will seek membership of the British Commonwealth.

Our Party will follow the ideal of 'Unity of Diversity' by respecting cultures, customs and traditions of all races and though a secular state it will foster equal respect for all great religions of the world represented in Fiji as we firmly believe that all religions have various ways to reach the same God. In this context I wish

48   Ratu Julian's other brothers, William, David and Josua, were the leading lights of the Alliance Party. According to Harish Sharma, Ratu Julian joined the Federation Party after listening to Patel's speech in the Legislative Council rejecting the electoral recommendations of the 1965 Constitutional Conference (Document 32). Ratu Mosese was a Master of Arts in Economics from Hull University and half-brother to Ratu Mara's wife, Ro Lala, who later became the head of the Burebasaga Confederacy.

to make it clear here and now that this Party is not anti-European as it is often misrepresented by its enemies, but it is most emphatically against colonialism and supremacy of any racial group. The Federation Party assures all people born in Fiji or who have continuously lived for seven years and made Fiji their home of full citizenship rights. Fundamental human rights will be safeguarded by a Bill of Rights entrenched in the Constitution which shall be enforceable by the Courts of Law so that no individual or minority may be oppressed by a majority.

In the economic sector our major task will be to raise the standard of living of the masses by development of our natural resources, by improvement and increase in agricultural production, by encouraging manufacture of local goods and by import substitution to the extent it is practicable and economically beneficial. We cannot raise the standard of living of our masses only by increasing production. It must be accompanied by a just and equitable distribution of the economic fruits of production among those engaged in the industry.

Our government, industries and commercial concerns are saddled with top heavy staff mostly recruited from Australia, New Zealand and Great Britain at salaries which compare favourably with those prevailing in those highly developed and affluent countries and far in excess of what our local economy can stand and thereby depressing the wages of local workers to a level far below what our economy can pay if it was not saddled with such over expensive staff. It will be the policy of our Party to see that the locals are given preference in employment and even where it is necessary to employ people from outside because of the unavailability of persons of required skill and experience locally, such people will be recruited from countries with the scale of remuneration which is comparable with ours.

Under the existing economic set up, local people have to sell their services and produce cheap and are made to buy commodities and services dear, largely from Australia and New Zealand. Our trade policy with other countries will be on the basis of 'we buy from those who buy from us.' As far as the production of food is concerned the objective of our Party is to make this country self-sufficient and those items which have to be imported, will be imported from the countries which offer them cheapest. This Party strongly condemns the measure adopted by the present government to debar people from buying butter from Holland at a price which is far below New Zealand's.

The Party appreciates the importance of capital in the economic development in Fiji and will encourage[the] formation and investment of local capital to the maximum and will also create favourable conditions to attract foreign capital for undertakings which require large capital. Though it is in favour of a fair and reasonable return to the investors it will not allow unfettered exploitation by monopolies and cartels. Wherever it is possible the Party will take steps to introduce and encourage competition to loosen the hold of such monopolies, as for instance, our Party will help and encourage and assist farmers to establish and operate co-operative sugar and oil mills in sugar and copra industries. We shall also prescribe a minimum basic living wage for the workers and minimum fair prices for agricultural produce such as sugar cane and coconuts to protect the farmers. The farmers of this Colony are by and large thrifty and careful in their expenditure. Their poverty and indebtedness is largely due to having to sell their produce like sugar cane on credit and at an uneconomic low price. This Party will introduce measures to ensure prompt payment of fair and economic price.

With a view to alienat[ing] the Fijians from the Indians, the colonialist diehards carry on a mischievous propaganda of lies to the effect that if the Federation Party comes into power it will take away lands from the Fijians. I appeal to our Fijian brethren not to allow themselves to be taken in by such a propaganda of lies. Even before going to the constitutional conference, the leaders of Federation Party had assured Fijian leaders that right of ownership of Fijian lands were not in question. The ownership of their lands is acknowledged and will be respected. Let me declare publicly that the Federation Party is against nationalization of land. It respects Fijian rights of ownership. As a matter of fact, under present law Fijian owners don't enjoy the same rights in respect of their lands, as the owners belonging to other races do in respect of their freeholds. Our Party will be prepared to confer the same rights on them if they so wish.

The agriculturists of this Colony are mostly tenants and it is the declared policy of our Party to provide them with security of tenure on fair rents and in the event of the termination of a lease payment of compensation for the unexhausted improvements effected by the tenant on the land. This is now an established practice in all enlightened and progressive countries. We cannot protect and promote agriculture which is so vital to the prosperity of all, if we do not create a sense of security and fair dealing in the minds of the tenant farmers.

The existing fiscal structure is heavily in favour of rich individuals and companies and the burden of taxation falls oppressively on the poor. The basic tax which is unfairly deducted at the source from the earning of workers and farmers without giving them anything in return, is an outstanding example of oppression and injustice. The Federation Party will abolish basic tax, and remove duties on necessaries of life. We shall revise and radically change the whole system applying the principle that the 'wealthier a tax payer the more he pays in taxes.' This principle will be applied to companies as well as individuals. In devising a new system, the requirements of capital formation and incentives for economic development shall be also borne in mind.

Lot of public money is wasted in the name of economic development. The most glaring example of this extravagant waste is the Lomaivuna project which is carried on to satisfy the fad of the Chief Minister. Membership of the Natural Resources Council largely consists of the representatives of the vested colonialist interests and it in fact discourages, impedes or slows down any projects of development which are likely to compete with or conflict with the interests of their companies. The Department of Agriculture which spends so much of the taxpayers money has so far shown very disappointing results. It is therefore necessary to effect a complete over-haul of the Council and the Department of Agriculture. The existing set back in land development projects is largely due to the restrictions and rigid control imposed upon practical and experienced farmers by raw and inexperienced government servants who are mostly based in theory.

Our Party is of the view that the success of such projects depends on the willing co-operation and initiative of the farmers engaged in them. Our Party also attaches great importance to the manufacture of consumer goods locally in the private sector and will do whatever it can for its speedy promotion. Sugar, being Fiji's largest and most important industry which plays a vital role in the economic life of this Colony, deserves special and particular mention. The Party is firmly convinced that the Eve Commission's Report, the Ordinance and the machinery set up under it viz the Sugar Board and the Sugar Advisory Council have all proved to be of one-sided benefit to the C.S.R. Co. Ltd which now operates under the name of South Pacific Sugar Mills Limited to the entire detriment of farmers and workers, reducing them to the status of serfs and slaves.

This party would scrap the Ordinance and all that goes with it and devise a system by which the miller will be bound to produce only so much of sugar as may be sold at an economic price so that the farmer can be assured of a fair and economic price for his cane and utilize the remaining land for other produce which will augment his income and diversify agriculture in cane growing areas.

Gold Mining is another industry which will receive special attention of our Party. Gold is a commodity which plays a very important role in international trade. Gold and other minerals belong to the state, and mining is a wasting asset. It is silly to allow a foreign private enterprise to dig out and take away gold from this country and for the government to subsidize such operation. Gold belongs to the state and it should be mined and used by the state for the benefit of the people of Fiji. Our Party therefore stands for the immediate nationalization of Gold Mines.

The basic ideal of the Party is to make Fiji a Welfare State in which no citizen, however poor or incapable, would have to go without food, clothing, shelter and medical care. Medical services shall be provided free to the patients. The Party also aims to introduce old age pensions and unemployment benefit schemes. Education will be free and compulsory for all children between the ages of 6 and 16. The Party will completely overhaul the existing educational system, which is geared to the requirements of a colonial set up, to make it suit the political, economic, social, cultural and spiritual needs of a free people.

The farmers are the economic backbone of this country and it is the duty of the government to see that the backbone is healthy and strong. The main causes of his poverty are low and uneconomic prices of agricultural produce and their late payment. The Party will adopt such measures as are found necessary to improve the economic condition of farmers.

This Party believes in the dignity of labour and in securing a rightful place for it in the community. Our Party would grant them protection against exploitation by prescribing a minimum basic living wage. The trade unions are at a serious disadvantage in bargaining with large and powerful employers because the workers receive wages which are barely sufficient for a hand-to-mouth living and they have no funds to provide even minimum necessities of life to the worker and his dependents during a strike. It is further weakened by the division of workers on racial lines into racial unions in the same industry. In these circumstances the trade unions are at a serious disadvantage in bargaining with the employers. Our Party will take necessary steps to strengthen the unions and devise ways and means to reduce or eliminate present handicaps.

The policy of the colonial government not to compete with private enterprise will be drastically revised and competition will be introduced by establishing undertakings owned and run by the state on its own or in partnership with private share-holders if it is deemed necessary in the public interest.

The Party believes in introducing local self-government in cities, towns, townships and rural areas, securing autonomy in local affairs. The Councils and Boards shall consist wholly of representatives elected by the residents of the area under a common roll. Every member in such Councils or Boards will be free to speak in any one of the three languages, namely Fijian, Hindi and English.

Now I come to the tasks which immediately face us. As you very well know the bi-elections will take place in the near future and we should organise our campaigns and leave no stones unturned to win in all constituencies and send our candidates to the Legislative Council with thumping majorities. Our Fijian brethren are gradually understanding and appreciating us and since Ratu Julian Toganivalu and Ratu Mosese Veresikete joined our Party Fijians are rallying to our standard in large numbers. Our Indian brethren have also woken up and risen to a man to support us and our Party. Both Indians and Fijians realise that unless both these communities joined together in this hour of crisis, they will be lost forever.

This is also a crucial year for our economic future. Whatever our race, religion, sex or station of life, we all—including the government—depend upon the income from sugar cane. If the farmers are prosperous we all can prosper. But if they are ruined economically, all of us will have to face ruin. It was the cane farmers who gave birth to the Federation Party and our Party, as it is in duty bound, pledges its full and whole-hearted support and help in securing a fair and favourable contract which would bring prosperity to the farmers and to the people and government of this colony for at least ten years to come. We all know what a hard and unscrupulous bargainer the Company is, and how all the colonial vested interests and the Alliance Government support it. It is therefore absolutely necessary that all farmers stand together and offer a determined front to achieve their goal.

All these entail heavy expenditure and require large funds. This is the time for all to donate liberally so that we can meet the crisis squarely and gain victory which rightfully is ours. My fellow members, I thank you for your patient hearing. May Almighty God guide our deliberations and strengthen our resolve to work courageously together for the political, social, economic and spiritual uplift and unity of our people and liberate our country from political and economic bondage.

Resolution on Independence, NFP Convention, 28-29 June 1968, Ba

This convention is firmly of the view that this Colony is fit and ready for Political Independence and requests the United Kingdom Government to convene a Constitutional Conference as soon as possible to prepare a Democratic Constitution based on one man, one vote constituencies and transferring power to the representative elected under such a franchise. This Convention emphasises the urgent need for immediate independence in order to remove all Political, Social and Economic impediments which obstruct the development of the country and thereby come seriously in the way of raising the standard of living of its inhabitants.

39: Political Statement by A. D. Patel, 30 August 1968

'You have experienced the work and achievement of the Alliance Party in the last two years. We all know now that Alliance is a block of white imperialists and those who serve them. These imperialists have kept the Indians and Taukeis, the people of Fiji, in the chain of slavery for the last 90 years and are now trying to keep them under bondage. Do you want this?' said Mr. A D Patel in his Radio Broadcast on Wednesday last.

He continued: 'Federation is a party of people who are hungry, poor, under slavery and down-trodden. It is a party of Indians and Taukeis who have been denied equal rights. It is the party of the people of Fiji. It was created by the farmers of this country. Federation has been serving the farmers, the workers, the little businessmen in the fields of politics, economics and social aspects without any prejudice or discrimination. Federation has been fighting for the people within and outside the Legislative Council.

Imperialist Alliance talks a lot about unity on the one hand but on the other hand keeps the Taukeis and the Indians divided and governs in a one-sided way for the benefit of the Whites. It makes rich all the richer and poor all the poorer. When Federation tries to bring national unity by having the Taukeis, the Indians, the Part-Europeans and the Europeans together, then the Alliance accuses it of creating disunity. When Federation tries to throw some light on the imperialist Alliance's dictatorship, colour bar favouritism and warns the people, then they clamour that the Federation Party is creating disharmony. When we ask for full self-government and democracy, then the Alliance people say that there are many races and unless they all get together this country will not be ready for independence. But when we want to bring everyone together under common roll then they oppose it. They do not tell us that most of the countries of the world are multi-racial and yet independent, like the United States, New Zealand, Australia, India, Trinidad, Jamaica, Malaysia, Singapore, Mauritius, etc., are all multi-racial but yet independent. In New Zealand there are more Whites than Maoris, in Australia there are more Whites than the natives, and in Singapore there are more Chinese than Malays. But all these countries are independent.

The Taukeis and the Indians have lived together for 90 years as brothers in peace and love. They participate in [each other's] happiness and despair. The example of peace, love and brotherhood created by the Taukeis and the Indians in Fiji cannot be found in any other place but the Alliance tells the world that there is harmony between the Taukeis and the Indians [because they are apart] and have created disunity amongst Indians and as a result have ruled both of them.

The Indians are awake now, the Fijians are awakening. Everyday the Taukeis are co-operating with the Federation in increasing numbers. They are joining the Federation Party. The Alliance now is shivering. The Taukeis know that Indians are their true friends. The Indians and the Taukeis know very well who their enemy is.

According to Ratu Mara, we cannot create one nation without one language. This is completely untrue. There are many languages in India, Singapore, Malaya and Switzerland. All these nations are independent and developed. It is not necessary to have blood and bullets for the creation of a nation as it is important to have unity of the hearts. [If] the unity between the Taukeis and Indians is good, we can create a beautiful and developed nation. The policy of the Federation party is to make Fiji a democratic nation and its president an elected *Taukei*. This is our policy. The Federation claims that Fiji become independent immediately and a Taukei should become its president. Will this policy bring unity or disharmony? You can think for yourself! The policy of Alliance is to distort and misinform [people] about whatever I say. It is the policy of the Alliance to bring disunity amongst Indians. Our Indian community now understands Alliance very well. That is why even after a lot of effort, Indian community will not intricate itself into the Alliance's web. Ratu Mara visits every home, shakes hand, has pictures taken. He spends the tax payers' money. Even after this the Indian people will not side with the Alliance. The candidates of the Federation Party have full faith in the people and the Indian community has full faith in the Federation candidates.

You all know the cries and the false preaching of the Alliance ministers and candidates. This is why even after all their efforts they are unable to succeed. Economic, social and spiritual developments depend on independence. This is why it is essential to have democratic independence in Fiji. Two things are dearer than the life itself to human beings—self-respect and freedom. Respect is in equality and freedom. This is why Indian community wants independence on a common roll for the Indians and the Taukeis. It is clear from the present constitution that the White imperialists while dividing the Taukeis and Indians have the reign of government in its hands. If independence is given to Fiji on this kind of constitution which divides people on racial basis, then it will bring destruction to the Taukeis and the Indians. By putting Fijians and Indians against each other, the Whites will rule and Fiji will become another Rhodesia.

Independence can come to the Taukeis as a boon when it gets equal rights under common roll: one man, one vote, one value. It does not matter whether he is a European or Fijian or Indian. Indians and Fijians make 94 per cent of the population of Fiji. Fijians and Indians comprise the country. They make the nation. If the Alliance people want independence and equal rights and accept these values, then it becomes their duty that they co-operate with the Federation for this good cause. Independence and equal rights is the cry of the awakened people of Fiji and Federation is a Party of the awakened people. Therefore, those who oppose Federation oppose the people. The effect of non-co-operation of the Federation Party has been considerable on the British Government. This is why the Alliance people now say that we shall have another constitutional conference and then we shall have common roll. If you look at history, you will find that people of many countries have shed blood, have lost everything to achieve freedom. Even the little courageous Vietnam fights one of the most powerful nations for this freedom. This it is doing by the sacrifice of its people and its children. The poor Negroes of America are sacrificing for equal rights. Federation worships peace and non-violence. Federation loves everyone. Federation hates injustice, not the people. This is why the Federation has entered the fight for equality and freedom for the down-trodden people. It has taken non-cooperation and non-violence as its aims.

Some of you voters have sent Mr. Vijay Singh, Mr. KS Reddy and Mr. Abdul Lateef to the Council.[49] What have they done for you? This is for you to judge for yourselves. If they have not done anything then is it possible for these amateurs to do anything? Can a tail wag the dog?

The times in Fiji are going to change. New Fiji is being created. This is why we have to reject the elements of disunity and imperialism and create a new nation. Ladies, and Gentlemen, rise, awake, vote Federation candidates and take steps to make your children, your community and your country free and march forward.

40: Final Letter from Sir Derek Jakeway, 7 November 1968

Dear Mr. Patel

I write, first of all, to say how sorry I was to hear that illness had struck you once again, and again at a most inopportune time. I was nevertheless glad that you were able to meet and talk with Mr. Hathi and Mr. Manjit Singh.[50]

I expect they impressed you, as they did me, not only by their sincerity, courtesy and friendliness but by their evident desire to be of disinterested assistance in closing the divisions which have so unfortunately appeared in the body politics of Fiji over the past 12 months, and which can become progressively more damaging to the national interest if they continue.

---

49 All members of the Indian Alliance.
50 Sukhlal Hathi was an Indian Government Minister and Manjit Singh was a senior official from the Indian Ministry of External Affairs.

Mr. Hathi felt that his talks with you and the Chief Minister and with other leaders in the Alliance and Federation Party had made some headway in this direction. If so we all have reason to be immensely grateful to our visitors. At our last meeting Mr. Hathi urged that I should carry on the good work where he had left off. Nothing would please me more, for if there is one thing of which I am certain it is that the ruination of this country could be strife carried to the point at which it destroyed racial harmony. Recent events have proved that there remains a serious risk of its doing so, by showing how easily emotions can be aroused and angry reactions produced. But, as you know, I leave Fiji in a few days and you are not yet fully restored to health.

All I can do now is to urge on you the importance of resuming your dialogue with Ratu Mara (which began promisingly early this year). Opportunities for this can easily be found—for instance whilst you are in Suva for the forthcoming meeting of Legislative Council. With goodwill on both sides it should not be impossible for agreement to be reached on changes to the constitution which remove the elements distasteful to your party and at the same time preserve safeguards which the Alliance regard as essential.

I know that my successor will be anxious to offer whatever help he can in this matter, and very much hope nothing will be done or said before his arrival to complicate the task facing him.

I have expressed similar sentiments to Ratu Mara and I know that he is prepared to resume discussions.

Yours Sincerely
Derek Jakeway

41: Pre-Independence Talks, Suva, 12 August 1969[51]

AD Patel

I think the views of the Federation Party on the constitution are very well known. As regards success or failure of this constitution, you have given the opinion of your Party and the opinion of our Party is that it is a failure, so there is no agreement on that issue. As to whether the constitution has worked or not, we consider that it has not. Had it worked we would not have had by-elections. Still, if you wish to know what our views are, my Party considers that this country, just the same as other countries in the British Empire, has got to be independent at some time or another. There is no getting away from that fact: it is just a question of time as to when it should, or when it would, be independent.

---

51   Opening excerpts from a full volume of confidential verbatim reports in my possession.

In our opinion, this country has reached the stage where it could immediately be independent. In comparison, many countries in the Empire are far more backward than Fiji, economically as well as educationally, and they are all independent. So, if fitness is the test for independence, then we hold that we are fit enough; we show responsibility.

Now, as regards the constitution, we have all along, all these years, made it quite plain that an independent country can only enjoy its independence and attendant prosperity through national consciousness amongst its citizens. But we have seen, unfortunately, in this country [people] kept on the racial hook too long and the responsibility for it rests on the shoulders of the Colonial Office. But because the British Government kept us on the racial hook it does not mean that we should also be an instrument or a party in either continuing or perpetuating it, and therefore, in our constitution the basis for elective representation in parliament should be on a national basis, not on racial or inter-racial basis because inter-racial in itself preserves a racial-political outlook. Therefore, we have always advocated the system of one man, one vote, one value, with geographical constituencies. This type of constitution is not new; it has been in existence and tried in many countries. The fashion is to describe it as multi-racial. There is no country in the world which is not multi-racial.

We would be better advised to follow the types of constitution which have proved successful and beneficial over a large number of years, rather than make ours and our people the guinea pigs of constitutional experiment. New adventures by constitution makers in recent years in this field should be carefully avoided. We should be rather careful of accepting anything from outside which has either not been successful in that country or has not had sufficient test of time.

The next point is: on the basis of such a national franchise, what should be the constitution of our country? The first question should be whether it should be unicameral or bicameral. Now considering size and population and our economic resources, in the opinion of our party a unicameral form of government is better. There is unanimity in this country amongst all political parties that there should be a Bill of Rights enshrined in the constitution to safeguard the minority. As far as that goes, there is no difference of opinion, as I understand it, amongst any group in Fiji. At the last constitutional conference we found ourselves entirely in agreement. As to what should be the optimum number of members in the parliament in a country like ours, we are of the view that number should be between 40 and 60, 60 would be an optimum number. I think I have offered you enough substance to chew on.

Ratu ETT Cakobau.[52]

I would like to go over that part of your statement where one man, one vote system has been introduced throughout the Commonwealth. This is generally in a homogenous community, and where you have a party system of two, three or four, the aims of each party are very much the same. The method of achieving the aims may differ but when one party moves out and another moves in, there is a common denominator. Yet in African colonies bloodshed is taking place, there is trouble and disunity. Where we have multiracial group care has been taken to ensure that there is unity amongst the people, apart from the unity of the political leaders. Again, there has been trouble in Malaya. From our point of view, instead of one man, one vote, we are thinking of extension and enlargement of cross-voting so as to at least keep some uniformity, some consistency.

AD Patel

I am afraid that anything more than a one vote system has not proved successful here or anywhere else. At the last conference, I asked whether it [cross voting] had been tried and we were told that it had been tried in Tanganyika, or one of the South African colonies. And they admitted it had not worked there. One of the UK people expressed the hope that although it had failed it might succeed in Fiji. But in our opinion it has totally failed; it is too complicated. Voters are querying so many things—identification and everything else with four voting slips in their hands. And I shall tell you about an instance in where wives of two European officers—one the District Commissioner's—they frankly expressed that they found it difficult to follow the system. Our opinion is that, after all, all you want is a man's opinion as to who he would like to represent him, and as long as he has only one vote he can give it. To call upon a man to vote for one race, another race and then another, perpetuates and accentuates racial differences in voters and candidates.

Ratu Sir Kamisese Mara

Where have you abolished race—that it can be ignored.

AD Patel

I am not saying that you can ignore it, but it should not be the main point. If you do that, there will be trouble and difficulties.

Ratu Sir Kamisese Mara

---

52   Ratu ETT Cakobau was the chair of the confidential talks.

When you generalise, 'It works everywhere else in the world,' can you give an example?

AD Patel

As far as humanly possible, it has worked in many countries where national franchise is in existence, even India.

Ratu Sir Kamisese Mara

But it has divisions. You cannot say even now that it works.

AD Patel

The constitution has not been an obstacle; even now, other countries pay tribute to the Indian constitution.

Vijay R Singh

Is it that ethnic differences come into the formation of these various states?

AD Patel

That is because of the large size of the country, and not because of the basis of franchise. Suppose ours was a large country and we had our states: that happens in every country, including Australia and the US. That is in the nature of a federation.

Ratu Sir Kamisese Mara

You said the Indian constitution is perfect but it does recognise classes [such as the scheduled castes].

AD Patel

The principle of franchise is not challenged: common franchise. It is a different thing altogether. Say, for instance, any community feels that because of its backwardness [it needs special assistance], there is well-known device in a constitution that there should be certain seats reserved. When these groups feel confident, and they are sure that they have nothing to fear, no reservation is necessary.

Ratu Sir Kamisese Mara

Is not cross-voting a system of reservation itself?

AD Patel

No, because as I see it you call upon a voter to elect more than on representative and each of them should be of a different race and he must racially vote for them. The system of reservation as it is in India, in particular, only a member of a scheduled caste can be a candidate for election but all will vote.

Ratu sir Kamisese Mara

It is still a reservation of seats whether it is given by the President or by the constitution. We have reserved seats for Fijian, Indian and European.

AD Patel

There is no racial representation [in India], but here in our Council we are described as Fijian, Indian or European. That is the label that sticks to us right throughout our tenure of membership in the Council and that is the basis on which we are elected. In India, it is totally different. Say, for instance, this country is divided into geographical constituencies, then you might reserve a certain number of constituencies for certain groups or communities. That is to create confidence; as soon as there is trust it is not intended that they would be permanent. If you voted on these lines here with certain seats reserved for Indians, reserved for Fijians and Europeans, and certain number thrown open, then these seats are reserved seats and designed to create confidence and trust among the various groups for which seats have been reserved. Say, for instance, that there was no reservation; the Fijians mistrusted and the Indians were strong as is being very often said, though I am quite prepared to convince you if you go through our census that it is for the time being only) when national consciousness becomes more or less widespread in the country, immediately the Indians will be the losers under common franchise because they are not spread out all over the country as the Fijians are. Their population is concentrated in certain areas only, the cane areas generally. Indians though larger in number will only have votes in these areas and will have surplus votes.

Ratu Sir Kamisese Mara

That is what we do not want; we do not want anyone to be losers, Indian losers or Fijian losers.

AD Patel

That is what I said. If you want nobody to lose then for the time being you have reservation of seats to assure a community in this national system that they are not going to lose anything. But these five unreserved constituencies will help the group, that if they—for instance the Europeans—say that they are grossly outnumbered and can never have a chance under common franchise. Out of five constituencies, 1 retained 1 European, 2 retained 2 Fijian and Indian, than that will prove that in spite of unreserved constituencies not being reserved the way their electors exercise their votes is above consideration because eventually these parties will have to develop not on racial lines but on some political ideology. One party might stand, say Conservatives as in England for certain things; Liberal for certain things; Labour for certain things. We have only made a start but even now we can see differences in outlook between the two parties and as time goes by, the country will be divided on these economic and political issues rather than racial lines.

Ratu Sir Kamisese Mara

When you say independence, you mean there has been a suggestion from your party of a republic...The Fijians particularly feel that there has been real meaning for them in the link with Great Britain because of Cession and this is what they would rather have developed to full internal self-government [rather than full independence].

AD Patel

The link will be there as Fiji remains in the Commonwealth. There are so many other members of the Commonwealth and yet the Queen is accepted as the Head of the Commonwealth and they have that link with Britain. The only difference is to have an elected Governor from Britain and those elected on their own. If a Governor or a Viceroy is appointed by the Crown, it will be on the advice and recommendation of the Prime Minister of the country. Whether you call him a Governor General, as in Australia, whether he is appointed or nominated by the Prime Minister, or whether Australia declares itself a republic, it does not make any difference to her relations with Britain. [On whether going republic would lead towards the American system] We unanimously agreed at the last conference, and I have not noticed any deviation on that score here, that as [far as] the system of government was concerned, we were all in favour of the British system and not the American system. [On the implications of the United Kingdom joining the European Common Market] If the UK gets the opportunity to get into the Common Market, she will throw the Commonwealth out in her own interests. And we might have to form new alliances ourselves with new groups. It is just a matter of time, and probably it might take its own course. The only difference is the link is still there. People might feel that instead of a Prime Minister they would like a Head of State. The people by vote should decide who should be the Head of State. But if there is no Commonwealth, there is no question of a link with the British Crown—either for Australia or New Zealand. This is just a marriage of convenience, frankly.

NB: This was the first and the last meeting Patel attended. When the committee convened in October, he was dead.

Part II. Bitter Sweet: The Politics of the Fiji Sugar Industry, 1943-1969

The 1943 Strike: Contemporary Documents[1]

The dispute between the cane farmers and the Colonial Sugar Refining Company Limited has entered the seventh month. There is a statute in force in this Colony, namely, The Industrial Disputes (Conciliation and Arbitration Ordinance, 1941), under which the Governor could have, as soon as the dispute came to his notice, appointed a Conciliation Board to bring about conciliation between the parties or compel the parties to go before the Court of Arbitration. The Governor has persistently refused to follow the Ordinance and has even tried to make out that there is no dispute between the Company and the growers and has even gone to the extent of asserting that the Company is only an agent of the Food Ministry.

To give necessary information on the subject we are enclosing relevant documents and papers, which are arranged in chronological order.

The growers never asked for the appointment of a Commission. In fact Mr. BD Lakshman2 and a few others secretly sent a memorandum in the name of the Kisan Sangh, the contents of which was unknown not only to the members of the Kisan Sangh but also to some of the signatories whose signatures were obtained by fraud. When the Government announced the appointment of a Commission, the growers informed the Government that they wanted a Court of Arbitration as the Company was definitely against paying a higher price and was not prepared to negotiate about the price. The Growers' Counsel repeated the same request for the appointment of a Court of Arbitration before the Commission at Ba. Instead of appointing a Court of Arbitration, the Governor embarked on a course of repression prohibiting meetings of the growers in Ba and Ra districts, unlawfully arresting and sentencing growers and their leaders. The defendants appealed and their sentences had to be suspended under the then existing law. The Governor and his legal advisors were so anxious to put people into prison rightly or wrongly that they hastily put through an amendment to the Appeals Ordinance so that whatever the result of the appeal the person would have to undergo punishment pending the decision of the appeal. When the Supreme

---

1 These documents come from a file on the strike kept by the late Swami Rudrananda who intended it for publication. I was given the file some time in the 1980s. These introductory remarks are from the file.
2 BD Lakshman (1900-1981) was elected to the Legislative Council in 1940, replacing Chattur Singh, with the support of the Kisan Sangh, and represented the Sang in negotiations with the CSR. He was later active in the trade union movement and served in the Legislative Council for a term in the early 1960s.

Court of Fiji decided against the Government and squashed the convictions, the Governor again hastily promulgated new regulations to suit his policy of repression.

The growers were prepared to sell their crop to the Government and leave the price to the conscience of the Government. But the Governor announced his intention of taking the cane by compulsion and refused to accept this voluntary offer. The Governor could have accepted the offer and compelled the Company to process the cane for the Government and paid the Company reasonable processing charges.

A careful study of these papers will make it quite clear that if the Governor had followed the law which was specially enacted and passed through the Legislature of the Colony for the special purpose of bringing about settlement of disputes such as this, the present dispute would have been settled long ago. When the growers are asking for a Court of Arbitration on their dispute with a powerful monopoly, such as the Colonial Sugar Refining Company Limited, they are not asking too much from the Government. It is the barest minimum which not only the Government of Fiji can afford to give but is also their duty to do so. It is hoped that reason will prevail and the Governor of Fiji will be persuaded to do at this late stage what could have been done easily at the beginning.

42: An Open Letter to Governor, 12 August 1943

Your Excellency,

The present measures adopted by your Excellency's Government as regards the Industrial Dispute existing between the cane growers and the Colonial Sugar Refining Company compel us to address the following to you in the form of an open letter.

When Your Excellency met the growers' representatives at Lautoka on the 19th July, you were good enough to inform the growers that as the owners of their crops they had every right to do what they like with it. You also promised them that you would set up a Board to bring about conciliation between the growers and the Company. You informed the growers that you were not sure what such a Board is called under the Trade Disputes Ordinance. Even if Your Excellency were not quite sure as to what such conciliation machinery is termed under the Ordinance, it showed clearly that you were at least aware that there is an Ordinance already in existence providing for settlement of Industrial Disputes such as this one during these times of war. In ordinary times there was neither obligation nor duty on the Government to intervene in the dispute and bring about an amicable settlement. Because of the war, there has been a duty placed upon you under the Trade Disputes Ordinance passed in 1941. That duty is not discharged or satisfied by merely appointing a Commission, and because the Commission was not acceptable to the growers, not taking any further steps for conciliation as provided for under the said Ordinance [was an error of judgment]. The law provides that if a Commission fails, you may still appoint either a Board or a Court of Arbitration whose decision will be final and binding on the parties to the dispute.

The growers had made their representations to the Company and to Your Excellency's Government that in view of the high cost of production and exorbitant cost of living, the present price was hopelessly inadequate to meet the present situation and that it should be raised to 30s a ton. Your Excellency's Government since April last has time and again informed the growers that you are in communication with the Secretary of State and through him the Ministry of Food. Although several months have elapsed the growers have not been yet informed of the reply.

Instead of following up the provisions of the law or taking any further steps to bring about conciliation Your Excellency's Government has embarked on a course of repressing the growers, and shown utter disregard to the merits of their claim. The growers have been, right throughout, peaceful and law abiding citizens and have not allowed as much as even a tone of bitterness to creep into this dispute. In comparison to what happens in such disputes in other countries, the behaviour and conduct of the growers have been a credit to them and to the Indian civilization and culture. Against such groups of poor but peaceful people, Your Excellency has seen fit to post and employ units of Fiji Defense Force in certain districts to frighten and terrorise them into harvesting and selling their crops to a profit making concern at a price that it dictates, even though such price is hopelessly inadequate to meet the present high cost of cultivation and harvesting, and the exorbitantly high cost of living. The Deputy Commissioner of Police in Ba has in his possession many facts as regards the incidents of provocation given by the members of the Defense Force to the growers.

Your Excellency has also seen fit to intern us and make a humiliating order against us to go every day and report ourselves in person at the Nadi Police Station as if we were ordinary criminals and suspects. The very fact that Your Excellency had to use your Emergency powers in an arbitrary manner and specially amend a Regulation in order to deprive us of our freedom and subject us to such humiliation, vindicates our honour as law abiding and respectable citizens of this Colony. When the head of a Government makes a Regulation in haste and punishes people even before anyone has an opportunity of knowing what new

Regulation he has made [is], such an act in our humble opinion loses all the respect and dignity that law is entitled to exact from the citizens and it merely becomes the will of a despot. We who believe in the highest and noblest ideals of democracy and who sincerely put our faith and trust in the four freedoms promised by President Roosevelt to the world, find it extremely difficult to bow to such auto-drastic edicts. And yet we politely informed the Superintendent of Police and through him your Government that though we cannot see our way to humiliate ourselves and report in person everyday at the Police Station, we are prepared to give your Government our word of honour that if we ever decided to break your order and go out of the prescribed radius of five miles from our respective residences, we would first inform the Government before taking such a step. The only reply that we have so far received to our request is a prosecution for disobeying such a humiliating and unreasonable order.

When we consider all this in the light of recent declarations made by Lord Moyne, the Secretary of State for the Colonies through a White Paper, that trade union movement in the Colonies will be fostered and encouraged and the Colonial Governments will undertake the obligation to raise the standard of living of all classes whose standards are below the minimum that can be regarded as adequate, our imagination is staggered, and the words escape our lips. 'Is this really the practical interpretation of Britain's New Colonial Policy?'

We are,

Your Excellency's Humble Servants

Swami Rudrananda

AD Patel

43: The Statement Made By A.D. Patel in Nadi Court, 12 August 1943

I wish to make it clear first that what I am about to state before the Court is not by way of mitigation but only by way of explanation. Since the Labour Tribunal was appointed under National Service Regulations, I was engaged on the said Tribunal as one of its members and after the Tribunal gave its award and adjourned since then I was at the Circuit of the Supreme Court of Fiji, right until yesterday acting either in capacity of Crown Counsel or Counsel for Defense. The Order that was served on me was served on my way to the Court while I was engaged in the Supreme Court of Fiji on a very important case, involving several charges of felony. Still to respect this order, I made an application to the Chief Justice to adjourn the Court, which he was kind enough to do. On the day the order was served on me and perhaps at the time it was served, I would be safe in saying that there was no mortal man on this side of the Island, who had seen this latest amendment, and in fact I came to know of the amendment, though I am a regular subscriber to the Royal Gazette of Fiji, for the first time on the 10th—Tuesday. So as far as facts are concerned, the Government of Fiji punished me first and told me of the law several days later. As far as the legal fiction was concerned, the Governor was in the right but morally in the wrong. On the 7th when Supt. Kermode rang me up and wished to know whether I would report at Police Station at Nadi in accordance with that part of the order, I informed him that my conscience and my self-respect will not allow me to submit myself to that part of the edict, and asked him if he would be good enough to convey to the Governor that I am prepared to give him my word of honour that if I ever decided to break or disobey the Order as regards my internment within five miles radius from my residence, I would first inform the Government before doing so. The only reply I have so far received to that request is this present prosecution. When I consider that not only I am an officer of the Court and a part of the administration of justice but the President of the Bar Association of Lautoka, President of the Indian Association of Fiji, President of the Indian Chamber of Commerce, the General Manager of the Then India Sanmarga Ikya Sangam and unanimously elected counsel of the growers in this their present dispute with the Company, my conscience tells me that I am not an ordinary criminal or a suspect to undergo the humiliation that His Excellency under that order expects me to undergo and in such circumstances I believe that it becomes the duty of every self respecting citizen to disobey such an iniquitous, unmerited, arbitrary humiliating Order.

44: Report of the Commission: Letter to Governor, 12th August 1943

May it please Your Excellency,

The long awaited report of the Sugar Cane Commission is now published, and we beg to take this opportunity to place our views on the matter before Your Excellency.

The feelings of the Commission in effect amount to what is stated as follows:

The average size of the cane farms of the Company's tenants is around about 12 acres in Sigatoka, Nadi, Lautoka, Ba, Tavua and Raki Raki districts and in the Rewa district the average size of the tenants' farm is approximately 9 acres. The average size of the farm of the contractors is still less; namely, between 10 and 11 acres in Northern and Central districts and $5\frac{1}{2}$ acres in Rewa district.

The estimated gross cane proceeds the present price from a 12 acre farm in 1945 comes to £129.3.0 and according to the findings of the Commission, it only leaves a margin of £6.15.0, if a grower also grows £10.0.0 worth of paddy in addition to produce of cane, and if it is possible for him to produce cane within the extremely narrow limits of cost as laid down by the learned Commissioners in the report, and neglect his farm by personally engaging himself in the cane cutting gang during the crushing season in case if he is not fortunate enough to secure a labourer to work as his substitute on a bonus of £10., and if he can further manage to live with his wife and four children on the budget prescribed by the learned Commissioners.

In our humble opinion no Indian farmer in spite of all the thrift at his command has managed or can manage to produce the present crop from a 12 acre farm at the cost of £58.4.7½ that the learned Commissioners have estimated. Assuming that such a farmer does exist, which we extremely doubt, he would have to manage within the following budget laid down by the learned Commissioners:

1. He should be content to feed himself and his wife and four children on 2½ lbs potatoes, 2 lbs onion, ½ bottle ghee, ¾ bottle coconut oil, 7 lbs sugar, ¾ lb Tea, 4 lbs Dhall, 1½ lbs salt, 5 oz garlic and other condiments, 9 lbs rice and 18 lbs sharps a week, with milk and vegetables of his own.

2. He should clothe his wife with one skirt of six yards of print or hair cord, one blouse of 1½ yards print or hair cord, one calico slip and one 3 yards muslin ornis a year;

3. Himself with 2 pairs of khaki trousers, 2 khaki shirts, a pair of canvas shoes and 2 singlets a year;

4. And his four children between themselves with 6 khaki shorts, 6 khaki shirts and six singlets a year.

5. He should have household drapery only worth £1.10.0 a year.

6. He should allow himself and family 3 boxes of matches, 2 bottles of kerosene, 1 bar of soap a week and no blue.

7. He should have household utensils limited to 4 enamel plates, 4 enamel mugs, 1 hurricane lantern, 4 enamel eating bowls, 1 kitchen knife, 1 basting spoon, 1 frying pan and 2 billy cans.

8. He should have housing of a yearly value of £6 only.

9. And by way of all expenditure for himself, his wife and four children should spend only £1.17.6 a year.

Poor and thrifty as they are, the Indian growers are not accustomed to live on such a standard as the learned Commissioners have prescribed for them. In the case of growers of Rewa district, it is impossible to make both ends meet even at the cost of production estimated and the minimal standard of life prescribed above.

We humbly beg to state that the Indian farmers do not propose to subject themselves and their families to such a standard.

We growers are also human beings. We also live in society. We also have to meet our social, economic and religious obligations and keep up social appearances just the same as any other people. We have to educate our children and give them better opportunities in life. We have to entertain friends and relations and visit them on occasions. We have to dress properly befitting our status in the community and meet a host of social expenses in our modest way. Our children also like to have sweets and relishes occasionally. Majority of ourselves like to eat and do eat meat and fish. Our families, though not as frequently as other races, go to pictures or at least to a Ramlila or a Tirunal. Our children have to be married like those of any other society.

We have as much right to be prosperous and happy as anybody else in the world with decent housing and better comforts.

The learned Commissioners, in order to justify the present price and condemn us to the realm of animals and cattle, have adopted the price paid for sugar cane in 1939 as a fair and adequate price for the propose of comparison with the present price.

We respectfully beg to point out that the price paid in 1939 was not just or adequate and the growers during that year clamoured for a rise in the price and a substantial number of them even went to the extent of ploughing out the cane and giving up further planting as a result of which the Company introduced the present scale of price in 1940.

The Indian growers as a class are ignorant and disorganized and for a number of years they have been under-paid by this powerful monopoly and thereby were forced to get into debts to meet the deficits even to maintain their present meagre and thrifty standard of life. Most of the Indian growers are heavily in debts in this Colony on account of the steady exploitation by the Company. We, the growers, have every right to have sufficient income to pay our liabilities gradually and some reasonable amount of saving for emergencies and old age.

The learned Commissioners are therefore wrong in adopting the price of 1939 as model and applying the same method and procedure as is done in case of unskilled manual labourers.

We appreciate that these are the times of war and during the four years of war the cane growers have voluntarily fulfilled their duties and obligations as patriotic citizens of this Colony.

The method of granting bonuses to cover only a part of the increase in cost does not apply to the price of sugar cane any more than that of the sugar or other commodities.

In this Colony, the Company is a strong and influential monopoly and the only buyer of cane. The element of competition amongst the buyers which usually determines the fair market price for sugar cane in other countries, is totally absent in this Colony. The only criterion therefore is not on how little the farmer can manage to live and supply cane but how much at the present price of sugar and other by-products of cane, the Company can afford to pay, after making a due allowance for a margin of profit which can be considered fair and just during war time. If the Company is making more profit now than what is was making before the war, then there is no justice in saying that the growers must sacrifice so that the Company's share holders may prosper.

Your Excellency has declared sugar cane as a service essential to the life of the community and we humbly submit that it is a duty of Your Excellency's Government to see that the growers who are engaged in this service are given and ensured a standard of living befitting civilized human beings. We also consider that the cane growers are a major and all important section of the community; we go further and say that it is not merely a duty but an obligation on the Government's part [to settle the dispute].

We therefore humbly suggest and request that Your Excellency be pleased to appoint a Court of Arbitration to ascertain immediately the maximum price of sugar cane which the Company can afford to pay to the growers in the present state of sugar industry; and further, to obviate disputes in future and the exploitation of an important portion of the community by a profit making concern, to takeover and nationalize the sugar industry in Fiji; and, if through some valid reason such a take over and nationalization is found impracticable at present, to pass legislation and appoint a Sugar Industry Control Board to inspect and examine the accounts of the Company and work out and declare the price of cane every year based on the following formula:

> The value of sugar plus the value of molasses and other by-products if any— minus manufacturing cost, depreciation and a reasonable margin of profit divided by the number of tons of cane crushed equal to the price of sugar cane per ton.

In the event of the price arrived at by the above method of calculation at any time falling short of the price necessary to meet the cost of production and cost of living, such deficit should be met pro-tem by the Government by way of a subsidy.

We respectfully beg to point out that in India and other colonies where there are a number of sugar manufacturers paying competitive prices, there have been boards appointed by the Government to give further protection to the growers with powers to inspect the accounts of the manufacturers and declare the price of cane every year worked out as mentioned above. Here we are all placed at the mercy of a sole buyer and therefore the need for such a control is greater and more urgent than elsewhere.

The Akhil Fiji Krishna Maha Sangh

Head Office, Nadi

The Kisan Sangh, Lautoka

President

Secretary

The Rewa Planters' Association, Nausori

45: What Happened in Suva? 21-26 August 1943

For the information of those anxious to know what happened in Suva, I am giving a summary and substance of the events as they took place in sequence.

Saturday 21. 8. 43

On Saturday the 21st August, I received a message from Mr. Said Hasan that His Excellency at the request of the Indian Members had agreed that the Counsel for the Growers should go into accounts with the Company's counsel and whatever figure might be agreed between them for the cost of production of sugar cane would be accepted by the Government, and the Governor would, by cable, get in touch with the Ministry of Food and endeavour to obtain direct relief for the Growers. I received a message from Superintendent Kermode that he was asked by the Governor to issue a permit for me to travel to Suva to attend the Conference. This was necessary because I am still an internee.

Monday 23. 8. 43

On Monday the 23rd I went with Mr. Hasan to Sir Henry Scott's Chambers. Sir Henry told us that the Company would require the growers to commence cutting their cane before they went into accounts with us. He also mentioned that the cane was deteriorating and the sooner it was cut and sent to the mill the better for everybody concerned. I informed him that it seemed to me that a settlement of the dispute was the only way left open for getting the cane harvested quickly. The sooner we reached a settlement, the sooner the cane would be harvested. We should therefore hasten with our settlement. Sir Henry then arranged for me to meet Mr. King Irving, the Company's Attorney, on the following morning.

Tuesday 24. 8. 43

On Tuesday the 24th Sir Henry Scott, Mr. King Irving, and myself met at Sir Henry's Chambers in the morning. Mr. Irving informed me that the Company held the view that unless the farmers started cutting their cane, the Company was not prepared to go into accounts with us. I told him the same thing that I told Sir Henry the previous day and added that we were there with a will to arrive at a settlement and that we could assure them that in dealing with the accounts they would find us reasonable. Mr. Irving believed that going into accounts might take a few weeks as there were four mills concerned. I offered to sit day and night and go into accounts to save delay, and to curtail the time further, I suggested that Mr. Hasan should go into accounts of the Rewa growers with the Nausori Mill and simultaneously I should go into accounts with the Manager of the Lautoka Mill. I further suggested that the figure arrived at for the Lautoka Mill might be accepted as the figure applicable to the growers of all the six districts on the other side of the Island as conditions of producing sugar cane were more or less the same in those districts. Mr. Irving and Sir Henry were favourably inclined to accept the suggestion. Sir Henry however expressed his pessimism over the suggestion that the Ministry of Food would give direct relief to the growers.

Sir Henry was of the opinion that the Ministry of Food would not consider any such relief and he himself personally preferred that the sugar industry sank in Fiji rather than the already overburdened taxpayer in England was called upon to bear an additional burden for the sake of growers in Fiji. We then adjourned as Mr. King Irving had to attend the Legislative Council. In the afternoon Sir Henry, Mr. King Irving, Mr. Hasan, and myself met again at Sir Henry's Chambers. Mr. Irving told us that the Company insisted that the growers must commence cutting their cane before going into accounts and he had to carry out his instructions. Mr. Hasan pointed out that that amounted to laying down a condition precedent while His Excellency had made it clear that there were no conditions attached to these negotiations. All the four of us regretted the deadlock and Sir Henry suggested that we should consider our conversations still open and that he would send me a letter of introduction to Mr. Smith and that I should go to Lautoka and have further discussion with him. We accepted the suggestion. Sir Henry also authorized me to mention this matter to the Attorney General if I so wished. From Sir Henry's Chambers I went to Attorney General's Chambers and informed him of the situation. The Attorney General rang up His Excellency and informed him what had happened. He then told me that His Excellency had asked him to see Sir Henry in the matter and to tell me that it was not necessary for me to go to Lautoka and that Sir Henry would be asked to call Mr. Smith to Suva if necessary. He would inform me of the result of the interview with Sir Henry.

Wednesday 25. 8. 43

The Attorney General informed me at his Chambers on Wednesday morning that Sir Henry had telephoned to Mr. Smith asking him to come to Suva and a cable was sent to Sydney. They were awaiting a reply.

Thursday 26. 8. 43

I was informed by the Attorney General that there was no reply to the cable so far and that Mr. Smith might be expected to arrive soon. Mr. Irving who was also present informed me that Sydney Office gave prompt attention in such matters and a reply might be expected quite soon. The Government tabled a White Paper on the Cane Growers Dispute in the Legislative Council that day. At about 4:30 in the afternoon I received a message asking Appabhai Patel, Mr. Hasan and myself to see His Excellency at the Government House at 5 pm. When we went there, His Excellency, Attorney General, Colonial Secretary, and Mr. BD Lakshman were present. I am reproducing the substance of what His Excellency told us. It is as follows:

> I have seen the Counsel of the Company on the matter. The Company is not going to make any condition as to the cutting of the cane but the Counsel has pointed out to me that it will not be possible to reach agreement between the parties as to the cost of production of the sugar cane and I am also of the same opinion. I am prepared to appoint a Commission and the growers and the Company can take the accounts before it. I am not going to appoint a Court of Arbitration because in the first place I do not consider that this is a dispute between the Company and the growers. The appointment of a Court of Arbitration will serve no useful purpose because the Company may have their books in Sydney and considering the time it would take for the Company to

obtain the books from Australia, it may take about two years before the Court can give its award. Some people seem to think that the Company is making big profits in Fiji. I do not know what profits the Company actually makes and I do not believe that a Company like the c.s.r. will like to disclose their profits. The Ministry of Food however functions continuously under the limelight of public criticism, and searching questions in the Parliament, in England, and I do not think that the Ministry of Food will give a price for sugar which will enable the Company to make profits.

I was previously a Governor of a Colony in Africa which produced sugar and from my experience there I am prepared to stake my reputation on my belief that the CSR Company is not making a big profit. I am not going to lay down a condition that the farmers must cut their cane before I appoint a Commission. I did say on a previous occasion that under the British rule they were not bound to cut their cane if they so wished. The reason for my saying so was that we have not got a sufficient supply of labour in the Colony and it would therefore be difficult to enforce my powers. The growers must realize that the cane is deteriorating and their not harvesting the cane through pigheadedness or obstinacy or refusing to produce properly attested evidence before the Commission will not bring them any relief. This is war time. I know that Cuba is producing considerable amount of sugar which is at present dammed up, so to speak and which can be immediately released and then Fiji Sugar may have no use and it may become difficult to find a market. If the growers do not harvest their cane and deliver it to the mill I shall take their cane under my powers and get their Labour Battalion to cut it and send it to the mill. Perhaps it may be painful to some of you who are present here but I wish to make it clear that I have got the Appeals Ordinance amended and interferences with the harvesting of the case will be promptly dealt with by the Government. I am satisfied that there is more than the dispute over the price of the sugar cane in this matter. There is a proverb in Africa that when Elephants fight the grass gets trampled. In the present dispute the growers are the grass. I am satisfied that if you gentlemen tell the growers to accept the Commission and harvest the cane, they will do so.

Mr. Hasan pointed out that the opinion of the Company's counsel that an agreement on the accounts was impossible was premature since we had not even started going into them. The Governor replied that he was quite satisfied that a Commission was the only proper course. Mr. Hasan reminded the Governor that he had told the Indian Members that he was willing to appoint a Board of Conciliation if they so wish. Would His Excellency appoint a Board of

Conciliation? His Excellency replied that he did say that he was prepared to appoint a Board of Conciliation but he had no power to appoint a Board unless both the parties agreed to it. When it was pointed out to him that he had powers to appoint a Board consisting of one person even if a party did not agree to it, His Excellency said that though he had the power, he was of the opinion that a Commission was the proper way. He was prepared to enlarge the Commission and have one representative from each of the three farmers' organizations or if they liked have a Commission consisting of the Attorney General Mr. AL Patel for the growers, and Mr. Smith for the Company. Mr. Hasan pointed out that we did not think that the growers would agree to that course. We were prepared to convey his message to the growers and send their reply. I tried to explain how misunderstanding had risen over the appointment of a Commission and to place the Growers point of view, but His Excellency was not in a mood to listen.

He indicated that he was not prepared to believe me and thereupon I preferred to remain silent. I left the Government House with a definite impression that the interview was arranged for the sole purpose of coercing me into asking the Growers to accept the Commission and harvest cane irrespective of whether I agreed with it or not. An interview took place with His Excellency at the Legislative Council Chambers in the morning. His Excellency, Attorney General, Mr. Hasan, Mr. KB Singh, Mr. Vishnu Deo, Mr. BD Lakshman and myself were present. We suggested that as His Excellency considers that there is no dispute between the Company and the growers, will he appoint Dr Jack to check the accounts of the growers and to certify what amount he thinks fair and reasonable for the cost of production of sugar cane. His Excellency replied. 'I shall appoint a Commission consisting of the Attorney General, Dr Jack and an accountant.' Mr. KB Singh told the Governor that he has seen the growers on the other side of the Island and in Rewa and he did not think that the growers would accept a Commission. If any coward has told His Excellency that if Mr. AD Patel told the growers to accept the Commission, the growers would accept it, such information is wrong. Even Mr. Patel would not be able to persuade the growers to accept a Commission. He pleaded with His Excellency to appoint Dr Jack to go into accounts with the growers as suggested. His Excellency replied, 'I am prepared to appoint a Commission consisting of the Attorney General, Mr. KB Singh for the growers and Mr. Smith for the Company'. Mr. KB Singh pointed out it was not the personnel but the machinery that the growers were objecting to. His Excellency replied, 'It is getting to ten o'clock and we should not spoil our record for punctuality in the Legislative Council.' We then left.

AD Patel

46: Growers Advised to Cut, nd.

The following important announcement regarding the sugar dispute on this side of the island was made by His Excellency the Governor at the close of the business of the Legislative Council this morning.

In the Council Paper laid on the Table yesterday,[3] Members have all the known facts in the dispute about the price of cane. While Council have been sitting I have, at their request, met the Indian Members, and I have also seen a number of other gentlemen who, either as leaders of one or other of the farmer organizations, as representatives of the CSR Co, or as counsel, are closely associated with the industry and with the dispute at present paralysing it. It may therefore be useful if I add a few words to bring the matter up to date.

In the first place I have ascertained that the Colonial Sugar Refining Company, while holding strongly to its view that cane cutting ought to start at once, will nevertheless not hesitate to co-operate with the Commission, if it is reconstituted, and will not insist that cane cutting must first be resumed. That is a reasonable and helpful attitude and I am obliged to the Company for taking it.

In the second place I think I may say that there is a wide-spread realisation today among the farmers and those who speak for them that there is nothing whatsoever to gain by continuing to refuse to harvest the cane crop which is standing ripe in the fields and which will mean a dead cash loss to the farmers of very large sums of money if it is not cut and cut soon.

Thirdly, I hope and believe that there is an equally widespread realisation that a mistake was made when, at the last minute and after the matters set out in the Council Paper, the farmers' leaders decided not to co-operate with the Commission or offer any evidence.

And lastly, it is now also widely understood that there has been in this unhappy dispute a good deal more among the Growers and their Associations than the issue about the price of cane; these matters are not my business and I propose to say nothing about them. But I may perhaps quote an apposite Swahili proverb which says, 'When the elephants fight the grass gets trampled.' It seems to me that the farmers are the grass in this case.

There is thus no longer any reason in which any one has faith or belief why the farmers should not come forward at once with the proof for which I have been waiting for well over a month, if they have that proof, and establish the validity of the case which they say they have, but which they have made no attempt to establish by properly attested evidence. Nor is there any reason that makes

---

3   Legislative Council Paper 16/1943.

any kind of sense why there should not be at once a general resumption of cane cutting. The sugar industry is, as everyone knows, an essential war industry and it is the duty of everyone connected with it to do his utmost to promote its immediate resumption, and as the farmers' case will not be affected in any way by cutting, it is clearly their duty, as well as, most emphatically, their interest, to start cutting now. If they do not do that, the date being what it is, they will incur grievous losses which may mean ruin for many of them and may seriously hamper the general war effort.

I should perhaps add that any man in a position to understand in full all the issues involved who at this juncture still advises the farmers not to cut their cane is doing them and the Colony a grievous wrong.

47: Inaccuracies and Omissions in the Council Paper: 'Dispute in the Sugar Industry', 1 September 1943

Inaccuracies

The statement in paragraph 9 that 'The Governor met the representatives of the Kisan Sangh and the Maha Sangh at Lautoka on the 19th July to discuss the request for a Commission of Enquiry contained in the foregoing letter' (The alleged letter written by the Kisan Sangh to the Governor on the 11th of July), is not correct. The Maha Sangh was not informed and was not aware of any request made by any person or organization for a Commission of Enquiry. The Growers belonging to the Maha Sangh who were present at the meeting had not gone there as a deputation from the Maha Sangh nor had they made any request to the Governor for an interview. The Maha Sangh growers were informed by Mr. Caldwell that the Governor is going to address the growers at Lautoka and the meeting is open to all the Growers who wish to remain present. The Maha Sangh growers had gone to hear what the Governor had to say on the present dispute, not to make any representations.

'Today at noon I met at the District Commissioner's Office at Lautoka deputations from the Kisan Sangh and the Maha Sangh.' This is not correct. No deputation of the Maha Sangh met the Governor at Lautoka on the 19th of July. If any person misinformed him only such person is responsible for misleading the Governor. 'They were introduced briefly by Mr. Lakshman, who said that what they wished to ask for was an increase in the price of cane, and further the immediate appointment of a Commission to enquire into the matter.' (Para 9, lines 11 to 14). This is not correct. On the 25th of August when Mr. BD Lakshman was confronted with this statement by Mr. Patel, he denied having used the words 'and further the immediate appointment of a Commission to enquire into the matter' and he further said that he is going to rebut that statement. The Growers who were present at the meeting are definite that no mention was made of a Commission either by Mr. BD Lakshman or any body.

All the reference about the appointment of a Commission or a Committee of Enquiry contained in the Governor's reply in paragraph 9 is not correct. All the Growers present at the meeting are emphatic that the word 'Commission' was never mentioned by the Governor at the meeting and the Governor definitely said that he would appoint a Board though he qualified it by saying that without the law books he cannot say what it is called in law.

Omissions: Paragraph 12 contains:

'On the 25th of July the Colonial Secretary met Sri Swami Rudrananda, Mr. AD Patel and the Hon. Mr. BD Lakshman at their request.' Mr. Appabhai Patel who was also with Mr. AD Patel and Swami Rudrananda and who also associated himself with the request asking the Governor to reconsider the appointment of the Commission and to appoint the Court of Arbitration, is not mentioned in paragraph 12. The omissions appear significant in as much as Mr. Appabhai Patel was one of the members of Commission appointed by the Governor. Does not the Government desire the world to know that the only Indian member on the Commission and incidentally the only cane grower on the Commission, also associated himself with the request?

No mention is made in paragraph 12 or any where of the request made by Mr. AD. Patel to the Colonial Secretary to suggest to the Governor to appoint some capable officer to act as an intermediary to negotiate a settlement between the Company and the growers. No mention is made of the fact that the Colonial Secretary had promised Swamiji, Mr. Patel and others that he will convey the representations of the above persons to the Governor by telephone. No reply was conveyed to Swamiji and Mr. Patel and others. No mention is made of the fact that regulation 17 of the Defense (General) Regulations of 1942 was specially amended on the 6th of August for purpose of interning Swamiji and Mr. AD Patel.

In the paragraphs 20 and 21 'Swami Rudrananda and Mr. Patel were sentenced to imprisonment' Why are words 'hard labour' omitted? No mention is made of the Police raid on Mr. Patel's office and residence, Swamiji's ashram and the Maha Sangh office. No mention is made of the reply given by the growers to Dr McGusty.

48: Can You Blame the Growers? 6 September 1943

The Colonial Sugar Refining Company Limited is a gigantic monopolistic concern in Fiji with large reserves of capital wielding more power than the Government over some ten thousand Indian and Fijian growers who are mostly small holders burdened with debts.

1. In 1940, the Company issued a memorandum of purchases of cane to the growers whereby the Company undertook to purchase sound cane grown and delivered under certain conditions mentioned therein. A copy of the memorandum is annexed hereto.

2. By virtue of that memorandum the growers received £1-7½ per ton for cane supplied to Lautoka Mill, £1-9½ per ton for Ba Mill, £1-1 per ton for Penang Mill during 1940.

3. In 1941 though the cost of production of cane and the cost of living was steadily rising, the Company arbitrarily and without the consent of growers paid only 11/- per ton for Badila cane, and 10/- per ton for other varieties in respect of the one third of the cane supplied by each farmer to the Company and also reduced the Imperial Preference Bonus from 3/6 per ton to 2/6, resulting in the average price for the cane of £-.17.11½ per ton for cane delivered to Lautoka Mill, £-17.10½ per ton to Ba Mill, £-18.5 per ton to Penang Mill during 1941. The protests from the growers to the Company and the Government were of no avail.

4. In 1942, the Company paid a surprisingly low p.o.c.s.[4] Bonus viz, 2 per ton for Lautoka Mill, 1/3½ per ton for Ba Mill and 5½ per ton for Penang Mill. No satisfactory reason is given to the growers so far for such unusually low p.o.c.s. The growers have received so far only 17/2 per ton for Lautoka Mill, 17/3½ per ton for Ba Mill, 17/5½ per ton for Penang Mill for cane sold to the Company during 1942. Cost of production and cost of living rose higher than the previous year.

5. During 1943 cost of production and living soared still higher and on the 11th March 1943, the Kisan Sangh requested the Company to raise the price of cane. The Company refused to raise the price and told the growers that the increased costs and difficulties were war burden for which it cannot be held responsible.

6. On the 20th April 1943, the Kisan Sangh approached the Government to obtain a raise in the price. During the month of May, the Growers had to

---

4   Percentage of cane sugar.

make arrangements to supply cane cutters for the gangs to harvest cane as the crushing was to start in June. The Company was also trying to find labour for their Mills. On account of the shortage of labour in the Colony, the growers had to pay a premium varying from £20.0.0 to £30.0.0 on top of the usual wages, while in the previous years this premium was only £8.0.0 to £15.0.0

7. The Growers have to supply one can cutter to the gang per every six acres of cane. The yield per acre has substantially decreased this year on account of the lack of manure. Besides his normal wages, the cane cutter has to be paid a premium of £20.0.0 to £30.0.0, plus a pair of cloths, a cane knife, and a file, and a billy can which cost at present approximately £5.0.0. The wages was increased by twenty-five per cent this year by the Company to bring down the premium. But in effect the growers are forced to pay not only the increased wages but also high premium. Things have reached a breaking point and meanwhile neither the Government nor the Company did anything to raise the price of cane.

8. The Government has declared sugar industry as an essential service to maintain the life of the community, but for three years, neglected their reciprocal duties to the growers.

9. The Company was adamant and the Government was silent over the growers clamouring for a rise.

10. All this resulted in the Growers' decision not to harvest and sell their cane to the Company until the price was raised to double the prewar level.

11. The Maha Sangh on the 21st June 1943 informed the Company and the Government of the situation, and urged them for an immediate increase in price. The Company from Sydney informed the Maha Sangh by cable that the present price was fair and reminded the growers that cane had no value until it was crushed. It would be like a rice miller telling the paddy grower that his paddy has no value until it was hulled in his mill. No rice miller dare make such an answer. The Company being what it is and the sole buyer of cane in Fiji, overlooked the fact that the value was in the cane and they were merely extracting it.

12. Though a similar letter was received by the Colonial Secretary from the Maha Sangh on the 22nd June 1943, it merely remained buried in official archives until at the Labour Tribunal the attention of the Attorney General was drawn by Messrs AD Patel and AL Patel to the dispute and to the urgency of the settlement. Until the Attorney General rang up the authorities in Suva, they appeared to be in the dark, in spite of that letter. It shows that the Colonial Secretary's office did not attach any importance to the letter.

13. Agriculturists refusing to harvest or sell their crop to a buyer is not a strike and there was no legal obligation on the part of the growers even to inform the Government of their decision. The sole purpose for informing the Government was to induce the Government to intervene in the dispute and set up a conciliation or arbitration machinery under the Industrial Dispute Ordinance forthwith to bring about a speedy settlement and yet several precious days were lost through the Colonial Secretary's office not attaching any importance to the information given.

14. The Attorney General lost no time in bringing the matter to His Excellency's notice and made the following announcement from the Bench at the sitting of the Tribunal in Ba: 'Gentlemen, I have already mentioned during the sittings of this Tribunal the question of the price of cane and on behalf of the members of the Tribunal on Saturday, I saw His Excellency the Governor on this particular question in which of course the growers of cane are particularly interested. His Excellency the Governor has authorized me to announce that he is in communication with the Secretary of State on the question of the price of cane. His Excellency the Governor has also authorized me to announce that he is prepared to set up conciliation machinery if necessary to deal with this matter as soon as possible.'

15. In the Kisan Sangh no elections have taken place for three years. The Central Board has divested itself from reflecting the desires, wishes and opinions of the members of the organization, whom they claim to represent. The Kisan Sangh had become merely a name in the hands of certain parvenus to exploit for their own personal advantage. This had become a matter of common knowledge on this side of the Island. It could not [have been] unknown to the District Commissioner Western and District Commissioner Central that the President of the Kisan Sangh was exploiting the name of the Kisan Sangh for his personal betterment and he had no influence left with the growers, nor could they have been in the dark over the hunting with the hounds and running with the hares policy of Mr. BD Lakshman. Unfortunately for the growers, the 'Eyes and Ears' of the District Commissioner Western, the Indian Assistant Mr. AG Sahu Khan, happens to be a son-in-law of the President of the Kisan Sangh [MT Khan]..

16. During the sitting of the Labour Tribunal at Ba, Mr. BD Lakshman and the President of the Kisan Sangh interviewed the Attorney General. If they had suggested at the interview that a Commission be appointed by the Government, this suggestion was never mentioned by the Attorney General to Mr. AD Patel and Mr. AL Patel though they were colleagues and though he was aware that both of his colleagues were greatly concerned in the matter. The Growers, their leaders and their legal representatives, were all

in the dark about the request of the Central Board of the Kisan Sangh for the appointment of a Commission.

17. Some of the Maha Sangh and other growers happened to attend the meeting at Lautoka on the 19th July 1943 through an oral message passed on by Government Officers that the Governor will address the growers in Lautoka and those who wished to hear him might remain present at Lautoka court. About 30 growers attended the meeting. No deputation was sent by the Maha Sangh to the Governor as stated in the White Paper. The Growers who attended the meeting are emphatic that no mention was made of a Commission. The Governor told them that he would appoint a Board and Pandit Hardayal Sharma asked if the Governor would accept a single representative if all the growers elected one. The Governor agreed to the suggestion.

18. On the 16th July 1943 the Central Board of the Kisan Sangh appointed a Hartal Sahayak Committee[5] to assist in every way those growers who were not prepared to cut their cane and also to carry on peaceful propaganda amongst those cultivators who were opposed to the Hartal. The funds of the Kisan Sangh were to be at their disposal for the necessary expenditure. Mr. BD Lakshman and the Central Board were appointed to help the Committee in their work. This notice was printed in Mr. BD Lakshman's press and under the name of the General Secretary of the Kisan Sangh and widely circulated amongst the Growers. While every pamphlet that was published by the Maha Sangh was promptly sent to Suva to the authorities, some even by aeroplane, the 'Eyes and Ears' of the District Commissioner Western appeared not to see or hear about it and it was kept away from the authorities. The only reason one can see behind it is that the President and Mr. BD Lakshman wanted to show to the Government that the Kisan Sangh was with the Company and to the members of the Kisan Sangh that they were with the growers.

19. The growers who were in the belief that the Governor has promised to appoint a Board held meetings in 6 Districts to elect one sole representative to the Board, Mr. AL Patel was unanimously elected as the sole representative of the growers.

20. On the 22nd July 1943 while they were holding a meeting at Raki Raki the Growers came to hear of the appointment of a Commission by the Government, instead of a Board. The meeting unanimously decided to accept the Commission. In subsequent meetings held at Nadroga, Maro and Nadi the growers unanimously decided not to accept the Commission.

21. On the 24th July 1943 the growers' representatives informed Mr. AD Patel and Swami Rudranadaji that the growers were not willing to accept a Commission. On the same day they also informed the Secretary for Indian

5   Strike Assistance Committee.

Affairs at a meeting at Nadi that the Governor had promised a Board. The appointment of a Commission was not acceptable to them.

22. On 25th July 1943 Swamiji, Mr. AD Patel and Mr. AL Patel, who was one of the members of the Commission, met Mr. Newboult, the Colonial Secretary, at Lautoka and informed him of the views of the growers on the appointment of the Commission and in order to avoid any unpleasantness, requested that the matter may be reconsidered and a Court of Arbitration appointed in lieu of it. Mr. AD Patel frankly admitted that the machinery provided under the Industrial Disputes Ordinance is being tried out for the first time in the Colony and he was aware of the difficulties and complications involved in the settlement of the present dispute. If the scope of enquiry of the Commission was wide enough and if the Commission had enough powers to have the necessary evidence required by the parties produced before it as in the case of a Court of Arbitration, it necessarily followed that the investigations of a Commission would take as much time as the hearing by a Court of Arbitration. At the conclusion of the investigations, a Commission can only make a report of their findings to the Governor, while the Court of Arbitration can give an award binding on both parties and thereby bringing the dispute to an end. It was pointed out to Mr. Newboult that there is another factor involving further delay, viz, having to submit the report to the Ministry of Food through the Secretary of State in London. It may turn out that the Ministry of Food may reply that under the present circumstances, it is of opinion that the consumers' interest should be considered first, and that though it sympathises with the growers in Fiji, it is of the opinion that the deficit in price should be met by the Company. In such an eventuality, we will be no better off than what we are now. It was suggested to Mr. Newboult that if any other amicable and quicker way of settling the dispute is found by the Government, the growers were ready to consider it. Mr. Newboult's reply was that once the westerner has made up his mind, he is not likely to change it. However, agreed to convey the representations to the Governor by telephone. What reply the Governor gave is not known to the Growers because it was never communicated to Swamiji, Mr. AD Patel or Mr. AL Patel. Mr. BD Lakshman who was present at the interview associated himself with the representations.

23. In the afternoon of the same day the Growers' representatives had a conference over the question. Every member present was asked to give his frank and personal opinion as to whether the Commission should be accepted under the circumstances or not. All present including Mr. BD Lakshman expressed the opinion that the Commission should not be accepted and no evidence should be offered before it. The counsel were instructed to convey the decision of the Growers to the Commission at Ba.

24. The Commission held their sittings at Ba, Lautoka and Nausori and not a single grower appeared before it to give evidence.

25. On the 30th July 1943, a very insignificant number of farmers in the Ba district began harvesting their cane. It may be remembered that the Governor in his address at Lautoka [had] told the Growers that 'As regards cutting their cane or not cutting their cane they had the good fortune to live under the British Government and could, therefore, feel at liberty to dispose of their own property as they wished' He further told them, 'It was their cane if they did not wish to cut it, they could let it rot.' Thus the Governor made it plain to the Growers that they had a right under the British Rule not to cut their cane if they so wished. He told them that if they exercised their right in such a manner he would call it exceedingly foolish. He did not tell the Growers that it was their duty to cut the cane as the Government later tried to make out when they decided to embark upon a policy of repression.

26. There was not a single case of intimidation or violence to the Growers who wished to cut their cane to justify posting Military in Ba or Ra.

27. On the 6th August 1943 the Governor amended regulation 17 of the Defense (General) Regulations 1942 for the purpose of interning Swami Rudrananda and Mr. AD Patel and the internment order was specially flown from Suva and served on them even before the amendment appeared in the Gazette. They were ordered not to go beyond a radius of five miles from their residences in Nadi and were ordered to report their movements in person each day to the officer in charge of the Police Station at Nadi.

28. Mr. A.D Patel and Swami Rudrananda had conveyed a message through Superintendent Kermode that they gave their word of honour that if they ever decided to go beyond five miles from their residences in contravention of the order, they would first inform the Government before doing so but they were not prepared to carry out the order of reporting in person to the police officer as it was humiliating their self-respect. Though they have been kept continuously under supervision by the police, they were prosecuted on the 12th of August and sentenced to a fine of £20 or one month's imprisonment with hard labour. Again they were prosecuted on the 17th for a repetition of the same offence and sentenced to two months imprisonment with hard labour. Their counsel gave notice of intention to appeal and they are now on bail. Swamiji was prosecuted under Regulation 22 at Ba and sentenced to 3 months imprisonment with hard labour. Mr. Krishna Reddy, the General Secretary of the Maha Sangh, Mr. Mehar Singh, Vice President of the Kisan Sangh, Mr. Ramcharan Singh, a member of the Central Board of the Kisan Sangh, Mr. Ramnivas, Vice President of the Maha Sangh, Pandit Har Dayal, a member of the executive committee of the Maha Sangh, Mr. Ramsumer, Mr. Ramjes, Mr. Kedar Singh and Mr. Sadasivan, members of the Central Board

of the Kisan Sangh, were prosecuted and sentenced under Regulation 22. Mr. Krishna Reddy was fined £50 or in default 6 weeks' imprisonment with hard labour and the rest two months imprisonment with hard labour without the option of a fine. Notice of intention to appeal has been filed in all cases. Arrests are still being made and prosecutions are still being continued.

29. Whether harvesting cane comes under Regulation 22 in a matter sub-judice and therefore we refrain from making any comments on it.

30. On the 20th August 1943 the Indian members of the Legislative Council saw the Governor and suggested to him that the counsel for the Growers and the Company should go into accounts over the cost of production of sugar cane and the amount agreed to by counsel should be accepted by the Governor as a basis for his recommendations to the Ministry of Food for a rise in the prices and obtain by cable the necessary relief to the Growers. The Governor accepted the suggestion and instructed Superintendent Kermode to permit Mr. AD Patel to go to Suva for the purpose. What took place in Suva has been published by Mr. Patel which statement is annexed hereto.

31. The Growers' dispute never was nor is with the Government. The Growers sell their cane to the Company. They have every right to ask for a price from the Company that they consider fair and have every right to withhold the goods until the Company agrees to the price they ask. The Company was approached as early as March for a rise in the price but has consistently right till now refused to consider any rise whatever and have told the Growers that their claim is not against the Company but against the Ministry of Food. Imagine a cloth manufacturer telling a cotton planter that if he wanted to have a rise in the price of cotton he should approach the buyer of cloth and that the cloth manufacturer is not responsible for it because the price of cloth is fixed by those who buy it.

32. What is described by the Company and the Government as a contract is in fact merely an undertaking by the Company to purchase cane under certain conditions.

33. The Growers had approached the Government as early as the month of April but no attention was paid to [their petition] until the 16th of June 1943, and even then all that the Government did was to request information from the Secretary of State abut remedial measures which might have been taken in other sugar growing colonies. The harvesting of sugar cane was to begin on the 21st of June 1943. The Government that considers sugar industry as a service essential to the life of the community since the 8th of December 1940 did not do a hand's turn to settle the question of the price before the harvesting season, though they had more than two months to solve the problem without the harvesting being delayed even for a day. It just shows what vigilant attention the Government was paying to a service which

143

they consider so essential to the war effort. Surely the Government has a reciprocal obligation towards those whose work is considered essential to the life of the community, to see constantly and with concern that they receive a fair return for their services. Had the Government wished to appoint a Commission they could have easily done so as early as the month of April and the whole problem might have probably been solved without any loss either to the Growers, the Company or to the Colony.

34. Industrial Disputes (Conciliation Arbitration) Ordinance was passed in 1941 under which any difference or dispute between the cane Growers and sugar manufacturers was included.

35. The reasons and objects for passing this Ordinance in the words of the Attorney General, Mr. EE Jenkins, were as follows: 'This Bill makes provision for the investigation and settlement of Industrial Disputes. The main object of the Bill is to bring the disputing parties together to arrive at an amicable settlement by discussion. If machinery for settlement does not exist in any particular district in which a dispute occurs, the Governor is given power to bring parties together or to appoint a Conciliation Board and refer the matter in dispute to such board for settlement. If a settlement is arrived at by the board, it is binding on the parties until notice of termination is given. During the continuance of the settlement and within one month after Notice of Repudiation any person concerned who violates the settlement is guilty of an office. If no settlement is arrived at by the parties the Board may recommend a settlement and the parties may accept or reject the recommendation. If the conciliation methods outlined above do not succeed, or if the parties to the dispute so request and the Governor in Council deems it expedient in the public interest so to do, he may require the parties to submit their dispute to a Court of Arbitration. The decision of such court is binding upon the parties and any person concerned who commits any act in violation of the decision is guilty of an offence.'

36. The scope of a Commission under the Ordinance is to investigate into any matter relating to industry and to report to the Governor. The Conciliation Board is provided to bring about conciliation. A Court of Arbitration is provided for an arbitration on the dispute.

37. The Government did not wake up to their duty until the middle of July and then decided to have an investigation instead of employing methods of conciliation, arbitration or negotiation to settle the dispute as quickly as possible.

38. The Government was notified as early as 25th July that a Commission was not acceptable to the Growers.

39. On the 3rd of August 1943, the Government announced that as the cane farmers have made no attempt to substantiate their case before the Commission that the price of cane is insufficient, Government sees no ground for taking further action. Was that the way of bringing about a speedy settlement of a dispute in an industry which the Government considers as essential service? Nearly a month was allowed to elapse and in the end the Government still insisted that the farmers should accept a Commission. What is more important in the war-time insistence upon so-called 'saving of face' on a minor issue, or a speedy settlement of the dispute?

40. The Growers still wish to make it clear that they have no dispute with the Government and they have never had and still not have the slightest intention to embarrass the Government in its war effort. The Growers are immediately prepared to harvest and sell their cane to the Government who can make their own arrangements with the Company for milling it and give the Growers a fair price that would cover the cost of production and a reasonable margin of profit commensurate with the present cost of living.

41. The Government has four ways open to settle the dispute:

    1. To buy the cane directly themselves from the Growers which is the quickest way of settling it.

    2. To act as a mediator and negotiate a settlement between the parties. That is the wisest way which not only would settle the present dispute but would also prevent disputes in future.

    3. To exert pressure on both parties to quickly arrive at a settlement. That is an unreasonable way because it would leave dissatisfaction on both sides and will sow seeds for future disputes.

    4. To exert pressure only on the weaker and poorer party to the dispute, namely, the Growers. This is both an unreasonable and unfair way of settling it; for it will leave not only dissatisfaction but a sense of injustice behind it.

42. The Growers will welcome either the first or the second method, will unwillingly submit to the third, but will oppose with all the moral power at their command to the fourth.

The grower's Stand

We sell our cane to the Company. We do not sell it to the Ministry of Food. Our dispute is with the Company. We have no dispute with the Government or the Ministry of Food.

We do not want an enquiry. What we want is conciliation or arbitration. A Commission merely enquires. A Board conciliates. A Court arbitrates. Let the Government give us a Board or a Court. Today sugar cane is cheaper than fire-wood in Fiji. It takes two years hard work and heavy cost to produce cane.

The Growers do not wish to impede the war effort. If the Government needs the sugar cane, let them buy it from us and give us a fair price.

Let the Government not put forward the war as an excuse to shield the Company.

(Sgd) Krishna Reddy

49: Letter to Colonial Secretary, 20 September, 1943

Sir,

Though the growers placed their demand before the Company as early as the 21st June last, and even earlier, for a rise in the present price of sugar cane, it has so far completely ignored the just and reasonable demand of the growers and has right throughout the dispute adopted the same unreasonable and dictatorial attitude towards the growers as it has been used to in the past.

The Company has persistently gone on reminding the Growers that it is a business concern whose main object is to make profit. At the same time it has ignored the equally patent fact that the sole aim of the Growers in producing sugar cane is also to make profit. Unless the Growers obtain a reasonable margin of profit consistent with the work and capital they put in and the risk and patient waiting they take in the production of cane, there is no justification for them to continue cane farming.

The Company has right throughout this dispute clearly shown to the Growers that it is worth its while to produce sugar even then comparatively a very small quantity of cane is crushed and processed in its two mills which must necessarily involve considerable overhead expenditure. The Company has further shown that it would rather undergo loss at present and keep the Growers in the position of serfs so that their exploitation may remain as easy in the future as it has been in the past, than give them a reasonable deal which would make the preservation and continuation of sugar industry worthwhile both for the millers as well as the primary producers of cane.

In order to bring additional pressure on the Growers the Company has so far withheld payment to the cane Growers of the price bonus which they are entitled to for the crop sold by them to the Company during 1942. The Company is withholding payment obviously with a view to starv[ing] the Growers into selling their cane to the Company at its dictated price.

The Company has gone still further and has now issued a veiled threat to the Growers that unless they begin to harvest their cane within next few days, their cane may not be bought by the Company at all, and at any rate, as far as their ratoon is concerned, even in the event of their commencing to harvest cane immediately, it may only be bought if the Company considers the quality good and the weather suitable at the end of the year.

In the above circumstances there is no guarantee that the whole crop for this year will be bought by the Company or the price increased of the present or future crops and there is a hint that in order to keep the Growers perpetually under the break line and submissive, the Company may as a disciplinary measure refuse to buy the cane of those Growers who do not obey immediately its dictates.

The attitude taken by the Company being such, the Growers owe a duty to themselves and their families to look for and resort to the farming of such crops as would make their lot easier.

The Government of Fiji has consistently advised the Growers to plant as much as food crops as possible so that the Colony at least may become self sufficient in food. So far the Growers did not pay sufficient need to this advice in the hope that the cultivation of sugar cane to which they have been used to for so many years may bring a better return.

The Company has made it abundantly clear that the only way left open for the Growers is to throw themselves on the charity of the Ministry of Food and obtain some relief. While other sections of the community, including the Company, are making larger profits on account of the war, there is no valid reason why the cane farmers of Fiji should make themselves objects of charity when they can also make larger profits by resorting to the cultivation of some other crops which are at the same time more vital and essential to the war effort of the United Nations and especially to the life of the community. Indications are that this is going to be a prolonged war and if Fiji becomes not only self-sufficient in food but also an exporter of the same, it would bring timely succour to the heavy drain on the food resources of the United Nations.

If the Growers by force of necessity have to switch on to the farming of food and other crops it is imperative that they must have their farms clear and made ready for planting during the month of October.

It is therefore resolved at a conference of the Growers' representative held yesterday that unless the Company,

(a) pays the price-bonus due to the Growers [for the] 1942 crop immediately,

(b) opens negotiations before the 30th instant with the representatives to be elected by the Growers for the purpose of settling the price of the present and future crops of cane,

and

(c) gives a guarantee to buy entire crop due for harvesting during this year,

and the Government withdraws all the prosecutions, orders and internments, and remits sentences of all those who are engaged in this dispute, the Growers will begin to plough out young plant cane on the first of October in order to make their lands clear and ready for planting food crop in time for the coming season.

50: Telegram to Secretary of State for Colonies

Cane dispute still unsettled. Future of sugar industry and Colony's economic position will suffer serious setback. His Excellency refused appointing arbitration court under industrial dispute ordinance settlement of dispute more urgent and import than inquiry. Governor himself admitted in Council that Commission was not intended to settle dispute yet more than six months allowed to pass insisting on inquiry by attested evidence which has proved utter failure. Respectfully submit present issue not likely to be settled by resorting to repressive measures and passing regulations under special powers curtailing civil liberties as Governor has done so far or even by directing as has been done that cane must be delivered not to government but to Company under Company's unilateral cane purchase undertaking especially when the undertaking is subject of unsettled dispute. Governor is wrongly advised that the undertaking is binding contract and insistence on Governor's part to treat it as such is injustice to Growers.

Growers have always been willing and anxious to settle dispute speedily but their representations ignored. When His Excellency would not appoint arbitration court Growers in order not to impede war effort offered as early as August their entire cane crop to Government leaving question of price to be agreed upon between Government and farmers representatives and expressed their readiness to harvest and deliver cane wherever Government instructed. Government could have arranged with Company for processing but Governor refused to accept this reasonable offer by dismissing it as impracticable. Disheartened Growers began clearing and planting food crops thereupon and because Supreme Court in appellate jurisdiction holding that Growers were under no legal or contractual duty to cut and deliver cane to Company set aside sentences of Ba magistrates court Governor made regulations declaring sugar cane and vegetables essential services thereby creating absurd position in war time showing that cane and vegetables more essential than even food when Colony depends on foodstuffs from outside.

My motion by way of amendment for appointment of arbitration court or sugar control board was voted for by all Indian members of Legislative Council but was opposed by Government without putting forward any alternative constructive proposal for settlement of dispute. Governor's attitude supported by European members one of whom is Company's employee and four others inclined towards vested interests of sugar monopoly against growers almost all Indians. One European member who depends largely on Company for votes even advocated in Council deportation of Indian leaders. What Governor stated on twenty-third December as decisions of council was self-assumed and arbitrary. In fact after the debate in council on sugar dispute growers feel very strongly and more than ever that there is no future prospects for cane industry and no impartial authority in Fiji to regulate relations to settle disputes or set up arbitration when circumstances so require.

Consequently Growers in despair are making no preparation for future planting.

At the request of SB Patel and with the authority of the Governor Honourable Ratu Sukuna interviewed Swami Rudrananda and AD Patel and entered into an agreement on 26 December setting out two broad principles for basis of settlement of dispute firstly Growers should offer their cane to government who will be responsible for payment of fair price and secondly government should appoint price fixing board.

51: Negotiations 26 December 1943

At the request of Mr. SB Patel,[6] and with the authority of the Governor, the Honourable Ratu JLV Sukuna on 26th December visited Nadi to discuss with Mr. AD Patel and the Swami Rudrananda proposals for the settlement of the sugar dispute.

---

6   In a letter to historian KL Gillion, SB Patel denied that the request came from him. The request, he insisted, came from the Government side.

It has in consequence been agreed by Mr. AD Patel and Swami Rudrananda that they will advise those who look to them for advice that the cutting and planting of cane shall be immediately resumed, upon the understanding:

a). that such cane as may be found to be fit for harvesting this season shall be delivered by the Growers at designated points on the main tramway or at the mills and that the price paid for it shall be calculated in accordance with the terms of the existing agreement between the Company and the Growers;

b). that the sole test applied in selecting the cane to be harvested must be its fitness for crushing and that of this the Company's experts, in accordance with accepted practice, must be the judge;

c). that the mills must be closed as soon as the sugar content of the cane reaching them falls to a point at which further crushing would be unprofitable for all concerned; and

d). that the Secretary of State is giving urgent and careful consideration to the whole problem of the dispute about the cane price including the request of the Growers' associations for the introduction of price-fixing legislation.

Owing to the extreme lateness of the season, it is unlikely that more than a small part of the cane still standing will be fit for crushing in its present condition; but it is understood on good authority that, if adequate care is taken of the unharvested cane throughout the period between now and the next crushing season, its sugar content may be then have increased, although there will have been an inevitable decrease in weight. The farmers may thus recover next season some proportion of the loss they can not now avoid incurring as a result of the present dispute.

As soon as there is evidence of a general resumption of cutting and planting, His Excellency will receive at Government House Mr. AD Patel, the Swamiji and all other farmers' leaders who may have to make for improving conditions in the sugar industry generally in the future years.

It is His Excellency's earnest hope that all Growers, irrespective of their attitude during the unhappy dispute which has clouded the past few months, will now unite in an effort to save what can be saved from the wreck of this season crop and to plant a new and full crop for later harvesting.

For his part His Excellency gives them an assurance that in future negotiations their interests will be diligently protected.

Agreement:

After considering the interest of Growers, the sugar-industry and the economic welfare of the Colony, we the undersigned agreed that it is in the best interests of all parties concerned to settle the present dispute over the price of cane immediately in the manner following that is to say:

1. The Growers would offer their cane to the Government who will be responsible to the Growers for the payment of a fair price.

2. The Government should appoint as early as possible Price Fixing Board to determine price of sugar cane from year to year.

These are the broad principles on which the dispute can be settled. If these two principles are acceptable to His Excellency, the details of the settlement may be discussed with His Excellency by us and may be agreed upon.

Nadi,

26th December 1943

JLV Sukuna

Swami Rudrananda

AD Patel

SB Patel

52: Ratu Sukuna to AD Patel, 28 December 1943

Dear Mr. Patel

As soon as I returned to Suva I called on the Governor and handed to him the document which was signed jointly by ourselves, the Swamiji and Mr. SB Patel at Nadi and which embodied your proposals for the settlement of the sugar dispute. His Excellency has now consulted his advisors and has directed me to reply to your proposals in the following terms.

(i.) <u>Delivery of cane to Government</u>. As was explained in His Excellency's telegram to you dated the 4th of September, there is only one organization in Fiji capable of processing cane and that is the Colonial Sugar Refining Company. Any arrangement for the delivery of cane to Government would, therefore, in effect, have to mean delivery to the Company, as I made clear to you in our conversation. Moreover, as no properly attested evidence has yet been adduced to show that any increase in price is justified, the price paid for this year's crop must be calculated in accordance with the existing contract between the Growers and the Company. Any guarantee would therefore have to be made within the framework of the contract. This point we also discussed and agreed to leave the question of price to Government.

(ii) <u>Price-fixing legislation</u>. The Governor made it clear in his opening address to Legislative Council that this suggestion, which was originally made in a joint letter from the Maha Sangh, the Rewa Planters' Association, and one faction of the Kisan Sangh, was among those to which the Secretary of State was giving careful and urgent consideration. No guarantee that such legislation will in fact be introduced can be given by His Excellency until the Secretary of State's decision is known.

As for your request for an interview with His Excellency, I am to say that, with the Company's mills likely to close down in the near future, there is no time to be lost in further negotiation. In any case, the decision of the Legislative Council clearly was that any resumption of negotiation must be preceded by a resumption of cutting and planting. You have possibly read the reports of His Excellency's closing address, from which the following is an extract:

> Honourable members who have raised these matters by means of motions have had their answer without doubt of equivocation at the highest level of constitutional authority in the Colony. I hope and believe they will accept that answer, understanding that beyond the limits of the authority of this Council there lie only the dark and dangerous ways outside the law. I hope they will go to all the people for whom they have spoken in this dispute and say: We have taken your case as we know it to the Legislative Council of the Colony and have fully expounded it there; these are the decisions of Council on it: that you harvest your cane and plant new crops of cane, working with zeal to repair the damage and loss which have been done; that you await patiently and lawfully the decisions which the Secretary of State is now deliberating and accept them loyally in the confidence that they will be based on full consideration of your welfare.

The Governor and I discussed this morning with Mr. Irving King ways and means of getting to the mills as much as possible of such part of the standing cane as may still be fit for harvesting. We agreed on the following arrangements:

(i) The sole test applied in selecting the cane to be harvested must be its fitness for crushing and of this the Company's experts, in accordance with accepted practice, must be the judges.

(ii) The mills must be closed as soon as the sugar content of cane reaching them falls to a point at which further crushing would be unprofitable for all concerned.

(iii) At Lautoka and perhaps at other centres the Growers must provide such extra labour as may be necessary to enable the mills to deal with all the cane selected for harvesting. Within these limitations the Company is willing to accept all the cane that may be offered.

Mr. King Irving made the interesting and reassuring point that if the cane which is not worth harvesting, or which for some other reason cannot be harvested this year, is given adequate care between now and the next crushing season, its sugar content may then have increased, although there will have been an inevitable decrease in weight. The farmers may therefore be able to recover next year some measure of the loss they cannot now avoid incurring as a result of the present dispute.

Although the above arrangements refer only to cutting, it is, of course, assumed that your advice to the farmers will include an exhortation that they should at once begin to prepare their land for the planting of a new and full crop,

The Governor authorises me to say that, if you and other spokesmen for the farmers, will give evidence of your good faith by bringing about an immediate resumption of cutting and of preparations for planting, he will be ready to meet them at any time and to receive from them further representations that they may wish to make.

It may be of interest to you to know that I saw at Government House this morning a telegram in which the Secretary of State expressed the hope that, as a result of the full discussion in Legislative Council, saner counsels would now prevail, and the farmers would realise that their immediate duty was to resume cutting and harvesting.

His Excellency's offer seems to me to afford a very satisfactory hope that you will lose no time in demonstrating your own good faith and loyalty of the Indian farming community by accepting it in the spirit of co-operation and concern for the public welfare in which I know it has been made. If you do so, I have not the slightest doubt that in all the ensuing negotiations the interests of the farmers will be fully prected.

Yours sincerely

(sgd) JLV Sukuna

53: AD Patel to Ratu Sukuna, 28 December 1943

Dear Ratu Sukuna

We received your letter addressed to Mr. AD Patel of even date for which we are grateful. In reply we have to inform you:

1. <u>As for delivery of cane to Government.</u>

We realise that the delivery of cane to Government would be in effect delivery at the Company's tramline as agreed amongst us during the discussion. We also discussed and agreed to leave the question of fixing a fair price to the conscience of the Government. It would, therefore, be for the Government to decide the manner of fixing such price.

2. <u>As to price-fixing legislation</u>

We appreciate that His Excellency cannot give a guarantee to introduce such legislation until the decision of the Secretary of State is known. However, in order to reassure the Growers and encourage them to plant cane, His Excellency, we think, should make an announcement to the effect that the Secretary of State is giving careful and urgent consideration, and early steps will be taken to introduce legislation as soon as Secretary of State's decision is known.

We agree that the sole test applied in selecting the cane to be harvested must be its fitness for crushing. But we suggest that such tests should be carried out with proper safeguards against any possible victimization.

We agree that the mills must be closed as soon as the sugar contents of the cane reaching the mills falls to a point at which further crushing will be unprofitable for all concerned.

We appreciate the difficulty the Company may have in obtaining extra labour but unfortunately the Growers themselves will be faced with the same difficulties in a more acute form in harvesting their cane and therefore they will not be able to provide any labour to the Company.

We realise that no time should be lost. But we felt that a personal discussion with His Excellency of the details would have been a much quicker method of approach.

We have read His Excellency's address to the last Council with deep interest. We are constrained to say that unfortunately His Excellency did not offer any constructive suggestion towards settling the dispute except the oft repeated advice to harvest cane.

Yours sincerely

Swami Rudrananda

SB Patel

AD Patel

54: Ratu Sukuna to AD Patel, 29 December 1943

Dear Mr. Patel

I received your letter of yesterday's date just before noon this morning and at once sent it to His Excellency, who has authorised me to reply in the following terms.

(i). <u>Delivery of cane</u>. As it is agreed that delivery of the cane to Government must, in effect, mean delivery to the Company, there appears to be no point in maintaining the fiction that Government is to be a party to the transactions, except as a benevolent onlooker.

(ii) <u>Price</u>. The question of the price to be paid is one, not of conscience, but of contract. The agreement between the Company and the Growers must be regarded as remaining in force until it is superseded either by a new agreement between the parties or by a decision of the Secretary of State. The price for cane harvested this seasons will therefore be calculated in accordance with the terms of the agreement at present in force.

(iii) <u>Price-fixing legislation</u>. His Excellency can for the present say no more than that the Secretary of State is giving urgent and careful consideration to the question of introducing such legislation.

(iv) <u>Victimisation</u>. His Excellency has received from the Company an assurance that there will be no discrimination between Growers in the selection of cane to be milled and he is confident that this assurance will be scrupulously honourd.

(v) <u>Labour</u>. It will be appreciated that, if the Company cannot obtain additional labour, the amount of cane it is able to handle at the mills will be reduced. Government will, for its part, do everything in its power to overcome this difficulty.

Subject to your signifying agreement with the clarifications above set out, His Excellency accepts your proposals as a basis for the settlement of the dispute and, so soon as he is satisfied that advice to the farmers to resume cutting and planting has been given and is being acted upon, he will be prepared to receive at Government House for discussion yourself, Swamiji, Mr. SB Patel and any other farmers' leaders who may care to be present.

I enclose a copy of the statement which the Governor intends to issue when he has heard from me that you have agreed to its terms. I should be grateful if you would notify me of your agreement by telegram.

Yours sincerely

JLV Sukuna

55: AD Patel to Ratu Sukuna, 30 December 1943

Dear Ratu Sukuna

I received your letter of the 29th instant this morning and I at once got in touch with the Swamiji and Mr. SB Patel.

Mr. [SB] Patel is unfortunately laid up with dengue and I had to send him a copy of your letter by special car to Lautoka. Hence the delay.

I am authorised by the Swamiji and Mr. SB Patel to reply in the following terms:

1. <u>Delivery of Cane</u>. It was made clear in our discussion that the Growers will sell their cane to the Government and deliver it to wherever the Government instructs them to do so. It is the first condition agreed upon amongst us and expressly mentioned in the agreement dated the 26th instance at Nadi from which we quote:

> '1 The Growers would offer their cane to the Government who will be responsible to the Growers for the payment of a fair price.'

As the Government will be taking cane for the sole purpose of processing it into sugar and will, therefore, have to send it to the mills of the Company which is the only processing agent in the Colony, the government naturally will have to instruct Growers to deliver the cane at the Company's tramlines or at the mills. This, however, does not mean that the delivery is made to the Company. The Growers will offer their cane to the Government and the Government will be responsible for the payment. The Government, therefore, is not a benevolent onlooker but the other party to the transaction.

2. Price. When we discussed and agreed to leave the question of fixing a fair price to the conscience of the Government, it was understood amongst us that the Government will pay whatever price in their opinion they consider fair. As this is a transaction between the Government and the Growers, the Growers would leave the question of price to the Government without any reservations as a patriotic gesture towards the Government.

We accept paragraphs 3, 4 and 5 re: price-fixing legislation, victimization and labour.

Paragraph (a) of the statement which the Governor intends to make and of which you have very kindly sent me a copy should be modified as follows: 'That the Growers would offer their cane to the Government who will be responsible to the Growers for the payment of a fair price. Such cane as may be found fit for harvesting this season shall be delivered by the Growers at the designated points on the main tramway or at the mills, and the Growers shall leave the question of the price to the Government without any reservation as a patriotic gesture towards the Government'.

I regret that I could not communicate the contents of this letter to you by telegraph on account of its proxility.

Yours sincerely

AD Patel

56: Ratu Sukuna to AD Patel, 31 December 1943

Dear Mr. Patel

Your letter of yesterday's date was a great disappointment to me, for I had hoped that we were at last on the verge of reaching a settlement.

I have discussed the matter again with His Excellency, who directs me to write to you in the following terms.

As it has been agreed between us that what is in fact to happen, under the proposed settlement, is that the cane shall be delivered to the Company and that the payment shall be made for it in accordance with the terms of the existing agreement, Government cannot be a party to the publication of a statement which could be considered as having quite other implications and which therefore could serve only to cloud the issue and mislead the farmers.

In the circumstances, His Excellency can see no object in our further protracting this correspondence. Time is pressing and the over-riding necessity, in the interests of all concerned, is that there should be an immediate resumption of cutting and planting. As soon as there is evidence of such a resumption, His Excellency will be prepared to meet any farmers' leaders who may wish to discuss with him matters connected with the industry.

Yours sincerely

JLV Sukuna

57: Ratu Sukuna to AD Patel, 2 January 1944

Dear Mr. Patel

After speaking to you on the telephone I recorded your message as follows:

The Growers will cut their cane and deliver it to the CSR Company's main tramlines. After paying harvesting and other expenses the Growers offer the proceeds to government as a free gift.

I immediately got in touch with the Governor and communicated it to him. He has authorised me to reply in the following terms:

It is quite clear that we are all in fact agreed that what is now immediately necessary in the interests of all concerned, and particularly in the interests of the farmers, is a resumption of cutting and planting. His Excellency is not prepared to assent to any general formula which might mislead the farmers by encouraging them in the belief that in consequence of Government intervention the existing cane agreement had been terminated. In any case the assumption you now make that the farmers, after paying their expenses, will have something left over to present to Government as a free gift conflicts with the assertion so frequently made in the course of this dispute that the price at present being paid for cane makes it impossible for it to be grown except as a loss. But there is no time to be wasted in argument over this or any other formula. It is now too late to save this year's crop; and at this eleventh hour His Excellency can do no more than repeat his assurance that, if cutting and other normal activities are resumed, he will be prepared to meet the farmers' leaders to discuss with them any matters connected with the industry. The farmers may have full confidence that tin all ensuing negotiations their interests will be diligently protected by His Excellency, by the Legislative Council and by His Majesty's Government in the United Kingdom.

I am sure that, if this assurance were given to farmers at their meeting tomorrow, they would be ready to listen to the only useful advice which at this stage can be given to them, namely, that they should begin to cut and plant at once.

I hope that in addition to giving them this advice you will also make it clear to them that the various suggestions which have been made are still under consideration in London and that they should not assume that the decisions of the Secretary of State will be unacceptable to them.

Yours sincerely

JLV Sukuna

58: AD Patel to Ratu Sukuna, 3 January 1944

Dear Ratu Sukuna

I received your letter of the 2nd instant for which I thank you.

It is apparent that you have completely misunderstood my conversation with you over the telephone which is not surprising in the present state of telephone service, where we could hardly make each other hear as the line was faint and inaudible.

My suggestion was as follows:

> The Growers will make a gift of their standing crop of cane which is ready at present for harvesting to the Government. Is the Government prepared to accept this gift? If so, the Govt. would naturally like to cut it and get it processed into sugar. In order to further assist the Govt. in their problems to obtain sufficient labour to cut the cane, the Growers will cut it for the Govt. upon payment by the Govt. of the cutting expenses.

The Company has persistently refused to buy crop from the Growers at the price the Growers ask for and insists that the Growers must sell their cane to the Company at the price offered by it under the so-called contract. The Growers refuse to sell to the Company at that price. This is the dispute right throughout between the Company and the Growers. The Company has persistently refused to revise the offer to the Growers. The Govt. has all along refused to set up conciliation or arbitration machinery under the Industrial Disputes (Conciliation) Ordinance in order to bring about a speedy settlement and has alleged that the Growers and their leaders are impeding the war effort of the Colony. In order to assure the Govt., the people of the Colony and the world, that the Growers have not the slightest intention to impede the war effort of the Colony, they have right throughout been willing to sell their crop to the Govt. and accept whatever price the Govt. chooses to pay them. This responsible and patriotic offer has been rejected by the Governor. In order to demonstrate their bona fide the Growers will this crop as a gift to the Govt.

I am sure you will appreciate the difference between the Growers' willingness to undergo sacrifices to assist the war effort and unwillingness under pressure selling their crop to a private profit making monopoly at the price dictated by it for the sole purpose of making as much profit for its share-holders as possible.

If my suggestion is accepted it would have the following beneficial results:

(1) It will show to the Growers that the Govt. is not siding with the Company but is acting purely in the interest of war effort.

(2) The Growers will have an opportunity to prove before the democratic world that their dispute with the Company has no ulterior or sinister motive of impeding the war effort.

(3) This will greatly promote mutual confidence between the Govt. and the Growers which is so important for solution of the present deadlock and for the preservation of the industry.

Yours sincerely

AD Patel.

59: Ratu Sukuna to AD Patel, 4 January 1944

Dear Mr. Patel

1. I find your letter of the 3rd January very disappointing, for I was under the impression that you wanted normal activities to be resumed. Your letter contains so many mis-statements of facts and misleading phrases that, before discussing the matter further, it seems necessary to set down once more the facts as they really are.

2. The Growers have persistently refused either to sell their crop at the price negotiated by themselves for a period of ten years, of which seven are still to run, or to continue production or negotiate until their demands are granted. The Company, on the other hand, has never refused to perform any part of its function.

3. But this was not the 'original dispute.' The matter originated because the Kisan Sangh in writing asked for the appointment of a Commission with a view to making a case for an increase in the price of sugar, to be laid before the Ministry for Food. A few days later a letter was received from the Maha Sangh, containing the same general argument—namely, that the increase in the price paid for cane had not kept pace with the increase in living and production costs. On the 19th July the Presidents and Secretaries of both Associations discussed this with the Governor and agreed to appoint representatives to the Commission. On the same day the newly formed Rewa Planters' Association asked to be represented also.

4. The Government has never refused to set up conciliation or arbitration machinery under the Industrial Disputes Ordinance. On the contrary, it

appointed a Commission under section 5 of the Ordinance, with which you and your associates have consistently refused to co-operate.

5.   The Growers and their leaders have been impeding the war effort of the Colony for five months by refusing to continue production in an essential industry unless and until their demands are granted. The Government and the people of the Colony know the facts and no new formula now will mislead them; and anyone one in the outside world who learns of the farmers' attempt to obtain an increase in price by stopping production will not be at all impressed by this last-minute zeal for the war effort, If you, or the growers, have any last minute zeal you have only to resume production to show it.

6.   The Growers may, as you now claim, have been right throughout willing to sell their crop to Government but in your telegram to the Governor of the 7th and 10th September you made it clear that the minimum price they could be persuaded to accept would be 25/- a ton, and this 'without prejudice to their case for a 100% rise.' You know and the farmers must know, that Government can do nothing with sugar cane and that it must in fact be sold to the Company to be turned into sugar and sold at the officially fixed price to the Ministry of Food: and you have shown in our discussions that you never intended the offer to the Government to be anything more than a face-saving device.

7.   You have deliberately brought a vital industry to a partial stoppage and inflicting grievous losses thereby on the farmers and some damage to the cause of the United Nations; large numbers of farmers, advised by you and your friends, are still refusing to resume production; and now, after one mill has closed and the others are with in ten days of closing, you make the suggestion that the farmers should prove their zeal for the war effort, in which they have shown no interest for five months, by delivering, in theory to Government but in fact to the Company, what little remains of this season's crop.

8.   I do not think you can really expect me to continue this correspondence. I have shown your letter and this to the Governor who agrees with my reply. He asks me to say in conclusion that there is only one way to show zeal for the war effort and that is to resume at once production and planting of cane. If you decide to advise the farmers to do this, your genuineness and that of your friends can be shown by the use of the following formula:

The growers have informed the Governor that they do not wish their dispute with the Company to impede the war effort and have asked what they do to ensure that there is in fact no such impediment. His Excellency has replied that they should resume normal planting and should deliver to the Company, in accordance with the existing agreement, such of the unharvested portion of this season's crop as may in its present condition be fit for crushing. In the interests of the war effort, the farmers are loyally accepting His Excellency's advice.

Yours sincerely

JLV Sukuna

60: Reforming the Sugar Industry, 21 December 1945

We must first consider the fundamental clash of interests which exists between the C.S.R. Company and people and Government of Fiji. It is to the Company's interest, being an outside concern, to produce sugar here in Fiji as cheaply as possible and to sell it abroad as dearly as possible, and the margin between the two is the margin of profit that Company pays to its shareholders in Australia. They have no interest in this Colony as far as marketing their product is concerned; therefore, the buying power of the people of the Colony is immaterial to them.

On the other hand it is very, very material that there is no competition in the labour market, that they command their labour at the cheapest possible rate, that there is no competition in agriculture so that no other product in Fiji can be more paying to the primary producer than the production of cane, so that they can obtain cane as cheaply as possible. After all, the Company, as time and again we have been told, is a business concern and we cannot blame them for the view that they take of their own business interests just as any other private business concern in the world, but we are certainly entitled to consider the interests of this Colony.

Mr. Vishnu Deo pointed out to us how far-reaching and wide is the economic influence of the Company over the Government and people of Fiji. He has also mentioned how jealously this concern guards against any other rival industry being set up in Fiji which might seduce labour or primary producers away from the sugar industry. That is how one previous effort of Government in establishing and starting the cotton industry was brought to ruin. It was brought to ruin, as is well-known in Fiji, by the dog-in-the-manger policy of the C.S.R. Company. Now we have heard a lot about the wonderful things the C.S.R. Company has done for the people and the Government of this Colony. Let us consider them. I do not wish to minimize their services to this Colony, but I would like to point out with all due respect, that they have been amply paid for what they did for the people and the Government of this Colony, not only amply paid but paid over and over again.

Now the Government has to consider whether Fiji has arrived at a stage where it can stand on its own and look to its own salvation. It has been suggested that it was the C.S.R. Company who taught the Indian community here farming and especially the cultivation of sugar cane. I join issue on that argument. As a matter of fact the Company brought these labourers from the United Provinces and Bihar, the majority of them, and even from South India, from those districts that grow cane. It is overlooked here that India is the largest producer of cane and sugar in the world and the Indians that came here were not novices in the cultivation of cane. It stands to their credit that where the Company failed as a primary producer, and where the European planter failed as a primary producer, the Indian succeeded and kept and maintained that industry as the main industry of Fiji.

It has also been pointed out that it is through the efficient management of the C.S.R. Company that we have got such a prosperous industry in Fiji and the prosperity that we enjoy. I am afraid that when that argument is put forward we overlook a very, very important factor in our prosperity, namely, the subsidy that we get from the poor taxpayers of England through the Imperial Preference. When the Growers of cane ask for a reasonable price and request the Imperial Government that if the Government cannot make the Company pay it, then it should devise some way of granting a subsidy from England, European Members are up in arms to say to the Indian Members: 'Look here now, you should not beg.'

It is sheer effrontery on their part to do so and they overlook the fact that this well-to-do concern with all its ramifications that we have been reminded about, retains 60 per cent of this subsidy that comes out of the pockets of the British taxpayer by way of Imperial Preference and passes on 40 per cent of it to the primary producer. So it is not as if it were through the wonderful and most efficient management of the C.S.R. Company that we are enjoying this prosperity here in Fiji. We enjoy this prosperity in Fiji because of the goodwill of the Imperial Government and the sacrifice that the British people make for the people of this Colony and this wealthy concern, I submit, steals a substantial portion of that subsidy. We have been told in this Council that if a concern like this was nationalized it would be difficult for us to find markets, but as it is it is the Imperial Government that is finding the market for the sugar of Fiji, this Australian concern cannot sell its own sugar produced in Fiji even in Australia or in the neighbouring Dominion of New Zealand. It is the Imperial Government that has already taken the responsibility and burden of finding a market for the sugar produced in Fiji. That to my mind cannot be a difficulty to discourage such a step as nationalization.

Much has been said about what took place during the sugar dispute in 1943. That showed to the people and the Government of Fiji and to the world abroad how desirable it was that there must be some form of government control over an industry like the sugar industry in Fiji. As was pointed out by Mr. Vishnu Deo, the government was trying to introduce industrial legislation in this Colony and every time the C.S.R. Company and their henchmen were trying to obstruct that legislation and denied the rights of collective bargaining to the primary producers and working classes of this Colony. They did their worst and in spite of their opposition, thanks to the Imperial Government, this Government was pressed into bringing that legislation into operation. But it was too late. The war had gone on for nearly three years, the cost of living was mounting up all the time. The Government had completely ignored the question of having any cost of living index prepared for the working classes of the Colony and they were left entirely to the mercy of the employers, and the employers themselves had thought that they were strong enough to suppress this growing discontent, resentment and dissatisfaction amongst the working classes and primary producers. Notes of warning were sounded now and then but neither the vested interests nor the Government of Fiji paid any heed to those warnings. In 1941 while the cost of living was going up unfortunately on account of the lack of shipping for which we cannot blame the C.S.R. Company, one-third of the sugar in Fiji we are told had to be destroyed.

But it was all done without even bothering to explain to the primary producers whose pockets were affected by the destruction of one-third of the crop; they just declared that one-third of the sugar would be destroyed and that they would be paid only the basic price for it. The notice was published in Hindustani in such ambiguous language that the people themselves did not understand what it was, and when Mr. Vishnu Deo approached the then Colonial Secretary to explain the contents of the notice, the Colonial Secretary referred him to the C.S.R. Company, saying that he himself did not understand it and did not know anything about it. All this was ignored. Dissatisfaction and discontent amongst the primary producers and working classes on the other side of the island were mounting up and the government and vested interests of the Colony were just burying their heads in the sand like an ostrich and believing all the time that everything was well with Fiji. It all came to a head in 1942. As early as February in that year, the Growers approached the government as well as the Company for a higher price of cane because the cost of living had suddenly soared up. The Company gave them an abrupt reply and the Growers approached Government and requested government to approach the Right Honourable the Secretary of State for the Colonies to grant some relief to the Growers. In these circumstances, it was not until some months had elapsed and the crushing season had nearly arrived that the government thought fit to post that request on to the Secretary of State.

Before the crushing season was to start the Company, because its labourers were asking for a higher wage, thought it could join hands with the Growers in trying to keep the wages of the labourers down, and with that view convened a conference of the Growers and tried to persuade them that they should try to cut down the premium that they were paying to the labourers to £10 and give them a 25 per cent rise in wages. The Growers could see through this because that was a time when it was difficult to get labourers for anything less than a premium of £20. Only in the previous year, that is in 1942, the Growers had paid as much as £16 premium and when the Company raised the scale of cutting charges, it meant that the Growers had to pay £20 premium plus a higher rate of cutting charge for the harvesting of their cane. The grower straight away asked the Company what was to happen about the price of his cane, whether he was going to get a higher price or not.

The Company point blank refused. They sent a cable to Sydney and they were told that they would not get even a penny more, and they were reminded that their cane had no value until it was crushed. Of course it had no value because there was no other buyer in the Colony to buy it from the grower and their helpless position was quite apparent to the Growers. The Akhil Fiji Krishak Maha Sangh wrote to the government. That was three weeks before the crushing season was to start. They explained the whole position and informed the government of the decision of the Growers that they would not sell their cane to the Company for a price lower than 30s a ton. A reply was received from some section of the Colonial Secretary's Office which was responsible for handling such correspondence that the matter was under consideration and that phrase turned out to have the same meaning as the Second Indian Nominated Member a few days ago told us it had in official phraseology, viz., 'filed and pigeon-holed.'

There was a labour strike and a National Service Tribunal was appointed of which I was a member. When the Tribunal was sitting at Lautoka and when Mr.. King Irving was insisting that the Tribunal should take a stand that it would not hear the labourers' case unless the labourers went to work, I reminded the Tribunal and Mr. King Irving that there was no work for them to return to because they were overlooking the fact that the Growers had decided not to cut cane; so how were we going to force the labourers to go back to the mills? Was the Company going to give an undertaking that if we compelled the labourers to go to the mills and if there was no cane cut and no cane delivered at the mills that it would undertake to pay wages to those labourers? It was then that Mr. Jenkins, who was the Chairman of the Commission, asked Mr. King Irving if that was the position and he confirmed what I had said. Mr. Jenkins expressed his surprise that nobody in Suva in the government service knew anything about it. I informed him that a letter had already gone to the Colonial Secretary. He rang up the Colonial Secretary's office in my presence after I produced to him a copy of the letter that was sent and it was after that that the Government woke up to the fact that there was not only one dispute, that is, between the labourers and the Company, but another and a far more serious dispute, between the producers of the cane and the Company. What followed was an unfortunate chapter of misrepresentations and misunderstandings. The then Governor of the Colony called a meeting of the Growers at Lautoka and told them and assured them that he would appoint what he called a Board of Arbitration, and then a Commission was appointed.

There were others at the meeting and it was well thrashed out. There was a report taken by the District Commissioner and a report taken by the Police and it was confirmed that there was a mistake which was admitted afterwards. When the Commission was appointed it was faced with the difficulty from both sides. The Growers were not prepared to accept the Commission, but the Company had informed the Commission that if it wanted to go into the accounts of the Company, the Company would also boycott it. The Commission gave them an assurance that they would not go into their accounts. That just showed how helpless the position was as far as the Government of Fiji was concerned in an important dispute in an industry which was the key industry of this Colony. When the Commission failed, Mr. Said Hasan, who was a member of this Council, then approached the Governor and the Governor agreed that the counsel for the Growers and the counsel for the Company should go into the accounts and ascertain the cost of production of cane and if there was a sufficient case he himself by cable would forward it on to the Secretary of State and obtain a rise in the price of cane for the Growers. I was summoned to Suva from my internment to go into these accounts. Mr. King Irving and Sir Henry Scott for the Company, and Mr. Said Hasan and myself for the Growers, met and had preliminary discussions and when we were discussing the manner of approach to this question of going into all these figures, the Company's Attorney, Mr. King Irving, and the Company's solicitor, Sir Henry Scott, told me that they had no authority from the Company to go any further and that I would have to go to see Mr. Smith at Lautoka whom the Company had sent from Sydney before they could go into those accounts with me. Sir Henry Scott sent to me a letter of introduction.

I returned to the Attorney-General's chambers and informed him of the position and Mr. Jenkins in my presence rang up Sir Philip Mitchell and informed him as to what had happened. His Excellency said: 'Patel, all this time I thought the Company was in the right and you were in the wrong but now I think you are in the right and the Company in the wrong. There is no necessity for you to go to Lautoka. You remain here and we will ring up Sir Henry Scott and ask him to get Mr. Smith on this side of the island without delay.' I was asked to wait in Suva and I waited for one day. The next day I was asked to go to the Attorney-

General's office, which I did. Mr. Smith had not arrived then but in the afternoon when he did arrive he told the Attorney-General and the Governor that he had not got any instructions from his office in Sydney and he would have to wait for them. Again I was asked to wait in Suva and then the strangest thing happened. The Governor and the Attorney-General who not only thought but had actually expressed to me that in that particular chapter at that particular stage they were of the opinion that I was in the right and the Company in the wrong, summoned me all of a sudden to Government House and there the Governor told us: 'Oh no, it is no use going into this matter, I do not think any useful purpose can be served because the Company will not go into the accounts with you and if you have any applications to make you had better come before the Commission (we will appoint a Commission again) and make your application there.'

That again showed the position clearly, that the Governor who thought the Company was in the wrong was not in a position to persuade the Company to be in the right. It had become an open secret in this Colony that the industrial legislation which had been passed during the war period, a few months before this dispute started, the Governor was fighting shy of putting it into operation, and employing other conciliation machinery by way of appointing a Board of Conciliation or a Court of Arbitration, because, as was well-known right throughout the Colony, the Government was afraid that the Company might refuse to produce their accounts and that would mean a loss of face for the Government. Under one excuse or another, the Government thought fit to save their faces by suppressing the Growers and their leaders, being the weaker party. It has been said that the situation [was] just on the verge of bloodshed in this Colony. Who was responsible for it? At the time when the military were posted, there had not been a single case of intimidation on record. The Police had never approached the government with a request that the situation had gone out of their hands and they could not control it, and with the advice of the Attorney-General of the Colony, of all persons, approached the Governor over the head of the officer who is responsible for law and order in this Colony, the Commissioner of Police, with a request that the military should be posted in certain areas because the Growers were intimidated and frightened of cutting cane and in need of military protection. It was only the level-headedness and restraint on the part of the Growers that saved the situation.

With all the provocations and insults they were subjected to, they showed admirable restraint and sense of responsibility. In Korovutu they were trying to employ the same tactics. In order to frighten those Growers into cutting their cane in the holy name of protection, the military were posted there and the Growers went to the District Officer and told him: 'For God's sake, take away these military. We are not in need of their protection, the sort of protection the police are giving has been enough,' and the military had to be removed from there. I have been accused of misleading the Growers. Well, I am convinced that I was taking up a true and a just cause and I am convinced that the stand I took was the right one, that the advice I gave to the Growers was right and I am proud of the part I played in that dispute. The Governor of the Colony [was misled], creating a difficult situation for the great man, whom I admire though I was once his prisoner, who before leaving this Colony expressed these words to me, which mean so much: 'Patel, you would never be able to convince me that I was in the wrong, and perhaps I would not be in a position to convince you that you were in the wrong, but I wish you to know that I respected you all along for the manner in which you opposed me.' If that conveys anything to an Australian, let him take it.

The Imperial Government during the wartime have made promises to the workers and primary producers of the British colonies, that ways and means will be found to improve the economic condition of the workers and primary producers in the Colonies. When a strong and mighty concern like the Company will defy the local Government, there is only one way in which the Imperial Government can keep its promise if that promise was sincerely meant, viz., to introduce some measure of control over a monopoly like that by which the Government will be in a position to see that the conditions of the workers and primary producers in that industry can be improved.

We have been told how much revenue the Company has been contributing to the finances of the Colony. Well, if the Company's concerns are nationalized, it would not make any difference to the revenue derived from that source; on the other hand, it will augment the revenue. Doubt has been expressed as to the practicality of this suggestion on the grounds of where is the Colony going to find the finances. Well, Mr. Vishnu Deo has showed one manner of acquiring the assets, that is, provided the C.S.R. Company are prepared to negotiate and come to some arrangement for accepting the consideration by installments, if not by raising a loan. After all it will be a productive debt and the industry itself will gradually pay itself back. All the income from that industry is prosperous and can make more revenue and if the conditions of the primary producers and the workers can be improved, business all around will prosper in the Colony because with more buying power in the hands of the people, everybody will be well off in the Colony.

We must not overlook the fact that not only is the socialist government in England nationalizing the Bank of England, which does not only provide England with its services but has got its services right throughout the world, not only the coal mines of England, which do not produce coal only for home consumption but also for overseas market, but it is going a step further and the President of the Board of Trade, whose name has been invoked in this debate, Sir Stafford Cripps, has got what he calls a tripartite plan for the rest of the industries, under which the Government, the employees and the employers will control those industries. Here there is an alternative way, if nationalization of that industry cannot be effected straight away at least a measure of control can be brought over it by bringing it under such a tripartite plan. It is not going to do any harm to a wealthy concern like that because perhaps we will be relieving that industry of its responsibilities outside Australia and it will result in the prosperity of this Colony, not only Indians but the Fijians, the Europeans and the Government all will benefit equally from a concern that does not belong to the Indians when it is nationalized but belongs to the Government of Fiji as the national representative authority of Fiji.

61: A Commission at Gunpoint? 6 June 1960

The Colonial Sugar Refining Company is the largest monopoly dominating the life of the people of this Colony. Being the only buyer of cane, it has always taken advantage of the cane growers' helpless position and paid him as little as possible. The Company knew that the 1950-60 agreement for purchase of cane was to expire this year just before the opening of the crushing season. Only the C.S.R. knew how much total area of cane it got the growers to plant. It was to the advantage of the C.S.R. Co. to get the growers to plant more than what it was prepared to buy. It knew that it required only 199,000 tons of sugar to fill this year's quota. But it got the growers to produce enough cane to manufacture 300,000 tons of sugar. It ensured that the supply of cane was far greater than the demand. It tells the growers that it will buy only that much cane as is required to produce 199,000 tons of sugar. The growers will have to destroy the rest of the cane. It offered a price which is about the same in percentage as it used to the growers before the Second World War. It wanted the growers to plant and grow more cane every year than what the Company would buy and destroy the surplus. If an opportunity like the Suez crisis occurred again the C.S.R. may take advantage of such a standing pool of surplus cane and profiteer, at the cost of the grower.

The growers naturally do not agree to subject themselves to such conditions. They are neither slaves, servants, nor serfs of the Company. As far as they are concerned there is no going back to the pre-world war conditions. They naturally want to hold on to what they have and to advance. They are asking for the same percentage that the C.S.R. is paying to growers in Australia.

There is no reason why it cannot pay a similar percentage in Fiji unless it wants to differentiate on the grounds of the colour of the skin of the cane growers. The farmers also realize that they cannot carry on with such wasteful husbandry of having to always produce more than what they can sell every year. The Company made a record profit last year. It never publishes what profits it makes in Fiji. But it is admitted that under the 1950-60 agreement, it made profit every year.

In 1957 the Company valued all its assets in Fiji at about five million pounds. In 1958 it boosted the value of the assets to thirteen million pounds. These assets include its 75,000 acres of freehold and 50,000 acres of leasehold land. It includes its non-sugar processing ventures. The C.S.R. wants profit from the sugar cane farmers on its boosted value of all these assets. In the circumstances, the only alternative left for the cane growers of Fiji is to get out from the clutches of this ever hungry wolf who keeps on whetting its appetite. His Excellency the Governor called a conference of the representatives of the Company and the growers. It went for 11 hours. It was a veritable conference between the wolves and the lambs. The growers' representatives did all the conceding and went as far as they dare go. The Company was prepared to meet the growers but only on one condition viz, the growers must agree to accept a Commission of Enquiry.

The growers have previous experience of such Commissions in the past. They know how the Company bamboozles such Commissions to its own way [of thinking]and how abortive and expensive they turn out in the end. Such Commissions go further and treat the farmers as if they belonged to a lesser species than the Europeans and go to the extent of laying down the size of the farmer's family, what he and his wife and children should wear and eat and what they should not. Only their physical needs are taken into account. The Commissions have only added insults to injuries. The farmers belong socially to the middle class of Fiji—the same class to which the Company's officers and managers belong. If buying cane is Company's [business], selling it is the business of the growers. And farmers have the same freedom to sell as the buyers to buy.

The Company is trying to ram the Commission down the throats of the growers by laying down the condition that unless they accept it, the Company will not buy their cane. The time has now arrived for the parting of the ways. The growers must prepare to stand on their own feet, establish their own co-operative mills and become the processors as well as producers of their cane. That way they will emancipate themselves and this country from the economic bondage of such ruthless monopoly. It can be done. It should be done. It must be done if the growers and their families want to live in security, peace and freedom.

62: A Drive for Disunity, 30 June 1960

Unlike free countries, where matters of vital importance affecting the welfare of the community such as economics, education, health and standard of living, etc., are decided by the institutions based on democratic principles, any important subject of the above nature is always arbitrarily dealt with in the dependent countries and colonies like Fiji.

The semblance of Councils, Assemblies and Advisory Bodies are merely kept as a show in these countries in order to keep the ignorant people in satisfaction and to show the outside world that people live in these places a very peaceful, contented life and that their way of life is a democratic way of life.

But in fact there is no real democracy in any dependant country or a colony, which fact is very well understood throughout the world today. That is the very reason why the world opinion is tending towards doing away with this old pattern which is outmoded and found ineffective in this advanced and enlightened scientific age.

However, even in these apparently peaceful and contented parts of the globe which are considered to be paradise on earth by some people both inside and outside, there arise times of dissatisfaction and discontentment. On those occasions, instead of making proper effort of taking steps to remove the root causes of the trouble, only superficial methods are being adopted just to top dress merely the surface and to paint it with new colour and make the old look fresh and bright for the time being.

On such method is appointment of an Enquiry Commission. Of course, this is not the only method. There are very many methods similarly adopted to suit the circumstance and the time.

We often hear of a Commission being set up for this and for that and there is no end of it. The news of appointment of such Commissions always go on the air and in the press and some times people get tired of such news. Such Commissions become so many at times that people forget some of them and there is no more talk about them. When the people hear of appointment of one Commission they get busy talking of the new Commission and give up discussing on the old Commissions. In that way we find some Commissions go into oblivion and their findings never see the light of the day.

Of course, an appointment of a Sugar Commission will not be forgotten like that. On the other hand, people always remember Sugar Commissions, especially the farmers, simply because they had to take insults and degradation and injustice at the findings of such Commissions in the past. The farmers had been treated in the past not as civilized human being but had been dealt with as lower being and considered only fit to be treated as slaves and serfs.

171

Under these circumstances we can never expect the sugar cane farmers in Fiji whole-heartedly to give consent to an appointment of Enquiry Commission to deal with their affairs and to give evidence before any such Commission jeopardising their own self-respect. Hence any attempt at forcing the Enquiry Commission on the unwilling throats of the farmers is an useless attempt. The farmers of Fiji and the millers should negotiate as sellers and purchasers amongst themselves in a decent way exactly as commercial concerns do all over the world. All other attempts to interfere will only end in a failure.

The main issue is that the Company during the years 1958 and 1959 encouraged growers to plant more, and supplied the services of soil scientists free of charge to show the growers the ways and means of increasing yield per acre. Thus the Company deliberately and with set purpose extended the area of planting, and also got the farmers to resort to improved methods of controlling, cultivation and fertilisation of land to obtain more produce. Now when the sugar cane is ready for harvest, the C.S.R. is trying to wriggle out of its obligation and leave a substantial portion unharvested. On this issue the farmers are and should remain firm. The growers' leaders in their over-anxiety to reach a settlement have allowed the Company to get out of this obligation. The Company has shrewdly taken advantage of this and is trying to side track people's minds by remaining silent on this all important matter and drag in the subject of instituting a government enquiry to fix the price and terms for 1961 harvest.

It should not be overlooked that the immediate and all-important issue is to have the entire crop harvested at the 1950-60 Agreement price.

The Company and the government are working hand in hand to cause disunity among the growers and their leaders. They are trying to separate the Fijian growers from the Indian. They are seeing the leaders of the growers separately and are desperately trying to bring about a division among them. There are indications that some of the leaders are being bamboozled into the trap. It is more important than ever that the leaders must stick together. If there is any difference of opinion among them, they are bound to refer such differences to the farmers. They must bear in mind that the ultimate decision must rest with the growers.

There is nothing new in what the Company and the Government are doing. They are doing the same thing as they did in the 1943 dispute. People earnestly wish that the leaders will not play into the hands of schemers as some of them did in the past to the general undoing of the farmers.

The all-important thing for the present is for the leaders to preserve their unity and for the farmers to see that they and their representatives stand together.

It must not be forgotten that the C.S.R. has many weapons to deal with the farmers. The only weapon the farmers have to defend their interests is their unity. If unity is lost everything will be lost.

It is, therefore, essential to take a firm stand on the main issue, i.e. the Company must buy the entire crop which is due for harvest this season. Consideration for 1961 crop must be postponed until the dispute over the 1960 crop is satisfactorily settled.

While the farmers stand firm and united it would be wrong for the leaders to weaken and betray their trust.

63: Negotiations and a Plan for the Future, 7 July 1960

No binding contract exists between the C.S.R. Co. and the cane farmers of Fiji for sale and purchase of sugar cane for the present, since a 10-year contract has expired by the 31st May, 1960. But this state of affairs does not absolve the C.S.R. Co. from its moral obligation of buying the cane from the farmers, as they planted and cultivated according to the advice of the Company.

However, for an amicable settlement, the whole of the 1960 sugar cane crop should be harvested by the farmers and bought by the C.S.R. Co. at a price based on the price clause in the recently expired agreement and also other clauses contained in the expired agreement should apply to the present crop. It is true that the farmers claim a higher price while the Company wants to pay a reduced price. For smooth running a middle path should be taken. But the C.S.R Co could so adjust the crushing that this 1960 crop itself may be partly utilized and used to make up the 1961 sugar quota of Fiji.

Seeing the existing condition of production, the cane farmers themselves have offered not to plant any new cane this year which means a great sacrifice on their part, considering their loss of future income and means of maintenance. As it is, 1961 ratoon crop must be enough for the C.S.R. Co to make up the quota, besides the surplus and the extended harvest of the 1960 crop in 1961. (This with the whole crop of 1960 and the ratoon crop of 1961 the farmers of Fiji and the C.S.R. Co. in co-operation will be fulfilling Fiji's quota and obligation with a little sacrifice).

In this the Company does not lose anything. It amounts to a friendly settlement of the immediate problem by extending the time of the expired contract for two years which the Company should gracefully agree and can afford to.

The Company says that by doing so it is losing a substantial bit in its profit. Whether it is true or not, the farmers are definitely losing their income itself in the immediate future. But, if the above suggested and only workable and feasible understanding is not arrived at through the present negotiations, there is going to be a catastrophe which will put every party into a great loss and Fiji itself will fail in its obligations. Even from a common sense point of view, a friendly and amicable settlement will surely yield good returns to both sides and that is the only proper solution. No doubt, this will also pave a smooth way and a proper approach towards working out a satisfactory long-term agreement.

It appears that the Company is sensible enough to see the soundness of the proposal and seems to appreciate the practicability of a settlement of above nature. But the trouble is, due to its over enthusiasm and anxiety in striking at a favourable long-term contract, using the present unsettlement as a key, the Company is pressing for appointment of an Enquiry Commission by the Government immediately.

Evidently, the idea behind such a move is that the farmers will find no other alternative before them than swallowing at once the pill prescribed by the Commission as a remedy for the illness. Also the Company seems to have forgotten the long history of its own tradition of adopting a give-and-take policy of the past and to have become eager to take to the new way and method of a drastic nature at once. It seems to be neither aware of modern progressive ways of life which are taking root throughout the world by which all those who take part in any concern are to be taken and treated as partners and not any section of them as mere instruments.

Unfortunately, the Company does not realize that merely the findings of a Commission of Enquiry which would probably say that this or that should be the price of the cane or certain percent of profit should be allowed to the Company, are not going to bind either the Company or the farmers in any way. You may lead a horse to the trough of water, even by force, but drinking or not is entirely the affair of the horse. Unless the farmers are given an attractive price and favourable terms, they are not going to accept any proposal or findings of a Commission. While all other sections of the community make money and profit, why should the farmers alone toil and suffer?

The crux of the problem is from now onwards who is going to shoulder responsibility of supplying sugar to the British Commonwealth from Fiji and shall fulfill the obligation of maintaining Fiji's quota? In other words, who is going to be the owners of the whole sugar production, from sowing the seed up to the export of the grain of sugar and converting it into cash?

There are three alternatives:

a). The C.S.R. Co. whose roots are in Australia, who shall not and need not bother about Fiji's progress, and whose profits are wholly distributed among all the shareholders in that country and none in Fiji, in partnership with the farmers of Fiji, who are in reality the producers of the wealth, although one is a sleeping partner and the other is a toiling one;

b). The C.S.R. Co. exclusively, without the farmers in Fiji having anything to do;

c). The Fiji farmers themselves without C.S.R. Co. having anything to do.

Among the above three alternatives the first one is a possibility. The second one is an impossibility, and the last one is both a possibility and a probability. It is always practical for the farmers to take upon themselves the task of processing of sugar also, by co-operating among themselves and starting their own mills.

Of course it is not proper to make the Australian capitalists suffer in Fiji by asking them to continue and carry on their venture as a losing concern. In fact, the C.S.R. Co. has always been threatening the farmers of Fiji and the Fiji Government, saying that it would fold its bag and baggage and go to Australia and put a stop to its business in Fiji if the farmers and labourers of Fiji did not listen to it. Indeed, the Nausori mill of the C.S.R. Co. has been closed because there was not enough profit over there. This is an indication of how the wind is blowing.

For the farmers of Fiji this is a good opportunity. They should organize themselves and start their own mills and be free from worries and anxieties for all time. This kind of uncertainty about their life and upset of their conditions every ten years is of no good to them. They must endeavour to plan and arrange definitely for their welfare for the present and future. Eventually this is certainly going to happen sooner or later. Let them get ready for the same even from now.

64: Memorandum to Mr. Julian Amery, 14 October 1960

Sir

We the undersigned members of the Cane Growers Federation Committee have great pleasure in extending to you our most hearty and sincere welcome on behalf of the Federation Committee of the Cane Growers' associations and farmers whom we represent and request you to accept our grateful thanks for readily consenting to meet us today.

We also request you to convey our greetings to Her Majesty the Queen, the Prime Minister, the Secretary of State for the Colonies and other members of the Cabinet.

We like to make it clear at the outset that the announcement made simultaneously both in Fiji and in England of your arrival to this Colony during your sojourn in the Pacific, was heartening news to us and to all the sugar cane growers of the Colony. The growers have great expectations in you and the Colonial Office and they hope that your arrival would bring about a speedy settlement of the present sugar cane dispute.

We believe that with sympathetic consideration and co-operation from the Colonial Office, a definite improvement in the present situation can be brought about and at the same time a foundation can be laid for a change in the structure of the sugar industry to enable this Colony to develop rapidly on progressive lines.

The Purpose of this Memorandum is to place before you the history of the present cane dispute and to make suggestions for its settlement and for the re-organization of the industry with a view to eliminate causes for such dispute and to ensure peace and prosperity to the cane growers who are the primary producers of the wealth of this Colony.

We wish to point out that refusal on the part of the Colonial Sugar Refining Company Limited even to discuss and consider the Federation Committee's proposal of the 1st August 1960, is the real stumbling block in the settlement of the present dispute.

The Federation Committee has always been reasonable in its negotiations and went as far as it could to reach a settlement for the immediate harvesting of the 1960 crop on reasonable and just terms and keep at the same time the door open for further negotiations in regard to future crops. But in spite of all our attempts the Company refused to change its attitude. Any compromise which the Committee offered was construed as a sign of weakness on the part of the growers, and instead of taking advantage of the offer, the Company has taken a rigid position and refused to discuss any compromise with the Committee.

Before we submit our suggestions for the settlement of the present dispute, we beg to narrate the history of our negotiations with the Company and the Government:

> i. The last contract for the sale and purchase of sugar cane for a period of 10 years was negotiated in the year 1950. The growers faithfully carried out their obligations under that contract. The Company on the other hand did not carry out its obligations under it. It made certain

unauthorized deductions, sold molasses to itself at a nominal price of £1 per ton and thereby paid a smaller price to the cane growers than what they were rightly entitled to under the contract. It also made long delays in making payments for the cane. For instance the Company has not even now fully paid the growers for the cane it purchased from them last year.

ii. During the years 1958 and 1959, the Company brought about overproduction of sugar cane by extending sugar cultivation to new areas knowing fully well that production and sale of sugar was limited by the Commonwealth and the International Sugar Agreements. We believe that this was deliberately done to weaken the bargaining position of the growers in the negotiations for a new contract in 1960. These new contractors had to make their own roads and deliver their cane to the Company by lorry transport at their own cost. Thus the Company obtained cane from these new contractors at a cheaper price and at the same time created a rival block of sugar cane growers with a view to use them if necessary against the growers who were already producing cane in the old areas. As a result there emerged a group of about 3,000 new growers who are known as lorry contractors.

iii. At the end of the 1958 crushing season there was 24,000 tons of surplus sugar. At the end of 1959 crushing season the surplus rose to 110,000 tons.

iv. In January 1959 the Company circulated a new draft contract among the growers for the purchase of sugar cane. Copies of the draft contract and explanatory notes are annexed hereto and marked (1) and (2) respectively.[7]

v. Since the terms in the new draft contract were worse for the growers than those of the previous contract the growers' associations envisaged the difficulties which lay ahead and in order to combat them joined together and formed a Federation Committee to negotiate a new contract with the Company.

vi. The Federation Committee countered with a new draft contract from the growers side and submitted it to the Company in the month of October, 1959. The copy of the draft agreement is annexed hereto and marked (3).

---

7   These annexes are omitted here for reasons of space, but will be found in the original document deposited with the Australian National University.

vii. A conference was held between the Company and the Federation Committee on the 5th and 6th January, 1960 at Lautoka. All the clauses of the draft Contract submitted by the Federation Committee were discussed at length. When the question of over production during 1960 was under discussion, the Committee suggested that in order to get over the surplus the growers should not plant any cane during 1960. The Company strenuously objected to the suggestion. The conference was then adjourned to 2nd February, 1960 at the request of the Company.

viii. Further conference was held between the Company and the Committee on the 2nd and 3rd February, 1960. At this conference the Company placed further amendments to its original draft contract which is annexed hereto and Marked (4). This made the Company's draft contract even worse from the growers' point of view. The Company's proposal was rejected and further discussion took place on the growers' proposed contract. Conference was adjourned to 29th February, 1960 at the request of the Company. Owing to the absence of the Company's Chief Manager from Fiji, the conference was held on the 14th March, 1960 instead of the 29th February.

ix. At the Conference on the 14th March 1960, the Company withdrew its previous draft contract and submitted a new one in its place, a copy whereof is annexed hereto and marked (5). The term in the new offer was reduced from 10 years to 2 years and several more stringent provisions were added which would enable the Company to compel all growers to deliver their cane to the mill at their own cost by lorry contract. Naturally this could not be accepted by the Committee. The Company's Chief Manager thereupon unilaterally declared a deadlock and said to the Committee that he will report to His Excellency the Governor that the parties had reached a deadlock and will ask him to appoint a Commission. The Committee submitted that the Company had so far only resorted to shock tactics and had not seriously commenced to negotiate. The Committee was willing to negotiate further, if such negotiations were carried on in a fair and business like manner. He was also informed that the growers will not agree to the appointment of a Commission.

x. On the 7th May, 1960 His Excellency the Governor met some members of the Federation Committee at Lautoka. At this informal meeting His Excellency informed the members that the Company had reported to the Government that a deadlock had been reached and had suggested the appointment of a Commission of Enquiry. His Excellency stated that the Government proposed to set up a high powered Commission to enquire into the economics of the industry. In view of the past experience of

Commissions appointed in disputes between the Company and the growers and the Company and its workers, the members informed His Excellency that a Commission will not be acceptable to the growers. His Excellency also [said that during his] proposed visit to Australia he would communicate with the directors of the Company in Sydney.

xi. Certain correspondence then ensued between the Government and the Committee, which is annexed hereto and marked (6).

xii. A conference was held at the Government House on the 8th and 9th June, 1960, under the Chairmanship of His Excellency the Governor. The Committee in order to effect a speedy settlement and harvesting of 1960 cane offered to sell sufficient cane to manufacture 199,000 tons of sugar under the terms and conditions of the 1950-960 contract. This offer the Company did not accept. The Company's representative said that the Company would look into such a proposal only if the growers representatives agreed to accept a Commission of Enquiry.

xiii. Up till this date all the negotiations had taken place between the Company and the Federation Committee as the representatives of all growers irrespective of their race or creed. But after the Company declared a deadlock, a defunct union of Fijian growers was hastily revived and two small new unions of Fijians were formed in Ba and Sigatoka districts through the instrumentality of the Fijian Administration and the representatives of these three Fijian unions for the first time appeared on the scene at this conference at the Government House.

xiv. The Committee held meetings of growers in all important centres to obtain the views of the growers on the government's proposal to appoint a Commission. The growers at each centre unanimously rejected the proposal and His Excellency was advised accordingly.

xiv. On the 27th June, 1960 the Federation Committee at the invitation of His Excellency the Governor met him at Suva. His Excellency expressed the views that the present deadlock in the sugar industry would harm Fiji as a whole and said that the grower's proposal to set up co-operative Mills in Fiji has been taken to mean in some quarters that one section of the community was attempting to take over the entire sugar industry and that it would lead to political strike and bitterness among different races in the Colony. His Excellency further added that if the present deadlock continued, Fiji will face an economic disaster and this will cause the authorities in the Colonial Office and other officials in United Kingdom to be alarmed and it was possible that a Royal Commission may be set up and the people who have unreasonably withheld support or opposed a Commission of Enquiry may not come out well.

His Excellency submitted a proposal and asked the Committee for its reply as soon as possible. A copy of His Excellency the Governor's proposal is annexed hereto and marked (7). This proposal is vague and ambiguous in many respects. Clarifications on certain points had to be obtained and growers had to be consulted before replying to this proposal. This was taken unfortunately by His Excellency the Governor as delaying tactics on the part of the Committee. In the absence of the Committee's chief spokesman Mr. AD Patel, certain correspondence passed between the Government and the Committee, copies whereof are annexed hereto and marked (8).

xv. On the 12th July, 1960 the growers' and the Company's representatives met at Lautoka where the Company put forward conditions and demands in respect of sale and purchase of 1960 crop which in effect reduced the price and nullified certain advantages which the growers possessed under the 1950-60 contract and in its place imposed certain monetary obligations on the growers. The meeting was then adjourned.

xvi. On the 20th July, 1960, the Company and the Committee together with the three new Fijian Unions sat in a conference to negotiate agreement for the sale of 1960 crop. The Committee from its side readily conceded the Company's demand for a share in the deductions for the burnt cane and also undertook to share liability for the loss suffered by a grower through lightening strikes. The Company stuck to its other demands. Talks went on till 23rd July, 1960. However no agreement was reached for the following reasons:

a) The Company insisted that the mills should close on 22nd January, 1961 even if all growers' quota was not harvested by then. This was contrary to practice and to the terms of 1950-60 agreement under which the Company was bound to buy all growers cane.

b) The Company refused to accept obligation to buy from each and every grower a fixed quantity of cane.

c) The Company refused the allocation of the quota on an area basis.

The Conference was adjourned to enable the Committee to hold a conference of its members at Nadi on the 24th July, 1960. The meeting did not take place because one member was late in arriving. It transpired later that one of the members, Mr. JP Bayly, had already arranged a meeting with the Company that afternoon without any prior consultation with his colleagues of the Federation Committee.

xvii. On Sunday the 24th July, 1960 five out of the nineteen members of the Federation Committee broke away and separately signed terms and conditions for the sale of 1960 cane on behalf of the Fiji Kisan Sangh and the Labasa Kisan Sangh. The signatories agreed to recommend these terms and conditions to their growers.[8]

xviii. On 24th July, 1960, mass meetings of growers were held in Nadi and Ba. The growers unanimously rejected the 24th July, 1960 arrangement reached between the Company and these five members viz: Messrs JP Bayly, Ayodhya Prasad, DS Sharma, Shiunath and Vijay Singh.

xix. On the 2nd August, 1960 a written proposal signed by the representative of all Unions of the Federation Committee, including the Fiji Kisan Sangh and with the approval of the President of the Labasa Kisan Sangh and the President of the Vanualevu Farmers' Union, was handed to the Company's Chief Manager at Nausori. A copy of the proposal is annexed hereto and marked (9). Though the growers were not willing to accept 24th July Agreement and though the representatives of the Fiji Kisan Sangh and Labasa Kisan Sangh had joined in the new proposal, the Company rejected it summarily and the deadlock continued.

xx. On the 11th August, 1960, the Company opened its Labasa Mill. The growers gradually through economic and other pressures began to harvest cane though they are against the 24th July arrangement.

xxi. After holding meetings of growers in various districts Mr. Bayly returned to the Committee.

xxii. On the 19th August, 1960 Messrs JP Bayly, AD Patel and SM Koya interviewed His Excellency the Governor. Mr. Bayly informed the Governor that the growers were not willing to accept the 24th July arrangement and that the Government should undertake to pay for any cane which may be left out from a grower's allotted quota by reason of the Company closing the mills on 22nd January. The Governor refused to accept this suggestion.

xxiii. On the 31st August, 1960 the Committee placed another proposal before His Excellency the Governor through the kind offices of the District Commissioner Mr. [QVL] Weston, a copy of which is annexed hereto and marked (10). This proposal was not accepted.

---

8 According to the Agreement, enough cane would be harvested during 1960 to produce 199,000 tons of sugar. The cane left standing would be added to the tonnage quota for 1961. Half the area of standing cane would be cut in the first round, while the second would be based on tonnage. The mills would close on 22 January, 1961. Patel's group wanted the second half to be cut on acreage basis and the mills to remain open until an equal proportion of each farmer's cane was harvested.

xxiv. On the following day at the suggestion of His Excellency the Governor, Mr. AD Patel, Mr. SM Koya and Mr. SB Patel went to Suva and signed a proposal which emanated from official sources and to which His Excellency the Governor and his official advisors appeared to be favourably inclined.

A copy of the proposal is annexed hereto and marked (11). This proposal was rejected after two days. We have reasons to believe that this proposal was rejected due to opposition of the unofficial members, three of whom were either directly or indirectly concerned in bringing about the 24th July arrangements.

xxv. Between 1st and 31st August the growers in public meetings held in all centres again confirmed the rejection of the 24th July arrangement and decided to send a deputation to the Right Honourable the Secretary of State for the Colonies. Thereupon the Government posted military and special constables in large numbers in all cane growing districts and the three mills in Vitilevu were opened. In spite of a lot of pressure, harassment and coercion only a small number of growers harvested cane. If no agreement is reached about 80% of this year's crop will remain unharvested this year.

From all this it will be seen that the Federation Committee has left no stone unturned to resolve the present deadlock. According to our information, out of 12,500 cane growers about 11,000 growers are still not harvesting cane. For the small amount of cane which is being harvested the Government is incurring huge expenditure in maintaining military personnel and Special Constables and the Company is also losing heavily on account of not being able to operate their mills at full capacity.

The growers only ask that the quota for this year's harvest to be fixed on an area basis and that an assurance be given by the Company or the Government that every grower's cane will be purchased to the extent of the fixed quota. Giving such an assurance is not likely to cost much (if at all) to the Government and the benefit which will accrue therefrom to the Government and the Colony through a full scale harvesting of cane and through the friendly relations re-established between the growers, the Company and the Government will far outweigh the sacrifice which it may involve on the part of the Government and the tax payers of this Colony.

We respectfully beg to point out that the present expenditure incurred by the Government will only result in economic disaster for all parties concerned, including the Government of Fiji. If you can see your way to persuade the Government to take a slight financial risk in the direction to alley fears of the growers, some £4,000,000 worth of crops can still be harvested and favourable conditions created for future negotiations.

The dispute can also be settled if the Company can be persuaded to withdraw its insistence on closing the mills on a particular date regardless of whether all growers' cane has been harvested or not and agree to fix the quota for harvest on an area basis. Even if the dispute in regard to the standing crop is settled there remains the question as to what is to be done about the future. Unless this is settled immediately the growers cannot cultivate the ratoon after harvesting this year. They cannot plant cane next year for the 1962 harvest.

Unless the contract for 1961-63 is immediately settled or some alternative arrangement is made the sugar industry for the coming three (3) years will be in doldrums. The appointment of a Commission of Enquiry does not at all help this immediate problem because:

a). The Commission of Enquiry will have no jurisdiction over the Company's head office in Sydney. It will have, therefore, to depend on the good will of the Company to supply information to the Commission or to produce its books of account. The offer by the Company to make their books of account available to a Chartered Accountant nominated by the Commission is not very helpful in the Commission's investigations.

b). If the Company refuses to produce its books of account to the Commission or to the growers' representative at the enquiry for inspection and cross examination, the Commission will not be in a position to enforce its production and inspection by the other side.

c). The growers' case cannot be adequately put or the facts and figures submitted by the Company challenged properly unless an expert is brought from overseas. This would mean considerable expenses to the growers.

d). The enquiry cannot be carried in haste if it has to be correct and thorough.

e). The findings of the Commission even after the expenditure of all the money and time involved in such an enquiry, cannot be binding on either party. The parties will have to come to a negotiating table to settle a contract in any event.

The Company has tremendously boosted up the book-value of its assets in Fiji in the last few years as the following figures show:

Year	Book-Value
1955	4,888,993. 0. 0
1957	5,895,521. 0. 0
1958	13,622,326. 0. 0
1959	14,037,759. 0. 0
1960	14,058,381. 0. 0

If the Company wants to increase its profits in the same proportion by reducing the price of cane or only enter into contract from year to year, neither the growers nor the Colony can maintain their present standard of living and they cannot afford to face such disputes every year. The problems facing the sugar industry can only be solved:

a). by the United Kingdom giving assistance to the growers in setting up co-operative mills;

b). divesting the sugar quotas for Fiji from the Company and vesting it into the Government;

c). insisting that as long as there is sugar cane available in Fiji that the Company fulfill the quota only from sugar manufactured in Fiji and not from Australia or any other country;

d). by Government nationalizing and taking over the sugar mills;

e). by establishing a statutory corporation in which the Government should own 51% of the total shares and the growers the remaining 49 percent. Such corporations to set up and run its own mills;

f). by helping the growers to form a joint stock company with 51% of the total shares allotted to the growers and the balance to be made available to the public;

g). by controlling or prohibiting monopolies by legislation as is done in the United Kingdom, United States and many other countries.

Sugar industry is the economic backbone of the Colony and the growers are contemplating to send a deputation to England to wait upon the Right Honourable the Secretary of State for the Colonies and your assistance in making necessary appointments will be gratefully appreciated.

This Memorandum has become rather too long. However, as the matter is of vital importance to the growers and to the people of this Colony, you will appreciate that this was unavoidable. We hope and trust that it will receive your sympathetic and favourable consideration.

In conclusion we thank you for affording us this opportunity to present this memorandum to you on behalf of the Federation Committee and the cane growers of Fiji.

AD Patel et.al

65: Submission to the Eve Commission, 9 March 1961[9]

Fiji is probably the only country in the Commonwealth which supplies sugar under the Commonwealth Sugar Agreement which has only one sole manufacturer. It is a monopoly which holds the quota on behalf of Fiji but, because it has monopolistic position, it treats Fiji as a closed shop for all time to come. This monopolistic position gives the Company certain advantages with the other parties engaged in the industry which manufacturers in other countries do not enjoy. They and the growers are 'married.' If the growers do not enter into a contract with them or accept their terms, then they find there is no other buyer. Because of that monopoly, they are in a position to dictate terms to the growers; because they are a monopoly they are in a position to dictate terms to their workers; because they are a monopoly, to some extent they can dictate terms to the Government on account of the important position of the sugar industry in the economic life of Fiji.

It does not stop there. This monopoly operates by remote control. Their headquarters are in Sydney. All their books are in Sydney. The monopoly is of such a nature that one of its outstanding examples is right here. It is that even the Sugar Industry Commission will have to go to Sydney in order to check and probe into the accounts of the Company. If the Commission cannot have the Company's books produced in Fiji, I very much doubt whether the Commissioner of Inland Revenue can get them here. That means that this position seriously affects the revenue of this Colony and thereby directly the Government and indirectly other taxpayers and the people of Fiji. [Patel quoted the price of molasses as one example of the results or remote control].

On the question of introducing an element of competition, I would suggest that if co-operative sugar mills were established where members of the society are growers themselves, it would solve many problems and difficulties that we have to face in Fiji. In the very first place, we cut out the processor middleman. We produce the cane but because somebody else processes that cane, we have got to give him a profit. The co-operative mill will then get all the profits.

Another advantage will be that with these co-operative mills we will be in a position to start mills in rural areas. Just now our biggest problem in Fiji is the

---

9   The Commission comprised Sir Malcolm Trustram Eve QC, JS Wheatly of the Colonial Office and JM Bennett, an accountant. See Report of the Fiji Sugar Industry Inquiry Commission, Legislative Council Paper 20/1961. The Commission found nothing seriously wrong with the CSR's operations in Fiji. It endorsed the CSR's proposal for a wholly Fiji-owned subsidiary called South Pacific Sugar Mills Limited. Predictably, it fingered Patel as the chief villain of the piece, saying 'We are satisfied that this leader is a very able man, and that he could provide sorely needed leadership of the right kind.'

problem of unemployment in rural areas. If these mills were located in rural areas, there would be considerable savings on the transport costs of cane. While we have to transport 7 tons of cane to a distance of 80 miles for turning into a ton of sugar, if we had a mill in Sigatoka, we would have to transport only one ton of sugar to the Lautoka wharf. It would cut down the transport costs to practically one-seventh. The mills should have a capacity of 600 tons. Any mill with less capacity would not be economical. There will be some difference in the cost of production but all the proceeds will remain in Fiji and this will help the government and people in Fiji and solve the problem of unemployment in rural areas.

The idea of establishing new sugar mills is not new. There are co-operative mills all over the world, especially in countries where they are producing sugar. There are co-operative mills in Australia and 34 already in operation in India. The mills cannot be built immediately. We have to wait for finance, arrange for purchase of machinery and so on. It would be about two years before we start production. Therefore, establishing co-operative mills is not an immediate solution of the problem but it is one of the best long term solutions.

[Regarding measures to control the industry] my first suggestion is that legislation should be passed compelling the Company to keep its account [of its Fiji operation] in Fiji. Since this is a national industry the books of account should be subject to audit by the Audit Department of the Government of Fiji. It should be made obligatory on the Company to produce their book of accounts before Commissions of Inquiry or the Commissioner of Inland Revenue, or any such body like a court of arbitration, if they are required by them.

The next measure of control should be the constitution of a Sugar Board. In all the sugar producing countries of the British Commonwealth which are under the British Commonwealth Sugar Agreement, probably Fiji is the only country where the Government exercises no control over the industry. The parties have been trying to reach an agreement for the last two years. The Company placed their proposed contract before the growers in January 1959, and from that time up till now, no agreement has so far been reached. The growers have complained that this is largely due to the monopolistic attitude of the Company of 'take it or leave it.' Now after all sides have placed their proposals before the Commission, and there is no agreement, we are all most anxious to save the industry because that is the very life blood of our economy. If an agreement is arrived at, there is still great need for supervision over the working of that agreement by the Sugar Board to see that both sides faithfully carry out their obligations under the agreement.

In the event of no agreement being reached, the Sugar Board should take over the control of the industry on the same lines as those prevailing in, say, places like Queensland and Mauritius. That is, the millers will go on with their milling operations and the growers would go on with their operations of producing sugar cane, and all the production of sugar and other by-products will be put on the market by this Board. They will decide a fair and equitable division of the proceeds between the growers and the millers, and they themselves will pay these proceeds to the respective parties. If these suggestions are carried out, a lot of misunderstanding and mutual suspicion can disappear between the two important sections of the industry, namely the millers and the growers. It can establish industrial peace and good relations in the industry, and it could ensure a fair and equitable distribution of rewards to both sides.

That brings me to the next question of quota. In 1950, when the conference was held in London for the negotiation of the Commonwealth Sugar Agreement, delegates were invited from all sugar-producing countries. Fiji's quota was fixed at 170,000 tons. Then after that, at these meetings to revise and fix the price of sugar cane for the ensuing year, the government did not send any of its own representatives. So it was all left to the good offices of the CSR. The Commonwealth Sugar Agreement was signed by the CSR on behalf of Fiji. We [growers] are included in the sugar industry [on whose behalf the CSR signed the Agreement] and that is why I contend that the Fiji sugar quota is held by the Company on behalf of the sugar industry of Fiji and not as their personal individual property. I therefore say that it is necessary to divest the quota because at this inquiry, now, the Company has gone to the extent of saying that the quota absolutely belongs to them, and that it is their own preserve on which nobody dare encroach; they hold the growers of the Colony as hostages that 'if anybody tries to take away any portion of our quota, we stop buying cane from each and every one of you.' In the best interests of the sugar industry and of the Colony, these quotas should be divested immediately from the Company and vested in the Sugar Board.

Next, I come to the Price Stabilisation Fund. At the time when this Fund was established, the growers were not consulted. After the establishment of the Fund was announced in Fiji, the growers opposed it. The Fund was established by conference between the United Kingdom government and the CSR. Our share of the contribution to the Fund came to 75 per cent and the Company's 25 per cent. When the legislation was passed and when some of this Fund was to be refunded, returned to the growers, the statute did not provide for returning to the growers the same share of the contribution which they made to the Fund. We recommend that the Fund should be divided in proportions, the Ordinance should be repealed and that the funds should be divided in the actual proportion in which it was contributed to by both the growers and the millers under the Agreement and that further collection or deduction of the Price Stabilisation fund should be discontinued. [It was]

Over a number of years, the Government has been collecting a direct tax in the form of sugar export tax and it does not give anything in return to the industry. The Government provides disease control to the copra industry, the banana industry, and for the production of rice. As far as sugar cane is concerned—the main industry of the Colony—the Department of Agriculture does not do anything. If the measures of control are carried out in respect of the Company's account, there is every likelihood that the Government's revenue may increase. It will not be necessary to levy this tax on the industry especially at this time when it has been agreed all round that one section of the industry is heavily indebted and in financial difficulties, and when it is said that indebtedness is increasing at an alarming rate. I want the export tax repealed.

It is admitted all around that the relations between the farmers and the Company and the cutters have deteriorated considerably in the last couple of years. In these circumstances, what is the best way to re-establish good relations between growers and the Company? I wish to submit that the only way is to have properly elected representatives of the growers to negotiate with the Company. The growers can be divided into seven constituencies—Nadroga, Nadi, Lautoka, Ba, Tavua, Ra and Labasa. Each of these should, by secret ballot, elect one member as a representative and those seven should constitute the leaders of the growers. Their term should be for two years and there should be an election every two years. We feel that a Board with growers' representatives as we suggest would be fully empowered to carry on negotiations with the Company and also with the growers and any agreement arrived at between such a Board of representatives of the growers and the Company or the Sugar Board would be binding on the growers. It is suggested that there should be only one Union of the growers and that they should have the power to speak on behalf of all the growers.

There are quite a substantial number of growers who would prefer not to join any organization and in the present state in which some of the unions are run, I don't blame the farmers who do not wish to belong to any of the unions. Our other trouble is with our national or racial traits. Indians are known as the world's most extreme individualists. Alone we work very well, but find it difficult to work in groups. It is unfortunate, but we have to accept it. We have tried for a number of years to work together. We wish we could learn to work in groups, in cooperatives as it were, but we have not reached that state of self-discipline and the disinterestedness necessary for any such cooperative help. In these circumstances the only alternative left is the way I suggest—to elect representatives for each area.

[Referring to the varieties of cane] we give the Company the right to select a list of varieties of cane and when they are choosing these varieties, they would naturally have their own interest in mind. If they are fair enough they would also try to consider our point of view and offer varieties that would be suitable and fair to both sides. We think that the growers should be given that same right of selection. I think that will be fair because both parties have got a say in the choice of cane. The Company has the first choice and the growers the second choice. If any party is going to be adversely affected, it is likely to be the grower and not the Company.

The price of cane should be estimated before the commencement of the crushing season and paid within seven days from the date of delivery. Any balance which may be found due to the grower should be paid, with interest, within two weeks of the closing of the crushing season. We contend that we are the sellers and the Company is the buyer. This is the raw material which we are out to sell and which the Company is out to buy. In our present condition, we would like to get the estimated cash price for the whole amount sold to the Company. It has been emphasized all along that the growers are heavily in debt. Some of the items of debt such as having to buy goods on credit because he has to wait for the proceeds of the cane, he has to pay for his children's school fees and for this he has to borrow money because he has to wait for the cane proceeds. He borrows money at a high rate of interest to pay his cane cutters by way of bonus and premium. If he was receiving his payment in cash on delivery or as soon as possible, he would not have to go to the storekeepers to buy on credit and he would not have to go to the moneylender to get a loan for payment of bonus to cane cutters. As I understand it, where the processor is buying the cane directly from the grower, he either pays the whole amount in cash or he pays interest on the balance of the amount which he pays at the end of crushing season.

66: Reforming the Sugar Industry, 2 May 1969

I move that in the opinion of this Council the Sugar Industry Ordinance should be repealed. For the purposes of this motion, I would first like to go back to the origins and through the history of the existing Ordinance, and then comment on the deficiencies and defects in this Ordinance to meet with the exigencies and requirements of the industry. It is well known that this Ordinance was based on the report of the Fiji Sugar Inquiry Commission which was headed by Sir Malcolm Trustram Eve as he then was and who is now Lord Silsoe. The Ordinance was enacted at the time when the dust was raised by the sugar dispute which ranged over a period of more than two years. The dispute started in 1959 and had not ended even in 1961. In the Report, the Commission went as far back as the sugar dispute in 1943 and also took into consideration some of the recommendations made by Doctor Shepherd in his Report.[10]

---

10   Cecil Y Shepherd, *The Sugar Industry in Fiji* (London: His Majesty's Stationery Office, 1945).

As far as the present Ordinance goes, the Report of the Fiji Sugar Inquiry Commission has been enshrined as the Holy Bible of Fiji's sugar industry, so much so that the Ordinance expressly lays down that the Report shall be followed as far as practicable. In carrying out the respective functions under this Ordinance the Independent Chairman, the Independent Vice-Chairman, the Independent Accountant, the Board, the Counsel and officers of those bodies or the Government shall be guided generally by the Report of the Fiji Sugar Inquiry Commission. And this happens to be a report, the first recommendation of which has been rejected summarily out of hand by Her Majesty's Britannic Government in London. I refer to Chapter Two of the Report:

Fiji Quota for Sugar.

> Throughout most of the world the export, sale and purchase of sugar is rigidly controlled. About 30 million tons of cane sugar and 24 million tons of beet sugar are made every year. Of this, Fiji makes just over 200,000 tons of cane sugar or 1 ton in every 270 tons of world sugar production. The greatest single benefit to the sugar industry and to the economy of the whole of Fiji would be to allow to be exported and sold to the United Kingdom, 50,000 more tons of sugar every year. (I emphasize the words, 'more tons of sugar every year'). Fiji has the working population and suitable land. We say with all sincerity to the power that be in London and Suva that if they can find a way to do this they will in the long run make more people happy with a worthwhile job and at cheaper cost than probably in any other island country in the world.

And then he goes on to say:

> We develop the subject in Chapter Five. We make, as the first of many recommendations, a strong plea that somehow and very soon Fiji might get this 50,000 tons; so small in relation to the world, but very important to these small islands.

We had a Development Commissioner in Fiji who also held the same opinion and thought that Fiji's quota and production should be gradually raised by 50,000 tons a year till it reached a half million tons. We have so far seen no indications of London attaching any importance to this most important and first recommendation of the Report which our local laws make a holy book to be followed by all those office bearers and bodies which were created by that law. The most important creation under the statute following the recommendations in the Report is the Sugar Board. The Fiji Sugar Inquiry Commission accepted the recommendation contained in Doctor Shepherd's report as a guide for the creation of such a body. In 1943-1944, when Doctor Shepherd was sent by the

Secretary of State for the Colonies to make enquiries in the industry and make his recommendations, the most important and burning topic of the day was how to check and scrutinize the price which the Colonial Sugar Refining Company paid to the cane growers for the purchase of cane. The contract existing at the time was based on the price of sugar obtained by the Company together with the price of molasses which was bought by the Company itself at a nominal price of £1 per ton.

As the price was based on the price of sugar which the Company received, the only way the growers could find out whether they have received the proper price or not would depend on whether the figures on which the Company has ascertained the price are correct and accurate. The Company, being a monopolistic concern carrying on its operations in this country over a large number of years, had more or less in its own estimation and in the estimation of the colonial government established itself as Caesar's wife who was always above suspicion. It had taken the attitude that whatever it said must be accepted as gospel truth without any question, that its modus operandi should never be questioned or suspected. And the Company refused to change its attitude and adjust to the fast changing times. It wanted to remain where it was in its privileged position, even though the whole world was changing and adjusting itself to the new conditions and requirements of life all the world over. In order to create a sense of confidence in the minds of the growers that they receive a fair and accurate price under that contract, Dr Shepherd recommended that there should be a Board which would go into the necessary accounts ascertaining the price and to certify whether the price declared and paid by the Company was correct.

Dr Shepherd's recommendation was strongly opposed by the Colonial Sugar Refining Company, and the Secretary of State, Oliver Lyttleton, made a solemn promise to the growers in this Colony on the floor of the House of Commons appealing to the growers and the leaders to have trust in him, to go before an investigator that he was sending, and to place all their complaints before him. He promised that justice will be done. In spite of that public declaration, Dr Shepherd's report was put away somewhere on the shelf of the Colonial Office, the Colonial Sugar Refining Company's voice proved stronger than the recommendation of the person whom the Colonial Office had selected and in whom they wanted the growers and the leaders in this country to put their trust.

When the Sugar Inquiry Commission held its hearing, this matter was placed before the Commission by that large section of cane growers whom Mr. Koya and I represented before the Commission. The Commission in its report recommended that a board be set up which was to be known as the Sugar Board. But strangely enough the Commission, could not get rid of its preconceived motions about the treatment of subject races in the colonies. The report suggested a nomenclature which in itself could appear very strange and naturally raised questions in the mind of an independent person. Right throughout this world, we have boards and the boards have their chairmen and their vice-chairmen and their accountants, but nowhere in the world will you find this particular and peculiar nomenclature—'Independent Chairman,' 'Independent Vice-Chairman,' 'Independent Accountant.' One would think that since the word 'independent' is used, there must be a provision in the law providing sanctions to ensure that the Chairman, the Vice-Chairman and the Accountant really act independently. They would, in fact, be independent and will have to be independent.

But strangely enough, in the Ordinance, there is nowhere any requirement or any sanction which binds the Chairman, the Vice-Chairman nor the Accountant to be really independent and impartial. We have got legislation in this Colony creating a Broadcasting Commission. The law has placed an obligation on that Commission to be impartial and for any breach of impartiality, they are liable to punishment. But as far as the Sugar Industry Ordinance goes, none of these luminaries are in any way bound by law to carry out their duties [impartially] and in the event of any breach of independence making them liable to punishment with the result that there is all the time repetition ad nauseam of this nomenclature in this country—Independent Chairman, Independent Vice-Chairman, Independent Accountant—without any guarantees that they are, in fact, independent. And in the working of this Ordinance over all these years, the growers have found to their dismay that these luminaries are not, in fact, independent or impartial.

The very first Independent Chairman of the Board was selected from England. He was a retired Vice-Air Marshall.[11] And this contract which Fiji Sugar Inquiry Commission had drafted and incorporated in its report, was put through in such a way that it became a contract of general application against the wishes of the majority of the cane growers. I shall deal with that in detail later on, but for the present, it is not only the creation of this Board with this strange nomenclature and no obligations [that is of concern] but also the creation of another advisory body called the Sugar Advisory Council. The law provided for such machinery and I say that that was provided deliberately to strengthen the position of the Company and weaken that of the growers and the workers engaged in the sugar industry. The five representatives who are appointed on the Council to represent the millers are appointed in consultation with the Company by the Governor.

There is no doubt that as far as the Company's representatives are concerned, they will truly and completely reflect and voice the millers on the Council. But as far as the growers were concerned, the law created again such a peculiar machinery which would give a facade of democracy and in fact introduced conflicting and contradictory elements both on the growers' side as well as the

---

11 Sir Arthur Sanders GCB, KBE, 1898-1974, retired in 1956 after serving as Deputy Chief of Air Staff.

workers. By some strange logic, the Commission recommended that the sirdars of the cane cutting gangs should elect a panel of representatives on behalf of the growers and from that panel the Governor would nominate five members on the Sugar Advisory Council. It was a well known fact then, as it is now, that by and large the sirdars of the cane cutting gangs were more or less pro-Company men. And even to this day, under some excuse or another, the sirdars of the cane cutting gangs are invited and entertained by the Company at its various functions.

Throughout all these long years, the Company never found it necessary to hold seminars for the sirdars. But now it has and the growers are not blind. They know and they see what the real reason behind it is. Naturally, they all question that a man who is elected for one particular purpose, namely to act as the foreman of the cane cutters and to see that the cane is properly harvested, loaded and delivered according to the programme, should be presumed to be a man who represents the growers' voice in all respects in the industry. But this absurdity was introduced for one reason alone, that this college of electors, if I may so describe them, should be pro-millers' men. They were not satisfied only with that manipulation. They went further, that even with the sirdars of the cane cutting gangs, they were not to be allowed one man one vote system which is the established normal democratic method of electing a representative. They introduced a loaded system by which [for] all the candidates appearing on the list, the points will be counted in accordance with the number which the sirdar votes for each of its candidates, with the result that the people who were supported by small minority of growers scored quite a large number of points and the candidates who enjoyed the support and confidence of an overwhelming majority of growers scored less number of points. And the outcome right throughout has been that in the council, the majority of growers are represented by a minority out of the five.

A situation is [thus] created in which all these members are presumed to represent the cane growers and they give their diverse and conflicting opinions in the name of the representatives with the result that the Company's opinion and advice as to what would be the true and genuine and real opinion of the farmers would prevail in the eyes of the Independent Chairman as against the conflicting views of the so-called farmers' representatives. The same thing has happened about the workers' representatives. In the sugar industry there exist two unions. The Sugar Workers' Union which is a large body and which is non-racial, has from time to time endeavoured to see that both unions are amalgamated and there is one Workers' Union so that their voice and their bargaining position may be strengthened. Unfortunately, one union which is described as the Tradesmen's Union is in fact an overwhelmingly racial union consisting of one particular race. And on the workers' side, the representatives of the workers on the Council have at least two or three divisions; one, the Tradesmen's Union representative who is elected on the democratic basis, (one man, one vote) and two, representatives of the Sugar Workers' Union one of whom is elected from the Western Division consisting of workers in the six districts in the west of Viti Levu and one from Labasa. There again, they have to submit a panel of names with the result that the people who are elected and whose names are submitted are not both elected with the majority of votes, but one with the majority and one with the second largest majority will be there. And the Governor has got the discretion as to whom he will appoint and the discretion has not always worked in favour of the workers. This Advisory Council, therefore, is in fact a packed council and the most important sections of the industry, namely the real producers of sugar and the workers who process cane into sugar, are submerged and the voice of the milling Company is strengthened and fortified.

The question then was [whether there was sufficient work] for the three members of the Board, namely the Independent Chairman, the Independent Vice-Chairman, the Independent Accountant, the Secretary of the Board, the interpreter, the clerical staff, and other appendages required for the office? I say, 'No.' The question of going into the accounts of the Company by the Independent Chairman assisted by the Independent Accountant as is provided in the existing law, commences at the close of the season. It does not entail the whole year's work. So, in order to create a resemblance of work for this Board, the system of allotting quotas to each farmer is introduced. Since the creation of the Board and since the coming into effect of the existing contract, there has not been a single year when the Company has not harvested and taken the entire crop for that year, regardless of the quota allowed or allotted to each individual grower.

The quota, therefore, is just a fictitious machinery which keeps the Chairman and the staff of the Board occupied in fixing what the national quota for the year should be, how much of that quota should be allotted to which grower, and how much tonnage the Company should crush during this season. This is all theory, but in practice every year the Company crushes all the cane produced during that season and the quota has no practical value or effect on the crops. It reminds me of a story of a devil who made a contract with his disciple saying that he would work for him on one condition that the moment he was without work he would eat him. The disciple then assigned all sorts of jobs to this devil to save himself from being eaten. Even then his resourceful mind could not cope with his other jobs, so in the end he just said, 'You keep on climbing up and down this staircase.' That is how the provision of a quota system has worked for the farmers as far as the Sugar Board is concerned.

Then has this law really been observed by the members of the Sugar Board, the officers of the Sugar Board, or by the Governor in his appointment of these officers? I say, 'No.'

I mentioned previously that our first Independent Chairman came from England, but he did not remain long here. He left the service and went back home. He had no experience or knowledge of the sugar industry and as often happens in this country, the only repository of knowledge and experience in the sugar industry is this one sugar Company. That Independent Chairman had to get his knowledge and his advice for every little thing from that Company, because over all these number of years, even the government and even the Department of Agriculture whose duty it is to have some knowledge and experience of the main agricultural produce of this country, have themselves been blissfully innocent of all knowledge or experience. Should any visitor from outside come to this country and go to the Department of Agriculture to find out something about the sugar industry, he would be referred to the Company's officials. It has happened in the past, it happens now and until the system changes, it will go on happening for ever.

His successor who came, with all due respect to his judicial ability and experience, I am pained to say that he also did not have any knowledge or experience, either in the sugar industry or any branch of that industry.[12] What is more, the Government by then had found out that even though these provisions are made to keep the Sugar Board officers busy, the work was still insufficient to keep the Independent Chairman occupied full time, with the result that his services and time are used in all sorts of stop-gap requirements. He sits as Judge of a Court of Appeal; he sits on a Tribunal on the Immigration Appeals, and also on the Income Tax Tribunal. Here is an officer who is to act as an Independent Chairman who has neither the knowledge nor the experience of the industry which he is supposed to guide and control. This is his part-time work for which the industry pays him full-time salary.

In the ordinary course of business, everyone believes that he who pays the piper has got the right to call the tune, but not so in the case of the Independent Chairman, Independent Vice-Chairman and the Independent Accountant of the Sugar Board. Even those who pay him have no voice or say in how much he should be paid, what should be his terms and conditions of employment, how many other services he is bound to give daily. But all this is fixed by the Governor and there has not been a single occasion that I know of when the growers who meet the major share of the expenditure have ever been consulted on the matter. The Independent Vice-Chairman, according to the report of the Fiji Sugar Inquiry Commission, should be a senior Fijian who is neutral, on the

---

12 Justice CJ Marsak, former Chief Justice of Western Samoa.

ground that the larger part of the land on which the sugar is grown is Fijian land! Firstly, in compliance with that recommendation, the Minister for Labour was appointed as the Independent Vice-Chairman [Ratu Edward Cakobau] but as soon as he vacated the post, this recommendation was blissfully forgotten. The Ordinance which prescribes that all these officers of the Board directly or indirectly, and through them, those who are engaged in the industry, are bound by the Report and every word of that Report is to be treated as holy, does not seem to bind the Governor or the Colonial Office in London. The result is that the successor to the Minister for Labour is a non-Fijian, he is a practising lawyer and a politician who is temporarily out of the political arena, not by choice but necessity.[13]

When you put all these factors together, what do you expect to come out from such a Board? Nothing which will create any satisfaction or remove any grievance or discontent from the farmers or the workers who are the most important sections of the industry. Coupled with this is the fact that the headquarters of the Sugar Board are located in Suva, away from the sugar districts. When it was decided that the headquarters should be in Suva, the then Independent Chairman gave these two reasons for his choice: one; that the Colonial Sugar Refining Company's Head Office is in Suva, so he would be near to the Company's office; and the second reason he gave was that as far as he was concerned, if the headquarters were established at Lautoka, he would not have any company or social life as the only man he could mix with socially was the Governor of Fiji. These were the two reasons given by the person himself to me, as to why he preferred Suva to Lautoka. We were of the opinion that as far as the Sugar Board is concerned, Lautoka would be the proper location for the headquarters. The result is that all these years the growers and workers find themselves too remote from the Independent Chairman and the Independent Vice-Chairman who are supposed to look after their interests.

The Independent Chairman is not only close to the millers' headquarters in Suva, but he is socially close to the millers officers both in Suva and in the sugar districts when he goes there. With the growers and the workers he is remote socially and otherwise. How can you expect the growers and the workers or the public at large to believe that here is an Independent Chairman who keeps himself completely neutral and aloof, and who is ready to serve and assist anyone in that industry, however small or insignificant his position in that industry may be?

---

13 The person referred to is Andrew Deoki who lost the 1966 elections to Federation Party's Irene Jai Narayan.

Now, I come to the most important provision of the existing law. The very raison d'etre for which this law exists is to see that a contract is amicably and peacefully negotiated between the millers and the growers and for that purpose the law provides—

> That for the purposes of this Ordinance no dispute shall be deemed to exist in the sugar industry until the Independent Chairman certifies that he has endeavoured to obtain agreement between the parties concerned and has failed.

Then it goes on—

> Whenever the Independent Chairman grants such a certificate he shall notify the Chief Justice forthwith and the Chief Justice after such consultation as he may think fit, with the Governor and subject to the provisions of subsection 6 of this section, shall appoint a person or persons to decide the dispute. The Chief Justice, if he thinks fit, may direct that the senior representative of the millers and of the growers or mill workers or both as the case may be on the Council, shall sit with the person or with persons appointed to decide the dispute to act as advisers without a vote.

This law further provided: 'That two years before the expiration of the present contract he should take steps to bring about a new contract between the growers and the millers.' Negotiating a contract has proved a matter of serious importance not only for those who are engaged in that industry but also to those people at large and the government of this country as the sugar industry happens to be the first and most important industry in the Colony. The most important reason for the establishment of all these Sugar Boards and for the engagement of the Independent Chairman is to see Chief Justice and the Governor so that some sort of machinery should be employed to resolve the dispute and bring about a contract which would be binding on both sides. It is unthinkable that any careful officer would overlook or forget that duty of over-riding importance. But let me say that neither the growers' representatives nor the growers know anything about any contract for which the Independent Chairman was going to take any steps to bring the two parties together for purposes of negotiations. On the other hand, the cane growers were astounded that the Independent Chairman went around holding meetings. One such meeting of the growers was held and a limited number of selected growers were called into the 'Bamboo Room' of Nadi Hotel. Most of them were called and selected from a particular group of farmers.

And what is more, when he was discussing the question of the contract and praising the virtues of the existing contract some of the growers had the courage to tell him that the cane growers did not want this contract. He just told them summarily—'I am not here to discuss anything about the contract and I do not want to have any questions being asked,' with the result that the growers felt that as far as the Independent Chairman of the Sugar Board was concerned, he was standing by the existing contract which the Company wanted to be extended without any change. If that is called impartiality or independence, I will have to revise my knowledge of the English dictionary.

It did not stop there. The Independent Chairman, as is required under the Ordinance, submitted his report to the Government. In that report this is what he said:

> Applications for Contracts—Despite the views expressed in some quarters that the present contract is not satisfactory to the growers applications for contracts keep coming in to the office of the Sugar Board in a steady flow. These applications for the most part come from former cane farmers whose contracts were cancelled on the termination of their leases or other forms of tenancy. And from persons who had worked for years on cane farms without holding a contract of that owner.

I ask what is behind this statement? When a new contract is being negotiated and the Independent Chairman, as he is duty bound under the law, brings two parties to the contract in the Sugar Advisory Council, he made a public statement upholding the existing contract which the growers unanimously do not want and unanimously rejected in the Sugar Advisory Council on the grounds that those who are squeezed out of the industry because they lost their tenancies or leases or those who want to enter the industry to which the entry is denied at present, are willing to accept the present contract. If I was to paraphrase this report in blunt language it would only mean—'Well, if the existing farmers do not want this contract there are blacklegs to take their place.' I have already mentioned the one-sidedness of this legislation. The legislation strengthens the hand of a powerful Company against small growers and workers whose number is counted in thousands, and it is humanly impossible for all those thousands to make representation with one voice or one mind. That is why all over the world we employ democratic methods that the majority voice may be taken as the voice of the whole class or community as happens in this very Council Chamber. When the 20 shout 'aye' and 9 say 'no,' the legislation is passed and has to be observed by those nine who also said 'no.' That is considered right and proper and should be considered right and proper everywhere.

Another loophole in this law which has been taken advantage of in the past and which has not been sealed even though it was used and seen by everybody, is that there is no time limit as to when the Independent Chairman should certify and declare that a dispute exists. Time is of the utmost importance, because by 30th March, 1970 the existing contract will expire and if no contract has taken its place, accepted by more than 66 per cent of the growers and thereby becomes a contract of general application, whether you have it or not there is a dispute and there is a strike in the industry. How do you expect the grower to harvest and send his cane to the mill at the strict mercy and dictate of the buyer, without any contract? If such a position arose, the vested interests will start clamouring for the heads of the growers' leaders as they did in the past saying that they are creating strife in this country. 'They are causing instability in the industry and the growers should quietly harvest their cane and send it to the mill, and trust in the millers and God for what they will receive.'

That is the position that you may have to face unless steps are actively and promptly taken to bring about either an agreed contract or a contract by arbitration and the law. Every day that passes gives advantage to the millers and disadvantage to the farmers. The millers have a ready-made machinery. They have got expertise at their command. Even if the Government was to appoint a Court of Arbitration, say in February, and the arbitrator called the parties before him in March, the Company has all its case ready. Their representative already has everything for his brief. All he has to do is to place it before the arbitrator. It is the grower who is at a disadvantage. He has no assistance, no expertise and he [does] not [have] any means by which he can quickly collect all the necessary material to put before the arbitration fairly and properly so that the growers' interests receive a fair hearing and just consideration.

Every day that passes draws the industry nearer to where the Company can feel that these people in haste and hurry will have to give in either under the machinery of arbitration employed by the Government at the eleventh hour or through the pressure from the miller, from the Government and from the public. I say that this has been going on for long enough and the time has come when due consideration must be given to the interests of the farmers. It is they who produce this wealth. Without them this Colony's economy can be seriously hampered. Those people whose efforts and work lead to general prosperity of others, expect some consideration from others too. Already the farmers' representatives have given notice that the farmers will not accept this contract after two years and that a new contract should take its place. The growers' senior representative on behalf of the growers [Swami Rudrananda] put forward a contract for the consideration of the other side as a basis for negotiation. That contract was rejected out of hand. The farmers have made it plain by unanimous will that the existing contract is not acceptable to them and just on this the Sugar Board has already wasted more than a year. Notice was given to the Independent Chairman before the 20th February, 1968. Already more than a year has passed. If a matter of such importance is going to go before the arbitration, it is only fair that there is a fair trial and hearing. This involves sufficient and adequate time for the parties—and both parties ought to prepare their case and adequately represent their case before the arbitration. Even in an ordinary civil action in the Supreme Court, decisions are sometimes not reached even in a year or two. On a matter of this magnitude, is it too much to expect that at least the party should have eight months to a year to prepare its case in the full knowledge that they are going before the arbitration? It will help both the arbitrator and the growers and will bring satisfaction on both sides if we were given sufficient time and opportunity to prepare our case and present it. This would lead to a more satisfactory and voluntary acceptance of all. On the other hand if the time is wasted like this and the parties are hurriedly pushed before the arbitrator at the last moment, you can rest assured that whatever the award of the arbitrator you will not be able to force it down the throats of the farmers.

The next serious iniquity existing in the legislation which hampers and impedes the growers as well as the workers is in the representation of their interests on the Sugar Advisory Council. Outside Fiji this particular piece of legislation will startle the readers and that is section 13 subsection (6) which says: 'No person who is a practising barrister and solicitor and no person who is a member of the Legislative Council or a professed candidate for the Legislative Council shall be eligible to be appointed or to remain as a representative of the millers, growers or mill workers on the Council.' As I have already mentioned, the millers are blessed with competent and well experienced staff who can adequately represent the millers, secure the necessary benefits advantageous for themselves; they not only assert their rights but help in overcoming the fair and just rights of the growers and the workers, even if the millers do not have lawyers or members of the Legislative Council or a professed candidate for election for the Council to represent them.

The absurdity of the whole thing is obvious. When we see that the important members of the Sugar Board who are also the ex-officio members of the Sugar Advisory Council, one of them is a lawyer with the experience of being a Judge and a Chief Justice in Western Samoa before she became independent, a territory where not a stick of cane is grown. The Independent Vice-Chairman happens to be a practising barrister and solicitor, an ex-member of the Legislative Council and an ex-professed candidate for election to the Legislative Council.[14] Surely if these worthies can be members of the Sugar Advisory Council, considered fit and proper persons to safeguard the interests of all sections of the industry, it is difficult to understand why the same worthies or their fellow professionals, or fellow members of the Legislative Council, cannot fulfill the functions and do justice to the interests of the farmers and the growers. This provision is definitely made to weaken the growers and workers' representation on the

---

14   The reference here is to Andrew Deoki, who lost the 1966 elections to Federation Party's Irene Jai Narayan.

Advisory Council and as very often happens where any Legislative enacts a law to prevent a particular individual or set of individuals, that law invariably results in a bad and iniquitous law. As far as this provision is concerned, my remark that this legislation was enacted before the dust raised by prolonged dispute in the industry had settled down had relevance and direct relevance to this piece of legislation on our statute.

Anyone who goes through the debate would find out for themselves who or what was at the back of the mind of the legislators when they were supporting that lawyers should not be allowed to represent the farmers or the workers on the Advisory Council and why the Legislative Council members and the Legislative Council candidates should not be allowed to do so. The members of the Council and the professed candidates are supposed to be politicians. Now, everyone knows that the members of the Legislative Council are politicians. It is their sphere of activity. But it is not only members of the Legislative Council who are politicians; there would be hundreds and thousands of politicians outside the walls of the Council. Party members, party officers, people who are actively engaged in party politics or politics of any kind in the country, people who are agitating for political reforms or social reforms or economic reforms: they are all politicians. And by what strange logic a candidate when he announces his candidature suddenly becomes a politician and a sort of untouchable for the purposes of the Sugar Advisory Council membership and, as soon as the election is over and he is defeated, he regains his self-respect and his touchability? The sort of absurdity would be extremely difficult to find elsewhere and everyone knows why we have incorporated it in our statute book. It is time that we remove such things from the statute book as soon as possible.

That brings me to the last objection to the existing law. And that is this law places powers in the hands of the Sugar Board, and especially in the hands of the Independent Chairman, to stop any competition entering in the sphere of the millers as far as the sugar industry is concerned. He has been given wide powers. Even if a farmer was to make gur for his own use and for a limited purpose of selling it to the other people and making some money on the side, the Independent Chairman can put a stop to it, he can even confiscate that gur. If a man starts planting cane without any contract, the Independent Chairman has got the right even to destroy his cane. And we in this country have recently seen one benefit resulting from competition. That is in the rice industry. When the Colonial Sugar Refining Company's mill was the only mill in Rewa, the price they offered was very small. Another competitor entered the field, established his mills, and the price rose almost to double. That is a fact before our very eyes. But, this legislation even prevents farmers from organising themselves and establishing and running co-operative sugar mills which is being done in many sugar producing countries, including Australia, the home country of the millers. So, this Ordinance gives protection to a monopoly from competition and by means of one-sided legislation, by weakening and introducing disunited elements on the other side on the Sugar Council, has worked to the detriment of both the growers and the workers.

As far as this Ordinance goes, it is undesirable because it originated and was founded in misconception, it has suffered from misconstruction and it has worked by way of misapplication. No amount of amendments of patching up would be able to set this legislation right. If justice is to be done to the industry and [to] all [the] people engaged in that industry, we will have to have a proper form of legislation which will be run something on the lines of the Sugar Board in Australia or along the lines of the Sugar Syndicate in Mauritius, some legislation which will provide for fair and just terms for purchase and sale of cane.

67: Ending Eve's Legacy, 12 May 1969

From the grower's side, I have played a prominent part in negotiating three contracts. The first was in 1939 when the director of the Colonial Sugar Refining Company sent its General Manager, Sir Philip Goldfinch, to negotiate a contract with us; and in 1939, I was the principal negotiator for and on behalf of the farmers and we amicably and peaceably agreed upon a contract for the sale and purchase of cane. So because there was no trouble in the industry, because everything was done nicely and smoothly, naturally nobody was going to give me any credit for it. My name was also not worthy of mention but I do not mind that, I never minded. I must say that that was due to one factor, and that was the difference in the directorate at each time of the negotiation in Sydney. Those directors in 1939 were more reasonable and responsive to my way of thinking and it was a pleasure to discuss and negotiate with a man like Sir Philip Goldfinch who could discuss everything in a nice, smooth, persuasive manner and not try to make out that they are the strong party and we have to listen to what they say, and to say anything in reply or make any counter suggestions or counter offers would be short of blasphemy. That is why the first contract was negotiated nicely.

The second contract was negotiated in 1950, and again I was the principal negotiator for and on behalf of the cane growers. The principal negotiator on behalf of the millers and Mr. Rourke who was again guided by the Sydney office and we had many discussions, many offers and counter offers and when it appeared that we might have reached a deadlock, Mr. Rourke undertook to make a last effort and send a cable to Sydney and get the reply if they would increase the price of cane to meet our demands to successfully negotiate the contract. The reply came promptly which enabled us to reach an agreement, and that was the agreement which brought a measure of prosperity to the growers from 1950 to 1959. No one in this country even knew what had happened and naturally who was bothering about who had negotiated the contract then or what part he had played. The thing was that there was no trouble, everything was running nicely and smoothly so there was no question of giving credit to anyone and naturally no one claimed any credit for it. But when the 1959 contract expired and the dispute started over the negotiations of the contract, there was another set of directors in Sydney and the chief negotiator representing the Company at the Conference table. At that time the position taken by the Colonial Sugar Refining Company was intransigent: they would not budge an inch from the position they had taken, even though the Governor himself called both parties for mediation at Government House and tried for two days to bring about some sort of settlement. Every time it was the growers' side which was making a concession and moving forward but the Company's side refused to move and join us somewhere so that the Governor can succeed in his mediation and the dispute may be avoided but he failed.

In 1943, as the Member for Natural Resources [Ratu Mara] mentioned, there was a disaster. But in both of these disputes, one significant factor and fact which has gone unmentioned and undisclosed is that in the 1943 dispute, Ratu Sukuna brought about a compromise. He came and saw us on behalf of the Governor and the Government and our compromise was reduced into writing and on behalf of the growers, I and Swami Rudrananda and Mrs. SB Patel at the behest of Ratu Sukuna signed that compromise and Ratu Sukuna signed it on behalf of the Government. He took it back to the Governor but because the Colonial Sugar Refining Company was not amenable to the Governor that the Governor, instead of standing by the compromise, sent me a letter saying that this compromise was not acceptable to the Government because the most important condition was that the growers will sell or hand over their cane to the Government and leave the price to the conscience of the Governor and whatever the Governor gives us, we will accept. Sir Philp Mitchell replied saying that this was a business matter, it was not a matter of conscience and the Government does not want to take this responsibility. If it was a lesser man than Ratu Sukuna he would have got into trouble later over the compromise. But Ratu Sukuna was too strong a man both for the Government and the Colonial Sugar Refining Company.[15]

But what happened in 1960?[16] Mr. QVL Weston, who was the District Commissioner, brought about a compromise. Again, that compromise was reached at the behest of Mr. Weston in consultation with the Government. The compromise formula was drafted, mutually between Mr. SB Patel, Mr. SM Koya, Mr. Weston and myself. Mr. Weston arranged that he would take this to the

15   See Document 51.
16   See Document 64.

Governor and wanted us to come to Suva so that we could discuss it further with the Governor if he so pleased. We came to Suva. Mr Weston saw the Governor, Sir Kenneth Maddocks; he came back and suggested that the Governor would like to have certain words changed. We readily agreed and changed the words. He again got it approved by the Governor who said that he would like us to discuss it in private with him. The three of us discussed the matter in private with him and it was his suggestion that we should come and put this proposal adopting it as our own before himself and his official advisers of the Executive Council.

Again, in the afternoon we were summoned to the Executive Council chambers in which we submitted these proposals from our side as suggested by the Governor, and his official advisers present there were the Colonial Secretary, the Financial Secretary, the Attorney-General and, if I remember right, the Secretary for Fijian Affairs. Again, Mr. Greenwood there suggested certain changes and wanted and he wanted to have certain words changed. We even agreed to that. It was again changed and re-typed, again we signed it before him. That was that whatever the Governor said we appointed him as our spokesman, as our arbitrator, that he had full authority; he could contact the Colonial Sugar Refining Company and whatever he told us to do after discussing with the Colonial Sugar Refining Company, we would do. What happened? As his predecessor had got the rebuff from that Company, Governor Maddocks also got the rebuff from the Company. Otherwise, it would have been smoothly settled there straightaway. But who would disclose all these matters in this country? We have a saying in our language that a poor man's wife is everybody's sister-in-law, and the position of the poor farmers in this Colony is that the farmers should be blamed for everything. This is the monopolistic power of the Colonial Sugar Refining Company, operating from a remote control. We have got the South Pacific Sugar Mills operating in this country, a locally registered company with a local Board of Directors. But those who are directors are completely under the control of the Sydney office. They have not got a free hand; they have not got full authority to negotiate independently with the growers here, with the result that [while] this sort of dilly-dallying is going on, valuable time is passing and no agreement is reached. Let me tell you that it is not a joke. One of the honourable members pointed out that we all benefit from that industry. Yes; and that is why nobody wants to kill the goose that lays the golden egg. Credit us with some sense! The whole thing is that what we want is that the people who are responsible for all this prosperity of all of us are not getting their fair deal and that is what we want to see that they should get. The price that is paid to them under the present contract is far from an economic price. I will tell you how that came about.

We spent a whole day before the Eve Commission and went into the cost of production of sugar cane, but if you go through the Report you will not find a word mentioned about what it would cost to produce sugar because the plain fact was that if the cost of production of sugar cane was taken into account and arrived at in the same way as the cost of production of cane is worked out in Queensland, Australia, by the Board, then obviously the farmers were working at a loss, with the result that the Report does not mention anything about what it cost the farmer to produce the cane, and whether the share that he would get under the contract that the Commission recommended would benefit him; and if so to what extent. The unpleasant side of the industry he totally ignored. What he did instead was to resort to an inflated basic cost on manufacture of sugar which was the result of the Colonial Sugar Refining Company giving the Commission figures which proved by experience false and they, in dealing with the Commission, did the same sort of thing that some businessmen do when they deal with their customers—they quote an excessive price. So if he is going to beat you down, still you will be getting more than your fair price, and that is what happened in that Commission. The basic cost that the Commission arrived at and on which they made the very foundation of this contract was a grossly inflated price. In spite of the cost of living increasing, cost of things increasing, bills of wages increasing even in the sugar industry; still over all these years the Colonial Sugar Refining Company has not reached that basic figure of manufacturing costs which the Eve Commission allowed them as a proper and reasonable cost of manufacture. As the Indian Member for Ba pointed out, the average basic manufacturing cost still comes to about 24 point something per cent of the gross proceeds and not 30 per cent. This is one of the ways of concealing the profit; the difference which they received by way of what they call difference in distribution; that is not the only way.

The General Member Northern claimed that he was one of the shareholders in the South Pacific Sugar Mills and the profit that that Company made is not high. He is quite correct. The concealed profits are high and those profits go to the shareholders of the Colonial Sugar Refining Company in Australia, not these few local shareholders that the Company has taken to give a facade to this industry that it has local interest in that industry. From the millers' side that concealed profit is concealed in several ways; for example, an arbitrary nominal price at which the Colonial Sugar Refining Company buys the molasses under that contract irrespective of the price which is prevailing in the world market. As members very well know, that price was published in the Fiji Times, too, at that time. The price of molasses went even higher than the price of sugar but we did not receive any benefit from it. From the enquiries that we made when the Eve Commission was sitting, and we were appearing before the Commission, the price of molasses was round about £10 a ton. Later on it rose to £15 per ton, but we got £2.10s a ton for the molasses and even from that £2.10s a ton, Port and Customs Service Tax and other Government dues were deducted, leaving a margin of about £10 a ton hidden profit to the Colonial Sugar Refining Company under this from molasses itself; and the Colonial Sugar Refining Company is taking 40,000 tons of molasses under that agreement, for its own subsidiary in Australia, which comes to £400,000.

Another avenue from which the Company directly benefits is the freedom it enjoys to sell sugar to whoever it likes. The Indian Member from Ba quoted that portion of the Report where the Company is praised [as one whose] activities of selling of sugar should not be controlled, and that it should be the duty of the Sugar Board just to certify the price. That leaves very serious loopholes open and that became obvious in the crushing season one before the last. The Colonial Sugar Refining Company sold a very substantial tonnage of Fiji sugar to New Zealand at £13 a ton. The only buyers who buy crude sugar are the refineries. So the Colonial Sugar Refining Company as the selling agent of Fiji's sugar in the name of the South Pacific Sugar Mills, which is the Colonial Sugar Refining Company under another name, sold this sugar at £13 a ton to New Zealand Sugar Refining Company which is again the Colonial Sugar Refining Company under a third name, with the result that our sugar was purchased by the Colonial Sugar Refining Company itself below cost because even on the Company's own figures, the manufacturing cost only came to £11.10s a ton. Add on that the 21/2 per cent guaranteed profit provided and what was left for the poor grower who is the real producer of sugar for his cane?

The surprising part was that though the Colonial Sugar Refining Company in New Zealand bought our raw sugar at £13 a ton, we would have expected that the refined sugar from New Zealand would have been proportionately cheaper and if it had been so there would have been an anomalous position in this country, showing that the Company was quite honest in its dealings and that would have been that the refined sugar from New Zealand here would have been sold at a considerably lower price than the raw sugar that the Colonial Sugar Refining Company was selling locally to us, which was about £35 a ton. But nowhere in New Zealand, whether the buyers were in New Zealand or Fiji, did the buyers of refined sugar receive any benefit from this crude sugar which the Colonial Sugar Refining Company sold to itself in New Zealand at £13 a ton. It would be the responsibility of the Government and of all the members of this House to ascertain whether the same Company (who are also the selling agents of Australian sugar) sold sugar from Australia to the New Zealand refinery both as to the quantity and the price. It sold sugar to Japan at £12 a ton, we do not know to which refinery in Japan this sugar was sold, why, and who has benefited from it. There is only one sugar refinery in Singapore. It would be interesting to find out whether that refinery received sugar from anywhere else in the world at £11 a ton, or was it only our sugar that it received for £11 a ton. If so, why?

These are various methods by which the Company's profits are concealed. It also raises one important point. That is: who owns the sugar? If the Company owns the sugar, how can the Company charge any commission as selling agents for selling our sugar to the outside world? It is a part of their business for which they are not entitled to any commission or any special remuneration; only the costs, not the profit, not the commission. On the other hand, if they are justified that they are entitled to a commission then the growers must have the control and a strong voice in the disposal of the sugar because in that case they are the owners of the sugar. Until these points are cleared up, until the very important point—that is the cost of production of sugar cane is seriously and fairly gone into, and the prices reached which would be equitable and fair to both, ensuring a reasonable margin of profit for both sides of the industry: that is the most important point to be decided and it has not been so far decided.

There has been always clamour about irrelevancies, clamour that I want to drive the Colonial Sugar Refining Company out of Fiji, that I want to bring some outside interests into Fiji, overlooking the fact that the Sugar Refining Company was not always a monopoly in Fiji. Everyone who is interested in the history of the sugar industry in Fiji knows that there were several companies operating in Fiji; there was competition before. By what ruthless and unscrupulous method the Colonial Sugar Refining Company happened to come on top and became the monopoly in this industry [is well known]. If an outsider was coming here, and starting a mill in the sugar industry which would introduce competition in the industry and thus raise the level of prices and wages in the industry and thereby generally raise the standard of living of the people in this industry: What harm or wrong is there? What harm or wrong is there if the farmers organize their own co-operative mills and cut out the middleman's profits, there would not then be any question of any middleman trying even to get more profits in a concealed manner by concealed devices, in a contract. They can have a fair remuneration, what harm is there? What is wrong there? But no, there must be one propaganda: anyone who is raising his voice against the Colonial Sugar Refining Company is a heretic.

As regards methods of selling of sugar under the existing contract, I have come across a very good example. In October, 1967 a firm of importers in Singapore wrote to an agent here enquiring about the f.o.b. and the c.i.f.[17] price of raw Fiji sugar. He intended to import 20,000 tons and wanted to have the sugar shipped by December, 1967. The agent wrote both to the Manager of the South Pacific Sugar Mills and the Ministry of Trade and Commerce enquiring about the price and whether the Company would sell and ship 20,000 tons of sugar to this buyer in Singapore. The Minister replied that the matter was in the hands of the South Pacific Sugar Mills and he should enquire from them but at the same

---

17   Free On Board; and Cost, Insurance and Freight.

time the Ministry would be glad if he would inform the Ministry of the reply he received from the South Pacific Sugar Mills. The South Pacific Sugar Mills replied that the sale of sugar was in the hands of the Colonial Sugar Refining Company Limited, Australia, and he should write to their Sydney office as it was not in their hands. When he wrote to the Colonial Sugar Refining office in Australia he received a reply saying that he should enquire from their broker in London. The broker's name given was Messrs. C. Zanikow Limited, Plantation House, Minching Lane, London, E.C.3 and the Company told him that they would be in a position to give him a reply.

He wrote to the broker and the reply from Messrs. Zanikow Limited was that the marketing agreement for the sale of the sugar in Singapore was well established and as they were already committed they were not interested in any other buyer. All this clearly indicates that even the buying operations are a sort of a closed shop. There does not seem to be any eagerness or keenness on the part of the selling agent even to find out or ascertain whether they can get a higher price from an outside buyer who is making enquiries and what they call the well established arrangements for a market in Singapore. The price at which that market was established was £11 per ton which is lower than what the Company pays. It costs them to process and turn sugar cane into sugar, viz £11.10s per ton. These are the sorts of handicaps that the growers face when they sell their cane under the present contract to the millers.

The Minister for Labour mentioned the desire of the Fijian land owners to have their rents revised and increased so that they could get a fair rent. We are all in sympathy with their desire and also in agreement that they should get a fair rent, but the rent more or less depends upon the price of produce from that land. If the economic return from that land is high, the rental value of the land will be higher, if it is less, the rental value would naturally be less. If the price paid for cane is uneconomic and low you cannot get a higher rent because the farmer will be squeezed out into bankruptcy. He cannot pay more than what he would get from his produce. So far in Fiji, the sugar industry has functioned and worked for the prosperity of the millers, both at the cost of the growers and of the Fijian land owners. As soon as the owners raised an outcry that the rents should be revised and raised, the Colonial Sugar Refining Company in haste surrendered all their leases of native land, creating a further chaos in the industry so that now the Company's tenants who are settled on those lands are sub-tenants and growing cane there are at a loss to know to whom to pay their rent, and what rent to pay. Even the Native Land Trust Board, as a matter of fact, does not know who are actually settled on those lands and what rent they are paying. It is quite clear that if the grower receives a fair and proper economic price that can bear a fair rental, then of course both the grower and the owner of land stand to gain. But if the price paid is uneconomically low, even if the land owner was to take the land back from the grower and grow the cane himself, he would be in the same predicament as the displaced grower, not in any way better. If the grower can make both ends meet, the same will happen to the owner who starts growing cane. Under the present contract, the owners of land, the growers, even the local shareholders of the South Pacific Sugar Mills Limited and the Government lose, and the people who benefit are the shareholders of the Colonial Sugar Refining Company and its subsidiaries abroad. So in the interest of everyone it must be seen that the price that is paid to the grower is fair and the conditions imposed are reasonable.

Now to consider a fair price and conditions for the farmer and a fair wage and conditions for the worker, no one can have anything to quarrel with this. Everyone would be in agreement that it is our duty to see that those who are engaged in the industry get their fair share and fair treatment. Insofar as that goes, I do not see any controversial point. That leaves the third to provide necessary measures of control to prevent the millers from taking undue advantage of their monopolistic position in the industry. I do not see how any reasonable or sensible or fair man can have anything to quarrel with that. We are not suggesting any provisions to control indiscriminately the activities of the millers but only to provide such measures as would prevent them from taking undue advantage of their position and the most obvious thing is they are the only buyers of cane. We have thousands of farmers producing cane and producers of cane are in fact the producers of sugar, which keeps this Colony going. The millers are quite conscious of their advantageous position and they have the attitude: 'Well we are the only buyers, they will have to come to us otherwise their crop has no value, they cannot sell it to anyone else.' That is why it is necessary in law to prevent them monopolising a single buyer to take advantage and have at his mercy thousands of farmers in this Colony. No one can have anything to quarrel with that, so in that case I do not see why that amendment should be unacceptable to the Government.

The Alliance Party time and again during the by-election campaign have said that the existing contract is not fair so there is no division or difference of opinion on that point, that the existing contract is not fair to the grower. Both sides are agreed on this as far as that goes. That leaves the Sugar Ordinance itself. Both the Minister for Natural Resources and the Minister for Labour freely admitted that this Ordinance, to put it most mildly, 'is not satisfactory,' that after trying out for a length of eight years it appears that this Ordinance should not be revised. So, as far as the views on the existing Ordinance are concerned, there does not seem to be any difference of opinion on either side of the House. That leaves this question of the repeal or the amendment of the Ordinance.

The Minister for Labour said that if this Ordinance were to be repealed, there would be a gap. There would not be anything to take its place and consequently there would be chaos in the industry. I would like to point out that had we stopped to have this Ordinance repealed immediately, there was nothing to prevent us from introducing a Bill in this House repealing that Ordinance. The very fact that we did not introduce such a Bill but decided instead that there should be a motion for the expressing of the view of the House so that time can be taken by both sides to go into the whole question of at what stage the Bill should be repealed and what should take its place. If both sides of the House are agreeable on this question that this Bill is not good and that something else should take its place, then I say that the foundation of this Bill is rotten. It is necessary to demolish it to the ground and have another edifice built in its place, a proper provision that would ensure fair play and justice to all who are engaged in this industry. Mauritius, for instance, has satisfactorily solved its problem so much so that the growers, millers and others interested in the industry are all safeguarded, are properly provided for and they all get their fair share. If the millers in Mauritius can manage to make a profit from their share which consists of 25 per cent of the gross proceeds, I do not see any reason why the South Pacific Sugar Mills or the Colonial Sugar Refining Company who boast of their efficiency, boast of their machinery or the sale and everything else, why they cannot make a profit with that percentage.

68: The Denning Arbitration, 19th August 1969

Lord Denning: Gentlemen of the Bar, may I add too the people of Fiji, I greatly appreciate the invitation you have extended to me to come and decide the dispute in the Sugar Industry. I am particularly grateful that you should have agreed on my appointment. It is a great responsibility and I shall endeavour to fulfill it to the best of my ability because I realise that the Sugar Industry is the backbone of the economy of these Islands. That the Sugar Industry is prosperous and the workers in it, the millers and the growers all receive their fair share for their labours then these islands, Fiji itself will prosper, and it will encourage visitors to come to your lovely islands and all other industries will flourish, but if the Sugar Industry should be torn with strife and dispute that will be bad for Fiji as a whole and everybody in it, so if I may say so, you have done well to refer the dispute to arbitration. The nature of it is well known. For some years now, millers and growers have worked under a contract which so far as I know worked, but on the other hand it is due to expire on the 31st March next year and efforts have been made to agree on a new contract on terms which are to govern the future but these efforts have been unavailing and dispute has arisen so it is very appropriate to solve it and let it go to arbitration and the Chief Justice has drawn up terms of reference which are my authority for holding the arbitration here.

The terms of reference are these:

1. First, to determine all issues which have arisen in the sugar industry over the terms of a new contract between the growers and the millers for the sale and purchase of sugar cane, general applications which expires on 30 March, 1970.

2. Second, to settle the terms which will be just and equitable and fair to all parties. So there is a task to settle, a contract to be just and equitable and fair to all parties and I myself as Arbitrator cannot hope to do this on my own, and that is why I am very pleased that the members of the Bar here are to help and they will, as always, each side put his case as strongly and as fairly as they can to allow me to arrive at a just solution and the witnesses then will give their evidence honestly and truly and will be treated with all the courtesy and consideration which their important role demands and then, having heard the arguments and heard the evidence it will be for me, with the help of the advisors to come to a decision, the Swami Rudrananda, the representative of the growers under the ordinance and Mr. [Stuart] Hermes, the senior representative of the millers under the ordinance, are with me as advisors without a vote and advising to help me in a decision. And importantly from London, Mr. McNeil, an accountant of the highest standing, who is to help me with the complex accountancy side. I can well see there are many questions of accounts which come into consideration and so without the help of all I cannot do anything by myself. With the help and support of all, I will try and undertake this responsibility to come to a decision as I have said before, that will be just, equitable, and fair to all parties.

Now as to the procedure which we will adopt, much of the evidence is bound to be tedious and complicated. As I understand it, at the moment the millers feel in substance that the existing contract should suffice with variations, but on the other hand, the growers feel there should be considerable alterations and considerable variation if justice is to be done. In these circumstances, I feel the growers should state their case first. I would ask Mr. AD Patel to open submissions first on behalf of the growers.

Mr AD Patel:

My Lord, allow me first to thank you for obliging us by accepting this heavy responsibility. This is indeed an historic event in the 80 years life of the sugar industry in Fiji. For the first time, the parties have decided that their difficulties in dispute should be submitted to an independent arbitrator like you. We are indeed lucky in having a man of your eminence and experience to be a judge in our dispute and all sides are confident that an award will be the outcome of this arbitration which will be just and equitable and fair to all parties concerned and satisfy both the needs of the growers and the millers and ensure stability and prosperity to this country as a whole. My Lord, you will appreciate that this is an uneven contest between the growers and the millers. The millers happen to be one of the largest companies in the world, a giant organization with its subsidiaries spread over many countries and especially as Fiji is concerned, and the sugar industry is concerned, it is a strong monopoly. They have all the information in their possession and so far, I regret to say, they have guarded that information very carefully and very little, if any, is allowed to get across to the growers who producers of the sugar.

We are of the opinion that it is Nature or God, as you may believe, who makes sugar, we produce as growers and the millers extract it. It is true that our sugar cane will have no value if there were no millers to crush it, but it is equally true that the milling plants will be useless unless they had sugar cane to cut, and that is why both sides of the industry are interdependent under the present contract. My Lord, a statement of price is published every year, certified by the Independent Accountant and the Independent Chairman of the Sugar Board. Now this statement is published every year to show what the price payable for that year's harvest is. Sugar making costs are given, but we have not been given breakdowns. And the same thing applies to manufacturing and transport.

denning: And you feel you should have a breakdown?

patel:

As regards the extraction of sugar we are in the dark as to how much sugar is manufactured each year at each of the four mills in Fiji, how much molasses, how much other by-products such as mill mud and megasse.

denning: Have you had an accountant look into these matters?

patel:

Without any accounts to look at, an accountant cannot do anything. We are asking for the accounts so that an accountant can look at them.

denning: Point taken.

patel:

Now My Lord, in any contract for the sale or purchase of a commodity, the price is the crux of the contract and in the sugar industry throughout the British Commonwealth, certain methods of arriving at price are, or have been, invoked and the oldest and may I say the most primitive method was the method of a lump sum, a flat price. That method has more or less been given up in almost all sugar producing countries in the British Commonwealth. The second method of arriving at price is a sharing of the cake—if I may put it that way.

denning: See what there is to be divided and share it in certain proportion.

Patel:

Yes, certain percentage to the growers and certain percentage to the millers. That method is in practice in two countries to my knowledge, one in Queensland and the other Mauritius.

denning: Established procedure.

patel:

Yes, but there the Government has taken full charge of the cane. In Queensland, the Government controls it, it obtains the cost of production of sugar cane from the growers on a certain basis, a schedule of which is provided by legislation.

denning: Material supplied from the millers.

patel:

The Government obtains costs from millers and growers and after that they go into the whole matter of the whole proceeds and a fair division.

denning: They get the proceeds and costs of production and share what is left.

patel:

An award is made every year. I have got certain information here from a fairly reliable source which says the division comes to about 70%, 30% to the millers. In Mauritius the percentage is still higher.

denning:

70% growers 30% millers? Does legislation prescribe the form of contract?

patel:

Yes and consequently there is no reason or no occasion or no room for either side to mistrust the other. We in Fiji have not got the benefit of such legislation so far, and consequently the formula that will be most suitable to us in our present circumstances is the formula of a basic price for sugar cane and linked with the price of sugar per ton on a sliding scale.

denning:

Basic price in having a sliding scale according to the general market—is that it?

patel:

The basic price would be the rock bottom price which under any circumstances the miller would have to pay.

denning:

I understand that, and then there is a basic price a sort of minimum price and there is going to be a sliding scale—is that it?

patel:

That would be on a sliding scale under the old contract. We say that the basic should be $10 per ton i.e. linked to $98 per ton for sugar. $98 per ton is the price per ton of sugar with the proceeds of molasses and other by-products thrown in, and for any price obtained above $98 per ton there should be a premium at the rate of 25 cents per ton of cane for every $2 per ton of extra price of sugar.

denning:

This is what you suggest as the right and fair way of doing it. It isn't so much sharing of the cake in the old days but going on a basic price ... In other words you are suggesting a different principle for dealing with it.

patel:

Because the other principle can't work here unless and until the millers are quite open and frank and treat the growers as partners and not merely as partners euphemistically and have access to all information, and if they are accountable to the partners i.e. the growers which in present circumstances in the absence of legislation appears to be impossible.

denning:

Supposing you had all the information you would like, would you think it right to go on to the sharing basis.

patel:

Not the existing way; the Eve contract stands on its own, in the British Commonwealth it is a unique contract. Before I go on to the Eve contract, may I be allowed to mention that we establish that £5 or $10 per ton we are asking for is quite fair and economic price and in present circumstances that this is the price in view of the present cost of production the grower ought to have.

denning:

Yes I suppose—in the course of time the cost will increase, probably the costs go up.

patel:

Both the millers and the growers are in business. The business of the millers is to extract sugar, and the business of the growers is to produce sugar cane, and the grower, therefore, cannot be treated as an ordinary labourer. In working out his cost of production, even his own labour and the labour of members of his family, should be taken into consideration at the market rate, to say the least.

denning: Yes, I see that.

patel:

Then on top of it, he will be entitled to a certain percentage, or a certain amount, for the risk he has to take in that undertaking.

denning: There may be calamities of some kind which overtake him.

patel:

There are plenty of those, My Lord. Firstly cyclone, for instance, and drought; we are going through one now.

denning: I understand.

patel:

The grower is also entitled to supervision and management costs the same as the miller. He has to supervise his undertaking and he has also got to manage his farm and the true measure of it would be again the market value, as to what a person who may be employed—

denning:

If he employs a supervisor or manager then he would have to pay him. He may do it himself, but he ought to have supervision and management.

patel: He would be doing it himself.

denning:

I understand. In other words you are working together the growers costs you have to add other ordinary labour charges, the risk he takes, the supervision and management charges himself.

patel:

As the mill plant is the indispensable asset of the miller and as it cannot accept sugar without it, land is an indispensable asset of the grower and he cannot do without because he cannot produce cane without it. And the depreciation and also the interest on the value of the land which he is bringing into use which he may have to pay for cane cultivation should also be taken into account in arriving at the cost of production of sugar cane. The argument I anticipate from the millers is that the price is not viable, that the industry cannot take, that if this price was paid there will be a serious loss to the millers. Now we will be rebutting that answer. We shall prove that it is viable and the industry can afford to pay it.

denning: That means looking into the millers' accounts I suppose?

patel:

It would be absolutely' necessary for the millers to produce their books of account, not the summaries of their estimate.

denning: Haven't you had access to these books of account then?

patel:

No My Lord, not even the Eve Commission had access to them and if your Lordship will read the report they give certain figures that even the Commission had to make allowance for it and reduce the amount of manufacturing costs and because of their Head Office expenditure.

denning: You mention that the Eve Commission didn't have access to them.

patel:

Yes, and according to the report, the estimates that the millers gave—or some parts of it—should be reduced in places and even then in actual practice it is found that even the figure the Eve Commission arrived at was a little bit on the boosted side than was actual and therefore we will have to call witnesses besides growers.

denning:

Growers to prove the cost of production—that's one angle of it to justify your basic price; then you will have to call someone on the millers' side.

patel:

Yes, to get this information out from the millers we may have to resort to interrogation and also subpoena some of the officers of the millers to give evidence and produce books of account and other documents and papers which are relevant to the issue.

denning:

Does Mauritius get more sugar than Fiji? How do you compare with total output? Sugar is the principal industry of Mauritius. At all events, you say that there are so many acres. The acre basis is adopted in Mauritius and it was so here until the Eve contract and then abandoned in the Eve contract and you want to restore what it was before. Is that it?

patel:

Because under the existing Eve contract, the entire risk is passed on to the grower i.e. the miller is not bound to take a single stick of cane more than he really requires.

denning:

For instance, under the Mauritius contract—under your previous contract, he was bound to take all that out of so many acres; of course I haven't studied it. Under the Eve contract he only takes as much as he wants. Is that right?

patel:

And the rest he can reject and all the risk again goes on to the grower. If he produces less than his quota, then he stands the risk of his quota being reduced under the provision of conditions at the time.

denning: Yes it's a quota basis, isn't it?

patel:

Now if he produces more than the quota, he takes the risk of his cane being left out.

patel: Land contract tenures.

denning:

What do you say about tenures is that it should give more stability over the period. Then we come to clause 5—delivery point.

patel:

The fundamental difference between the set up here and other Commonwealth sugar producing countries is that the distance that the cane has to be transported from the farms to the mill is very, very long. The crucial point is the question of risk after delivery under the existing contract; that is the difference made between the cane that is to be transported by lorry transport or tramlines.

denning:

So there are portable line and trucks taken to the farm and they have to be delivered to the nearest point of the tramline.

patel:

Now usually the distance is not very long, it might be at most 55 chains or even a mile but not any further than that. Under the present contract, it is delivered at this point. But then the question arises as to who is carting the cane to the mill. As far as the practice in other countries is concerned, it is that from the delivery onwards the miller is responsible. Here, although it is delivered at the tramline, it is weighed at the mill, which in some cases might be as far as 70 or 75 miles.

denning:

Although it is delivered to the tramline, it maybe 70 or 75 miles before it gets to the mill and it is not weighed until it gets to the mill? I suppose there may have been risks attached to it meanwhile for all that distance—who bears this risk? In other words, the growers say that once it is delivered on to the tramline then it is the miller's responsibility then and that's the delivery point, and the millers ought to accept this responsibility because I suppose it's their engines and their machinery that pick it up.

patel:

Now then the question of lorry transport. There the grower has got to deliver the cane at certain points near the tramline where they have got these receiving stations and in other cases they have to bring it over long distances to the mill itself. In certain areas no tramline is available and he has to transport his cane all the way from the long distance sometimes as far as 20 miles, weighed and delivered in the mill and the grower has got to bear all these transport costs.

denning:

Bear all the costs right to the mill? That is hard on the man who has got to take the lorry right the way through. What are you suggesting?

patel:

That the delivery points in the case of cane which is to be transported either by tramline or by truck or lorries should not be further than 3 miles away from the farm. Then we come to 'The Weighbridge.' Now in this country more than 2 million tons of cane are produced and weighed every year within a period of 20 to 24 weeks. There are only 4 weighbridges to weigh all that amount of cane within that period. There should be more weighbridges. As a matter of fact, there should be a weighbridge at every delivery point. When it is delivered that is the time that it should be weighed so that both parties know how much is bought and sold.

denning: Is it very expensive to install a weighbridge?

patel:

Not so expensive in the long run, considering that in other places they have to have so many mills in the vicinity of cane growing areas.

denning: 'Tramline and Trucks?'

patel:

Now the complaint of the growers is that at the beginning of the crushing, season, only a few trucks are allowed to the cane cutting gang with the result that the labourers who are employed to harvest cane that day, quite a number of them have to be returned because there is no work for them. Although the labourer returns home, the grower is bound to pay his premium which is what he calls bonus. Say, for instance, there is a gang of about 20 labourers and for these 20 workers at least 10 trucks are required, two of them are cutting and loading one truck. Instead of 10 trucks if they are only given 5 trucks, half of the workers have to be turned away.

denning: Why is it that there aren't the trucks available?

patel:

That is something we have not been able to understand all these years and we have kept complaining about it. What happens, surprisingly enough, is towards the close of the crushing season there is a liberal issue of perhaps more trucks than the gang can cope with.

denning:

What are you suggesting here? The Company should allocate sufficient daily quota of lorry loads, that is one—and also supply sufficient portable lines and trucks to enable it to be harvested without delay. In other words, you say there ought to be provision that the millers are to supply lines and trucks so the work can be got on with.

patel:

We go to Clause 9. Sugar cane to be cut level with the ground: it is a common ground on both sides it is not the issue. As regards extraneous matter the cane is dammed to be clean from extraneous matter, tops, trash etc. does not exceed 4%. If it exceeds 4% the Company should check this at point of delivery. In the existing Eve contract, it is 2%. In Queensland the Company pays premium for clean cane. If the extraneous matter is less than 4%, they give a bonus to the farmers but here they insist that the cane in Fiji should have extraneous matter of 2% and no more.

denning: 'Notice for Closing of the Season.'

patel:

The present practice of giving notice is too short, usually a fortnight or so, and even then sometimes it is not definite.

denning:

In each season they give a certain notice—we are going to close the mill down on such and such a day and sometimes it may be only two weeks. You say it should be 4 weeks. Why is that?

patel:

So that the grower definitely knows the area they are cutting in such a way without having to hurry. What happens is that short notice creates anxiety in the minds of the growers. When the cane is still uncut, they fear that if it is not in time, they might miss out and then they will have to wait until the next cutting season for that crop. We want that there should be sufficiently long notice so that everybody knows he can make arrangements accordingly.

denning: Clause 10—'No work on Sunday'.

patel:

Now that was the practice in Fiji right from the beginning. Then one year, there was a good harvest—the year was 1959. The Company persuaded the growers to work on Sunday so that the cane could be sent to the mill and the entire crop can be harvested, that was the understanding that these were special circumstances and this will not become established practice. Unfortunately, the Company from that time onwards can see that this is convenient for them, so they have carried on with the practice up to the present and though the Company in effect in so many words says you don't have to harvest on Sunday, but what they do is that the Company says today is Sunday and I am just going to work so you will miss your chance in the run, we will give it to somebody who is prepared to harvest on Sunday.

denning:

I see. The man who says I don't want to work on Sunday is at a disadvantage, because the next door neighbour who will work on Sunday will be given the tramline.

patel:

And then this man will have to wait until the whole programme is finished. They won't come back on Monday and harvest his cane; though in theory they say that they don't. And that is why we want to have it expressly stated in this contract. From 1879 when the Indians were first brought to Fiji right to 1959, they have not been cutting on a Sunday, and there is no reason why it couldn't go on now.

denning:

'Duty to extract the maximum sugar.' There should be an obligation to extract the maximum. On these matters did the Eve contract have anything in it at all? There should be an obligation to extract the maximum. On these matters did the Eve contract have anything in it at all?

patel: Yes, but it has become a dead letter because of lack of information.

denning: 'Duty to sell molasses at the highest price.'

patel:

Under the Eve contract, molasses is taken by the millers at a nominal price of £2.10.0 per ton, irrespective of the price on the world market.

denning: Do they use it themselves?

Patel:

Yes, My Lord, their subsidiary company in Australia uses it. So the c.s.r. sells molasses in the name of s.p.s.m to another subsidiary company.

denning:

In other words there isn't a free market, they almost can fix a price between themselves. What you say is it ought to be taken at the world price.

patel: Yes, My Lord.

denning: 'Prohibition on introduction of newcomers to the industry'.

patel:

This is to prevent the Company giving contracts to the newcomers to detriment of the existing cane growers.

denning: What is happening at the moment then?

patel:

When this dispute was going on when the grower's representatives and the Company's representatives could not come to any agreement in the Sugar Advisory Council, the Chairman of the Sugar Board submitted a report to His Excellency the Governor in which he mentioned that there are many growers who have either lost their contracts or have never gained contracts are prepared to accept the existing contract. This clearly showed a loophole that if the Company or the Independent Chairman wanted to thrust this contract down the throats of the growers, all that they have to do is bring these methods in so that if you don't take it he has another man who will.

denning:

So you want this clause in, that the Company shall not enter into any agreement with any person who has not at the moment got a sugar cane farm.

patel:

Yes, but we have made certain qualifications to accommodate certain genuine cases, and that is that those who held cane contracts and who have been evicted from their land should get lease on compassionate grounds, and lands which were under the sugar cane contract cultivation beforehand. As far as this contract goes, My Lord, it has been unanimously rejected by all the cane growers who found out to their own cost that this contract was a killer. Through this contract the growers are slipping further and further into debt. More bankruptcies have been filed during this period, more cane growers have gone bankrupt, than in a similar period in the past.

denning:

So in the last seven years there have been more bankruptcies than before. Is the rate of bankruptcies very high amongst growers? Do many of them get into financial difficulties?

patel:

That is so My Lord, there are many insolvents who are forced into bankruptcies because they are afraid they might lose everything, so they are just waiting to get something from it in case things change. The total indebtedness of the cane growers now is alarmingly high and we will seek to prove that before you.

denning:

And is that because the sharing arrangement is not fair to the growers, is that what you say?

patel:

Yes, what is happening here, if we compare the position of the two parties during this period, you will find a period of prosperity for the millers and a period of distress of the growers. The contrast is evident during this period. Quarters have been improved, amenities have been provided for officers of the millers, more equipment, better vehicles, amenities like the golf courses club houses, concrete roads and swimming baths.

denning:

What about the dividends? You do not know what dividends are declared in relation to the Company here?

patel:

No, as far as the Company here is concerned, it is the c.s.r. Company under another name, completely under the control of Australia. Even the rates and dividends and everything else is not decided independently by the Directors, but according to the instructions of their Sydney office. And this prosperity is due to, in our opinion, the Company getting the larger share than what it appears on the face of the price formula in the Eve report.

denning: $82\frac{1}{2}$% and $17\frac{1}{2}$%.

patel:

Yes, My Lord, this sum is a device cleverly built into that formula whereby there are what I call concealed profits. I will give you one example of the price statement regarding the sugar making cost and the farmers cost. The Eve Commission decided in this contract that it be incorporated that the millers should get 50% of the total proceeds for their sugar making costs, more or less divided into two parts—sugar making and farmers costs and further divided into head office and other costs. There are certain costs that the Company actually spends, but we do not know under which account it comes, but My Lord you will see that 30% was the actual millers' costs come to £9 a ton. To represent that as 30%, the price of the ton of sugar will have to be £30. Now, say, the average price received per ton is £50. Then 30% of that will be £15, my Lord. Now, the difference between the £9 and the £15 which is allowed to the Company is concealed profit.

denning:

So you say that if the actual cost is £50, and if you take 30% of it, it will be £15, so the difference of £6 would be concealed profit?

patel:

Yes, Another peculiar thing about that is, it is again divided into 10% and 20%, that 30%–10% for growers services is to be divided equally between the growers and the millers. It is half to the grower and half to the miller, and one is two-thirds to the miller and one-third to the grower. The miller has already covered his costs, which are actually £9. He has already received that and on top of that, as far as that 10% is concerned, he gets 50% extra and the grower's share of 50% goes into the residual pool. So, as far as that division is concerned in that account, the miller gets 50% not $17\frac{1}{2}$%.

denning: I see what you mean.

patel:

As regards the two-thirds and one-third, the miller gets 66-2/3 and the growers share goes into the residual pool, which is 33-1/3. They get 66-2/3, and in some portion they, get 50% which is net profit after all these costs which are included in £9. Then, there are certain things where they get 100%, and I will give one instance of that, as commission for the sellers. It is a very peculiar set-up, my Lord. The Colonial Sugar Refining Company are the selling agents of all our sugar here. But in one case we found there was an inquiry from an outside country to purchase Fiji sugar, and the agent here approached the Colonial Sugar Refining Company. The quantity was quite substantial—a few thousand tons. The agent told them that he had got this order, and would the Company consider fulfilling it. The Company said they could not sell, and that he could write to Sydney. This man wrote to Sydney, and the reply was that it is not in their hands, but that it was in the hands of the brokers in London—if I remember rightly the name was Zanikow Limited, the famous sugar brokers of London. So that shows that if any commission is charged by the c.s.r. Co, on top of Zanikow's charges, that is clear profit, it is concealed profit, in the guise of a commission.

denning: It is really profit to the Company, although it is down as commission.

patel:

Another source of concealed profit is in regard to the polarisation premiums. Whatever sugar we sell under the Commonwealth Sugar Agreement as well as the International Sugar Agreement, the standard price quoted is for 96 degrees polarisation and any degree of polarization over and above 96 draws a premium. Under our Commonwealth Sugar Agreement premium, I understand, is for every additional degree—1.4% of the price of sugar. The premium certificates are issued, and the millers get that premium. That is never shown in these accounts and it is not even shown in the Independent Chairman's Report to the Governor. As far as we are concerned, we think the premium ought to come into the accounts. I am told that in the United States the premium is higher than even 1.4% that is allowed in the United Kingdom. It is a concealed profit and it ought to be shown in the accounts.

denning:

You have got the commission, the polarization and the percentages. Your criticism is the way the Eve Contract has worked and the concealed profit or amounts going to their benefit which have not been going into the accounts.

patel:

Then, the Company sells quite substantial amounts of sugar every year to its own subsidiary in New Zealand. The prices are not disclosed. What we have got to see is at what time those purchases are made. Some information that came into my through the Statistical Bureau indicated that the sales made to New Zealand seem to synchronise with the price when the London prices are low. I cannot say much on this because we have not got sufficient information.

denning: You say the prices happened to be lower at that time?

patel:

Very often. Because when we see the cost at which this is sold—from the Statistical Office—we found Fiji sugar drawing good prices from local sales, from sales in other neighbouring territories, from sales in the United Kingdom under the Commonwealth Sugar Agreement, except in New Zealand where certain sales were recently made at remarkably uneconomic prices at £12 and £11; again our source of information is the Statistical Office. It covered only the millers' cost, leaving nothing for us. All the other sales were good prices and the New Zealand ones happened to be low ones. So we do not know if there is any agreement between that subsidiary and the c.s.r. Co. or whether there is an agreement between the New Zealand Company and the Fiji Company. We do not know anything about it. Because of all those things, the growers, as your Lordship would read from that Contract, will no doubt come to the same conclusion that we have come to, that it is beyond the comprehension of an ordinary small Indian or Fijian farmer, with the result that they have come to thumb-mark this agreement after someone telling them that this is good. Over this period of time they have found out where the shoe pinches by experience, with the result that in the Sugar Advisory Council, unanimously, this Contract was rejected. There was no difference of opinion amongst the farmers then and even now, and that is because of all these reasons that I have mentioned.

denning: I have the clause about burnt cane here.

patel:

Now, the sale of burnt cane or firing cane before harvest—that clause proved oppressive to the growers. As it happens in other countries, too, I found out in a.c. Barnes' book 'Sugar,' that somehow there are these fires taking place, either accidentally or as acts of incendiarism. But usually in all countries they seem to take place after the crushing starts and before it is closed. Usually there are several causes. One cause is even opportunity for the labourers. We had some years ago a case in Nadi Court where a labourer was actually caught setting fire to the cane. In that case it turned out that this man had done it with a view to approaching the owner after it is burnt and offering himself to work as a cutter at a higher rate. Indeed there may be other causes. There may be some enemy. It may be accidental fire but in every case, instead of the man being helped, he has to be exposed to all these severe penalties. There is a serious deduction. The millers have the right to withhold his proceeds for 3 months, without payment of interest. And besides that, there is another penalty as regards the normal harvesting expenses of unburnt cane, or of cane with authorized burning, which is very rare.

denning: Burning is sometimes authorized?

patel:

Most often it is unauthorized. Towards the end of the crushing season before the closing of the mill, the farmers feel that unless and until the cane is burnt they cannot send it quickly to the mill. In such cases, they call that unauthorized burning of the cane. It may be incendiarism but then they do not advance the harvesting expenses which they do for other farmers.

denning:

They advance the harvesting expenses in other cases but they do not pay to him.

patel:

With the result that this man is forced to go to some money lender who raises the advance at a usurious rate of interest in order to get it cut and pay a premium wage so that it can be cut as quickly as possible and sent to the mill to save heavy commitments as the scale is laid down there. So by experience, farmers have found that clause oppressive. And we will be calling witnesses of those victims whose cane was burnt. Some of them had cane burnt over a series of years, practically ruining them. There are other clauses which are also objectionable to the farmers, but

I will come to them later. I have already taken sufficient time. Is there anything your Lordship would like to know on what I have already submitted?

denning:

I think you have submitted it very well Mr. Patel. Thank you very much indeed. Such is the case which Mr. Patel presented.

Editor's Note:

Denning was deeply impressed by Patel's advocacy. In a private note to me, he wrote: 'Of all the lawyers who appeared before me, AD Patel was the most outstanding; intellectually the most brilliant, as a character the most honourable, and as an advocate the most persuasive. Quick in mind, fluent in speech, he stood out above all. He even outshone Mr. Brennan [later Chief Justice of Australia]. It was his persuasive advocacy that led me to my report which was in favour of the growers and against the millers.' Denning rejected all the central tenets of the Eve contract. His contract gave the growers 65 per cent and the millers 35 per cent of the proceeds of sale, each paying their own costs, instead of the 57.75 to 42.5 per cent ratio. The growers were also given the power to appoint an independent accountant to inspect the books and accounts of the millers. The sale included not only sugar but its by-products as well. Finally, the growers were to receive a guaranteed minimum price of $7.75 per ton, $5.75 paid within five weeks of delivery and the remaining $2.00 within six weeks of the end of the crushing season. Patel prophetically said that this would be his last fight with the CSR. It was. He died soon after the arbitration proceedings concluded. Peter Westwood, Commissioner Western, wrote on 3 October 1969: 'I greatly admired the ability and eloquence with which he opened the sugar arbitration. He was a great advocate.'

Part III. Land and Livelihood

69: All-Fiji Indian Conference, 30 October 1938

The All-Fiji Indian Conference met on October 30 at the Lilac Theatre in Suva, wherein representatives from all parts of Fiji participated. The theatre was crowded to full capacity. The Honourable Pandit Hriday Nath Kunzru, B.A., LL.D., B.Sc., presided.[1]

Mr. AD Patel, President of the Indian Association of Fiji, said that the Indian community was indeed fortunate in having such an eminent personality as the Hon. Dr Kunzru to preside over the Conference.

The learned chairman spoke forcefully and dwelt on many problems affecting the Indians in Fiji. He appealed for unity and closer co-operation between the different communities living in Fiji. The chairman further emphasized the greater need for female education. After the chairman's speech, the following papers were read and discussed:

1. Paper on General Economic Position by Mr. AD Patel.
2. Paper on Land by Mr. R Parmeshwar.
3. Paper on the Indian cultivator and his problem by Mr. Ayodha Prasad.
4. Paper on Health and Hygiene by Dr CM Gopalan.
5. Paper on Education by Pandit Amichand.
6. Paper on Commerce by Mr. Hargovan Gangaram.
7. Paper on Indians in Fiji and their rights and disabilities, by Mr. AD Patel.

The Following resolutions were unanimously adopted by the conference:

1. This All-Fiji Indian Conference is strongly of the opinion that an enquiry into the economic conditions of the Indian community in Fiji which was promised to the Government of India several years ago, but has not as yet been carried out, is essential, and urges the Government to appoint as early as possible a Commission of Enquiry, containing representatives both of the Indian community and the Government of India.

2. This All-Fiji Indian Conference requests the Government of India to delegate representatives expert in land matters to assist the Indian community

---

1 (1887-1978), elected President of Servants of India Society in 1935, an organization founded by Gopal Krishna Gokhale in 1909.

when the Government of Fiji will appoint a Committee for the proposed demarcation of native reserves and alienation of lands for leasing purposes.

3. This All-Fiji Indian Conference draws the attention of the Government to the great difficulties experienced by the Indians, who depend to a large extent on land for their livelihood, in obtaining leases of agricultural land and requests it to take immediate action to protect Indian interests on the following lines:

    (a) Leases of lands at present cultivated should be renewed.

    (b) Suitable provision should be made for obtaining fresh land.

    (c) Subject to regular payment of rent and the right of the Government to revise rents after prescribed period, Indians should not be disturbed in their possession of agricultural land, the system followed by the Government of India in those provinces where land is directly held from the Government should be adopted in Fiji.

4. (a) This All-Fiji Indian Conference impresses on Government the urgent need for legislation to regulate the relations of landlords and tenants and to allow to tenants the rights and protection enjoyed by them in all civilised countries. The present position is giving rise to widespread and acute discontent and unless dealt with fairly and boldly will prove seriously detrimental to the future development of Fiji.

    (b) This All-Fiji Indian Conference is further of the opinion that Government should take early action to prevent tenants from being forced to work for any individual or association.

5. This All-Fiji Indian Conference authorises the Indian Association to make suitable representations to the authorities for the:

    (a) Training of more Indian medical students.

    (b) Establishment of hospitals in the districts in which there are no proper medical facilities existing at present.

    (c) Establishment of Indian child welfare centres and training of Indian nurses.

    (d) Provision of pure water supply in the districts in which such supply is not available.

    (e) Establishment of a sanatorium for t.b. and such diseases, and

    (f) Arrangement for necessary instruction to Indian Dais, mid-wives, attending confinement cases.

6. This All-Fiji Indian Conference registers its strong dissatisfaction with the present educational facilities afforded to the Indian children and strongly urges the Government to put into effect as soon as possible the recommendations contained in Mr. Mayhew's report on the following points:

    (a) Introduction of compulsory education.

    (b) Provision for technical and vocational training.

    (c) Establishment of intermediate and secondary schools.

    i. This Conference, while welcoming the fact that the Government have adopted the Mayhew recommendations in principle, is of the opinion that the provision made for carrying them is quite inadequate specially in view of the neglect of Indian education in the past by Government notwithstanding the keenness of Indian parents to educate their children.

    ii. This Conference further records that (1) as in India a prescribed percentage of Indian children should be admitted to the European Grammar Schools and that (2) efforts should be made to obtain trained women teachers from India.

    iii. This Conference, while approving of Mr. Mayhew's recommendation that scholarships for higher education should not be confined to Europeans only, is strongly of the opinion that in view of an increasing number of Indian boys ready to profit by University education, that adequate provision should be made for giving them higher education outside Fiji.

7. This Conference authorises the Indian Association to make necessary representations to the authorities to facilitate importation of Indian patent medicines and matters connected therewith and to remit import duties on foodstuffs.

8. In view of the fact that the Indian community has vast interests in this Colony, this Conference strongly requests the Government to appoint an Indian elected member to the Executive Council which consists of Europeans only at present.

9. This Conference requests the Government to expedite the publication of the report of the committee appointed to consider the question of passports and domicile and urges the Government to remove the disabilities under which Indians labour at present.

10. This All-Fiji Indian Conference considers that the time is opportune for the appointment of an Agent of the Government of India in Fiji and urges the

Fiji Government to give facilities for the purpose in the interests of both the Government themselves and the Indian community.

11. This Conference strongly urges the Government to repeal the Masters and Servants Ordinance and to introduce legislation to facilitate registration of agricultural and trade unions in Fiji.

12. This Conference is of the opinion that the provisions of the Workmen's Compensation Ordinance be extended to the Indians and Fijians in this Colony at an early date.

13. This All-Fiji Indian Conference records its emphatic protest against the racial discrimination made in the Fiji Civil Service against Indians and Fijians and urges the Government to take immediate steps to give equal opportunities to the members of different communities for careers in the public service of the Colony on the ground of personal [merit].

The Chairman, in his summing up, said that he was grateful to the audience for their contribution and patience. He was particularly happy to find that none of the resolutions will do any harm to the Fijians. The Government of Fiji had promised to pass an Ordinance giving equal rights to Indians. Fiji was their home where they wanted to live as free men, equal in every respect with those of other [communities] residing in this Colony. While exhorting the Indians to serve not merely their own community, but also the Fijians and others with whom they live in this Colony, he said, in conclusion, that through the Indians this Colony had benefited to a great extent, and their contribution to the Colony's present position entitled them to enjoy equal rights and privileges to those enjoyed by other subjects of His Majesty.

Mr. AD Patel then moved the following resolution, which was seconded by Mr. JF Grant, and was carried unanimously:

'This Conference records the thankful gratitude and appreciation of the Indian community to the Hon. Dr Hriday Nath Kunzru for the trouble he has taken in enquiring into the conditions of Indians in Fiji and for presiding over this conference.'

70: Economic Condition of Indians in Fiji Paper read at the All-Fiji Indian Conference by AD Patel, 30 October 1938

I hope you will understand that the subject which I am supposed to deal with is one on which books may be written to do it full justice. In the short time which is at my disposal, I can only give you a general outline of the economic problems that face the Indian community in Fiji and their possible solutions. It is not claimed, however, that the solutions which I may venture to suggest are infallible.

The Indian community may be classified into three groups, namely labourers, peasants and traders. The labourers, as is the case all over the world, form the majority of the population. The ordinary Indian labourer in this Colony receives a wage of 2/- to 3/- a day. The biggest employer of Indian labour is the Colonial Sugar Refining Company Limited. Labourers working under the CSR get 1/8 a day and free quarters in the labour lines. Those that are signed under the Master and Servants Ordinance by the Company receive a small bonus at the expiry of the terms of the contract. The new labour lines are certainly a considerable advance on the old ones as far as accommodation and sanitation are concerned, but the daily wage of the worker has remained unchanged. The wives of the workers in the lines have no occupation and they and their children are entirely dependent on the meager wage that their husbands earn. An income of 1/8 to 2/- or even 2/6 a day would be in this Colony just hardly sufficient to satisfy the primary necessities of life, such as the cheapest goods and clothing. There are no facilities provided for the education of the children of workers at the mills.

The lot of the agricultural labourer on the farm is hardly better [as] he receives about the same wage as his fellow worker in the mill. He and his family, however, have some scope of supplementing their income by keeping a cow or growing a few vegetables, and if they possess a small plot of suitable land of growing paddy or some other food crop. His children in some places attend school and acquire a bare knowledge of reading and writing. The skilled Indian labour, which forms a very small part of the working class, manage to obtain better conditions of life. Their wage, however, is considerably less than the half caste or the European worker of the same class.

Though the wage is meager and the general conditions are unenviable, there is no unemployment or starvation. It may, however, be observed that even a little unemployment or starvation for a few, if most of the workers are well fed and gain better conditions of life, is preferable to a whole class having to live and work on a small wage and bring up under-nourished and uneducated children. The employers of the Colony hardly realize that they not only exploit the peasant workers but also drain the future manpower of the Colony. Fiji is perhaps the only country in the civilized world where the State has so far done almost nothing by way of legislation and administrative measures conducive to the welfare of labour.

The next largest portion of the Indian community is the cultivators. A great majority of these are engaged in the cultivation of the sugar cane. A small number grow paddy, maize, cotton, tobacco, etc. More than half of the cane growers are the Company's tenants. The average size of their holdings is about 10 acres and the net annual income about 50 pounds. The terms of the tenancy are stringent. Rest of the growers are mostly tenants of the Fijians. A small number hold land from European landlords of Indian tenants. There are very few Indian cane growers who are the owners of freehold lands. The land of the Colony is entirely owned by non-agriculturalists while the entire agricultural population consists of the tenants. One would naturally expect in such a country legislation to safeguard and promote the interests of the tenants. While the rights of the landlords and tenants in other countries have undergone a revolution, the landlords of Fiji in this fourth decade of the twentieth century enjoy the same absolute rights and privileges enjoyed by the landlords of England prior to 1875.

The Indian peasants of the Colony are mostly in debt. The indebtedness of peasants is a world-wide problem, and Fiji is not immune from it. The causes of the Indian peasant's indebtedness in Fiji are as follows:

1. The smallness of the holdings.

2. Purchase of cane growing land at reckless prices under sale and purchase agreements

3. Heavy rate of interest for expenditure on marriage and other social functions.

The cane growers appear to me to be more in debt than other peasants. That may be due in most cases to reckless buying of land and easy facilities of credit.

The Indian trading class of Fiji mostly consists of small shopkeepers and artisans. They are most industrious and thrifty and careful enough to provide for a rainy day out of their moderate income. Most of them carry on trade on borrowed capital. A substantial portion of their earnings go to the landlord and the money lender. It is through the enterprise of this class that the imports from India not only of food stuff but also manufactured articles increase from day to day. Their thrift and industry enables them to sell their wares at competitive prices and thus benefit the previous two classes whose means are always limited.

The greater part of the revenue of the Colony is derived from indirect taxation in the form of import and export duty. The incidence of export duty on sugar indirectly falls on the growers and labourers engaged in sugar cane cultivation and sugar manufacture, which also to some extent contributes to their poverty. Duties on imported foodstuff for Indian consumption are mostly charged on a quantitative basis instead of *ad valorem*. Such method of taxation falls equally on the poor as well as the rich. An *ad valorem* duty on the other hand falls on the consumers in proportion to their means. A consumer who has to live on cheap food stuffs and clothing would have to pay less duty if it is charged *ad valorem* than one who lives on an expensive standard of life. The present system of tariff seems to have been devised to make the rich richer rand the poor poorer. Amongst direct taxes, the Residential Tax is another instance.

Lack of education is another cause contributing to Indian poverty. You cannot improve the economic conditions without efficiency and you cannot acquire efficiency without education. You cannot make a silk purse out of a sow's ear, nor can you make an illiterate and ignorant community wealthy. The causes of Indian poverty are:

1. Lower wages.

2. Smallness of holdings.

3. Unrevised law of landlord and tenants.

4. Reckless buying of land.

5. Expensive social customs.

6. High rate of interest.

7. Lack of education and training.

8. Lack of opportunities for those who get education and training.

9. Iniquitous method of taxation.

10. Lack of social and industrial legislation and lack of planned economy on the part of the state.

When the causes are known, one is naturally tempted to ask: 'What is the remedy?' The remedy, to my mind, lies in the hands of the state, the owners of the land, the employers of labour, and last but not least, in the hands of the people themselves. The state can help by:

1. Fixing a reasonable minimum wage.

2. Bring the law of landlord and tenant in line with other countries, such as England.

3. Opening up more land for settlement.

4. Controlling rate of interest and establishing credit societies.

5. Providing good education and opportunities.

6. Re-adjustment of the present system of taxation.

7. Planned economy.

The owners of the land and the employers can help by:

1. Payment of better wages and improving general conditions of labour.

2. Enlarging the holdings.

3. Affording security of tenure.

The people themselves can improve their conditions by:

1. Careful purchase of land.

2. Reforming social customs.

3. Education.

4. Cultivating a sense of social solidarity.

We must not forget that God helps those who help themselves.

71: The Misadministration of Land, 20 August, 1945

The land policy of the Government of Fiji has fluctuated over a number of years. No grower and, for that matter, no tenant in the Colony, has felt sure or secure as regards the land policy that the Government may at any moment adopt. As to the native lands, first we had an old Ordinance under which, if anybody required a lease of native lands, he had to approach the native owners, and if the native owners consented to the grant of the lease, he would have to put in his application to the Director of Lands. That is how he obtained the lease of these lands from the owners. Under that Ordinance, there was a safeguard to the effect that it was made illegal for the lessee or the owner of the lands either to pay or accept a premium, but in spite of that legislation, this evil grew as there was more demand for land and there was so much pressure on the agricultural areas of the Colony. It assumed such proportions that in 1935, when a large number of leases were about to expire or had already expired, the lessees approached the native landlords for the renewal of these leases and higher premia were asked and had to be paid. The evil grew to such an extent that both the Indian growers and the Fijian owners had a problem to face.

Fijian owners who were tempted by high premia recklessly disposed of their land, irrespective of any consideration of their own personal needs, present or future, and the Indian tenants recklessly paid premia by borrowing money at a high rate of interest. They borrowed recklessly without ever thinking whether they would be able to repay the amount. Representations were made by the Indian growers to Sir Arthur Richards when he was Governor and a new policy was enunciated. First, the leases that were to expire and the existing 21-year leases were extended for a further period of nine years and so all those leases were made 30-year leases. There was a provision made that if the native owners declined to renew the leases, then they had to pay the value of the improvements effected by the tenant on the land. Even that did not turn out to be satisfactory and in the end the Native Land Trust Board was created with three main objects, firstly to safeguard an adequate area of Fijian lands for the present and future needs of the Fijian community, secondly to confer a security of tenure to the tenants of the Fijian lands, and thirdly to keep up the fertility of the lands. There was a spirit of give and take on both sides. The Fijian owners agreed that after reserving the areas that would be necessary for their own immediate or future use, the balance of the native lands would be handed over to this Native Land Trust Board to be let out on leases. The Indian tenants, on their part, also agreed that as the security of tenure was acquired, there was no further need for a provision that an Indian tenant must be entitled to payment for the permanent improvements effected on that land.

Consequently, after the passing of the Native Land Trust Ordinance, the tenants lost their right of claiming compensation for all improvements effected on the land in the event of a non-renewal of the lease. All the while, there was a clause existing in the leases, as it exists at present, that no lease shall be transferred, assigned or sold without the consent of the Director of Lands. The Director of Lands, all these years right up to the year 1944, even four years after passing the Native Land Trust Ordinance, has gone on approving and giving his consent to the transfers, no matter how grossly excessive the consideration was. Through this shortage of land and the acute demand on the part of growers for land, right up to 1940, the Fijian landlords made gross profits by way of premia. Since 1940, moneylenders and other people profited from it, but all throughout, right from the beginning up to 1944, the Director of Lands and the Government of Fiji were a party to this exploitation. The Director always gave his consent and made it possible. Now, suddenly the Government awakens to this very difficult situation, but it is not as if no warning had been sounded by the growers or their leaders previously.

As early as 1937, we asked the Government for the appointment of an Economic Commission to go into the economic conditions of these people, because the Indian community, and the leaders of the community, even at that time, knew that the grower was slipping deeper and deeper into debt and it was high time something was done. Unfortunately, without making any enquiries, the Government somehow denied that request on one excuse or another and men were found in this Council in the year 1937 to make a remark to the effect that the Indian growers were quite happy, quite wealthy and that they were coining money out of cane. If you consult the figures given in Professor Shepherd's report, you will find that in 1935 the indebtedness under crop liens amounted to £189,446. By the time the Indian Members in this Council had asked for the appointment of an Economic Commission to go into their conditions, the indebtedness had increased to £271,898. By the time the Native Land Trust Ordinance was passed, the indebtedness of the growers had increased to the tremendous figure of £330,321. Of course, it is difficult to ascertain now how much of this £330,321 went into the pockets of the Fijian landlords by way of premia and how much went into the pockets of those intermediaries who were friendly with these landlords and who were always ready to take lands and pass them on to some unfortunate bona fide grower.

That is how we have got into the position in which we are today, and let no one think that he had no part in contributing a share to it. The whole question is that we have got this problem to face; what is the solution? What is the way out of it? The Director of Lands and the Government of Fiji say: 'We will stop the speculation in prices and reduce the price of land.' It is quite logical. In fact it is so logical that it falls in the same class as if, for instance, I went to my hatter and complained to him that my hat was too small and did not fit and he came to my aid and gave me a very precious piece of advice—that the problem was simply solved; all that had to be done was to chip a bit off my head and make it small and it would then be found that the hat would exactly fit the head. Of course the argument is quite logical, but it defeats the very purpose for which we are trying to prescribe this remedy. By reducing the prices of the land, are we helping the grower to reduce his debt? Are we helping the grower to improve his economic condition? The land has been an asset to him; not only has he borrowed money on it but he has put in his own savings without which the original loan would have been impossible. He put all that money in the land and now we say that the £100 which the land is worth to him is an extravagant price, an unproductive price, and that the productive value would come to only £20. 'You were a fool to buy that land for £100 and spend so much on improvements, but we will allow you to sell that land for £20.' What would be our reaction if we were in the place of those growers? Would we not say: 'What happens to my debt under your new policy? I am losing all my savings, but I do not lose my liability for payment of my debts.'

On the face of it, it might look as if we are now going to harm these so-called speculators and exploiters, and these rapacious moneylenders, and help the growers. But does it not amount to this, that even when the grower is sold up, if the Director of Lands does not allow him the full market price whatever it fetches, if there is a balance of debt that is left unpaid after the sale of the land, it is still on the head of the grower? The money-lender has got his remedy in law even if the security is extinguished or exhausted as a simple contract debt. He could sue the man and obtain a judgment for the balance of the debt at any time within six years. After obtaining that judgment for twelve years, he will be flourishing over the head of the farmer and that judgment will carry a rate of interest of eight per cent which means that by adopting this policy we are impoverishing the grower without giving any relief to him from his debts. After making him penniless, we leave his debt hanging over his head like the sword of Democles, at least for a period of 18 years. Perhaps it may be said that while he may not be able to help those who have made the mistake, we will save the occupants of the lands from committing or repeating the same mistakes if the buyers of land were to come from outside, if they were of a class separate and apart from the sellers probably it might mean the policy of robbing Peter to pay Paul.

As it is, the buyers and sellers are all in the same boat. They are in the same boat because the Director of Lands insists—and here I say quite rightly insists—that the buyer should be a bona fide grower. And where are we going to get these bona fide growers from, from the same existing lot that is in the Colony, already under this heavy burden of debt? It might only amount to, as we say in Hindustani, the changing of turbans. I carry my debt with me but when I sell my land to 'B,' he also carries his unpaid debt from the other block to this block and I carry on mine which the Director of Lands has been good enough to help me in buying at a cheaper rate, and the debt, this ever increasing burden of debt, still remains. If anybody can convince me that you can help a man and make him rich by making him poorer than what he is, only then would I understand that something good might result from the policy that the Lands Department has adopted.

Dr. Shepherd recommends that any grossly excessive price charged for land should be prohibited. There is a considerable difference between grossly excessive price and speculative price. What we can do is to prohibit profiteering, as we have done in the case of commodities, for instance. We may not allow any vendor to charge more than a certain percentage of profit, or no profit at all, but to turn around and say that he must sell at a loss and then to tell him that he has been a fool and so must bear the loss. The vendor would be quite entitled to say that in that folly the Director of Lands and himself are accomplices and partners. At the time when he bought the land the Director gave his consent to the transaction and did not warn him; now he wants to ruin him and call him a fool. I appreciate that there is a sincere desire behind the policy to help the growers; but are we really helping the growers? Mere sincerity is not enough; the cure that we prescribe should be an effective cure that will not hurt the patient.

The Director of Lands also quoted from Dr. Shepherd's report that there are unmistakable signs of lands being flogged as a result of this heavy indebtedness. It is very difficult to distinguish what is the real cause of the flogging of such areas. For instance, it is well known that all the contractors do not leave a portion of their land fallow every year, just as the Company's tenants do, but they also follow the rotation of crops: they harvest the crop from the whole area for three years and in the fourth year leave the whole area fallow. If they are flogging the lands unnecessarily to pay their debts, the production of sugar cane from the lands owned by contractors will not be so much as it is at present. Everybody in this Colony knows that the Company has got the best lands, rich, fertile, and nice flat continuous areas, while the contractors took leases of second class and third class lands, mostly hilly lands or lands that were under thick bush. They cleared the land of stones and boulders and bush and persistently went on cultivating it in spite of the failure of several consecutive crops, and built up the fertility to that pitch where it is at present, just slightly less than the productive fertility of the Company's lands.

No doubt in some particular instances, land has been flogged, but there is another reason that we have got to consider and to my mind this is the reason. Several leases have expired or are about to expire. People apply for the renewal of those leases but owing to circumstances created by the war, consideration of the application was postponed. We, by passing legislation, extended the term of the leases by small installments and those growers whose leases had already expired or were about to expire, especially the leases in the neighbourhood of Fijian villages, were naturally concerned and anxious as to whether their leases would ever be renewed. As they had no claim against the Native Lands Trust Board for permanent improvements done and there is a probability that these lands might fall within native reserves, these farmers think that instead of putting more into the land they should now try to get the utmost out of what they have previously sunk into it, and to my mind that is the real cause of flogging in several cases.

72: Post-War Agricultural Development, 20 February 1946

The Government presented to the Legislative Council its policy on agricultural development in Fiji, the course of action it proposed to realize those policies, and the capital and recurrent costs involved in the project. There has been a difference of opinion between the official and the unofficial side of this Council in regard to experimental stations. The question that comes uppermost, to my mind, is what could be the scope of experiment that should be carried out at such stations. I agree with the Director of Agriculture that the experimental work should be limited to those problems of practical utility, not matters of mere academic value or concern. In considering the question of establishment of experimental stations and in deciding the nature of experimental work, we have to refer back to the sugar dispute, which has been already referred to by many members in this debate. I am not surprised at the reference to the dispute because, as a matter of fact, this debate and this new policy is the offspring of it. The dispute gave birth to the Shepherd enquiry which in turn gave birth to Shepherd's Report on Agricultural Policy, which again brought Messrs. Paterson and Dodds to this Colony to implement the work done by Professor Shepherd, and this led to the appointment of a committee to consider those reports. Thus this Statement of Policy has been brought before the Council now.

It has been suggested that the experimental work should include all crops except sugar cane. I would like to remind this Council that when Dr. Shepherd made his recommendations as regards the investigation work by the Department, the need that was uppermost in his mind was the system of cane cultivation in this Colony, which is embodied in paragraph 86 of his Report. I would like to read out that paragraph: 'Only half the area under cane cultivation is cropped in each year and the system cannot be considered a highly productive one. During the war, part of the cane land has been planted in food crops, particularly rice. Normally the cane farmer either grows rice on swampy land unsuited to sugar cane or buys his supplies from rice farmers. The planting of rice on cane land is justified by the war emergency but the cultivation of swamp rice at least should be discontinued when this emergency has passed, for conditions favourable to swamp rice are not suitable to cane production. The reaping of a second ration of cane is considered by the Company's agricultural experts to be undesirable even on the most fertile soils because of the danger of disease. Experiments should be conducted to ascertain whether a food, cash or fodder crop can be obtained from the land between successive plantings of sugarcane. The first problem than will be to define and study, scientifically, various rotations of crops retaining sugar as the principal cash crop.

If the proposed experimental station or stations are going to be of any practical use, they must undertake the investigation work suggested by Dr. Shepherd. Reasons have been advanced as to why the Government should not undertake any experimental work in sugar cane, and why it should be left entirely to the C.S.R. Company. Before coming to the reasons why it should be taken over by Government, I first propose to examine the reasons put forward by the Director of Agriculture against Government undertaking to conduct research work in sugar cane. The first reason put forward is that the C.S.R. Company has better facilities, capable technical staff, knowledge, experience and finances. It has also been put forward that work of that nature in other parts of the world, such as Jamaica and Hawaii, has been conducted by the industry itself and has shown remarkable results. I would be first and foremost to congratulate the C.S.R. Company for the splendid achievements they have obtained in their research work, but I would like to point out that until Dr. Shepherd came to this Colony and mentioned this fact in his Report, very few people, if any, knew that the C.S.R. Company was conducting experimental work in various types of sugar cane, and had a breeding station of a first-class order in Ba. It was all right when the C.S.R. Company was both the producer and processor of the cane. In those days, it was entirely their own concern. They were conducting experiments from the producer's point of view, as well as the processor's; but of late the C.S.R. Company has ceased to be the producer of cane and is now merely a processing Company. Consequently, the experiments they are conducting are with a view to gaining information that would be useful and profitable to the processor.

I would like to give one instance in which the interests of the processor and the producer are in direct conflict. I refer to the variety of cane known as Badila in this Colony. The planting of that variety has been a continuous source of friction between the Company and the cane growers and for a very good reason: Badila has a high percentage of sugar content, but tonnage per acre is low from the producer's point of view. Another aspect that discourages the producer is that that variety is susceptible to weather conditions; it suffers if there is too much moisture and it suffers if there is too little, but from the Company's point of view and the way that contract has been drafted, if the whole of the Colony was producing Badila the producers would be suffering a loss, but the margin of profit to the processor would be even larger than it is now. The Company insists all the time that a certain percentage of Badila is grown by the growers: they have offered an additional price of one shilling a ton, which is not sufficient inducement to the growers. They are therefore pressing some of the growers to make up this difference between Badila and other varieties of cane, and to plant Badila.

This was one of the demands put forward by the growers before Professor Shepherd, that the growers should be allowed to plant varieties of cane according to the types of land, that is, considering the suitability of land. In one instance, at Tavua, while this enquiry was proceeding, Professor Shepherd had to intervene as a conciliator between one cane grower and the Company because the Company was pressing him to plant Badila on his land. Professor Shepherd inspected his farm during the course of the enquiry and there was a compromise between the Company and the grower that, in order to save the face of the Company, the man should plant at least one acre of Badila and the balance of the land could be planted in any other variety that would be suitable. Therefore it is not right to say that as far as the varieties of cane are concerned, the matter should be left entirely to the C.S.R. Company. Interests have changed and the growers naturally expect some sort of independent organization to undertake these experiments and provide necessary information for their guidance.

It has been pointed out that the Agricultural Society of Jamaica and the Sugar Cane Planters Association of Hawaii are carrying on splendid experimental work. I am acquainted with some of their work because I get their journals regularly.

As far as Jamaica is concerned, the Agricultural Society may be considered a co-operative enterprise by the Government, the farmers and the processors: they are all interested in sugar cane. The Governor of the Colony, if I remember right, is a Patron of the Society, and the Colonial Secretary is ex officio a member of the Board of Directors. Consequently the work of the Agricultural Society of Jamaica cannot be looked upon as work conducted and carried out by a private concern.

As far as the Hawaiian Planters' Association is concerned, the small peasants of this Colony cannot be compared either for knowledge or for means with the American planters of Hawaii. They have better facilities, better knowledge and sound finances to carry on the splendid work they have been doing. We need the same type of work in Fiji. For instance in one of the issues of the bulletins published by the Hawaiian Planters' Association, there was a report on some admirable research work done on the subject of soil moisture and irrigation. We have a similar problem in Fiji in regard to the cane, just as they have in Hawaii, and who is going to carry out that experiment in Fiji? I suggest the Government.

I now wish to put forward the reasons why they should undertake the experimental work in sugar cane. First and foremost, we ought to read the signs of the times. The peasant world is seething with unrest. If we in Fiji indulge in wishful thinking and just remain blind to such contingencies after the experience of 1943, it would be our own mistake. So many Members deplore the amount of loss that this Colony had to undergo. I believe that it was a costly lesson and that it should teach us something. Why did the Colony have to undergo such a heavy loss? It was merely an industrial dispute over the price of cane. The growers were quite agreeable that the Government should help them in working out the cost of production, allow them a reasonable margin of profit and fix the cost of [production] over all those years. The Government had left experimental work in the field of sugar cane in the hands of the C.S.R. Company: they, as a third party, were unable to do anything.

The Commission was appointed, but the C.S.R. Company held out the threat that if the Commission required them to produce their accounts they would boycott it. The Governor suggested a private compromise by the counsel on both sides going into this question of accounts over the cost of production and submitting the accounts to the Governor. That came to nothing because again the C.S.R. Company were not willing to go into accounts or disclose their cost of production, and consequently the dispute dragged on. Government did not have any independent information of its own, but if there had been such a Government experimental station in the Colony where had cane growing on a practical basis, producing it and supplying to the Company, the Government itself would have been in a position to know whether there was any money or profit or whether there was a loss to the peasant farmer in the growing of sugar cane. I suggest it is high time that Government undertakes it because that will at least help in averting such disputes in future.

I can understand why the C.S.R. Company would oppose such a project. But if the Government considers the welfare of the farmers of this Colony and the general interests of the Colony, it has an obligation to carry on this type of work on the experimental stations on a practical basis to ensure the largest measure of satisfaction to the primary producer and to ensure peace in one of the most important industries of this Colony. There has been some difference of opinion as regards the number of experimental stations and their location. It is agreed on both sides that there should be at least two, one in the wet zone and one in the dry zone. As regards the location of the station in the dry zone there is a tug-of-war amongst the Unofficial Members; some suggest that it should be located in the north-western part of Viti Levu, some that it should be located in Vanua Levu. My personal view is that if we follow the principle of maximum benefit to the largest number, the experimental station should be located in north-western Viti Levu, because the largest number of the farming population—may I say, the dry zone farming population—resides in that part of the Colony. As regards the finance of the experimental station, it has been suggested that these stations should be self-supporting. I am afraid I cannot agree with that view. If the Department is going to carry on experiments, it is bound to follow the ordinary scientific process of trial and error and elimination, and for the work to be of any practical utility at all to the Colony in conducting the experiments the Department has got to be prepared for some losses as well.

Coming to the next subject, which is conspicuous by its absence from the statement but which has been dealt with by Paterson and Dodds in their report, that is the question of agricultural banks. It is admitted on all sides that to ensure good farming the question of agricultural credit must be solved and it is not a question peculiar to the Colony alone. It is a question of worldwide importance; every country is faced with the question and every country has either solved it or attempted to solve it or is still trying to solve it.' We in Fiji also cannot afford to ignore it. I was wondering why it did not appear on this Statement of Policy. I thought that perhaps because Paterson and Dodds mentioned that this is not properly a concern that should be undertaken by the Department of Agriculture, it was omitted from the Statement; but to me that hardly seems a plausible reason. The question of land tenure does not fall within the province of the Department of Agriculture but it has appeared on the statement and the question of an agricultural bank which is interwoven with all the problems of farming, including the tenure of land, ought not to have been omitted from this Statement. Certain statements have already been made by Your Excellency in this Council regarding this subject. Your Excellency has already informed the Council that the Government is seeking expert opinion on the matter and I feel that it would have been right if it had been mentioned in this Statement.

The next important question is that of a soil survey. Everybody in this Council is agreed that it is a desirable recommendation. The difference of opinion is only regarding the limit and scope of such survey. I, for one, suggest that such survey should be limited only to those areas that could be thrown open for settlement in the near future or within the next five or seven years. To attempt any scheme of survey on an ambitious scale would be too much of a strain on the over-tried financial resources of the Colony.

The question of agricultural education has been one of the most debated questions in this Council. It has been suggested by the Director of Agriculture in his statement that such education should be limited to the candidates in the Teachers' Training College and to the subordinate staff of the Department. Some of the Members on the Unofficial side have suggested that agricultural education should be open to those young men who would like to adopt agriculture as their vocation in life, and it has been suggested by one of the Members that the standard of education to be given at such a school should be similar to the standard prevailing in the agricultural school at Drasa. My own view is that if we are going to just limit ourselves to that standard as far as Indian students are concerned, we might as well not have the school at all, because an Indian grower himself feels that he is competent enough to educate his son in practical work. He can teach him how to plough, how to harrow, how to hoe, how to use a sacrifier, and, when the proper time comes, how to harvest and deliver the produce. What he is looking forward to is scientific education; he expects that his son when he returns back from the college knows more about farming than he himself does, and unless we are going to teach him scientific farming and the elementary science involved in farming, any such agricultural schools will be useless from a practical point of view. I suggest that the standard of education in any such schools should be the same as or similar to the standard that we have achieved in this Colony in our medical school, as far as the subject of medical science is concerned. If we can give them the same knowledge in agricultural school about agriculture as we have been imparting to Indian and Native Medical Practitioners in our medical school this Colony would have made one big step forward. I, therefore, suggest that there should be a proper agricultural school there on the same lines as the medical school here in Suva, but it should be open to other students who will adopt agriculture as their vocation after they have finished their education with the training college, and this educational school should be located on the same farm. As regards the practical work, there might be one year's practical course in the dry zone where the students could go into projects and work either on the experimental station at Lautoka or anywhere on the north-western area of Viti Levu or any of the demonstration farms.

This brings me to the most debated and sore question of land tenure and the recent policy pursued by the Government. As far as the first part of the statement is concerned, everybody is agreed that the management of Crown land should provide for security of tenure for the tenant, so as to encourage good farming and maintaining and increasing the productive nature of the land. It is also agreed all around that the system of land tenure is not such as to create a feeling of security in the mind of the tenant, and that the problem of land tenure is one of great urgency. The experts also express the same opinion, and the man in the street holds the same view, but what do we find in part 2 of this statement? Paragraph 20 reads: 'The application of the following principles and procedures in the leasing of Crown Land for agriculture purposes: (a) the maintenance of control over dealings in leases, including the encumbrance of leases.'

The first question is, should this control be one-sided? And the second question is, who would be the competent party to exercise that control? And the third question: the extent and nature of that control? The present control is one-sided. It is the control of the tenant by the landlord. The new policy laid down by the Government does not bind the landlord; the landlord is not amendable to that policy or that control. I will give you a few instances, Sir. We have been advocating that there should not be undue fragmentation of the land, that the creation of blocks of uneconomic size in the Colony is impossible. If any tenant is trying to sub-divide his lease in such small areas which, in the opinion of the landlord, amount to dividing up the land into uneconomic blocks, the landlord can turn it down and stop such a subdivision. But what is there to prevent the landlord subdividing his land and letting these blocks out to the tenants in such uneconomic sizes? Undue fragmentation of land is not in the interest of the public good of the Colony as a whole, and if we are going to follow that policy we must follow it to its logical conclusion. We must apply it to whoever goes against it, but be the tenant or the landlord, otherwise that policy has no meaning.

Take another instance, this vexatious question of prices of leases and sale of land. The new policy gives power to the landlord to say 'No' to any transactions by the tenant, in a case where the landlord is of the opinion that the price the tenant is charging for his leasehold interest is excessive. It has been said that we are restraining the tenant and allowing the landlord to prevent him from selling his lease at an excessive price in the interest of the land itself. We do not want land to be sold at an excessive price so that it may be flogged by the buyers, thereby affecting the future of this Colony. I agree with that argument, but again I say that if we are sincerely convinced of the desirability of such a control, then it ought to apply not only to the tenants but to both parties concerned—to the landlord as well as the tenant. We ought to be in a position to restrain any landlord if he is charging a higher premium or rental for his lease that, in the opinion of the Government, would be uneconomic and excessive. We have done nothing of the sort. These are not merely questions of academic value: they are questions of daily practical importance.

I have one case in mind. There is a small block of land near the Nadi Hospital (it is native land), it was a swamp before. The Mosquito Control authority dug a big drain and drained this area. This land is surrounded by three tenants, two of whom are bona fide agriculturalists, and the third one a brother of mine in profession, a solicitor. During the war-time one of these agriculturalists, a cane farmer, took this land on rent from the native owners to plant rice, at the time of the campaign for growing more food. When the Mosquito Control dug out this drain they took it out of the block, which is also a small block of uneconomic size on which cane was growing at the time, of another adjoining tenant. He was not paid any compensation for the cane that was destroyed, which amounted to about four tons, nor for the area that was taken away in this drain, nor was his rent reduced. He is paying just the same rent now as he was paying before, but when that man applied for a lease of this adjoining area so that his own holding there might not become of an uneconomic size, so that he might be in a position to plant swamp rice on that area to supplement his income and have some satisfaction of getting some compensation for the land that he had lost, this application was turned down. The application of the other bona fide farmer was also turned down and agricultural lease was granted to the solicitor. I know of several instances where the same Board has refused transfers on the ground that the transferee is a store-keeper or a moneylender and not a bona fide agriculturalist. And he will see that the agricultural lands only remain in the hands of bona fide peasants. This shows that though the new policy is binding on the tenants, the landlords are free to follow or pursue whatever policy they like. Is that right? We are all agreed that there should be control, but we all say that such control should not be arbitrary, that it should be well regulated, that it should not be one-sided; it should be a control which will apply to all sides, and the control should be a judicial one controlled by the State, not by the landlord.

I remember the Colonial Secretary once saying on this subject that everybody is criticizing the Government and the Native Land Trust Board regarding this policy but that nobody is saying anything about the freehold lands. I, for one, advocate that freehold lands also should fall within the same category. If we say that this is an agricultural Colony, that it is in the interests of the Colony that the fertility of the land should be maintained and promoted, that the fertility of the land must be and ought to be the concern of the State, then it will be the duty of the State to constrain anybody, whether he is a landlord or a tenant, whether he is a freeholder or a leaseholder, from exploiting that land and thereby endangering the future of this Colony. The policy can only be a just policy but as it is it strongly savours, if I may say so, of a conspiracy of the three biggest landlords of the Colony, viz., the C.S.R. Company, the Fijian through the Native Land Trust Board, and the Government, to restrain and keep the tenant farmers of the Colony down by just putting forward an excuse that we are thereby trying to protect the farmers from such vultures and wolves as the financiers and the lawyers of this Colony. Of course, landlords do not like to place themselves in the same category, and they want us to accept as a presumption that the landlord is the best person in the Colony to look after the interests of the tenant and to safeguard his future, to ensure his happiness, comfort and convenience. I for one cannot accept that view.

73: Delay Is Dangerous, 3 September 1949

All persons in authority, from the Governor downwards to the smallest officer of the Native Lands Trust Board, have expressed sympathy for the Indian farmers who will be dispossessed of the lands which will be included in Fijian Reserves. So far it has only remained a lip sympathy. Nothing has been so far done for the unfortunate farmers except being told that there are hardships and difficulties in store for them.

The land belongs to the Fijian and he has every right to keep it for himself, if he so chooses. The Government proclaims this right from housetops. But as for the right of the dispossessed tenants to be compensated for unexhausted improvements, everybody in authority observes unholy silence. About the 80 per cent or so of good, diligent and hard-working Indian farmers, who with their sweat and money built up second grade, and sometimes even third grade lands, into really first grade cane lands producing anything from 30 to 50 tons per acre, nothing is said. But loud noise is made about 20 per cent or so who are lazy and careless, and all are condemned for the faults of a few.

Even first class lands were acquired originally by payment of quite heavy premia to the native owners and then brought under cultivation by uprooting and clearing thick jungles of guava, vai vai and such other bushes and trees which are hard and expensive to eradicate. In the first few years, the farmers had to struggle hard to be able to produce even enough to make both ends meet. It was years of intensive cultivation and heavy manuring with coral sand, chemical and green manures which have made some of their first class lands what they are at present. Besides building up the fertility of the land, the tenants have planted many coconut, mango, tamarind, orange, mandarins, jack and other fruit trees which for many years to come will yield rich harvest. Tenants have dug wells and built houses on the land. In many areas they have paid heavy costs for the building of the tramlines to enable cane to be taken to the main line and made roads, put up culverts and even bridges to make the land easily accessible. They have also been contributing substantial amount every year to the Sugar Price Stabilisation Fund, the benefit of which will be enjoyed by the dispossessing landlords.

The Fijian owners are not only allowed to take their lands back, but they are also allowed to confiscate these costly improvements made by the Indian tenants. The fact that the tenant is allowed to harvest his standing crops upon payment of rent before he is actually evicted, is being advertised, as if it was a great act of generosity, while absolute silence is kept over the whole-sale confiscation of improvements. The Fijian owners should be duty-bound to pay full value for the unexhausted improvements to the lands brought about by means of clearing the land, manuring it and digging drains or building up dams and retaining walls; for the fruit and other trees planted on the land by the tenants, for the wells dug and houses, out-houses, stables and other building together with hedges or fences erected and total amount of contributions paid to the Sugar Price Stabilisation Fund. Trees and wells cannot be removed and even if the buildings and fences are dismantled, removed and re-erected in another place, the loss to be incurred by the tenant is so doing will be as much as there being left on the land. The tenant is entitled for the payment of these improvements and it is the duty of the Government to see that the compensation is fully paid to him before he is asked to leave the land.

It is also the duty of the Government to see that the dispossessed farmer is re-settled on suitable and easily accessible land. Breaking new lands and making them productive is a long laborious and expensive job. The farmer must have some source of credit to carry him over this long, unproductive period. As the farmer will not be allowed to mortgage his lease and as there will be no improvements on the lands which he can pledge, he will be thrown on the rapacity of usurious money lenders. It must be the duty of the Government to provide these tenants with sufficient loans on long and easy terms.

The Native Land Trust Board has already made a start in evicting tenants, but no start has yet been made to providing the payment of the compensation or opening up new land and re-settling the displaced tenants or financing them to bridge over the unproductive period. This procrastination on the part of the Government has created deep resentment amongst the farmers. Unless the lip sympathy is quickly turned into fair play and effective aid, the Colony will be heading for trouble.

74: Their Darkest Hour, 17 September 1949

Fiji is predominantly an agricultural country, with this distinction that the owners of land are not agriculturists and the actual agriculturists are not owners of land. Most of the farmers are either the tenants of the Native Land Trust Board or the Crown or the Colonial Sugar Refining Company Ltd. The Fijian owners have approximately 3,770,000 acres of land in their possession out of the total area of the Colony of 42 million acres. As early as 1905, the Government was alive to the Fijian interests. Under the Native Lands Ordinance passed in that year, the Native owners could lease their lands to the non-Fijians only with the consent of the Governor-in-Council. The Governor-in-Council was empowered to refuse consent if in his opinion the land proposed to be leased was necessary for the maintenance and support of the owners was leased out. Thus all the lands that were considered necessary for the maintenance and support of the Native owners have been all the while reserved and preserved for them and only the surplus lands have been leased out to the non-Fijian tenants.

The tenants who took these unrequired surplus lands (in many cases on payment of high premia) were induced to improve them as much as they could by the statutory right conferred on the tenants to the extension of the lease upon expiry of its term, or in default of such extension, to compensation for permanent and unexhausted improvements. If the native owners refused to grant extension of a lease, the Governor- in-Council was empowered to call upon them to pay into the Treasury or to the District Commissioner of the district within a specified time such sum as the Governor in Council would decide to be the present value of the permanent and unexhausted improvements made on the leasehold by any lessee during the period of the expiring lease. If the Native owners failed to pay the amount within the specified time the lease was deemed to be extended on such terms and conditions as fixed by the Governor-in- Council. Thus the tenant was not only given the right of compensation in respect of his improvements but he was also given a fair chance of extension of the lease.

Most of the leases that have now expired, and very many of the existing leases have been taken by the lessees on the strength of this statutory assurance. This assurance also provided them with an impetus to improve and build up fertility and turn them into first class lands. The Native owner naturally coveted the improved lands back. When the time came for the tenants to demand extension of their expired leases or to cash in their improvement the Government blandly took away that right with a strike of the pen by passing the Native Land Trust Ordinance 1940. When tenants, all the world over were given special protection and privileges to the point of indulgence when, even in Fiji, the town-folks were given the protection against evictions or extortions by their land-lords which continue to enjoy right up to the present, the tenants of Fijian landlords were deprived of the rights they were titled to under the Native Lands Ordinance. The tragedy of it all was that even those members who were the elected representatives of the Indian tenants at that time in Legislative Council supported the obnoxious and unjust measure which swept away the tenants' right to compensate for permanent and unexhausted improvements.

When the Fijians were given this opportunity to take back well-developed lands without having to make any compensation for improvements, it was, naturally, to be expected that they would make most of such a golden opportunity. As a matter of fact the Fijian owners, like Warren Hastings, can very well claim to be surprised at their modern [good fortune] while the tenants stand aghast at this legalised confiscation of their just dues.

75: A Sop to Evictees, 15 October 1949

The Governor has appointed a committee for the Western Districts. Yes, the Governor has appointed the committee and the fact has been advertised in the *Fiji Royal Gazette* under the pompous title 'A Resettlement of the Persons Evicted from Native Reserves within the Western Districts.' The Committee consists of the District Commissioner Western (Chairman), District Engineer Lautoka, Mr. CL Langdale, Mr. CE Whitehead, Roko Tui Nadroga and Navosa, Mr. EA Potts and Mr. TR Sharma. These good men are appointed (1) 'to assist persons displaced from Native Reserves' and (2) 'to submit for consideration by the Central Committee,' which will be appointed shortly, 'proposals for making available for settlement new areas outside the Reserves.' How exactly this Committee is going to assist the displaced tenants we are not told. It is well known that none of the members of the Committee has the means, authority or power to procure resettlement of the displaced tenants even if they had the best intentions of being helpful to the unfortunate tenants.

In what way is this Committee going to help them? Is it going to intercede on their behalf and obtain compensation for the improvements left behind on the land or are they going to go around looking for some suitable but unoccupied land and obtain leases of the same? Or are they going to provide funds for the displacement tenant and his family to enable them to break new land and bring it under cultivation until such land can produce enough for their subsistence? Has the Committee been supplied with means to carry out all or any one of those tasks?

One of the objects and perhaps the foremost one in the establishment of the Native Land Trust Board was to constitute a body which would throw open for settlement Fijian lands not included in Native Reserves and provide settlement of farmers on a large scale. The Government also called experts like Dr Shepherd to advise them on land tenure and settlement of Indian peasants. It is nearly a decade since eviction of tenants from lands which the Fijian owners may choose to reserve for their own use and the resettlement of such tenants were contemplated. It is five years since the Government had the benefit of expert advice on the matter.

And yet at this late hour the Government is asking for proposals from a committee which is least qualified to do so. Has it not been the duty of the Native Land Trust Board to design new settlements outside the reserves and make them available to those who are in need? Neither the Government nor the Native Land Trust Board have made preparations to meet the present emergency which could have been foreseen at least ten years ago. Instead of following the only logical solution of the problem in the circumstances, namely persuading the Fijian owners of the Reserves not to hasten and take possession of their land before the Government has made adequate arrangements and found areas for immediate settlement of evicted tenants, they have put the cart before the horse and followed the policy of throwing the tenants out of their old homes first and look for new homes afterwards.

What the Government did not, or could not, provide in a decade the Committee is expected to produce like a conjurer out of its hat on the spot. Though we do not believe in magic, we wish it good luck.

76: Adding Insult to Injury, 26 November 1949

This is just like the Native Land Trust Board. For who else would put forward such an excuse as given by the Board in its latest circular to confiscate tenants' improvements. The circular reads 'The Board is of the opinion that, in general, past methods of farming on leased native lands have not led to any permanent improvements in such lands, and in consequence the Board is not prepared to consider the question of compensation for improvements to such lands.' If the Board really believes the correctness of its opinion, it would have certainly declared without beating around the bush that it was willing to pay for permanent improvements, if any, in the event of the non-renewal of the lease. Nobody then could have questioned the fair mindedness on the part of the Board and it would not in fact have to pay any compensation if no permanent improvements exist as they try to make out.

The Board blandly states that, in general, past methods of farming on leased native lands have not led to any permanent improvements in such land. Some of these lands have been leased to the Colonial Sugar Refining Company which has in turn sublet them to Indian tenants. Some lands are directly leased to Indians which have been developed and brought into sugarcane cultivation by them. So far the Colonial Sugar Refining Company as well as the Government of Fiji have taken pride in the methods of sugar cane farming prevailing in this Colony. Lands that were under scrub, stones and weeds when they were leased out, now produce in many cases 30 or 40 tons of sugarcane per acre. The lessees of the native lands in sugarcane areas have not only broken and developed wild country but they have also permanently enriched it. Lands that were not easily accessible have been made accessible by the roads and tracks made by the tenants. Their contributions in the past to the Sugar Price Stabilisation Fund will also benefit the Fijian landowners.

This is what the 'past methods' of farming have achieved in the sugarcane areas. Besides that, valuable fruit trees are planted by the tenants whose fruit will be enjoyed for some generations by the landlord. And yet the Native Land Trust Board claims that there are no improvements for which the question of compensation can be considered. Many native leases have been brought under coconut plantations by the tenants. It is their past methods of farming which yield such lucrative harvest of copra today. We know of a native lease on which the lessee had a rubber plantation. The Native Land Trust Board refused to renew the lease and did not pay any compensation for the value of the rubber trees which the Fijian owner took over with the land. Perhaps in the opinion of the Native Land Trust Board even a rubber yielding plantation is not a permanent improvement deserving payment of compensation.

If the Board does not like the native lands as they are at present, would they like the tenants, before they hand over the lands, to exhaust all improvements, cut down or dig out all valuable trees and turn it into a veritable bush as it was when originally leased? Expropriating landlordism never runs short of excuses to swallow up what rightfully belongs to its tenants. But the excuse put forward by the Native Land Trust Board is unique. It condemns its own creator.

77: Diversification of Agricultural Production, 4 November 1956

What stands out most prominently in the report of Sir Geoffrey Clay, Adviser to the Secretary of State for the Colonies, on his visit to Fiji in 1954 is his advice on the urgent need for diversification of agricultural production, a need which discerning students of this Colony's economy have felt, and to which we have had occasions frequently in these columns to refer. For no wise country should have all its eggs in one economic basket—and that is more or less the position in Fiji now.

Sir Geoffrey Clay spent five weeks in Fiji last year in the course of his tour. And after a study of the agricultural problems of the Colony, he sums up the present situation:

> Fiji's agricultural crop production is, in the main, confined to the flat alluvial lands and occupies less than 10 per cent of the total land area, is dependent very largely on sugar cane and copra, and with the exception of bananas and rice, which show welcome expansion, has remained static in volume over the past decade and half in spite of an expansion of population of over 50 per cent and an adult male population of at least 25 per cent during that period.

Faced with this situation, some publicists in Fiji used to raise the bogey of over-population and also blame it all on one particular race which happens to be virile and active. But a wise and unprejudiced authority like Sir Geoffrey naturally suggests the scope for development and the need for carrying out studies and field experiments in this behalf.

'To anyone acquainted with the other parts of the Colonial Empire,' states Sir Geoffrey, 'one's first major impression must be surprise that the interior of the mountainous islands has been almost completely neglected.' He suggests, therefore, that necessary soil survey and ecological study should be completed in these regions. For, it would appear that in many of these regions the climate and the soils may be suitable for tea and coffee. In the wetter zones cocoa should hold out excellent possibilities as the investigations already completed show; Sir Geoffrey suggests the advantages of under planting cocoa in the coconut plantations too. And in the intermediate as well as in the wet zone conditions could be found suitable for rubber and coffee. For the dry zone, cotton, especially the short and medium stapled varieties, could well form the basis of the farmers' crop. There are possibilities too of expanding rice production with irrigation, schemes for which could well be executed without very heavy investment.

Fiji is the nearest tropical dependency to Australia, New Zealand and (Western) Canada, three important members of the British Commonwealth. And this fortunate location should and can be exploited for the advantage of the Colony which can supply all tropical produce to these countries, as well as to America. Spices like pepper could form valuable dollar export crops. And with the rapidly developing air service between temperate countries passing through Fiji, tropical fruits like mango, often, called the king of the tropical fruits, should also provide as valuable an export crop as banana is at present. And in the case of the mango, there is the additional advantage that once orchards are planted with good varieties, the recurring labour costs are comparatively negligible. And the vast untapped Market of the temperate countries nearby should be able to absorb Fiji's exports, although these Market will have to be developed.

In dealing with the sugar cane, naturally and rightly Sir Geoffrey says that he was impressed with the organization of the sugar cane industry under the over-all management of the C.S.R. Co. He pays well-deserved encomiums to the scientific and field staff of the Company for their work. And he suggests that better over-all production might be obtained by limiting cane to the plant crop and practising 25 per cent rotation.

In dealing with this topic, Sir Geoffrey mentions how the application of quotas for sugar under the International Sugar Agreement makes development of crops other than sugar cane essential for the Colony. For already the Colony is producing, under the existing area under cane, an exportable surplus up to the quota limit. And in order to avoid over-production, at least so long as the International Sugar Agreement is in force on the present basis, it may even become necessary to reduce acreage under cane, when perhaps the Company might close their Nausori Mill.

The complacent cane farmer may not be worried over the situation. But an enlightened public and government interested in the welfare and progress of the people cannot afford to be complacent.

Diversification of Agricultural Products II (18 November 1955)

We have considered in a previous number the need for diversification of agricultural production in the Colony in the light of Sir Geoffrey Clay's report. How much diversification can well be effected is the next question to be considered.

Sir Geoffrey has some valuable suggestions to make in this regard too. In its position as the agency responsible for the control of all native land, the Native Land Trust Board. says Sir Geoffrey Clay, 'must play a major role in organising settlement and development of vacant lands'.

When the demarcation of Reserve Land is completed, a picture will be available of the nature and extent of the land available for development. Perhaps it should then be possible for giving the settler in the land a greater stake than is available at present. For the needs, present and future, of the Fijian having been provided for, it should be possible to give the farmer his due share of what he produces. Terms of land tenure and the basis of rent payable to the land owner should be all fixed in such a way that these will provide real inducement to the farmer.

In considering the suitability of climate and soils, especially in the interior of the mountainous islands, for particular crops the need for survey under able and experienced experts has been stressed by Sir Geoffrey. He has also suggested some suitable names for this purpose.

While discussing the recruitment of senior staff for the Department of Agriculture, Sir Geoffrey wisely said that 'it would not be in the interests of Fiji to attempt to make the Fijian service a closed service,' by confining the recruitment of officers domiciled in New Zealand and Australia. In fact he suggests that 'in the case of recruitment from Australia and New Zealand, some tightening up in the actual selection is required.' The advantages to be derived from transfers to and from the Unified Service of the British Colonies are great indeed.

It would, in fact, be to the advantage of agricultural development in the Colony if arrangements are sought to be made for getting the services of experienced officers from parts of the British Commonwealth of Nations, especially in the projects for development of new tropical produce like tea, coffee, rubber and spices. Experts from tropical countries like Ceylon, Pakistan, Malaya and India can render valuable aid. And the idea behind the Colombo Plan, which has shown such magnificent results all over South-East Asia, should be of benefit to the Colonies. And the spirit of amity and helpful co-operation, existing between the different members of the Commonwealth is an assurance that such help will be forthcoming, provided they are tapped.

Next only to the land suitable and available for the purpose, is the man power which is essential for the purpose of agricultural development. Sir Geoffrey Clay has some valuable suggestions for enabling the Fijians to play their part in such a development. Though 'speaking generally the Indian section of the population who are traditionally agriculturists have tended to regard,' as Sir Geoffrey remarks, 'agricultural development as synonymous with sugar cane farming,' it was no fault of the Indian farmer himself. We dare say the enterprising and industrious Indian, provided he is given the opportunity, will play his part creditably in any well-thought out scheme of agricultural development in the Colony. There is need for it. There are men ready for it. It is for the Government to do their part to enable and help the men to play their part for the agricultural development of the Colony.

78: Fruit Industry, 31 May 1956

The demand for fresh fruits and also preserved varieties is steadily increasing. Fruit contains some minerals and sugar, and is valuable for its roughage. Fruit has the additional advantage that it is frequently consumed raw, without any loss of Vitamin C. Sir Robert McCarrison, world famous for his research in nutrition in India, says that fruits are rich in alkali minerals.

No propaganda is necessary to make our people eat fruits, for they like them provided they can get them. Hence it is necessary to encourage fruit growing on large scale commercial basis and make them available to the poorest man. At present fruits form a negligible part of our diets.

At present we grow only bananas and pineapples on commercial basis. No other tropical or temperate fruit is grown for marketing though we have suitable land for growing such fruits. Such land is now lying waste. We depend mostly on imports for preserved varieties.

An intensive effort to introduce temperate-fruit growing is necessary in our Colony. In areas like Nadarivatu and other hilly regions, this variety can be successfully introduced provided we do it in the scientific way. A new variety of bananas, *Musa Sapidisloca*, which is sweeter and more nutritious, can be grown on hillsides 2,000 feet high.

Madras State has paid considerable attention to the development of hill fruits and has introduced varieties of exotic fruits. Southern California is another place where we have the organization of fruit orchards on large commercial basis. Countries like Switzerland, Italy and the United Kingdom have well developed fruit industries. Succulent strawberries available in temperate regions can be easily grown in our high hills as it has been done in the Nilgiris. Better strains of oranges and other citrus fruits may be usefully introduced.

There is no reason why Fiji should not be made self-sufficient in the matter of these 'temperate' fruits. The hilly region, which occupies the major area of our island and remains untouched except to some extent for manganese prospecting, favours the production of many kinds of temperate and sub-tropical fruits. Table grapes are grown in plenty in the plains adjoining the hilly regions of Southern India. The income per acre in such fruit growing areas is many times more in comparison with other produce growing areas.

Our Agriculture Department should lead the way by starting model fruit farms at different places in the western districts for demonstration purposes and teach our people modern techniques, and supply our farmers with saplings, seeds, plants and other material. This will induce at least some of us to be the pioneers in large scale fruit farming in Fiji.

Fruit shows, like flower shows, will serve as a fine instrument for propaganda. Quite apart from the temperate fruits we can grow a wide variety of other sub-tropical and tropical fruits, the chief of which is mango. Growing and eating more fruits would add to the pleasures of life. In New Zealand we can find good market for our new tropical fruits like mangoes, pomegranates, and plums.

79: Diet and its Effect, 3 August 1959

The diet of Magsaysay Peace Prize winner, Acharya Vinoba Bhave, indomitably energetic in his own way, consists, according to Arthur Koestler, of small cups of curd and molasses taken every three or four hours, a total of 1,100 calories a day. Yet his body is all muscle and sinew, his skin has a healthy glow, his gestures are vigorous, and he can out pace his younger disciples on his Bhoodan Marches.[2]

The influence of diets on politics must be considerable, if British poet Walter de la Mare is to be believed that whatever Miss T eats becomes Miss T. This is supported only by Hindu thought, which has drawn a sharp, if unscientific, distinction between vegetarianism and non-vegetarianism and in certain food stuffs in their effect on human qualities. Gita mentions this in Chapter 17.

This is different from the pre-Puranic Brahmanism of Emerson's Brahma who claimed that he was the slayer and the slain and did not bother what anybody ate or killed for eating. The trouble with modern vegetarians is that they have not been unanimous in defining vegetarianism. The London Vegetarian Society included some kinds of fish in vegetarian diet on the basis of its definition of meat.

The adherents of vegetarianism exclude even mild and other animal products. The vegetarian societies which grew in many European countries cited in their favour health, economy, race improvement, and character development in their tracts for the times. Not the least interesting argument was that if it required ten pounds of fodder to produce one ounce of meat, it was better to achieve caloric contentment through vegetables.

The great modern dramatist George Bernard Shaw put it in his topsy-turvy way by saying that he was a vegetarian because he would not eat dead animals. Hegelian dialectics led to both Prussian militarism and Stalinist communism, and it is difficult to say what vegetarianism or non-vegetarianism contributes to politics. The Brahminical tradition in India was strengthened by the Jain doctrines which in the name of Hinduism Gandhi propagated. He experimented with diet, but always within the limits of vegetarianism.

Nehru's biographers describe his breakfasts and not the rest of his diet, though it is widely known that he achieves a balance in his habits which could be called both vegetarian and non-vegetarian. The difference between vegetarianism and non-vegetarianism in the higher levels of thinking is the difference between Bernard Shaw and Bertrand Russell.

---

2   A movement started in 1951 by Bhave to get wealthy landowners to give a percentage of their land to the landless lower classes.

Non-vegetarians include men as various as Hitler and Churchill, though in the case of Western statesmen, what they drink matters as much as what they eat. Disraeli used to claim that he had taken too much claret whenever he had taken too much brandy.

The classic story from British public life is that of Pitt the Younger remembering, on his death-bed, Bellamy's pork pies, though it is widely believed to be an apocryphal story. Drinking is considered a worse habit than meat-eating in India, though they should go together, but the more sensitive set of public men consider that corrupt men are acceptable but people who drink are not.

There is no particular glory perhaps in any habit and man's metabolism has many contradictions. Learned Erasmus said his heart was Catholic but his stomach Lutheran. The metaphorical significance of meat-eating is greater than its protein and other values. Among the people, habits change, howsoever slowly: some get tired of eating meat and others of eating vegetables, as the Roman Empress, Valeria Messalina, got tired of adultery.

80: Fiji's Growing Pains, 17 December 1959

The Legislative Council of Fiji has 31 members, of whom 16 are official and 15 unofficial. The official members are bound to vote as the Governor directs. So the Government can never be defeated on any measure. Out of the 31 members 21 are Europeans while there are five Indians and five Fijians. Out of the 15 unofficial members, the Governor nominates nine, two of whom are Europeans, two Indians and all the five Fijians. Thus the Fijian members are appointed by the Governor and all of them invariably are subordinate government servants. No Fijian who is not a Government servant has ever been appointed to the Council. Never has a Fijian—whether a Chief or a commoner—from the Western Division has been nominated, although it is the most important division in the Colony in all respects.

The Fijian nominees by virtue of their position dare not open their mouths against the Government. They justify their appointments by praising the government and the Europeans and criticising Indians. Motions have been brought by Indian members from time to time for constitutional reforms. European members oppose any constitutional change because it can only mean curtailment of present European hegemony. Fijian members oppose because for them it means self-elimination from the Council. If the Fijians get franchise, then they being government servants, cannot stand for election. If any of them resign from government service and seek election, it is most unlikely that he will be elected. The Government and the European press represent to the outside world that the Fijians are completely satisfied with the present political setup and oppose any change in the constitution.

The Government and the press call the Fijian nominated members, 'Fijian leaders' and whatever they say in Council and in public is represented as the considered opinion of the Fijian people. But in truth these 'Fijian leaders' are not the leaders of the Fijians. They are paid government servants. The late Ratu Apolosi Ranawai, the leader of the Fijian people, raised a cry of Fiji's independence as early as the twenties of this century. But for a few intervals Apolosi had to spend most of his life in interment and exile. It is several years now since he passed away, but many Fijians still refuse to believe that he is dead. It would be a mistake to assume that since Apolosi's death the Fijians have no leaders.

The workers of Fiji comprise of Fijians, Indians, and part-Europeans, who are united in their demand for higher wages and better conditions of work. The employers and the 'Fijian leaders' try to disunite Fijians from Indians and part-Europeans. But the more they try to divide them, the more united they stand.

Last year's unrest among workers in the sugar industry gave sufficient warning and notice to other employers in the Colony to revise the wages of their employees. The C.S.R. quietly took advantage of the Honeyman Commission's majority recommendation and settled the unrest by giving a raise of three pence per hour to their workers. Other employers could have followed C.S.R's example and secured industrial peace for at least one year.

Christmas was drawing near. The shop windows were filled with expensive and glittering Christmas goods. The schools were closed for the long vacation. Fijian school boys were wandering looking at the glittering shop windows with bleak prospects for a merry Christmas in their hearts on account of unemployment or low income of their parents.

In this setting on Monday last week some 250 workers of the Vacuum and Shell oil companies working in Suva, Lautoka, Vuda and Nadi Airport went on strike. The smallest body of workers in Fiji went on strike against the biggest oil companies in the world. The Government promptly came out with a statement condemning the strike and asking the strikers to return to work. Right on its heels, the Native Land Trust Board came forward with an announcement that no rents will be paid [to the landowners] until transport situation improved. It meant that the Fijians will not get their own money to spend at Christmas. These two announcements created a widespread feeling among the general public that the Government was siding with the oil companies and bringing undue pressure on the workers.

The bus and taxi drivers in Suva replied with a sympathy strike without prior announcement. Men, women and children collected at the bus station looking for transport. The Secretary of the Wholesale and Retail Workers' General Union tried to address people who were there. The police thereupon used gas bombs and batons to disperse the peaceful crowd. This action of the police played the part of a spark. Widespread rioting broke out in Suva. Youngsters smashed shop windows and destroyed goods and hurled stones at passing cars injuring several people. It appeared as if pandemonium was let loose in Suva, but the rest of the Colony remained completely peaceful.

The Public Servants' Association made representations to the Governor requesting immediate settlement of the dispute and the establishment of peace and order. This body of Government servants condemned most strongly the action of the police in using the gas bombs and baton charges. It added that until the throwing of the gas bombs, the assembly was peaceful and if it were to ascribe responsibility for disturbances that followed, then it must rest on the shoulders of the policemen whose action actually provoked the feeling of the crowd.

To establish peace and order in Suva the Governor-in-Council clamped drastic regulations on the whole country and imposed curfew not only on Suva but on Lautoka and Nadi Airport as well. People were shocked at the outbreak of violence in a country which is normally so peaceful. There was no one who did not sincerely condemn the violence, and the situation became calm long before the promulgation of the curfew order.

'The winds of social change which are transforming Africa and Asia, blew even over Fiji,' commented London *Times* in its editorial on these disturbances. The editorial went further and said: 'Fiji which was aware of the rapid emancipation in other dependencies, was beginning to question a Crown Colony constitution which still gave a small permanent majority to the official side. There were complaints too that the five Fijians in the Legislative Council represented the Chiefs and not the people.'

The 'Times' hit the nail on the head when it further stated, 'Whether or not this diagnosis is right a general overhaul of the constitution and economy of the islands will not come too soon.' It is hard to say which perturbed the reactionary elements in this country and abroad more, the editorial of the 'Times' or the disturbances. To many of the diehards the editorial appeared to be a greater calamity than even the outbreak of violence. Their tune suddenly changed. They now try to make out that 'subtle minds have tricked the Fijians into a Ghana-like "out with the British" demand which they don't really want and which could only harm them.' They are trying to block constitutional changes by carrying on a propaganda in Britain, Australia, New Zealand and other countries to the effect that Fijians do not want any political change. The 'Fijian leaders' are vainly trying to support it by diplomatic anti-Indian utterances. But the Fijians are not as unintelligent as they think.

We are glad that the violent part of this big drama is over. We sincerely wish that it is over for good. It would be wise to remember that more can be achieved by touching peoples' hearts than by touching their heads. And this applies to everybody—as much to the members of the Government as to the people of this country. In this big drama all have a part. It will be admitted on all sides that the wages of workers in cities and towns are too low to provide themselves and their families with proper nourishment and even minimum comforts and social amenities of life. A general revision and fixing of a proper minimum living wage for all workers by government legislation will save the country all the unrest and damage which result from wage disputes.

81: The Medicine[3], 7 March 1960

The long awaited Report of the Burns Commission is now published. It has killed many expectations and put to rest many doubts and misgivings.

Fiji is a Crown Colony with meagerly developed natural resources and rapidly increasing population. To develop natural resources in such a way as to keep pace with increasing population, the things which the Colony most urgently needs are capital, technical know-how and remunerative market for the products. None of the members of the Commission was competent to procure these things or to produce a blueprint in the absence of their provision. If the cart was put before the horse, one can hardly blame the horse for it. The people who are disappointed because their expectations of a blueprint did not come true, should blame the Governor who appointed the Commission rather than the members of the Commission who did what they could under existing limitations.

Instead of a blueprint the Commission has provided the Colony with a prescription, which is a mixture of numerous ingredients, some of which are sweet and some bitter, some salty and some sour, some hot and some acrid. The ingredients include all tastes, and the mixture is, therefore, likely to leave, if not an altogether bad, at least a very disagreeable taste in the mouth.

The Commission warns that all the medicine has to be taken and it will not do just to take that which appeals and leave the rest. The Commission consists of two colonial administrators who were perhaps highly successful in their careers in the colonial service with minds securely closed against any chance of pollination by the winds of change which are blowing all over the colonial territories, and a learned professor ensconced in the academic sanctuary of a Scottish University.

---

3   Response to Sir Alan Burns, TY Watson and AT Peacock, Report of the Commission of Enquiry into the Natural Resources and Population Trends of the Colony of Fiji, 1959, Legislative Council Paper 1/1960.

They have rushed into the question of constitutional reforms with head long speed regardless of the fact that neither their competence nor their terms of reference allow them even to tread.

Usually a doctor takes into consideration the religious and other prejudices and sentiments of his patient in prescribing the medicine. The Commission has departed from this time honoured practice and has allowed their own personal prejudices and religious beliefs to influence them in determining their prescription for the patient. This is quite evident in the report when it says that Sir Alan Burns dissents from his two colleagues on the recommendation relating to family planning and birth control because of his religious belief. How many of his other peculiar beliefs have influenced him in arriving at the conclusions contained in the report are not very hard to surmise. The report can therefore be hardly described as a result of scientific investigation by impartial and unprejudiced experts. The reason for appointing such a costly Commission at the time when every penny is important to the Government and the tax payer, was to secure expert, impartial and unprejudiced minds to bear upon our problems in order to find correct solutions.

To point out these drawbacks does not, however, mean that the medicine is perfectly useless. If the Colony has not got its money's worth it has at least got something in return. The Commission has candidly pointed the impediments and disincentives which hamper production and development. The Government's land policy, the expensive inefficient and unnecessary Fijian Administration, the cramping communal system, the policy and undesirable functions and activities or the Native Land Trust Board, the lethargy and incompetence of the Native Reserves Commission which has not completed its work, which was intended to be completed within two years, even in 20 years, and many other things have been carefully scrutinized, exposed and suitable remedies are prescribed. On the other hand, the proposals not to incur any further expenditure on Health, Education, and other social services and failure to realize due importance of these in the development of the natural resources and economic improvement of the people are apparently the outcome of the minds preconditioned by the concepts of Colonial Administration prevailing in the pre-World War II era.

The salaries and allowances of expatriate civil servants are upheld and justified. People are warned not to criticize them too much lest it might hurt their morale and affect their efficiency. Religious, educational and political leaders are exhorted to exert their influence to restrain extravagance by persons of all races. It is not stated who the religious, educational and political leaders of the expatriate civil servants are. Many of the recommendations amount to supporting the findings and recommendations of previous investigators appointed by the Government, which are not so far implemented. The Colony has had many investigators and many reports since the last war. It is to be hoped that Burns Commission will be the last for many years to come, and instead of calling any more investigators, the Government will seriously and sincerely start to properly implement at least some of those reports.

The Burns Report does not claim to provide a cure. It leaves it to others to diagnose further and find the cure. It frankly admits that even after due administration of all the medicine the patient may keep on losing weight. Strictly speaking the prescription is more in the nature of a tonic than a medicine.

82: Landlord and Tenant Bill, 20 July 1966

The problem of security of tenure, of fair rent and of compensation for unexhausted improvements by the tenant on the expiry of the lease in respect of agricultural tenancies, has been with us for over 30 years now. As time passes, these problems grow in extent, in acuteness, and in complexity. Certain requests have been made for the postponement of this Bill. The Attorney-General gave very sound and excellent reasons why the Bill should not be postponed. There is one more reason that I wish to add to that long list. It is said that people whom this Bill concerns most have not been consulted, and they have not been given the opportunity to study this Bill: namely, the tenant farmers. I would like to point out that the request for deferment of this Bill came only from the merchant community through the Federation of the Chambers of Commerce, and the working community of the Law Society. As is well known, there are many farmers' organizations in existence and all these years we have been alive to the interest of the farmers and very active in championing their cause. There are Indian farmers' associations and there are Fijian farmers' associations. This problem has been exercising their minds all these years, and not one farmers' association has come with the request that they want time for further consideration of this Bill, and that this Bill should be deferred.

What is more, there are as far as the Indian side is concerned, at least four members in this House, who are active workers in farmers' organizations. I myself happen to be the President of the Federation Committee of several farmers' associations operating in the Western and Northern Divisions. The member from North Viti Levu is the Secretary of that Committee. The Indian Member for the Northern Constituency is also a prominent member of that Federation Committee and the fourth member is the First Indian Nominated Member who is a tenant of native land. He is a farmer who farms sugar-cane, who keeps poultry, who breeds, rears and keeps livestock. As far as the tenant farming community is concerned, it is well represented in this House and no request has come to any of those four members of this House that they want more time to consider this Bill and that it should be postponed. I, on the other hand, am of the opinion that the sooner we put the landlord and tenant legislation on the statute book, the better for the tenant farmers whose minds are acutely in distress. The sooner that alarm is allayed, the sooner relief is granted to their minds, by relieving their anxiety, the better for everybody. I, therefore, strongly support that this Bill should be put on the statute book as soon as possible.

As far as the tenant community of Fiji is concerned, I would say that about 90 percent of tenants are the tenants of either the native owners or of the Crown, or of the Colonial Sugar Refining Company. About 10 percent of the tenants will be tenants of individual owners of freehold land. There is a tendency in this country to presume that everything which is big is good and virtuous. I must say that it is not necessarily so. I must emphasize the fact that whether the landlords are the native owners or the Government or the Colonial Sugar Refining Company or the private freeholders, all of them have got skeletons in their cupboards and it is no use for any of them to feel more virtuous than the rest. Let me first take the largest landlord in this Colony, the Native Land Trust Board, and point out that the largest tenant of native land is the Colonial Sugar Refining Company. It was said that the Fijian owners have made a determination that they must use their land. I appreciate both their desire and their determination to make use of their land which covers from 80 to 83 percent of the total land area of this country.

But I must sound a note of warning. Good as this determination may be, if it is not used in a proper manner there are dangers that such a determination may lead their tenants and this country into a state of a chaos and may result in the economic and political ruin of this land. If their determination and desire takes the form of resuming lands from the tenants which have already been developed and are placed in the highest state of production, under the temptation of having land which has been already well developed and ready-made and requires the least amount of struggle and effort, it will only result in uprooting farmers who have been experienced over all these years, farmers who have specialized in growing particular crops which they are growing on those lands, such farmers will face utter ruin and the land which will revert to the Fijian owners will of necessity, go down in production until the Fijian owners gain sufficient experience and knowledge of that type of farming, which will affect the general prosperity of the Colony.

Another result will be that the present tenant farmers will be reduced to the position of 'nomadic farmers,' as I call them. In arid areas nomadic people migrate from place to place seasonally. Here, if I am to take the words of the Director of Lands seriously that 30 years' tenancy is adequate for purposes of all kinds of farming including copra planting, then it will amount to this: at the end of every 30 years, in spite of this legislation, the farmer must leave his land which he has occupied, used, cultivated and brought to the highest pitch of production and go somewhere on virgin, possibly marginal, land and again start breaking new lands and developing it, until the entire 80 or 85 percent of the land area of the Colony is developed by the unfortunate tenants. That sort of treatment will terribly shake the confidence of the farmers both as far as their own personal interests and their profession is concerned, and also in the training of the future generations. Every farmer will try to see that his son does not become a farmer and seeks employment in some other vocation or occupation, with the result that the agriculture of the Colony will sink to its lowest level and at the same time it will create an acute problem of unemployment in other walks of life. Instead of taking the Colony upward and ensuring a higher standard of living for everyone, it will result in lowering the standard of living for everybody—not only the farmers but everybody living in this Colony—to its lowest level. Luckily, in this Colony, as far as Fijian lands are concerned, only a small proportion of those lands have been actually leased out and there is still a vast proportion of land unleased, unused and if they turn their attention to the development of those lands, it will help them, it will help their tenants and it will help this Colony.

First, take the native reserves. There is quite a substantial acreage in native reserves. Should it not be the first objective to make the fullest possible use of those reserves before thinking of displacing tenants on other lands? I know there is quite a legitimate desire on the part of Fijian owners that they would like also to be cane farmers and share the prosperity of that industry. But if you look to the history of that industry it had its ups and downs and in future, too, there is no guarantee that it will not again have its ups and downs. Indians came as farmers when the sugar industry was on the rocks, when the big plantation owners had to get rid of plantations and get out of the industry. It was at that moment in the history of the sugar industry that the Indians became sugar farmers and kept that industry going and salvaged it from those difficult times. It was because of their innate temperament for hard work and for thrift. They know how to live on as little as they can get as well as live on the utmost limits of luxury and comfort that they can afford.

As far as the sugar industry is concerned, the Government hopes and expects that production will be increased and the area of sugar-cane farming will be extended. Before the War, this Colony was producing around about 100,000 tons of sugar. Now we are producing more than 300,000 tons and we are hoping that in the next few years, the production of sugar may be increased to 400,000 tons and, if possible, to half a million tons per year. Even in the sugar industry as far as the extension is concerned, the Fijian owners have got an opportunity without displacing the tenant to enter the industry and to try it out for themselves. I hope, and sincerely hope, that they will not find that it was distance that had lent enchantment to their view. Even after these lands are exhausted, there are such extensive unused areas for which we have made a provision in the development plan laying emphasis on forestry which is also included in this Bill as an agricultural tenancy. Even if they do not look at sugar-cane, there are still plenty of opportunities and plenty of scope for resorting to cash farming and to subsistence farming. That will be a great help to themselves, to their tenants and to this country as a whole.

As far as native leases are concerned, the most acute problem has been, and is, renewability of the leases on their expiry. When the Native Land Trust Ordinance was passed, people thought that the problem of renewability was more or less solved. But unfortunately we have that problem on our hands even now, and in a worse form. This Bill seeks to provide for two extensions, each of not less than ten years. As far as the existing leases are concerned, it means that on the extension of these leases, the tenant, if he is a good farmer, has got a very good chance of getting leases renewed twice each time for a term not less than 10 years. If the Native Land Trust Board and tenant agree to the term and if the tenant has no necessity to go before the Tribunal, there the matter stops, but if the Native Land Trust Board and the tenant does not agree, then the tenant has at least one remedy provided under this Bill: he can go to the independent Tribunal and have the term of his extension fixed.

Complaint has been voiced that if a Fijian owner wishes to resume land on the expiry of a lease for his own use, he will not be able to establish greater hardship than the tenant before the Tribunal. I would think that in that case the Fijian landowner is in a more fortunate position than the tenant and he should be thankful to Providence for it. As a matter of fact, as this Bill stands, it provides that if the Fijian landowner just wishes to limit himself within the provisions of this Bill, that provision in itself, to my mind, will supply an excellent reason for the tenant to establish greater hardship and that is the provision that the owner of the land, the landlord, has got to give twelve months' notice to the tenant of his intention to resume the land for his own use. The tenant has got a sound argument and case before the Tribunal. How can anyone expect an established farmer with all his fixtures and all his commitments to be able to get away and make provision elsewhere and get out and hand over the land without causing acute hardship on him? If the owners of the land are wise, this Bill provides for a better and easier reward than what they would get by using the land themselves and that is a fair market rent which can be re-assessed every five years.

This Bill will also obviate another problem which creates acute anxiety in the minds of holders of native leases; that is, when the lease expires and when the tenant has made an application for renewal or extension of the lease, and a document is issued to them which is interpreted as a tenancy-at-will. Some years ago, it was the practice of the Board that under this tenancy-at-will, the tenant was called upon to pay the rent monthly, knowing fully well that he has a sugar cane farm and it would take 18 months to harvest from the time it is planted. This absurd position went on for quite a long time. Later on, when it was pointed out and when there was a lot of criticism about it, then it has been changed to annual rent payable in two installments but still it is a tenancy-at-will.

Now, these tenancies-at-will are abolished by this Bill and the tenant has not got to worry about what will happen under such a vague and flimsy nature. At least he gains the chance of having his lease renewed for two terms each not less than ten years. What's more, if a tenant wanted to sell his lease, the Native Land Trust Board insisted that the price he could charge for the lease should be the value of improvements he has effected on the land and the crops and buildings which are standing on the land. Later on that was modified and the tenant was allowed to charge whatever price he could get. The power to refuse consent for transfer was used to re-assess and raise the rent on that lease with the result that the buyer of the native lease has got to pay a high price for the land as well as a higher rent to get the consent of the Native Land Trust Board to that transfer. This Bill removes that handicap. The Native Land Trust Board, or for that matter any landlord, cannot withhold consent. So as long as the choice of the tenant is a proper choice and there is no unreasonableness, this law provides that the lessee is free to sell his land at any price he can get on the market.

As regards security of tenure of native leases, there is one loophole and that is that the provisions of this Bill do not apply to land in a native reserve. The Governor, at the same time, has been given power to apply the provisions of this Ordinance, if he thinks fit, in consultation with the Native Land Trust Board, to the tenancies falling within such a survey. What some people are afraid of is the power of the Governor to take any land and put it into reserve at any time. Fears have been expressed by some people that there is nothing to prevent the Fijian owners asking the Governor to take that particular land into native reserves and thereby defeat the protection afforded under the clause providing for greater hardship. In the first place, I believe that no Governor would resort to such a devious method of defeating a legislation which is a Government measure specially designed for the protection of the tenants and I believe that that is sufficient assurance, and there is nothing to be afraid of on that score. As regards the problem of renewability of leases, that is by and large the problem of the tenants of the native lands and of individual freeholders. The security of tenure is adequately guaranteed by the provision of clause 5 and clause 13. All the annual tenancies in this Colony upon the passing of this Bill will be completely abolished and converted into leases for a term of at least 30 years. To my mind, it is a very substantial and radical change and considerably in favour of the tenants.

Provisions in regard to compensation only apply to any improvements which may be made after the passing of this Ordinance and those improvements are divided into categories, which means that the improvements which the tenants have already made on their existing leaseholds are not covered by this provision. They still stand to lose those improvements in the event of their not getting an extension as provided under clause 13. As against that, for very many tenants, there is more or less an absolute certainty that leases will be renewed or extended, at least for two extensions and that minimum period of twenty years may be sufficient for them to exhaust the improvements which they have already made. As far as that goes, it provides some sort of remedy which is better than what is the position under the present legislation.

I consider the provision for control of share farming and provision for maximum rent very important, safeguarding the tenants against excessive rents. There is a lot of pressure on the land; demand for land is increasing, especially in sugar-cane areas. Even at present on the majority of our sugar-cane farms, two or more families live on a size of farm which is adequate for one family. That, in itself, accentuates the demand which, naturally, would tend to send the prices as well as the rents of cane lands upwards. This ceiling on rents is an adequate safeguard against an evil which will naturally result from the present state of things unless and until steps are taken to relieve the existing pressure on cane land. The freedom to the tenant to sell his lease at the price it may fetch is also a very important change. So far, his right of disposal was seriously restricted, both in the case of native land, in the case of Crown land and in the case of Colonial Sugar Refining Company, as well as the land of private owners.

It is well-known in the sugar-cane areas that the Colonial Sugar Refining Company's tenant who wishes to sell his block has got to collect his premium under the table because under the existing law, the Colonial Sugar Refining Company has got absolute discretion to withhold consent to any transfer. Now, there will not be any necessity for such tenants to go about in a devious manner to sell their land and to collect their premium. The same will apply to the tenants of individual freehold lands. At the same time, while the numbers of leaseholds will go up because of this freedom, the price of freehold lands will come down because of the restraint provided under this Ordinance. I will not be surprised that in the near future, unless something is done to relieve the pressure, the price of leasehold will be higher than the price of freehold, which will amount to a reversionary interest which will revert to the owners after about 30 years. If the landlord is given the freedom to charge his premium for the lease, there is also a limit placed on it by providing that such premium will be taken into account in assessing the annual maximum rent under the formula provided under this Bill, to my mind, that is a very substantial provision which will operate and work in favour of the tenant and against the landlord.

Another very important change is in the field of relief for forfeiture. Under the existing law, if a tenant does not pay his rent regularly and is out of time, the landlord is free to re-enter and he is not bound to accept the rent if he offers it at that late stage. Now, under this Bill, the tenant gets three months' grace after the rent is due and within those three months' grace, the landlord cannot do anything. After the three months of grace has expired, the landlord can serve him with a notice to quit and after he receives the notice to quit the tenant gets one month more within which he can pay the rent and save his tenancy. I consider that is a very substantial reform.

Of course, with measures of this type, there is a wide diversion of views. The problem of law reforms is not only limited to Fiji; it is world problem. You come across that problem in almost every country in the world. All countries are trying to solve this problem in a manner suited peculiarly to its own circumstances. Some people may say that the easiest and best solution of this problem would be nationalization of land, that the State hold all the land and that all the people hold the land from the State as tenants. Some people may say that the Agricultural Holdings Act 1948 of the United Kingdom is the best solution, to convert all the tenancies into perpetual tenancies. Some people say that the best solution to the problem would be to follow the principle that the land belongs to the person who uses it. There are radical ways in which problems have been solved in various countries. As far as Fiji is concerned, we have to consider this aspect; Fiji lives on agriculture. Farmers are the foundation of Fiji's economy. The number of landlords is also large and strong. Naturally, the landlords want to preserve their own freedom of contract. The tenant, on the other hand, naturally wants protection of law against such freedom. Fiji has got to provide a solution whereby the conflicting interests from both sides are compromised.

I support this Bill because I look upon it as a compromise measure. It goes a fair way in relieving the immediate problem and the prevailing fear amongst the tenants that their leases may not be renewed. That, in itself, is a great thing. For the landlords, though it takes away from the sale value of that land, it provides them with a fair and reasonable return. It should not be overlooked that this Bill does not compel either the landlords or the tenants to secure or grant terms and conditions more favourable than this Bill provides. There is nothing to prevent a landlord and a tenant from amicably terminating their tenancy if they so wish. This is, as the Member for Natural Resources [Mara] pointed out, a code of behaviour prescribed by law both for the landlord and the tenant. I would say that it is a minimum code of behaviour prescribed for both. Ultimately, the problem depends upon the human relationship between the landlord and the tenant. If both the landlord and the tenant curb their greed, both consider their mutual interest as well as the common interest of the country as a whole, I do not see that there will be any serious difficulties in the administration of the Landlord and Tenant legislation in at least a few years to come.

We are not finding a permanent solution to the problem but we are, by this Bill, providing an immediate relief and remedy which may last for twenty years and within those twenty years this country, I hope, will make great advances in economic development which will result in relieving the existing pressure on the land and increasing the prosperity of the country, which will result in increasing the number of tenants of all races, including the Fijians, so that at the time when it comes to revise our thinking and to find a solution, there will be as strong and as numerous a body of Fijian tenants as there are of Indian tenants now. I believe that an increase in the number of Fijian tenants in itself will considerably help in securing a solution which will be of benefit to the tenant. I support this Bill with what I would call a feeling of ambivalence but it would be a miracle if a compromise was to completely satisfy both sides. If a compromise satisfied only one side, and left the other side dissatisfied, that compromise would be grossly unjust. But a fair compromise is sure to leave both parties partly satisfied and partly dissatisfied, and this measure falls within that category.

83: Nationalizing the Gold Mining Industry, 31 January 1968

The subject of nationalization is usually a controversial one even in countries where people are now used to various nationalized industries. Therefore, it is no wonder that in a country like ours, which is economically ruled by private monopolies and buttressed and supported all along by the Government, this motion appears to be something very radical. Before I deal with why the gold industry in Fiji should be nationalized, I will first of all reply to the questions asked by the Government speakers as to why it should not.

Now as to prospecting for gold, even the Tavua Gold Mines has a very interesting history. Tavua gold was not discovered by the Emperor Gold Mines by any manner of means. The original prospector to discover gold in Tavua was generally known as a man who lived and died in poverty. That man was Borthwick, who was financially aided and physically maintained by Mr. Pat Costello, who was then the owner of the Lautoka Hotel. When gold was discovered Mr. Costello and others who were aiding Borthwick helped to bring in Mr. Theodore who used to be an ex-Finance Minister of the State of Victoria and had many personal interests in the gold mining industry outside Fiji. As far as prospecting was concerned, Tavua gold field was discovered by an individual, and as has happened so often in history, such pioneers live and die without reaping any reward or the benefits that they confer either on the country, the community or even the world. If gold industries were owned and run by the State instead of by private corporations, this State could carry on with the prospecting in the same way as a private corporation and perhaps much more effectively. We have the example of India prospecting for oil fields. Britain has had a lot of experience in oil prospecting. Many giant oil companies belong to Britain. Even now Britain holds and owns very rich oil fields in the Middle East. So prospecting is no more a problem for the Government than it is for any private enterprise.

I come now to the point raised about the difficulties in acquiring the ownership of the oil industry which nationalization entails. We are aware but once we agree and once we make up our minds that the gold industry would and must be nationalized, then I say, where there is a will, there is a way, and constitutions all the world over are not so rigid and inflexible that they cannot be amended to meet the requirements of the country to a particular circumstance. As far as Fiji is concerned, our constitution is in a fluid state, it is not yet finally settled, we are just going on from mile to mile so that is not an obstacle which one could call insurmountable.

Now, I come to the Minister for Communications, Works and Tourism [JN Falvey]. One advantage he has over us is that he has settled ideas and settled views which probably no matter what happens, he would never change, but the reasons he put forward as to why the gold industry should not be nationalized were the product of a confused mind. In one breath he says that if the industry is nationalized, it will discourage prospective investors from bringing in their capital to Fiji. In another breath, he says that if we took such a step there would be nothing to prevent the Gold Mines from gutting the mines and from the shareholders filling their pockets with the loot and finding themselves in a far better position than they are. If one were faced with such an opportunity, one would think that instead of discouraging prospective investors it would rather encourage them. He went to the extent of saying that capital is shy. Let me say that shyness ordinarily arises and is the offspring of morality and modesty. In my opinion capital is a shameless, brazen immoral dame who would travel and go to any length if there was monetary gain at the other end. Nothing is going to discourage it.

Nationalization took place in Britain on a considerable scale but it did not prevent the hard-headed American investors from pouring their capital into Britain and establishing various factories and industrial concerns. Even India which had resorted to a modest programme of nationalization after the end of the British rule there, in spite of such nationalization today more new British capital is coming into India than was the case during the British Raj. So it is quite wrong to say that if a particular industry is nationalized in Fiji, capitalists abroad will not think of coming to Fiji and will simply dismiss the idea by saying 'Oh, they have nationalized the gold industry there so we will not go and start a textiles industry (for instance) in Fiji'.

The General Member for West Viti Levu said that we on this side of the House were utterly ignorant of the gold mining industry. He then enumerated certain members on the other side of the House as people who were very well informed and possessed expert knowledge on this industry. Amongst these formidable personalities, the member also included himself. I was, therefore, hoping to learn something from him in this debate which I did not already know. But to my utter disappointment, he only reiterated the same figures that the Gold Mines have kept on feeding to the public and to this House all along for a number of years. That is how much it pays in wages, how much it pays in taxes, how much even its employees pay in taxes, and then he tried to make out the case that because it was doing all this it was essential that the Gold Mining Industry should not in any way be interfered with and that the State should continue with this partnership.

I would have been interested to hear how much of this profit they had ploughed back into the enterprise. He could have given us the figures for every year; the way in which it was utilized, and how it was profitable. We did not hear anything on that score. They just kept on repeating in parrot fashion that 'Oh, the gold mine is here, it is giving employment to so many people; that mine has built up a town, and if the Gold Mine is taken over then all these things will somehow miraculously disappear, and this country will have to dream about a Gold Mine in the sky'. Leave the Gold Mine in the sky to those who are fond of it. We are dealing with the Gold Mine in Tavua and all the other gold mines that we hope we may be able to discover in the future.

Fear has been expressed that if the Gold Mines were nationalized the workers would be seriously affected and in his excitement [the General Member] went to the extent of saying that if such a day came they would not work for the Government-owned mine. We have had several transactions in this country before of change of ownership, and no one raised any outcry against such a change. Take for instance, Brown and Joske. When it was taken over by Carpenters, no employee of Brown and Joske complained or objected to such a takeover. They were, as a matter of fact, happier that they were coming under a large concern with better prospects. When Morris Hedstrom was taken over by the same company, there was no outcry anywhere, no voice was raised in opposition. Even the Minister for Communications, Works and Tourism did not have anything to say against that as to why the ownership should be changed. Now, if nationalization was effected in this industry, all that it would amount to would be this: instead of a small limited liability Company, which in modern parlance is called a corporation, will be replaced by the largest and the strongest corporation in the country, namely, the Government.

If the employees of Brown and Joske or Morris Hedstrom had no objections to being taken over by Carpenters, I see very little reason why there should be fear if the Emperor Gold Mines is taken over by the State of Fiji. The workers will be in a stronger position than now because it is the duty and will always remain the duty of the Government to be a good employer. It will not be dominated by profit motives all the time at the expense of the employees. There will be no discrimination and the dissatisfaction which prevails in the working force would not arise because the Government would always see to it that there was no discrimination. And since it is the duty and the onerous obligation of the Government to provide as much employment for as many people as it can, they will be securer in their employment than at present. Furthermore, it will confer upon them a higher social status as government employees. I do not see any reason why the staff or the working force should have any anxiety if the Gold Mines instead of being owned and run by one company, would be owned and run by the Government.

The Minister of Finance mentioned nationalization not having proved very satisfactory even in a country like the United Kingdom. Now the British people are known all the word over as a nation of shopkeepers. Economically they have stronger brains than probably anybody else in the world. They have enjoyed this privilege for more than a century. But in spite of a change of governments, both Labour and Tory, some of the industries which were nationalized have remained and continued to run as nationalized industries, with the exception of one, namely, the Steel Industry. This has become more or less a political football in British politics. Apart from that, because the owners in the Steel Industry are politically more powerful, they have more political influence and more power, as one of the speakers from my side of the House pointed out, in the House of Lords. I would go further and say even in the House of Commons. So to say that nationalization has not proved to be satisfactory in Britain is merely to express one's personal opinion. I am quite sure that there will be millions of Englishmen who would maintain that it has proved successful. That is again a matter of personal opinion and not a proven fact.

Turning to the subject of why we should nationalize the gold industry in Fiji, first and foremost, we must not forget that gold belongs to the State. It is owned by the State whether in Tavua or anywhere else in Fiji; it is the property of the Crown and what is the property of the Crown today when Fiji becomes a free and democratic nation will become the property of the nation—the people of the country. The question is, what would be in the best interest of this country: to extract gold and use it for the benefit of the Government and people of this country or should we just step aside and allow what rightly belongs to the people to be taken over by private concerns who would profit from it at the cost of the nation and at the cost of the taxpayers?

Another factor which has not been so far mentioned in this House is the capital gain that the shareholders have made in respect of the Tavua Gold Mines (besides all this profit which the Company has made over a number of years, the indirect tax free gain which the shareholders make on the original value of their shares). According to the editorial of the *Fiji Times* headed 'An Unfortunate Proposition' in the issue dated Saturday, December 7th, 1968, which was quoted and read out at length, 'Both Government and Company are gambling that the gold price will rise. When a report that gold would go free again swept across the world four months ago, Emperor shares rose on the Sydney share market from some 30c to 4 dollars.' (So even when this speculative rise took place it was three times its original value and it suddenly soared to forty times.) 'They went back to $1.75', (which means that even then it was 17 and a half times worth its original value) 'and have risen again to $2.30' which means at present the value of these shares is 23 times its original value. So for anyone to say that the poor shareholders will suffer a great deal if the enterprise is taken over by the State since they have done so much for us and they will get so little in return is all again, as I have said, without any foundation.

Gold is a commodity which is rightly or wrongly valued by mankind all the world over and highly prized. It is one asset that is most important in international trade, both in times of peace and in times of war. I, for one, would not [be surprised] if the Government of the United States of America or of the United Kingdom or President de Gaulle looked with alarm if there is some depletion in their gold reserves. Not only the monetary system but the country's strength, both in times of peace and in times of war, depends upon its gold reserve and that is why we find such a strange spectacle that the United States buys up and gathers as much gold as it can and then puts it under the sea and as some wisecracks remark 'What is the use of gold? It is taken out of the earth on one hand and it is sunk into the water on the other hand.' It remains the most coveted commodity internationally. This is common sense. Nature has bestowed upon us an asset which mankind values so much and looks upon as indispensable both for its own maintenance and for its own survival in political as well as economic vicissitudes.

Tavua gold field is known to have a rich deposit and is considered amongst the richest deposits in the world. What phosphate is to Nauru, gold is to Fiji. Nauru, even before it became independent, decided that it would nationalize the phosphate industry and she has already started negotiations with the British Phosphate Commission to take over the phosphate industry, with the result that in the very first year of its independence, the Nauruans found themselves a people who can financially help their neighbours living in the South Pacific, for instance, us. If the gold industry is nationalized we will be able to solve many problems. We are building a very imposing edifice just across the road and for the time being, we call it the Capital Development Bank [later the Fiji Development Bank]. I hope a day will come in the not too distant future when that Bank will become the Reserve Bank of Fiji.

Gold is universally in demand at all times and in all places while manganese is not. Now the advantage by nationalizing gold will be to spread out the benefits resulting from its production and use. Just at present, it only benefits to a limited extent those who are engaged in the mining of gold. As has been pointed out by some of the honourable members opposite, it helps about 5,000 people in Vatukoula. If it were nationalized it will help them more, it will better their conditions in many respects and the profits and benefits derived from gold through the State will benefit the entire population.

If we make good profits, it helps both in our economic development projects as well as in easing the incidence of taxation on the taxpayers. It strengthens the whole nation and it gives the nation a status and a place in the international world. We at present have three products mainly to offer to the outside world: one is sugar, another is copra and third is gold. As far as sugar and copra are concerned we have often met with opposition that if we produce more there is no demand, no market for it, and we had to, only recently, sell our sugar as a gift—free gift to certain countries. The same thing happens with copra. There is always a limit on the market, anything beyond that and marketing becomes a problem. And even within the limits, there is always the danger of a slump in prices. Gold is the only commodity in the world for which demand never fluctuates. No country has complained that there is nobody to buy its gold; and the price remains steady. As time goes on, gold remaining in the bowels of the earth gets less and less with the result that sooner or later gold can be even more precious and a more coveted metal in the world than it is even at present. Such a valuable asset can help the nation a lot because instead of leaving it in private hands to be sent to Australia and then for the Australian Government to decide as to how that gold reserve will be used once it is in Australia, while the Government of Fiji has not got even an once of gold on which it can in any way bargain with any other country. Nationalization of gold does not necessarily mean that the Government should sell either all its gold as soon as it is extracted, nor does it mean that it should store all its gold in reserve for the future but it certainly enables the Government to sell gold to whom it suits best considering the interests of the country and the government at the time or at the price or on a deal which the Government considers will be most profitable and favourable to the country.

Gold is an asset in the hands of the Government, an internationally coveted asset, which it can use when and if it finds it necessary. We must not forget that there is a vast difference between sugar, copra and gold, not only in marketing but in the very fact that we can replant cane and keep on producing sugar. We can replant our coconut plantations and go on producing copra, but gold is a limited and wasting asset. Whatever gold you take out from the ground and ship out from the country is a dead loss. Gold does not grow in the mines; it cannot be replaced, and this is the asset which belongs to the nation, not only the people who are alive today but it is a national asset that also belongs to the coming generations. The more we take out and ship out of the country the less there is left. In the hands of the Government you can regulate, you can decide how much should be used and shipped out, how much should be kept in reserve so that the future generations are not totally deprived of the benefits.

Another important reason why gold should be made a national industry is that, as I have already pointed out, gold is a sacred trust in our hands for the people of Fiji and for those generations who will succeed us. Some difficulties have been pointed out by some of the members opposite. One of the members read out from a book and said that one drawback of nationalization is lack of initiative. Lack of initiative is an established and outstanding characteristic of civil services right throughout the world. As a matter of fact, individual initiative is generally discouraged. A civil servant is trained to look for precedents, and rules and the orders, that he may be given from his superior officers for all his actions; any initiative which makes him depart from instructions, rules or practice is frowned upon.

I can understand the diffidence and the hesitance of the present Government because it is in fact a 'Civil Service Government' consisting of existing civil servants or civil servants who resigned and left the civil service after they were elected to this House and took their places on the Government benches and the fortunate ones inside Government ministries. But a government would be a poor government if it lacks initiative. Ability to take initiative, to have foresight and not to provide ways not only to meet existing challenges but to provide ways and means for future challenges as well, which means it is indispensable for any strong government to have both foresight and initiative and even if the present Government feels diffident, I am sure and I hope that the Government of Fiji will not all the time consist of civil servants and will be composed to people who have foresight and who have initiative. If the present Government feels that nationalization is beyond their capacity to undertake and handle it, this does not mean that there is anything wrong with nationalization. It only provides an argument for the change of government.

84: Agriculture Landlord & Tenant Ordinance, 30 January 1969

In the modern world, feudal landlordism is a matter of the past and, wherever the order survives, it is receiving strong and violent attacks. We, in this country, are moving towards democratic freedom and, in a democratic state, common good prevails over personal greed, be it the greed of the owners of land or the owners of capital, or the owners of personal labour; all have got to make their personal interests subordinate to that of the interest of the people as a whole and of the welfare of the country as a whole. Ours is a predominantly agricultural country. Therefore, our prosperity largely depends upon agricultural production and good management of agricultural land. So the prevailing and overriding demand on agricultural land is that the production should be maintained if not increased further. Also, agriculture should be carried on in a manner which will not only preserve the fertility of the soil, but will also further build it up and enhance it. And, for that, proper land usage is absolutely important. If a man happens to be the owner of land either by birth or by personal acquisition, in a modern State, it is his duty to see that the land is used in such a way that the production is maintained, if not enhanced and so also the fertility.

I, myself, have got a small bit of land in this Colony, but if I insisted on working that land myself, it will only lead to personal disaster economically and to the loss and inconvenience, not only of the tenants but the general prosperity of the country as a whole. I tried out an experiment on a very small scale. When the Labour Government in England was keen on the ground nut scheme in East Africa, I thought that I might also try it out on a small piece of my freehold land in Fiji. The area was very small, but instead of making any profit out of it, the loss came to £400. And, if I had been foolhardy enough to bring all the land under ground nuts, probably I would have sustained such a loss that it would have taken several years to recover from it. So, it does not necessarily mean that if a man owns land, he is fit to use and work on that land to the best advantage of himself and others.

In the modern world, serious strictures have been placed on the absolute rights of landowners practically everywhere right throughout the democratic world. Even the United Kingdom, whose example we very often follow in this country, is not exempt from it. Agricultural land in England is in the hands of a few fortunate owners. And, land is worked in the United Kingdom as elsewhere, very often by tenant farmers. But the law of the land has made it obligatory on the person who is working the land whether he is the owner himself or the tenant, that he can remain in occupation and utilize the land so long as he carries out the norms of good husbandry. And, if he fails in that duty, the County Agricultural Board gives him notice; first to set the matters right and

bring the production up to the norm and, if he fails to do it, then he is served
with a notice to vacate the land, even if he is the free hold owner of the land.
The Board would then give it to a deserving farmer who would carry out the
obligations of meeting the required target of production. And security of tenure
in the United Kingdom is secured in a manner which is more drastic than ours.
Though on the face of it, it appears to be an annual tenancy it provides security
of tenure to the tenants so long as they work properly. If the tenant is not
working the land properly, he can be ejected not only at the instance of the
owner but of the State.

Sir Malcolm Trustram Eve in his Report[4] from which the appointment of the
Agricultural Landlord and Tenant Committee took place, and which ultimately
resulted in this legislation, based his recommendations on the prevailing practice
in Great Britain. We, in many ways, are more fortunate than owners of land in
many other parts of the Commonwealth, including India. Under the present law,
if the owner of the land finds it difficult to get the land back for his own use, he
has also got countervailing advantages conferred upon him by the Ordinance.
Before, native leases of agricultural land were granted for a term of 30 years—
that was the normal term—and rent was reassessed in certain leases after a long
interval and, in some leases there was no provision for reassessment of rent at
all. Now, the landowners are in a fortunate position. Whether such a covenant
in the existing lease is there or not, under the existing law, every five years, if
he so wishes, he can go before the Tribunal and have the rent revised. It also
confers the same advantage and benefit on the tenant. If things have changed so
adversely that the existing rent becomes too high and onerous, he can also go
before the Tribunal and have the rent revised. So this is one advantage which
the owners as well as the tenants enjoy under the existing law which they did
not enjoy before.

Another advantage is that the landlord has the advantage of ensuring that the
fertility and the condition and the productivity of the land will be preserved
and maintained by the tenant properly from year to year. And, if at any time
he makes a serious lapse, he is liable to the termination of the tenancy and the
land reverts to the owner. In all the enlightened countries, security of tenure is
considered vital to the interests not only of the tenant, but also of the landlord
and the country in general. If a tenant feels secure on the land he will put his
heart and soul into his work and he will have an incentive to improve the land and
to increase the production of the land to the mutual benefit both of the landlord
and the tenant. If the fertility goes up, if the production goes up, the value of the
land goes up and, after five years, the landlord can take advantage under the law
and have his rent revised especially if the price of the produce soars high. There
are such circumstances where the landlord can, with advantage, share in the

---

4   *Report on the Fiji Sugar Industry*, Legislative Council Paper 20/1961.

prosperity of the tenant which is due to the circumstances which were more or less in the nature of a windfall; which he could not have done under the existing leases in the absence of that Ordinance.

A tenant has also got this advantage, that with the security of tenure, and with the assurance that whatever improvements he effects on the land, he will have the opportunity either to exhaust them or, at the end of the term when he has to leave the land, [receive] adequate compensation for such improvements effected by him [which] has remained unexhausted. In India the owner of the land is not in such a happy position. For instance, if I had land in India, not only would I not be able to take only a reasonably low or fair rent on the land that I have got there, but my land will be given to the tenant. The price will be fixed by the Government and installments for the payment of the price will also be fixed by the Government so that it does not become too onerous on the tenant to pay that price. Even in the case of owners of land who are present there, considerable strictures are placed on their rights of ownership. In very many cases they are compelled to sell their land to the tenants and the prices are fixed by the Government. There is a well known slogan in India now that the land belongs to its tiller.

We are lucky that we [do not] have any such radical reforms in this country. If we take a moderate and reasonable attitude and give little time which might satisfy the other side, it would be far better and far more sensible than what we may be compelled and we may feel is too much if it comes too late. I would ask and appeal to the *taukei* members in this House to take the excellent advice given by the Attorney-General to explain the law as it exists to people. I am quite sure that if that is done half of the misunderstanding and half of the fears will completely disappear. The other half of the fears arise not from the Ordinance or from the law but from the operations of the Native Land Trust Board and the owners of the land themselves, and the relationship between the two. Under the existing law, an individual owner has got to follow the machinery of the law; give the notice at the due time; put in his application whenever he wants to. In the case of other Fijian lands, it is not the owners who directly are entitled to do it but they have got to depend upon the machinery of the Native Land Trust Board as their trustees and agents to carry these requirements out for them. So the other half of the fears are due to the present position that though the *taukei* are the owners of the land their rights of ownership under this Ordinance have to be exercised through the agency of the Native Land Trust Board. If that relationship and if the working and efficiency of the Native Land Trust Board is improved many of the fears resulting from the second half can also disappear.

We have tried this Ordinance out over a short period now but during that short period we have discovered certain difficulties, certain undesirable side-effects which we had not anticipated before and certain new problems which have arisen out of the working of this Ordinance. These are all matters which can be conveniently gone into by the committee; it can make its recommendations after thoroughly going into all the matters and giving them full, deliberate consideration. I have no doubt that the work of such a committee would result to the benefit of the country, of the owners of the land, and of the tenants. And, considering the amount and nature of work this committee will have to do, I consider that it would be unreasonable to set a date and compel the committee to make its report on that particular date or before that date. I personally consider that we should not tie down the hands of the committee so much. It would serve our purpose and it would serve the urgency that this matter requires, if the motion is amended by deleting the words 'before the 31st March, 1969' appearing in the penultimate line of the motion, and substituting the words 'as soon as practicable.' The motion then reads 'That this House notes the resolution passed by Provincial Councils and the Great Council of Chiefs in relation to the Agricultural Landlord and Tenant Ordinance and in particular to section 13 concerning hardship, and having regard to difficulties which have become apparent in the first year of its operation, both for landlords and tenants, requests that the Governor be invited to appoint a Working Committee to study the Ordinance, including the Regulations made thereunder, and its operation, and to make recommendations including a draft amendment Bill as soon as practicable, to render the Ordinance more workable and more equitable.'[5]

85: Letter from Justin Lewis QC to AD Patel, 15 September 1969

Dear AD

I have been asked by all the members of the Working Committee on Landlord and Tenant matters to write to you and wish you a speedy recovery. I do hope you will soon recover.

In 1964 I myself had a sudden collapse due to overwork and I have the deepest sympathy with anyone who has suffered or is suffering in this way. I do suggest you take as long a rest as is possible.

I am very sorry to trouble you about the following matter. The next meeting of the above Committee is to be held at Lautoka on October 1st, 2nd and 3rd, 1969. These are to be discussion meetings.

I do not propose to hold such meetings in your absence nor in the absence of any member unless he absents himself voluntarily.

---

5   The Agricultural Landlord and Tenant Act was passed into law in 1976.

I would be grateful if you would inform me by sending a message through your wife or any other convenient means whether or not you will be able to attend on the above dates because if not, they will have to be adjourned.

Is it possible for you to give me any idea when you will be fit and well to attend these meetings?

We miss you very much and we look forward to your return.

Very best wishes

Yours sincerely

Justin Lewis

Attorney General

Part IV. Society and Culture

86: Swami Avinasananda to AD Patel, 15 October 1937

My Dear Ambalal

I am surprised very much to learn that you have not yet secured the Director's [of Education] approval about Ramakrishnan's appointment. A graduate, a degree-holder in the training (LT: Licensed Teacher) is to be employed. I do not understand what credentials more he requires. It is very annoying, especially this petty fogging pin-pricking affair. I would request you to seek an interview with the Governor and ask squarely whether he means to stand by the public and solemn pledges and promises made by his predecessor [Sir Arthur Richards], or is he going to allow the narrow-minded, spiteful officials to obstruct and nullify the concessions made to us. Ramakrishnan is formally sending something written by the Director, Madras. I think it is very essential that you should at once see the Suva fellows and get approval for both Ramakrishnan and Ganeshwar Rao whose papers will also be sent to you soon. Ramakrishnan's salary grant must be 144 pounds per annum, that is first grade, and Ganeshwar Rao's III Grade 75 pounds or 78 pounds per year. Please get this in writing and then cable to me. Ramakrishnan will have to wait for your definite reply before he resigns his post.

The eye is still the same and myself confined to bed. I cannot convey to you how much this teacher problem is worrying me.

With my best love

Yours affectionately

(sgd) Avinasananda

87: Letter to Swami Avinasananda, 30 September 1939

My dear Swamiji,

This will be a surprise—almost a shock—to hear from me after a long spell of silence.[1] I crave for your forgiveness for not writing before, but my mind was in

---

1   Swami Avinasananda died on 16 December 1958 at Vizagapatnam where he was head of the Ramakrishna Mission. AD Patel wrote: 'People of Fiji had never seen a Swami, especially of the Ramakrishna Mission, before. Indians had an impression that a Sadhu cannot be learned in English language, and why on earth should a University Professor, and a Principal of a University College at that, take a mendicant's life. To the rank and file, Swamiji was a living wonder, and wherever he went in Fiji, he simply stormed peoples' hearts and conquered them.'

a turmoil and I thought that I should not pass my troubles and worries on to my friends consciously or sub-consciously.[2] Thank God that I am gradually getting over it all, and am again able to see things in their proper proportions.

I am grieved to hear that your sight has not improved. It will be tremendous handicap in the cause of service to which you have devoted your whole life. I know you are brave, an eternal fighter, and even that handicap will not deter you from your life's mission.

I hear that our countrymen are treated in an ungrateful manner in Ceylon. I hear about Pt. Jawaharlal's visit to Ceylon and I sincerely hope that his visit has borne some fruit.

Though I have not written to you for a long time, I have often thought of you, wondering and worrying how you were and what you were doing. We here have been steadily plodding on. We were in correspondence with the Governor to obtain an interview for the purpose of making representations to him on various subjects as suggested by you. Unfortunately the war has intervened and the Governor's time appears to be fully taken up by matters relating to the defense of the Colony. In the circumstances, I suppose we will have to wait until better times come.

As you might have heard by now, we have got a five year's tenancy of the grazing land. We shall soon arrange for the cows and launch our scheme of the proposed model dairy.

Since Mr. Ram Krishnan took charge of the school, things have changed tremendously. It just shows what an enthusiastic and capable man can do when he is placed in a school like ours. I wish we had many more like him and we can easily make our institution … to move in the Colony.

The Sangam had advised the people to bring as much land as possible [under cultivation and plant] food crops and we also propose to see the Company and ask them to allow [them] to plant foodstuffs on certain portion of their holdings. How far we shall be able to persuade the Company is as usual a matter of doubt. Still there is no harm in trying and even that commercial organization may have conscience enough to realize the exigencies of the times.

Do favour me with a letter and let me know how you are.

With my love
Yours affectionately
Ambalal

---

2 Among his turmoil would have been the impending end of his marriage to Patricia Seymore who had left for New Zealand. Then there was his electoral defeat in 1937 to law clerk Chatur Singh and the unending parochial politics of the Indo-Fijian community.

88: Sangam Registration, 3 November 1937

May it please Your Excellency

I have the honour to apply on behalf of the Then India Sanmarga Ikya Sangam for your Excellency's licence directing that the said Then India Sanmarga Ikya Sangam be registered as a Company with a limited liability without the addition of the word 'Limited' to its name under the provisions of sec 22 of the Companies Ordinance 1913.[3]

The said society is in existence for 12 years and is carrying on educational and other useful work amongst the Indians in this Colony. It owns and conducts 21 schools in the districts of Nadroga, Nadi, Lautoka, Ba, Tavua, Ra, and Rewa.

In a general meeting of the said society held on the 31st of October 1937 at Nadi, it was unanimously resolved that the said society be registered under sec 22 of the Companies Ordinance 1913 without the word 'Limited' being added to its name. A copy of the Memorandum and Articles of Association is attached hereto.

For effectively carrying out the objects of the said society, it is absolutely necessary that it be totally exempted from the provisions of section 21 of the said Ordinance. I have therefore the honour to make further application that Your Excellency be pleased to grant a licence empowering the said society to hold unrestricted quantity of lands.

In view that this is purely a charitable society serving the needs of the people of this Colony, I hope that Your Excellency will see your way to exempt it from payment of the registration and other fees and confer such further privileges as may be within Your Excellency's powers to bestow under the said Ordinance.

I have the honour to be,

Your Excellency's humble servant.

AD Patel

Counsel for the Then India Sanmarga Ikya Sangam.

---

3   AD Patel was the General Manager for Sangam schools from 1937-1953, when Swami Rudrananda took over, and its Legal Advisor from 1937-1964. YP Reddy, longtime President of Sangam wrote on 3 October 1969: 'Mr Patel zealously safeguarded the tents of our religion and painstakingly devoted himself for the upliftment of our community. He will be quoted and re-quoted by generations to come.'

Among the objectives of Sangam at the time of registration were to:

- Impart and promote the study of science, art and industry;
- Establish, maintain, assist and carry on schools, colleges, libraries, orphanages, workshops, laboratories, dispensaries, hospitals, nursing homes, houses for the infirm, the invalid and the afflicted, boarding houses, hostels, and other educational and charitable works and institutions of a like nature;
- Train teachers in all branches of knowledge above mentioned, and enable them to reach the masses;
- Print, publish, and sell or distribute gratuitously or otherwise, books, pamphlets, journals, periodicals, that the Association may think desirable for its objects; and
- Impart and promote the study of Hinduism and its scriptures and the teachings of Ramakrishna Paramhans, and to promote the study of comparative theology in its widest form and assist and bring about the harmony of all religions.

89: Letter to Governor Sir Harry Luke, nd.

May it please Your Excellency

The following are some of the urgent needs of the Sangam to carry on and advance their activities. They are, in our humble opinion, capable of fulfillment, if sufficient understanding and sympathy is forthcoming from the Government.

Natabua Teachers Training School and other training centres in the Colony have been in existence since the passing of the 1928 Education Ordinance for the training of Hindi Teachers. Since the amendment of the Ordinance the medium of instruction can be the mother tongue of the majority of the children attending the School. While for Hindi schools there is not much difficulty to obtain trained teachers, the Tamil and Telugu schools have to depend mostly on the untrained recognized teachers on account of the lack of centres for the training of Tamil and Telugu teachers. His Excellency Sir Arthur Fredrick Richards promised to fulfill that want by opening a Tamil and Telugu Teachers Training Centre in co-operation with the Sangam in Nadi. So far nothing has been done to implement that promise. We realise that the establishment of such a centre might take time. There are, however, certain avenues open during the transitional stage. Hindi can be made an optional subject with Tamil and Telugu and other Indian languages at the entrance examination. Provision can also be made at the Natabua Training School for the teaching of Tamil and Telugu at a moderate cost. Until such provisions are made the recognized teachers of Indian languages other than Hindi should be given a Government grant [of] say 2 pounds a month.

More liberal financial assistance should be given for the importation of trained Tamil and Telugu teachers from India, and the teachers selected under such scheme should be definitely graded before they leave India as they are reluctant to come to Fiji without their being certain of the grade they would be placed in by the Education Department of Fiji.

As to the selection of the teachers the requirement by the Fiji Education Department of the report from the Director of Public Instruction in India as to the abilities of such a teacher is most unreasonable. The Director of Public Instruction of a big Presidency like Madras can hardly be expected to come into contact with teachers of elementary schools. There are thousands of such schools under him and they are entirely left under the control and supervision of Educational Inspectors and their Deputies. In such circumstances, the report by the Deputy Inspector should be considered sufficient by the local Education Department. So far only one out of the two teachers sanctioned by the Government has been imported. The Sangam is urgently in need of importing a Telugu teacher. The Sangam has selected one Mr. Ganeswar Rao. In his selection the Sangam has an extra advantage of having Mrs Rao's services who is also a trained teacher.

Besides teaching qualifications the Sangam have got to consider the adaptability of the teacher to the circumstances of the Colony and his fitness to work in different surroundings. Taking all that into consideration, Mr. Rao is the most satisfactory candidate we have got so far and his appointment should be approved by the Government.

The Sangam is running five big schools and four small schools in this Colony. They give education to one fifth of the total number of Indian children attending school. Yet the Government has not so far appointed their representative on the Board of Education, though organizations with less number of schools and pupils are represented. A representative of the Sangam should be appointed to the Board immediately. The Sangam should also be given a special grant on the same lines as given to various mission schools in this Colony.

Though the Education Ordinance has been amended, the rules thereunder have not been revised and brought up to date to conform with the amended Ordinance. The rule pertaining to the establishment of new schools, for instance, is not revised. It is unreasonably interpreted to the detriment of schools whose medium would be other than Hindi. The settlers of Ravi Ravi, which is predominantly a South Indian settlement, have been eager to establish a Telugu school in the settlement. There are 75 or more children of school-going age in that settlement who are not attending any school. The nearest school is the Government school at Karavi which is a Hindi school. The building is small. It is overcrowded and cannot take any more pupils. On account of the old rule, the Department insists that the proposed Telugu school should not be established within 3 miles of the Karavi school. This requirement pushes the site of the proposed Telugu school to the extreme edge of the settlement. The settlers rightly insist that it should be in the heart of the settlement. There is a suitable site available but on account of the obstinate interpretation of the 3 mile radius rule, the children of the settlement have been deprived of education which would otherwise have been theirs two years ago. We humbly request that the desire of the settlers should be acceded to so that an early start can be made. The parents are willing to make financial sacrifices and it seems pitiable that a mere technicality should deprive all these children of their education.

We have taken this liberty to place before you some of our immediate requirements. If Your Excellency may be pleased to find some time to discuss various aspects of the above requirements and our activities in general, the Sangam will be grateful to wait on you in a deputation in Suva where they can be dealt with in details. We hope and trust that Your Excellency will take immediate steps to meet these requirements and thereby earn the gratitude of our community and the blessings of our children.

90: Sangam's Petition to the Governor, 12 December 1947

May it please Your Excellency,

On 23rd November 1937, His Excellency the Governor, Sir Arthur Richards, stated in his address to the Legislative Council that, 'For many years the Sangam has shown a keen interest in education and it has established its schools at considerable financial sacrifice in different parts of the Colony. The Sangam has frequently approached Government in the past with a request for facilities for teaching of Southern Indian children in their mother tongues but, owing to the difficulty of finding suitable teachers for other Indian languages, the Government has been obliged to declare Hindi the medium of instruction in Indian vernacular schools'. And at the same time, he made a public promise that, 'It is now intended that, in selected areas where Indian communities whose mother tongue is a language other than Hindi are prepared to establish schools in which their children can be taught for the early stages of their education in the mother tongue, Government will encourage and assist them in their endeavours. In this connection the Government is now considering proposals for the establishment of a cultural centre for Southern Indians at Nadi, where it is expected that teachers competent to teach Southern Indian languages may be trained for the future. Both the Director of Education and I are in sympathy with these aspirations and I have undertaken to give practical effect to this sympathy at an early date'.

His Excellency the Governor further added that, 'Swami Avinasananda of the Ramakrishna Mission is at present in the Colony studying social conditions. He has made proposals for the social betterment of Indians which include education. As a Southern Indian, Swami Avinasananda has pleaded for facilities for the better teaching of the languages of that region. Honourable Members will remember that the matter of teaching Indian languages was referred to in Mr. Mayhew's Report and a promise was given that more latitude would be permitted in selecting the Indian language that would be taught in any particular school. Government views with sympathy the Swami's plans to make Nadi a centre for South Indian Culture and will assist and encourage the Sangam to give effect to it.'

In the same address, the Governor also said, 'In the debate on Mr. Mayhew's Report attention was called to the recommendation that in certain cases another Indian language should be substituted for Hindustani and it was pointed out that an amendment of the Education Ordinance 1929 would be required to permit this. The necessary amending Bill has accordingly been prepared and Council will be asked to pass it. The benefit will be felt mainly in schools for South Indians who naturally wish their children to learn a language which will enable them to keep in touch with their relations in India and to read the works of their great authors of whom they are justly proud.'

Again on the 22nd April 1938, the Governor, in his address to the Council said, 'I recognize that, in conformity with the policy which I enunciated last year towards the Sangam and Southern Indians, it will be necessary, initially, to import certain teachers from India, within the terms of the policy. The Director of Education has been instructed to give special attention to this matter, and societies wishing to import teachers should make their applications to him.' In accordance with the promise of help given to the Sangam by Sir Arthur Richards the Sangam was enabled subsequently to import two teachers special from India.

In order to implement the above promise, the Education Ordinance of Fiji was amended in the year 1937, and was made to read that, 'Vernacular shall mean the language commonly spoken by the pupil in every-day life' in place of 'Vernacular shall mean the language commonly spoken by the pupil in everyday-life provided that for Indian pupils the vernacular shall be deemed to be the Hindustani language'. While moving this above amendment, the Director of Education declared, 'The definition of vernacular in the Education Ordinance of 1929 made Hindustani compulsory in all Indian Schools. The object of this Bill is to permit the substitution of another Indian language. The reason for the amendment is the natural desire of certain sections of the community that their children should be taught in their mother tongue'. While seconding the above motion, the Secretary for Indian Affairs said, 'I would like to assure the Council that the taking of this step will give a great deal of satisfaction to a very large section of the Indian community of Fiji'.

In order to enable Indian children of non-Hindi speaking parents to receive primary education through the media of their mother tongues the Education Ordinance was thus amended and provision was made that the medium of instruction in an Indian school will be the mother tongue of the majority of pupils attending the schools. This was done to meet the requirements of the Then India Sanmarga Ikya Sangam to preserve and promote South Indian culture in Fiji amongst the people who come from South India and their descendants.

Unfortunately for the Sangam Sir Arthur Richards was transferred from the Colony before his Government could fulfill the promise he made. In-spite of repeated requests, the promise made by the distinguished Governor on behalf of the Government of this Colony has remained unfulfilled on the part of the Government and on that account we have been facing lots of obstacles in our work, and, in-spite of the enthusiasm and sacrifice of the South Indian community, we have not been able to make as much progress as such enthusiasm and support of the people warrant. In-spite of the Ordinance being amended the policy and activities of the Education Department have remained contrary to the letter and spirit of the amendment. No provision has been made for examination in Tamil, Telegu or Malayalam either in the School Leaving or Qualifying Examination, and our children are placed in an invidious position of having to learn Hindustani even in a Tamil, Telegu or Malayalam school for the purpose of these examinations. All the education received by a pupil through his mother tongue is rendered useless as far as such examinations are concerned. He is placed under a severe handicap in these examinations and in his further education in the Secondary School and Teachers Training College.

In spite of this apathy on the part of the Department of Education towards the South Indian Languages and the obstructionist policy pursued by it against preparing teachers in South Indian languages, the Government has depended on the Sangam for the supply of clerks and interpreters in South Indian languages required in the Civil Service. The Sangam therefore deserves the thanks of the Government for preparing local young men for these posts which they would otherwise have to fill from India. The Sangam is thus rendering a great service not only to the South Indian Community but also to the Government. We would like to point out that Tamil and Telegu are the languages recognized for literacy qualification for an Indian voter for Legislative Council elections. Though the Government needs Civil Servants well equipped with the knowledge of South Indian languages, and though it has acknowledged the necessity of education in South Indian languages such as, Tamil and Telegu to enable South Indian section of the community to earn and exercise its civil rights, it has not done anything effective to impart education to the South Indian children through the medium of any of the South Indian languages.

The Government has so far not made any provision for the teaching of the South Indian languages in the Teachers Training College, neither has it given practical effect to the promise made by Sir Arthur Richards to help the Sangam in training teachers in these languages. The Department of Education not only rendered no help to fulfill the promise made by Sir Arthur Richards but positively hinders our activities and defeats the very spirit of the promise and the consequent amendment of the Ordinance.

Even when there are a sufficient number of South Indian children of school going age in any particular locality, and the settlers through the Sangam try to establish a Tamil or Telugu school, the Education Department refuses permission to start such a school and brings pressure upon South Indian settlers to send their children to a Hindi school. We respectfully wish to point out that such a tyrannical imposition on our cultural life is contrary to British Policy as has been known to the world hitherto. England has never tried to interfere with the cultural and religious rights of other races living in the Empire and we urge Your Excellency to restrain the Director of Education from continuing with such an anti-British and anti-democratic policy. We are entitled as a minority to receive protection for our culture. British statesmen have assured us from time to time that no minority will have any reason to fear extinction of its culture in the Empire and legitimate rights of the minorities will always be respected and safeguarded. Even though Sangam manages nineteen temples in the Colony, and is affiliated to Sri Ramakrishna Mission of India, whose ideals are based on recognition of harmony between all religions of mankind and inculcating the spirit of broadmindedness, tolerance and respect towards all religions, the Education Department of Fiji arbitrarily refused to recognize the Sangam as a Mission, because in the words of Director of Education, 'The clause intended to refer to the staffs of Missions which are essentially religious bodies sent forth to convert people of other beliefs to their faith'. It is well known that the Sanatan Dharam Sabha, the Arya Samaj, the Sangam and the Muslim League are the chief religious bodies of Fiji established by various sections of Indians not in order to aggressively encroach upon other faiths and convert people from those faiths to their own but to save people of their own faiths being weaned away and proselytized by other faiths. These defensive Missions are therefore entitled to be recognized by the Education Department in the same way as Christian Missions and are entitled to similar consideration in respect of reservation of teachers.

We request Your Excellency to help the Sangam and thereby the South Indian section of the community by—

a). fulfilling the promises made by Sir Arthur Richards;

b). introducing Tamil, Telegu and Malayalam along with Hindi as optional languages in their School Leaving and Qualifying examinations;

c). providing for the teaching of Tamil, Telegu and Malayalam as second language in the Teachers Training College and Secondary Schools;

d). encouraging and assisting the Sangam in the establishment of new Tamil, Telegu and Malayalam schools wherever the number of the pupils available justify a school irrespective of whether there is a Hindi School in the vicinity or not;

e). the Department of Education taking a sympathetic attitude and rendering assistance to the Sangam which we regret to say it has so far neglected to do; and

f). furnishing scholarships and bursaries for Tamil, Telegu and Malayalam teachers to enable them to go overseas for higher studies.

91: To Drink or Not to Drink,[4] 25 November 1947

It has become a fashion in this Colony to invoke the Deed of Cession now and then and when that instrument is being invoked the contents of that instrument are totally overlooked. Let me remind the Council again that the Deed of Cession is nothing more nor less than an instrument of unconditional surrender of the lands and sovereignty of these islands to the British Crown in the hope that Christianity will be promoted, trade and industry will be developed and good government established in the Colony. This is the sum and substance of the Deed. It is quite clear that for over a thousand years in Europe, liquor and Christianity have lived side by side, and when Christianity came to Fiji it did not leave liquor: Bible and liquor both came into this Colony at the same time; and if it was considered not in the best interests of the people living in this Colony one would have certainly expected that liquor would have been left behind and the Bible would have been the only article brought to this Colony. Has that been done? People who are objecting to our right—whether we wish to drink or not—themselves claim the right to decide for themselves. They consider that they are responsible enough to use this freedom wisely. Without giving any reasons they allege that we are not fit to exercise our freedom or judge wisely. It is a 'call a dog a dog and hang him' sort of policy.

---

4 Patel's stand against prohibition proved costly to him. Patel's statement that even Hindu gods partook of alcohol was twisted in the quintessential Fiji Indian way to spread the word among the Indian electorate that Patel had claimed that Hindu gods were drunkards! It did not help Patel that Vishnu Deo, the staunch Arya Samaji leader, supported prohibition.

I have heard the argument that if the restriction is removed on the right of using liquor by the Indian community, there will be bootlegging, and they will sell liquor to the Fijians and spoil the Fijians. No facts or reasons have been advanced in substantiation of such a serious allegation. It takes all sorts to make this world and it takes all sorts to make a particular community. You will find the most honourable and venerable men and the most despicable ones in the same community, and it is neither right nor fair to pass sweeping judgments condemning any particular community. How would Members feel if I was to make such a sweeping generalization about their communities because certain people may have been caught bootlegging in this Colony, convicted and punished? Would that justify me in condemning the whole community to which such people belong? I would expect my colleagues to appreciate that and to refrain from making such sweeping allegations against other communities in future.

It has been suggested that Europeans should be free to use liquor because they are used to it; as the European Member for the North-Western Division put it, they are used to it by custom and usage. May I remind him that if custom and usage are going to be the test, our right to liquor goes further in the past than the claim of the European community wherever they are. Liquor is not a new thing for India or Indians. For the last 5,000 years, India has been using liquor. As happens in every country in the world, you may find arguments in favour of liquor and you may find arguments in favour of prohibition. But in spite of religious injunctions, in spite of all exhortations by moralists and advocates of prohibition, liquor has gone on and lived all these thousands of years in India just as in any other part of the world. If it was a new drink to us, the present Indian Government would not have had to resort to an experiment in a cautious manner, picking out districts here and there, in the hope of eventually succeeding in wiping out liquor from the country. That just shows how deeply rooted the use of liquor is in India just the same as in any other country in the world.

It is therefore not right to say that it is only the Europeans who are used to drinking liquor or that it is the European national drink. It is true that the Europeans came to this Colony with liquor but it is equally true that the Indians came to this Colony with the habit of drinking liquor, a majority of them, during the days of the indenture and since. If we analyse various groups and sections of the Indian community here, my point will be clear. Amongst the business sections of the community, there will be 80 per cent of the people who drink liquor and who are used to drinking liquor for ages. It is not a new thing with them either here or at home. If you take the Sikhs, the Punjabi section of the Indian community in the Colony, you will find invariably that almost all of them drink, restriction or no restriction. If you take the South Indian community in

Fiji you will find invariably more than 90 per cent drinking. Those who cannot obtain drink will resort to the methylated spirit cocktail; and the fourth section of the community, those people who have come from North India (the United Provinces), the majority of the people in that section drink. So it is not right to say that ours is such an abstemious community as it looks.

Unfortunately, as happens in any country where prohibition is enforced, prohibition breeds hypocrisy. People who drink have got to appear before others who do not believe in drinking, so that no suspicion may arise against them. Instances have been quoted here in which certain people at certain times have advocated prohibition for the Indian community. Mr. Vishnu Deo referred to religious groups, requesting the Government to continue the restriction of prohibition against drink as far as the Indian community was concerned. The petition was signed by Mr. Grant, Mr. Phuman Singh, Mr. JP Maharaj, and Mr. Kifayat Hussein. Now I know for a fact that Mr. Grant and Mr. Phuman Singh never have had any serious objections against drinking liquor, and I also know that the fourth signatory to that petition, Mr. Kifayat Hussein, who is dead and who happened to be my clerk, was not a particularly abstemious person either; but as the office bearers of that particular religious group they had to associate themselves with such a petition, in the same way as my Lords Spiritual of the Christian Churches of Fiji have had to endorse, whether they themselves are strict teetotallers or not, the request that the Indian community should not be allowed to drink.

Times have changed, circumstances have changed, and I am glad to find that even that staunch opponent has now seen the light of day and he also advocates that the restriction should be removed. Of course, we have now the last bastion left and that is in the person of Mr. Vishnu Deo, and that cannot fall. I know, because he sincerely and conscientiously believes that it is a sin to drink and he dare not say that liquor should be made free for everybody in this world; but within those limits, he certainly made one point and that was that racial discrimination even in the case of this Bill is not desirable. He is not in favour of the perpetuation of it, and as he cannot advocate the removal of restriction on drink because of his religious beliefs, the only way left open to him is to advocate that there should be total prohibition all round so that he can kill two birds with one stone, that is, he can secure elimination of racial discrimination which is now existing in the liquor laws of the Colony, and at the same time preserve his principle and his right to a better place in the next world.

The question remains, is prohibition in the best interests of the Indian community or not? And on that I have this much to say; we have tried out prohibition in this Colony for nearly half a century now—since 1884 Indians have been subjected to prohibition—and has prohibition succeeded? If it has not succeeded, it is not the fault of the law-makers or the administrators of the law. It is due to the inherent weakness in the legislation i.e., the people themselves were not prepared voluntarily to submit to the legislation. Where an overwhelming majority of the people do not subscribe to a law it only results in evasions and becomes a farce. Prohibition as far as the Indian community is concerned has consisted in thousands of people going and knocking at the doors of sly-groggers in liquor at exorbitant prices, consuming liquor at exorbitant prices, consuming liquor stealthily and on the quiet, and as they know it is a forbidden fruit, consuming as much as possible as and when they can instead of keeping to the golden path of moderation. That is what prohibition has resulted in as far as the Indian community is concerned. We have not been able to save the community from the evils of drink in the community.

We all overlook the fact that it is self-denial that turns a man into a saint, not prohibition; prohibition only succeeds in turning a man into a hypocrite. If a man wants to drink and you impose restrictions on him, all that he will be doing is to devise ways and means to evade the law and find some suitable place, time and opportunity to drink to his heart's content. And he will hide the fact that he drinks so that he may not be caught and punished. That is all that prohibition can achieve and has achieved in this Colony. Is that worthwhile going on with? Other countries better equipped and able to spend more on stricter control, with special excise police to enforce prohibition have failed. I instance the United States of America: that wealthy country could have spent any amount of money when the country went dry to see that prohibition was properly carried out and enforced. It employed special police and the result was that, whereas in Fiji people are resorting to methylated spirits, in America, they being more advanced, went to the length of resorting to Eau-de-Cologne.

India has been quoted as an example, but it is a well known fact that this very Government, during the last decade when the Congress was in office in the Provinces, tried out the experiment. They declared certain districts and areas as dry areas and that time they failed. The Congress Party felt that their failure was due to an unsympathetic third party, namely the British, that they were not in favour of prohibition and that that is why the experiment failed. They are trying it out again but even Pandit Nehru himself is not fully convinced and he wishes and hopes that the experiment will prove a success. This time when I was travelling through Southern India, through some of these areas now declared dry and prohibited areas, I had a very amusing experience: while travelling from Bombay to Madras, I found that at certain railway stations the waiters from the restaurant cars will come to the compartment and say 'Look here, Sir, if you wish to have a drink, come over to the restaurant now, because the next station is a dry station and you won't be served with a drink'. The train passes through dry areas and as soon as it has passed through the waiters will come and say 'It is now free, you can come to the restaurant car and have drinks to your heart's content'. That just shows how far it can be effective when the people themselves treat it as a joke.

We have got to consider one factor very seriously. In India, not only religion but society itself has created certain sanctions, especially in the higher classes and castes, against the use of liquor and thereby kept the use of liquor to the lower classes only. There are no liquor shops in villages and a man, if he wants to have a drink, has got to go to some town to obtain liquor. Public opinion among higher classes residing in the villages is against liquor and consequently even when the lower classes consume liquor, they have to do it on the quiet. In those surroundings and circumstances, there might probably be some chance of prohibition succeeding, but here, liquor has become the badge of respectability and wealth.

It has been said that young Fijian men were applying for liquor permits; but what else can one expect when these young men see that their high officials and their chiefs drink, the Europeans, who are the ruling community of Fiji, drink, when they find that amongst the Indians those that are considered respectable and affluent and hold some sort of social status, are allowed to drink? Naturally they aspire to enjoy the same privilege and be amongst the favoured few. If these youngsters are to be impressed with the desirability of remaining teetotalers, the only way to do it is to set a personal example. What is the good of going on drinking and holding total exemption permits and telling other fellows, 'Oh no, good fellow, you should not drink, it is not good for you'. He is not going to take your words, he is going to follow your actions in making up his mind whether he should apply for a permit or not.

Unfortunately prohibition has played havoc with the psychology of our young men. If people preach to them the desirability of avoiding alcohol they just turn round and say, 'You are talking like that because you cannot get a permit, but I can'. What else can you expect? Religious societies make petitions exhorting the Government to carry on the legislation that restricts the freedom of other people because liquor is prohibited and is against the tenets of their religion. They do not stop to ask themselves that if the use of alcohol is against their religion, the inhibitions and prohibitions laid down by the religious books and scriptures should be sufficient for their people to abstain from alcohol. How would anybody feel if some of the religious bodies came to this Council and said that because beef is prohibited by their religion there should be a law prohibiting people from eating beef. They will get a plain answer—'Well, it is a matter of your own conscience; you think that you should not eat beef, nobody forces you'; and the same thing be with liquor.

Removing the restriction on liquor does not necessarily mean that the Government is going to go from door to door exhorting people to drink or that they are going to go around in the schools and preach to students that they should consume more alcohol. The Department of Education puts placards in schools with the portrait of Lord Montgomery and words in bold letters: 'I do not smoke, and I do not drink, and I am 100 per cent fit'. The religious preachers belonging to every denomination go round and preach against the evil of drink. The campaign can be carried out successfully only if the restriction is removed, if the glamour attached to the forbidden fruit is taken away, and if people who are preaching abstention from drink set an example by becoming teetotallers themselves. So far, I am not aware of any requests being made by either the Indian Reform League or the Muslim League or Arya Samaj or the Gurdwara Committee who happened to be signatories to the petition Mr. Vishnu has referred to, that the office-bearers and members of their respective organizations should not be appointed as members of the Liquor Committees or granted permits or exemptions under the Liquor Ordinance or that they ever made a rule in their societies disqualifying people who drink liquor from holding office, leave alone being members of the societies. If they worked on those lines, they might find that the use of alcohol would disappear from their followers. I have never so far heard a request being made by any religious group in the Colony requesting their people not to accept membership on Liquor Committees. I have never heard any representation being made by any of these religious groups that if any follower of their religion applies for a liquor permit his application should be refused. Nobody dare go so far as that because they know that probably there would not be a single person left in their particular denomination. On the one hand, they allow people who drink to hold important positions and appointments in their societies, they allow such people to sit on Liquor Committees and they allow people who are leading members of their societies to obtain and hold liquor permits or total exemptions, and on the other they clamour for prohibition!

The present state of affairs has not only created a grievance in my community on account of racial discrimination, but has also created a further grievance on account of class discrimination. In one of the meetings I had in my constituency when a man said that everybody should be allowed a chance to have his views expressed on the Liquor Bill, one man stood up and said 'Look here, you just want to preach. You hold a permit, and you want that nobody else should be allowed to drink'. Prohibition has resulted in economic loss to the Indian community because those who drink, whether there is prohibition or not, have managed to find liquor somewhere, only at a forbidding and exorbitant price. It has brought about moral lassitude because in the present circumstances, people cultivate slyness and hypocrisy. It has created a sense and a feeling of humiliation and an inferiority complex in the community because all the while they feel that they are inferior to the other races who are privileged to have the freedom of drink in this Colony. These are the evils that have crept in and have played havoc with my community in Fiji.

I might further point out that though Congress advocates prohibition at home, Congress has never advocated that in Crown Colonies where Indians reside along with other races, where other races are allowed to have the freedom to drink, Indians should ask for prohibition, restricted to themselves. There are African Colonies, there is Ceylon, Malaya, Burma and other countries. There are not only Indian people residing in those countries, there are branches affiliated with the National Congress of India. The Congress Parties in these territories have never suggested that there should be restriction imposed on Indians. They have never said, 'We believe in prohibition and never mind whether Europeans or others are allowed to drink we should not drink and should not be allowed to drink'. Besides, the Congress and the Government of India expect that Indians who live abroad will behave and act as independent people ready to shoulder their own responsibilities, and this is not such a heavy responsibility that the Indian community cannot shoulder it. I have got full faith, trust and confidence in my people. They are a thrifty, industrious and abstemious race. They will always look after their families. As happens with every community, you may find a few renegades even in my community, but by and large you will find that this community even after the restriction is lifted will remain as sober and as responsible minded and as well-behaved as any other community in Fiji.

To Drink or Not to Drink, II (1969)

There is a story in Hindu mythology that gods and demons went into partnership and churned the ocean and brought out 14 jewels, and out of these 14 jewels, three happened to be potable substances—one was nectar, the second was liquor and the third was poison. The gods selected nectar as their share of the division; the demons selected liquor as their share, but neither side would have poison, so it was allotted to the god of death and it has remained his favourite drink. So, liquor in our religion is looked upon as a drink of the devil. I myself was once upon a time a strong prohibitionist, but, when I saw the results of prohibition from the example of a wealthy country like the United States of America and the consequences of prohibition which is at present prevailing in India, I find that the side-effects of prohibition are even worse than the effects on people who are allowed their own choice whether or not to drink.

In this country, since my arrival, I have always smarted under this discrimination and I have never made a secret of it. Those who are against liquor and who sincerely believe in liquor as the cause of the greater part of misery for mankind, the answer is, do not drink, keep away from it. Those who still believe as I believed once, that by total prohibition we can eliminate these miseries, I would say that for trial's sake, if you want to have it, have total prohibition in this

Colony. But, whenever I have spoken of total prohibition in the past, even some of the leaders of churches who are against drink, have admitted that that is not possible in this country, so far as the Europeans are concerned.

If that is so, then it is useless to expect other races to accept restrictions on the grounds that they do not have that highly developed sense of responsibility, or that much self-control as the Europeans have. No Indian or taukei would ever agree to such a proposition. I remember some years ago, I was discussing this discrimination in our law against Indian and taukei women with the then Commissioner of Police, and he told me that he agreed with me as far as discrimination against Indian women was concerned on the ground that Indians controlled their wives better than the Fijians. I thought this argument was quite ridiculous because it is not a question of race. Right throughout mankind in every home it is the woman who rules the roost.

The question was whether there was any justification or any need for imposing such restrictions on the women of the two major races in this Colony and, whether such discrimination was justifiable from any point of view. And further, whether the discrimination embodied in the existing Ordinance is enforceable. We are all free to buy liquor, to drink liquor and to keep liquor in our homes. And, as we know, in every home, the custodian is the wife. To enforce the existing prohibition against Indian and taukei women, the Government would have to post a constable in every home throughout the 24 hours of the day and night, and, even then they would not succeed because they would not have access to the bedroom. If the Government was logically going to carry out its obligations with regard to the enforcement of this Ordinance, the total existing revenue of this Colony will not be adequate. And, when one member here suggested providing a liquor squad to maintain good behaviour and order in public bars, it would need a regular army, considerably larger than the Fiji Military Forces, to supervise every home in this Colony both the taukei and Indian, to be able to exercise even partly the control which the law has imposed upon Indian and Fijian women. The present situation is that the statute book unnecessarily and stupidly outrages the self-respect and dignity both of the taukei and Indian, not only the womenfolk but also the men.

Just imagine if I received an invitation from Government House wherein both myself and my wife were invited and at the dinner table or at the cocktail party as the case may be, and she was told that she would have to take a soft drink as she could not take liquor, although I could. The obvious answer to that would be that I would turn such an invitation down. I would look upon it as a gross insult. And, under the existing law, at all the parties held at Government House, no one has ever raised any objection, nor can they out of any sense of decency or decorum, to Indian and taukei ladies taking either wine, beer or spirits in the same way as other ladies do, and if there was an outsider there who had been told that in Fiji there was a restriction on taukei and Indian women, as far as liquor is concerned, I think the only thing he would have to say would be, 'What a hypocritical lot you are in this country.' He sees Indian and Fijian ladies being entertained at Government House where liquor is one of the items of entertainment and at the same time he finds in law that as far as the Indian and Fijian ladies are concerned they cannot drink liquor.

The present situation is that the restriction imposed upon taukei and Indian women is to all intents and purposes a dead letter in the statute book just to be read, for we all know it cannot be enforced and is impossible to enforce and it creates unnecessarily a feeling of resentment against the other races whose ladies are not subjected to the same restrictions. I therefore, say, that the sooner we remove this discrimination from our statute book the better for all concerned. Some of the opponents to this Bill have expressed apprehension that if the restriction is removed it may lead to increased drinking amongst the womenfolk of the two races. This I say is absurd and groundless. If Indian and taukei women are not drinking at present, it is not because the law forbids them to do so, it is because their own culture forbids them to do so and because they have a sense of responsibility towards running the house and to making both ends meet. Liquor is as freely available to them in their own custody and they have opportunities throughout the 24 hours of the day and night, and if they wanted to do it, they would have done it long ago, in spite of this provision on the statute book. The very fact that they have not done so proves that they are as much responsible and as much culture conscious as we are. It is a common sight amongst Indians where the head of the house is entertaining guests, the wife, who might be a staunch vegetarian, will cook meat for the guests; she does not touch liquor herself, but the guests will be entertained with liquor. And if that does not tempt her in any way to take liquor herself, do you mean to say that the removal of this restriction from our statute book of which she has no knowledge as she does not even bother about what the law says about liquor; that because we pass this law today, she would change her mind and start drinking? I say that it is quite absurd and we are underestimating the sense of their responsibility, the sense of their dignity and pride that they take in their own ancient culture.

There is prohibition even in this Bill against taukei and Indian women from entering a public bar. Though there appears to be racial discrimination, culturally, whether there is such prohibition or not you would not ordinarily find Indian or taukei womenfolk going into the bar or being seen in the public bar. Their own sense of self respect, dignity and prestige prevents them from entering public bars. But, now that this country is trying to promote tourism there are benefits as well as disadvantages resulting from the tourist trade. In urban areas and centres where tourists mostly congregate there is a fear that some of our womenfolk belonging to the poorest stratum of society through economic need may be tempted to accompany tourists and take drinks in the public bar. This restraint safeguards our womenfolk from such temptation. And that is why the restrictions on taukei and Indian women from entering public bars may appear racially discriminatory but it has its justification.

At the last general elections some of our Indian women voters put forward questions as to why there was such restrictions upon Indian women and particularly asked me point-blank whether I accepted that Indian women were in any way inferior to the women of other races who have no restrictions against them on the statute book. I had to tell them that we would endeavour to remove these restrictions from the statute book and to say that discrimination for all practical purposes appeared senseless and unnecessarily outrageous.

92: Ring in the Saints, 6 January 1952

If the nineteenth century can be called the century of Great Britain, the first half of the twentieth century can be aptly described as that of the U.S.A. This is the century of doing more and more in less and less time. The twentieth century man is out to subjugate everything he can lay his mind upon. He has already mastered the air and conquered the skies. He has made ether his messenger boy. He has turned silver bromide and celluloid into the greatest entertainer of mankind. He has manufactured thunderbolts and lightnings which make him the envy of gods. He has invented new methods of surgery and found new drug to cure diseases which would have passed as miracles in the days of Christ. He has achieved all this and much more.

Equipped with his newly discovered knowledge, power, strength and skill, he has gone about feverishly to change everything. He has founded international organizations to wipe out scarcity and disease—two of the three chief enemies of mankind. He has recognized that poverty anywhere is a threat to prosperity everywhere. Concepts of imperialism and exploitory colonialism stand universally condemned and those who still believe in them have to invent new nomenclatures to hide them. The ideal of individual and racial equality is speedily taking root everywhere. All this is being achieved with surprising rapidness.

And yet, this is an age in which the common man enjoys more comfort but less happiness than ever before. Ways and means have been contributed to provide ice-cream and other luxuries to soldiers on the battlefield, but we have failed to abolish the battlefield and the havoc, misery and degradation it entails. We still rain bombs on women and children in the name of peace. War, the third arch-enemy of mankind, still baffles man's scanty wisdom and continues to keep him perpetually under its fearful shadows. The First World War was fought between those who exclusively owned the vast empty habitable spaces of this earth and those who wanted to have a share in them. The Germans called it a war for the place in the sun, the allies called it a war to end war. Those who professed to fight to end all fighting once and for all won. And yet all that mankind got out of the war was the poison gas, the bomber and the 'thieves kitchen'. It barely took two decades of uneasy peace to hurl mankind into the Second World War.

In this war one side professed to fight for the removal of an injustice, the other side for survival. The side which fought for survival won. All that mankind has got so far from the Second World War is the fear of the atom bomb and loss of peace and individual liberty. Those who fought for 'Survival' not only lost peace with their enemies, they also lost peace among themselves. And within five years of the conclusion of the Second World War, the world is brought on the brink of a third world war to be fought amongst the erstwhile allies, again for survival. [5] And all the while the means and modes of warfare are becoming more brutal and ruthless than ever. The fear of war has enslaved the people of even free countries to the chains of bureaucracies, and individual freedom has become only a dream. The individual has become the slave of State everywhere.

The first half of the twentieth century has proved that a saint who advocates non-violence and love gets murdered while the man who orders the use of atom bombs and prepares for war becomes a leader of the world. At this critical mid-century, humanity has two alternatives to choose from—Gandhiji's non-violence and Truman's hydrogen bomb. So far mankind in its international councils has shown predilection for the Truman way. Will it revert to the Gandhian way in time to avert the catastrophe of the third World War is a question which time only can answer. Since the members of the United Nations individually and in groups are feverishly preparing for a war among themselves, the U.N.O. has lost its credentials to lead man into the way of peace. We enter the second half of the century without a leader or an organization that can save the world from the oncoming disaster. What has been gained through knowledge may yet be lost through lack of political wisdom. The Brave New World must realize that the only road to survival is the way of the saints.

93: The 'Flowers' of Fiji, 20 June 1952

Accidents of history and the pursuit of profit have endowed Fiji with a mixed population mainly consisting of Fijians, Indians and Europeans. How this mixed population of different races will grow and become worthy citizens of this beautiful Colony will depend on the care and attention bestowed on the children here, who will become her citizens of tomorrow.

---

5   The reference here is to the Korean War.

Speaking recently on the care and affection that the children of a country deserve, Chakravarti Rajagopalachari, the wise statesman and last Governor-General of India, used a happy smile: he compared children to flowers and exhorted the people to treat the children with as much tenderness and affection, as they would delicate flowers. As the beautiful flowers, when properly and wisely tended, grow and develop into vigorous seeds which ensure the future of the plants, so do children, when carefully and intelligently brought up, become worthy citizens, who ensure the progress of a country.

What is the kind of attention our colonial government is paying to this important aspect of a country's life? All over the world enlightened opinion considers 'One World' as the ideal, and works, more or less, zealously towards that goal. Even in those parts of the United States, where colour prejudice is still strong, the general tendency of State action is towards the welding of the diverse communities and races into one united people. But here in Fiji the three communities are kept apart from each other right from the earliest years. Instead of allowing all children to grow up together in common schools, cherishing common ideals, they are kept apart, so to say, in water-tight compartments. And while in one case, the Government has recognized the need for compulsory primary education, they keep a blind eye on the needs of the other, with the result that more than ten thousand Indian children alone of school-going age are denied elementary education.

In civilized countries all over the world, the responsibility of the State for providing for every citizen's fundamental right to education of a secondary—in some cases, even collegiate—level, is recognized and is being discharged. Even in Ceylon, one of the youngest members of the Commonwealth, this right is recognized and provided for up to the highest stage. But in Fiji, secondary education, it would seem, is a luxury, towards the provision of which the State does not owe any responsibility whatsoever! What other conclusion is one to draw from the smug satisfaction that the Government seems to feel from the provision they have made in two secondary schools for a couple of hundred students. And that for a population of three hundred thousand!

Is it the idea that an educated young man will not become an efficient cane farmer? Or rather, that he will not be a willing and docile slave, working unquestioningly for the benefit of his master?

Flowers of Fiji! Your lot is anything but enviable.

94: Welcome, Mr. Dugdale,[6] 4 August 1952

British Colonies in the past have been ruled and governed in a single pattern with small local variations in details. It was not essential though that the Secretary of State who ruled over the far-flung empire should be equipped with first hand knowledge of the countries, over which he ruled. Whitehall was buttressed with a host of advisors and Secretary after Secretary went on ruling over the colonial empire with vicarious knowledge. The credit of breaking that tradition and taking a personal trip to the farthest colonial possessions of Great Britain goes to Mr. Dugdale.

In these days of quick communications during his fortnight's sojourn in Fiji Mr. Dugdale will be able to obtain a considerable amount of first hand knowledge and information which may, we hope, eventually benefit the people of this Colony. In the economic field the administration may well boast of the sound financial position of the Colony, and the flourishing copra, gold and sugar industries. It may proudly point out the fact that this Colony has not suffered from shortage of food, clothing, and other necessities of life, that taxation here is lighter than that prevailing in the neighbouring dominions or in the home country, that the largest amounts of expenditure from the general revenue are devoted to the maintenance and improvement of Health, Education and Agriculture.

There is no starvation or unemployment in Fiji. Relations between capital and labour though not exactly cordial are not so bad as to give serious headaches to the administration or seriously dislocate the economic set up of the Colony.

In the social and cultural sphere, the relations between Fijians, Indians and Europeans are peaceful and friendly. Rapid advance has been made in the primary education of Fijian and Indian children. Some schemes of child welfare work are already in operation. There are institutions like the Medical School and Makogai Leprosy Hospital of which the Colony may be justly proud. No doubt, all these and many more achievements will be pointed out to Mr. Dugdale by the administration.

It is the political sphere where the achievements of the British Rule in Fiji are so disappointing. The laws of Fiji are made in a Legislative Council packed with the nominees of the colonial administration. The administration of Fiji is therefore virtually a law unto itself. That does not mean that it is a lawless organization. In some respects it may be even more enlightened, efficient and wise than administrations in some of the politically independent countries. But still, it is not democracy. And what can be more painful to a minister championing the cause of democracy in domestic and world politics.

---

6 John Dugdale (1905-1963) was a Labour politician and in 1950, Minister of State at the Colonial Office. Whitehall was the location of the Colonial Office.

The civic affairs of towns and townships are managed by Town Councils and Township Boards. The civic life of the Fijians is governed by the Fijian Affairs Board and the Great Council of Chiefs. These civic institutions are either packed with or totally consist of the Colonial Administration's nominees. The Administration may claim to be more intelligent, wiser and more altruistic in the choice of their nominees than the common man. But there is certainly no local self-government in Fiji. Rights of free movement and free association are among the most fundamental rights of all human beings. And yet they are denied to the Fijian people in their own country. Fijians and Indians are subjected to controlled drinking, so that European dealers in alcohol may not lose their monopoly. The Exchange and Import Controls are administered to provide dollars and trade to British.

Britain has provided Fiji with a civilized administration. But that is about all. If the aim of British rule in Fiji is to develop the Colony into a self-governing territory, it is high time that a start is made.

18 August

Mr. Dugdale has completed his hurricane tour of Fiji and Tonga and left for the Solomons on Wednesday this week.

He must have seen all that he was shown but observed much more. The monotonous looking sugar and rice holdings dotted with miserable looking grass huts and deteriorated appearance of Fijian villages beside the roads must have presented to him a true picture of Fiji as a British colonial possession.

After meeting the representatives of labourers and farmers, Mr. Dugdale could not have failed to notice how docile our labour is and how gullible some of our farmers can be.

Meetings with Town Council and Town and Township Boards must have provided him a close view of the travesty which is imposed upon the people of this Colony in the name of local self-government.

Having not gone off the beaten track he would have no idea under what appalling conditions people have to live in the settlements. He would, however, know under what insecure conditions the farmers till their holdings and how unscrupulous landlords, like the government and the Native Land Trust Board, confiscate tenants' improvements without payment of compensation when they throw their tenants out.

What must be most striking for a visitor from outside is the complete lack of any man-made beauty in Fiji. We do not possess any works of art or architecture. There are no stately homes, or beautifully laid out farmsteads, gardens or orchards. With so much of natural beauty, man makes little attempt to paint or carve beautiful pictures or write inspired poetry or compose enchanting music. With abundance of stone everywhere there is no sculpture or architecture of any sort. Fiji has so far made no start even in the field of literature. Even legends, folklore and folksongs of poetic or historic merit which are usually found among primitive peoples are conspicuous by their absence. We even lack the simple art of self-adornment.

Nothing that is made or built in Fiji has got an appearance of permanence. People live and work as if they are mere sojourners in Fiji. Even the Fijians do not create or make anything which they can proudly pass on to their descendants.

Fiji has not so far produced a single man of high intellectual attainments or scholarship. Education is given and undertaken solely for the purposes of white collar jobs. We are therefore a Colony of mental and spiritual pygmies who neither live abundantly nor in abundance.

This is Fiji after seventy-five years of British rule. It is true that government cannot make the people. But it can create conditions under which indigenous civilizations and cultures of all communities can grow and flourish.

95: The Indian Problem in Fiji, 8 August 1952

Like the red rag to the bull, the Indian problem in Fiji seems to send some people into an excitement and rage which deprive them of the power of thinking. And obviously well-meaning friends, on whom the White Man's burden sits heavy indeed, are busy planning solutions to imaginary problems and tilting at windmills. While these prophets of doom are engrossed in their self-appointed task, a dispassionate observer of Pacific affairs, especially in Fiji, will admit there is an Indian problem in Fiji, but with a difference.

It is the problem of Indian culture. Indian labour has, along with European capital, been mainly responsible for developing this Colony. But the Indian element here is yet to make its contribution from their cultural heritage, that is their patrimony, to their motherland, Fiji. Only with the enrichment of the culture of this Colony can Indians feel they have done their duty to their motherland.

This cultural heritage of theirs, which places service above self, and things of the spirit above material things, which fosters a catholicity of outlook and a dynamic spirit of tolerance, is something of which they can be proud, any one can be proud. Centuries before the birth of Christ there flourished in India a civilization, which has been an enigma and a wonder to the historian.[7] And it is admitted that modern sciences like medicine and mathematics had their beginnings in India. On the sacred soil of India has been born a galaxy of world figures, like Ram and Krishna, Buddha and Gandhi, Ramakrishna and Vivekananda, who have made their impress[ion] on the thought and life of vast masses of men in the world.

And in recent times India's culture with its emphasis on moral values explains the singular manner in which India fought for and attained her freedom. With no material forces to back her, India not only wrested freedom from the mighty British Empire, but also in the process converted the Empire itself into the Commonwealth of Nations. And within less than five years of freedom, India has most successfully conducted the greatest democratic experiment in the world's history—the recent general election involving an electorate of more than 150 millions. The fact of their being illiterate did not prevent them from exercising their choice wisely, because, unlettered or not, they all shared the same great culture.

On Friday next when India celebrates the fifth anniversary of her independence, let Indians here pause and think over this problem: how they can worthily contribute their stream of Indian culture to the cultural life of this great Colony and the Pacific Isles. No divided allegiance or loyalty, as Pandit Jawaharlal repeatedly advises Indian settlers abroad. But as loyal citizens of this Colony, it is their proud privilege, nay, bounden duty, to enrich the culture of their motherland with their special contribution.

The vast distance from India, the circumstances in which the settlers grew here and the indifference of people in India to this problem, have all made it necessary that concerted attempts are made so that Indians can make a worthy contribution to the cultural life of the Pacific Islands.

That is the Indian Problem in Fiji.

96: Ramakrishna Mission in Fiji, 28 September 1952

After repeated requests and importunities of the Then India Sanmarga Ikya Sangam, the Ramakrishna Mission has at last been persuaded into establishing its branch at Nadi. The inauguration ceremony took place last Friday the 26th September. Though it was a week day and the day of cane payment, the attendance was large. People from all parts of Viti Levu had come to take part in this historic event.

---

7   This has been the subject of a great book by AL Basham, *The Wonder that was India* (1954 and subsequent reprinting).

For the past seventy years Indians came to Fiji in search of livelihood. They had very little else to give except their sweat, toil and tears. But of these they gave in abundance in return for a modest living. During the dark days of her political and economic subjection, that was all that impoverished India could give to the rest of the world. But after the advent of freedom India has been galvanized into a new life. India is now in a position to place her age-old spiritual wealth at the service of mankind which is groping its way in the deep fog of materialism.

Shri Ramakrishna Paramhansa is the prophet of awakened India.[8] His gospel of fundamental unity of all religions and faiths and of love and service of our fellow creatures has already spread far and wide. Big centres have been already established in America and various countries of Europe. The branches of the Ramakrishna Mission are rendering valuable service in Ceylon, Burma, Malaya, Singapore, Mauritius and various other places. The activities of the Mission are well known throughout the world. Wherever it has gone, the Mission has earned love and respect from people belonging to various races and different faiths.

One of its Swamis has been working in our midst for the last twelve years.[9] His untiring work in this Colony has served a double purpose. It has shown the people of the Colony, both by personal example and precept, what the Ramakrishna Mission stands for and it has convinced the authorities in Belur Math how badly we stand in need of their services.

For the further happiness and progress of the Colony, it is necessary, nay, imperative, that various communities and sections should realize and feel a deep and abiding spiritual unity. Once that is achieved, the rest should follow naturally as the Summer follows the Spring. And if there is any organization which can be of tremendous help in bringing about such spiritual unification, it is without doubt, the Ramakrishna Mission. The peoples of the South Pacific in general and the inhabitants of this Colony in particular will, therefore, welcome this piece of good news. For, in this part of the world as in many others, we have long enough missed the wood of fundamental oneness of humanity for the trees of merely skin-deep differences of colour, caste, and creed.

---

8 (1836-1886), born Gahadhar Chattopadhyay in Bengal. His best-known disciple was Swami Vivekananda. Paramhans means 'Supreme Swan,' which soars to great spiritual heights. See Harold W French, *The Swan's Wide Waters: Ramakrishna and Western Culture* (NY: Kennikat Press, 1974).
9 Swami Rudrananda. This is what AD Patel said about Ramakrishna on 26 March 1959: 'Sri Ramakrishna is a like a lighthouse in the modern world. He has taught us the harmony of religions. Whatever may be the source of rivers, he said, all join the same sea. All religions, wherever they flourish, lead to the same God. This is the essence of Ramakrishna's teaching.'

97: Fragments of a Diary 1952

22nd October — Wednesday

After bidding good-bye to our friends, we boarded the plane. We suddenly found ourselves transported from the warmth of friends to the coldness of the strangers. But we were too preoccupied with finding and settling down in our seats to notice the change. Atul and Dhimant were very much excited when the plane took off. They were very much intrigued by the scene below as the plane flew over Viti Levu. After it left Viti Levu in a few minutes, Atul dozed off and Dhimant started whimpering to go back home. I had to bribe him with sweets and pineapple juice to keep him quiet until he fell asleep. The food they gave on the plane was just enough to whet our appetites and we actually felt more hungry after we had our meals than what we did before! The flight was dull and monotonous. We flew most of the way through clouds. When the pilot announced that we were over the Mascot aerodrome, we could hardly believe it, for there was not a sign of anything under the white foamy clouds and it was hard to believe that a large well lit metropolis—in fact the third largest city in the Commonwealth of Nations—lay buried under the clouds.

The pilot announced that it would not be wise to attempt a landing and that he was heading for Dubbo aerodrome which was about 55 minutes' flight from Sydney. I whiled away these fifty five minutes in reading Neville Shute's *Far Country*. The book proved a welcome distraction.

When we landed at Dubbo, it was already 9 p.m. Sydney time. For the last fifteen minutes Dhimant was feeling thirsty and crying for water. I was told that there was no water on the plane. I tried to coax him into drinking some lemonade. But he must insist on water especially when none can be had! So as soon as we landed our first effort was to find some water for him after which we went into the small waiting room which was already packed with passengers who had landed from planes which like ours had to divert their course from Sydney. The Captain, poor man, was trying to find hotel accommodation for the passengers. It was midnight when the air hostess came in and jubilantly announced that accommodation was found for children, their parents and ladies. After the glad tidings we had to wait another half hour before the bus arrived. We boarded the bus and went to Dubbo. We drove from hotel to hotel knocking at the doors and receiving the stock reply, 'Sorry, we are full up'. At last our bus stepped near the Royal Hotel. The hostess went in for a short while and returned with the news that there were two single beds available in a three bed room which is occupied by one man, and that I and the children can go into that room. Leela and another lady were assigned another room. The rest of the party had to return to the aerodrome disappointed and spend the night in the plane.

It was through Atul and Dhimant, that I was able to spend the rest of the morning in the warmth of a bed while our fellow passengers had to keep vigil in their seats in the plane!

23rd October

Though we managed to find the bed, we could not get the breakfast there. The air hostess took us to a cafe for that. After our stomachs were full we took kindly to the town! We admired its wider and clean streets and its rural setting. I made an important discovery that the world looks beautiful only when the stomach is full. Even this 'one-horse town' as one fellow passenger called it, impressed its charm on me.

We took off from Dubbo at about 10 a.m. The weather was still cloudy. When we reached Sydney the pilot told us that he would try to break through the cloud and if he succeeded in the attempt we would land in ten minutes. And break through he did!

We landed at long last and were taken into the Customs shed. Mr. Mayne, that ministering angel of Indian travellers, was waiting at the gate to greet us. After medical and customs examinations we drove to the Wentworth Hotel. I have never seen Atul and Dhimant so excited before. It was a new experience for them. They were suddenly rushed into the brave new world. The double-decker buses intrigued them most and Atul called them 'lorries with driver on top and driver below'.

A short while after our arrival Odin Ramrakha's son Karamchand[10] came to our room. He had gone to the aerodrome to meet us the previous night, so he knew already about our misadventure. In the evening we had our meal at a restaurant in Hunter Street and went to Karamchand's house. We spent the evening in discussing various things. I was sorry to hear that the Australian press was carrying on propaganda against Fiji Indians, while our Fiji-born politicians were toying with their petty discordant fiddles. If Fiji Indians do not open their eyes in time, they will meet with the fate of an ostrich burying its head in the sand. Let them take heed.

24th October — Friday

We were told by the *P&O* people to get on board the *Strathnaller* before 3 p.m. Mr. Mayne advised us to get on the boat between 1 and 2 p.m. as there is usually a congestion of traffic between two and three o'clock. We had therefore no time

---

10   Karam Chand Ramrakha, who became a Federation Party parliamentarian in 1966 and remained a member until 1982. He was studying law at Sydney University.

to go sightseeing. Instead we went to Farmers to do our shopping. Farmers is all of these mammoth shops which sell anything from a hairpin to an elephant. Once inside this store and you forget that there is anything like want, poverty or shortage in this world. There is plenty of everything as well as the best. There seems to be nothing that a rich man's pocket cannot buy them. I thought I would allow myself the luxury of a gabardine overcoat. The attendant brought one out which fitted me perfectly. I asked the price. It was twenty nine pounds and something. I took the overcoat off quickly and told the attendant that my purse would not stand the strain of such a fine coat. He told me that I could have a cheaper one if I liked. I asked him the price of the cheapest coat he had in stock. It was sixteen odd pounds. Thus the cheapest price was too dear for me and I decided to forgo the luxury. Anyhow, I bought Leela a silk dressing gown, Atul and Dhimant two nice pairs of sailor suits and myself a woolen dressing gown. When we returned from shopping Mr. and Mrs Baijnath and their children with Rangaswamy Naidu were waiting at the hotel. Mr. Nicholls of the C.S.R. was also there. He entertained us all with a drink and as there was very little time left we had to bid them a hurried good-bye.

Mr. and Mrs Baijnath accompanied us to the boat. Later Rangaswamy Naidu came with Karamchand on the boat and told me that the passage order for the air ticket to Nadi was short by about fifteen pounds and wanted to borrow the amount. Unfortunately all I had was in bank drafts with very little cash. I realized his difficulty and would have gladly helped him out by advancing him the necessary cash. In the circumstances all I could do was to give him a letter to Mayne, requesting him to let Rangaswamy have the necessary cash. Knowing Mr. Mayne, I have no doubt about Rangaswamy reaching Nadi without any difficulty.

We left Sydney at about 5 p.m. It is Leela's first experience of a sea voyage. She did not have her dinner that evening, nor did she go on deck. Though she was not sea sick she appeared to be suffering from sea consciousness. The children however took it better than the mother, and felt quite at home in their new surroundings.

25th October — Saturday

It is a cloudy day but the sea is calm. I persuaded Leela to come out on the deck. It proved to be an essay in exploration. We discovered where the lounge, the library and the game decks were situated. While going around the B deck I came across a sailor who comes from Damau. From him I learnt that most of the crew consists of men from Damau, Navasari and Parad districts. He also told us that arrangement could be made, if we wished to have Gujarati meals. Naturally we preferred to have our own food. I asked the purser to make necessary arrangements. We were told that from next day we will have our Gujarati lunches and dinners in our cabin. For breakfasts and teas we would be going to the dining room.

I have spent the day in complete relaxation and purposeful idleness. It is a welcome change from the small vexations of life in Fiji.

In the evening children asked for some apples. I told the steward to bring some. 'Sorry, Sir, you can't have fruits in the cabin, now. They are strictly rationed', said he. Anyhow, he produced two apples and one orange from somewhere.

'What a downfall!' I thought to myself. 'Here is a shipping line which used to carry lordly satraps to the east in lavish circumstance. But now it is reduced to the state of one East End housewife scraping for one apple here and one orange there to make both ends meet!'

26th October — Sunday

We woke up in Port Melbourne. It is dull and cloudy morning. After breakfast we took a taxi to the zoological gardens. We passed the railway station. 'More people pass through the gates of this station at its peak period than those of any other in the world. It is claimed to be the busiest railway station in the world,' said the taxi driver. We drove on.

While passing a massive and imposing edifice the driver remarked, 'It is the gas house.' 'Gas house?' I thought I had not quite got him. 'Gas house, otherwise known as the Parliament House of the State of Victoria,' replied the driver.

Of short distance ahead he pointed to the left and said, 'This is known as the white elephant, though officially they call it the Exhibition'. After a lovely drive through parks and avenues, the taxi pulled up at the gates of the zoo.

It was a real treat for Atul and Dhimant. Of all the animals, the monkeys appeared to intrigue them most. What enchanted us were the beds after beds of beautiful roses large as lotuses. We spent the better part of the forenoon there, and returned to the boat to be just in time for the trip to the ranges.

While going to the bus we met Dullabh Mistri's son Shanti, who was looking for us on the boat. We told him that we were booked for a trip to the Ranges, and he readily joined us. We drove through the beautiful suburbs consisting of small bungalows artistically set amidst beautiful gardens. We came into the orchard country and what the Australians call the 'bush'. We stopped at a farm with a little tea shop. Leela, Atul Dhimant and two Shantilals had ice-creams while I feasted on milk-shake to my stomach's content! We bought four pounds of really first class Granny Smith apples. When I pointed at the apples and told the stall keeper that I wanted four pounds of those, he looked at me as if I did not know, and said, 'They are the most expensive of the lot, they are 1/6 a pound. 'It is alright. They will do me.' I replied.

After a stop of twenty minutes, we boarded the bus and continued the journey. After passing through a few miles of orchard country our bus started climbing up the Dandenong ranges. We drove through a beautiful forest of tall trees plumed with ferns and flowers. We went to the top of the hill. The place was crowded by trippers and picnickers who had come from Melbourne to wash off their blues. After half an hour of landscape gazing we descended on the plane. Coming down we passed through a dreamland of ferns protected by stringiest laws from human degradation.

We passed tail-waggers club. Anybody who wants give a holiday to his animals or pets has just to write to the club, and they collect them and give them really good time and rest. I wish the example would be copied everywhere. We returned to the ship. Shanti Mistry had a real Indian meal of chapatis, rice, dhal and curries with us after which he returned to his lodgings.

27th October — Monday

We went to Mayer's Emporium in Bourke St. to do our shopping. Whatever cash we had with us disappeared quickly and Leela put a veto on any further purchase! Upon return to our cabin Leela delivered me a curt lecture on economy and announced that from henceforth she is going to have complete control of the house.

Though the quantity and quality of the food on the ship has not sunk to the austerity level, it is quite evident that the halcyon days of British guzzling are now over. By arrangement with the purser we are having Indian vegetarian lunches and dinners in our cabin.

28th October — Tuesday

We went to Melbourne by train, and looked around. We ultimately landed in the art gallery. There is a good collection of old English Masters but it was already late and children were feeling tired. So after a hurried round we returned to the ship.

29th October — Wednesday

The passengers are distantly polite to one another. The social life has not yet begun. The weather is cold, cloudy and a bit depressing.

The Indian crew on this boat is mostly from the Portuguese territories of Damau and Goa. This was a puzzle to me as to why a die-hard British concern like the P&O should go all the way to Portuguese territories when there is so much manpower available within the Commonwealth itself. I tried to find out the terms on which labour is employed on this boat. The highest monthly basic wage is thirty-six rupees and the lowest is fourteen. Of course, they are paid a cost of living allowance. When totalled up, as one of the crew told me, he gets five wages a month meaning thereby that he was getting four times his basic wage in cost of living allowance! They have to bring their own uniforms. They don't get a holiday on full pay. And what's more, it is the *sine qua-non* of employment that they should not belong to any union. Indians of Damau and Goa being the political orphans of the world, no body—occupational, national, or international—questions the labour policy of this influential concern. It is a surprise to me that the Seamen's and dock workers' unions of India and Australia have not taken up this matter.

9ᵗʰ November — Sunday

This morning there were two remembrance services going on side by side—one in the lounge and one in the smoking room. Both were worshipping the same God, believing in the same prophet and remembering and praying for the same dead who lost their lives in the two world wars. And yet they could not sit together and join in the prayer! People who stand shoulder to shoulder in the business of killing their own fellow beings in wars and hob nob over a glass of whisky find it impossible to sit together in the worship of their Creator. How cheerfully Satan's followers unite while those of God always quarrel and wrangle among themselves!

Mr. Frisk who is going to attend the family planning conference in Bombay as an Australian delegate came and told me that Shroff wants to take a photo of Atul and Dhimant but feels too shy to ask my permission! I told him that if Shroff wanted to snap them, he was welcome to it.

We shall be crossing the equator tonight at twenty minutes past midnight. Neither the children nor Leela seem to be very much interested in the event. All that interests them is the fact that we are getting nearer and nearer to Colombo.

98: Divide and Rule, 15 December 1954

It cannot be denied that in the present socially and politically perturbed world, Fiji is perhaps the only country where the social and political waters are placid and calm. Where else in the world can be found a place where the relations between the rulers and the ruled, between capital and labour, or between the native and the immigrant races, are as harmonious and cordial as they are in Fiji? This happy position which should in fact provide satisfaction all round has actually resulted in giving headaches to the diehard imperialists who feel the ground slipping under their feet. Some of them have been persistently making frantic efforts for the last fifteen years to churn up racial hatred and bring about a conflict between Fijians and Indians. It stands to the credit of the members of both these races that they can see through the sinister designs of these mischief-makers and do not allow themselves to become tools in their hands. Ironical as it may seem, the more these diehards indulge in the propaganda of fanning hatred between Fijians and Indians, the closer the two communities come in the realization of the common danger. In their solicitude for their common welfare, both the races are becoming more considerate, both in utterance and action, towards each other than before.

The old bind of the policy of divide-and-rule, through its long over-use, has become so worn out and thin that anybody with a modicum of sense can see through it. Both Fijians and Indians realize that destiny has cast their lots together, for better or for worse, in this lovely land which is after all their land of birth, and it will be in their mutual interest to strive for making their common lot for the better and prevent it from being for the worse. Whatever the propagandists may think, the Fijians and Indians consider their persons and property as valuable as those of their European compatriots and under no circumstances are they going to offer their skulls to be broken, or their properties turned into bonfire by one another as a benefit performance for the delight of the diehard propagandists.

Do these propagandists ever stop to realize that the arguments they use to incite the Fijians against the Indians are in the nature of a boomerang with a tendency to recoil on themselves? For instance, when they talk of 'land grabbers,' the Fijians very well know who have completely gobbled up half a million acres of the best Fijian lands for almost a song. They know who fooled their fathers into selling hundreds of acres of their very best lands in return for a box of matches, a bottle of liquor, a musket or a piece of cloth? If the Fijians have only second best lands left for their own use, they very well know who licked the cream off their milk.

From this left over of their ancestral inheritance, they have reserved first rate land for their own use and rented out the surplus to the Indians through a board of trustees, of which the Governor himself is the president. When the propagandists talk of the exploitation of the Fijians' lands, the Fijians immediately think of the gold mines and all the gold taken out therefrom every year without payment of a single cent to the Fijian owners of the land. When they talk about the increase of the Indian population, their minds naturally turn to the great epidemic of measles which almost wiped out their numbers, and they also know who brought that catastrophe on their race. Even after three-quarters of a century, they have not been able to make up for the loss caused by that epidemic, and they know who are responsible for it. When these propagandists try to run the Indians down in the eyes of the Fijians, they overlook the patent fact that they and their forbears were responsible for the introduction of Indians in this Colony. The government of the day only did what the European planters asked them to do. If the Indians are such bad people as these diehards try to make them out, the guilt of introducing these people into Fiji lies squarely on the greedy shoulders of the European masters, who placed orders with the government for the importation of these labourers. In these days of fundamental rights of human beings the Fijian knows who denies him those rights and keeps him behind.

99: Fijians and Fijians, 29 January 1954

On Tuesday last, Australia celebrated her National Day and India observed the Republic Day with due solemnity. By a happy coincidence this year, the Indian Republic Day fell on the Birth Anniversary of Swami Vivekananda, the first cultural ambassador of India who went abroad to preach to a thirsty world the great truths of *Vedanta*, the quintessence of philosophic knowledge.

Both the members of the Commonwealth, Australia and India, celebrated the occasion with the pomp and circumstance it deserved. And as is usual all over the world, the nationals of the globe also joined in the celebrations inviting the local people to share in their rejoicings. And the official representatives of these countries in foreign lands naturally observed the day, too, and in the capitals of countries like U.S.A. and Russia, the heads of state and other leading figures joined in the celebrations and expressed the good wishes of their countries.

But Fiji is slightly different. Here we have some people who squeal over such an occasion. Or rather, we have a journal that cannot resist the temptation to use the occasion for its favourite pastime of trying to create discord between different sections of the loyal citizens of the Colony. A non-Fijian journal, writing about the celebration of the Indian Republic Day at Suva arranged by the Commissioner for the Government of India in Fiji, asks with uncontrollable indignation, 'why it should be thought necessary or even advisable to hold a flag-hoisting ceremony (complete with distribution of sweets for children) at Suva on that day?' And why not, any unprejudiced party might be tempted to ask these frogs in the well in reply?

Fortunately for the world, the paper admits that 'no thinking non-Indians in Fiji resent or question the right of the Indian people in the Colony to look to their motherland as the source of Indian heritage of culture.' Thanks for little mercies.

To what then is the objection? Perhaps another sentence in the article gives the clue. Referring to the recent speech of the Commissioner for the Government of India in Fiji, Dr NV Rajkumar, at Ba, the paper suggests, the Commissioner should leave the indigenous Fijian people out of his discourses. So it is the fear that Fijians of Indian origin and Fijians of indigenous origin are likely to fraternise on such occasions, that is at the root of the whole thing. But these Fijians and Fijians have many things in common: they all suffer the same disabilities; they have the same aspirations and hopes, they have the same warm heart under their black skins. But it is too late in the day for such vile attempts at creating discord and ill-will to hope to succeed. Yet it is a pity that such attempts are still made, and that such attempts are tolerated.

'If Fijian comments, written and verbal, are representative,' concludes the paper, 'the Fijian people, like a number of others, are not favourably impressed by the prospectus of celebrations on the occasion of India's parting company with the British Crown.' If the sample that found publication in the paper on the day before over the nom-de-plume, 'Plain Speaking,' is the specimen of the wide generalization, none is going to be convinced. So long as these anonymous writers do not have the courage to reveal their identity, few people will be taken in by these 'manufactured opinions.' The columns of our Fijian section reveal a different story, a more heartening story of fraternity of the people of the land to their brethren of Indian origin. The plenitude of wisdom that finds expression in the concluding part of the sentence that Republic Day is the occasion of India's parting company with the British Crown, is quite in keeping with the rest of the piece.

100: Segregation Stands Condemned, 11 June 1954

The Supreme Court of the United States of America has, in the course of its existence of 162 years, pronounced many important judgments. But none of them was, perhaps, of more consequence to the U.S.A. and the world in general than the recent one declaring segregation to be unconstitutional.

The question of the segregation of the Whites and the Negroes in the public schools came before the Court in cases from five states. In one judgment covering all these, the Court has unanimously pronounced its opinion in a forthright manner.

In a world which once had deep respect and regard for America as the country of liberty, equality and fraternity, this firm expression of the idea of the equality of man as the underlying basis of the American Constitution, will go far towards restoring her waning prestige. The red-baiting, which McCarthy has taken to fantastic extremes, has created doubts in the minds of thinking men all over the world about the existence of liberty in America. And the segregation of Negroes in different states was a blot against the professed principle of the equality of man.

This momentous judgment will affect the lives of more than 10 million school children in the U.S.A. And it will have a healthy reaction in the lives of more millions all over the world.

Let us hope that the principle upheld in this will be noted. For segregation of a kind is practiced in our educational and other institutions. Separate schools are run for the three main racial groups in the Colony. Whatever might have been the justification for it at some time in the past, everyone will have to admit that it prevents today the growth of a harmonious community is this Colony with a common outlook on life in an atmosphere of freedom and equality.

And in the 'higher' (!) stages of education, for which the Colony provides facilities, i.e. secondary education, the system of segregation now practised has another serious disadvantage as well. When public funds are utilised for starting and running separate schools for each of the three major races, there is a waste of human energy and precious money involved, institutions on which large funds are spent become more show-pieces if all the available accommodation is not utilised. If students of one community are not forthcoming, in sufficient numbers, it must be available to benefit those who are eager for it. And certainly the healthy influence of open competition and of rubbing shoulders with friends of differing races will help to raise the general attainment of all groups.

The plea may perhaps be trotted out that 'equal' but 'separate' facilities are provided for all the racial groups here. When one remembers that one institution for a community of 6,000, and an 'equal' number for another of 16,000, constitute 'equal' facilities, one can realise the hollowness of the plea. But even this myth of 'equal' but 'separate' facilities has been exploded by the Supreme Court judgment, when it proclaims, 'in the field of public education the doctrine of "Separate and Equal" has no place.' Separate educational facilities are inherently 'Unequal'. The sooner we recognise that segregation stands condemned, the better it will be for the progress of our country and peace in the world.

101: A Bogey Laid, 30 July 1954

For long it has been a fashion in Fiji, among some publicists, to raise the bogey of over-population threatening our Colony. They used to blame it all on one particular section of the people here, almost alleging that it was a sort of conspiracy on their part to multiply so fast and swamp the other sections of the population and bring down the standard of living. This, no doubt, gave an indication of the prejudice which was the real source of their propaganda.

No false modesty prevents us from starting that ours used to be the lone voice that would not concede that our Colony is overpopulated or threatened with overpopulation in the foreseeable future. We have never been tired of stressing that our problem is not overpopulation but under-development. And we have expressed the need for assessing the economic and other potentialities of the Colony and developing them on a rational and planned basis. Now our position has been vindicated, and by no less an authority than the Secretary of State for the Colonies.

Our readers may remember that among the resolutions passed by the last LegCo, in its closing sessions was one on this subject. Everyone was clear about the real subject of the resolution, which was this threat of over-population. As passed by the Council it urged that a 'Commission of Enquiry from the United Kingdom be appointed forthwith to enquire into the advise as to what steps should be taken to ensure that this Colony will not suffer from over-population to the detriment of the standard of living of all races in the Colony.'

As the Governor wrote to the Secretary of State for Colonies in forwarding this resolution, 'the proponents of the resolution felt that the necessary wide, independent and authoritative knowledge and experience is not to be found locally for the purpose.' This has been more than conceded by the Secretary of State. For his reply wonders at the wisdom of the step suggested and questions the advantages of such a Commission at this stage. In fact one should think that his reply should lay the bogey of over-population in Fiji, if not for all time, at least for a long time to come. The resolution requested the appointment of a Commission of Enquiry from U.K. And, for very weighty reasons, the Secretary of State has turned down this request.

The main reason is this: For any such enquiry to be useful, sufficient basic data should be available for the expert committee or Commission to do [work] upon. And these are not available here. As Mr. Oliver Lyttleton[11] says, 'There are at present so many unknown factors, such as the mineral potential, the forestry

---

11 (1893–1972); a businessman and Conservative politician appointed Secretary of State for the Colonies after the 1951 elections.

potential, the soil and ecology of the interior, and the basic data as to the development of hydro-electric power for such missions to work upon and form definite conclusions.' Unless basic investigations have been carried out before-hand, the value of the recommendations of a Commission, however expert, depends upon the outcome of further enquiries, and these, when completed have often revealed that the Commission's recommendations cannot be carried out because the assumptions on which they were founded were incorrect.

'The immediate need, therefore,' the reply concludes 'is for detailed surveys to supply the basic information about the economic potentialities of the Colony and that these should be carried out before consideration can usefully be given to the appointment of a more general Commission of Enquiry.'

Perhaps the Secretary of State had in mind something more than the resolution communicated to him when he says in his reply to the Governor, 'I also recognise the responsibility resting upon the Government of Fiji and Her Majesty's Government to ensure that the development of the Colony proceeds upon the right lines, so that its inhabitants of all races may live together in harmony and prosperity and with confidence in the future.'

Perhaps those who used to raise the bogey of over-population and try to create discord among the loyal subjects of Her Majesty the Queen in this Colony, will mark these words. It is to be hoped, in any case, that the bogey of over-population in Fiji has been laid to rest once and for all by the Secretary of State for the Colonies.

102: With Malice Aforethought,[12] 2 September 1955

Amongst the Bills that will be presented at this session of the Legislative Council is a Bill professing to make provision for certain control of companies and societies formed for the purposes of promoting commerce, art, science, religion, charity, or any other useful of social object or the like. In fact, this is a Bill which shows malice against certain countries of the British Commonwealth and certain religious missions. The countries discriminated against are India, Pakistan, Ceylon and all the Crown Colonies and Dominions except Fiji, the United

---

12   The Bill was brought before the Council by KS Reddy to try and prevent the Ramakrishna Mission from claiming any rights to property acquired by the Sangam. Sangam was operating within the ambit of the Mission with lack of clarity about who owned what property. The dispute was resolved when the management of the Sri Vivekananda High School was passed on to the Mission and Sangam operated schools under its own name.

Kingdom, Canada, New Zealand and Australia. Amongst the missions which are discriminated against are the Roman Catholic Mission and the Ramakrishna Mission, both bodies of international eminence and standing.

There is already adequate provision under the Companies Ordinance for the proper control and management of companies and societies incorporated under Section 22 of the Companies Ordinance of 1913 and of Section 19 of the Companies Ordinance Cap. 170 of the laws of Fiji. If such a society or company wishes to amalgamate with any other person or body it can do so with the consent of its members, of its creditors and of the Supreme Court. The Supreme Court openly hears the case and arrives at a proper adjudication. This Bill seeks to vest powers in the Governor-in-Council whose deliberations and meetings are held in strict secrecy and who is not bound to give any reasons for his decisions. The societies or companies are prevented from vesting any property even by way of lien, charge or encumbrance of any nature whatsoever, in any person, firm or corporation or association which is controlled from any country other than Fiji, United Kingdom, Canada, New Zealand or Australia. And 'controlled' under this Bill means controlled in any manner whatsoever, wholly or partially and even as to a matter which is not of substance.

If this Bill is enacted into law, it will raise a presumption that any institution, association or body, however eminent and respectable which has its headquarters in any country other than Fiji, U.K., Canada, New Zealand and Australia, is presumed to be undesirable for the purposes of this Bill unless and until the Governor-in-Council declares it to be desirable. If the Then India Sanmarga Ikya Sangam, which is expressly mentioned in the objects and reasons of the Bill were to vest any of its property in the Methodist Mission, or the Church of England or the Seventh Day Adventists or the London Missionary Societies, it will not come under this Bill; but if it wishes to vest the same in the Roman Catholic Mission or the Ramakrishna Mission, it will have to be first approved by the Governor-in-Council.

This amounts to a gross discrimination against two important missions existing in this country. And this discrimination and indignity is sought to be imposed upon them for no other reason than that the headquarters of one happens to be at the Vatican in Rome and of the other happens to be at Belur Math in India. By implication this Bill is creating a presumption that any person, association or body controlled from U.K. Canada, Australia and New Zealand, however disreputable and undesirable is presumed to be desirable for the purposes of this Bill and is not subject to the control of the Governor-in-Council. On the other hand, a person, body or association from other parts of the Commonwealth and even friendly countries like the U.S.A., France and Italy—even the UNESCO—are presumed to be undesirable unless and until the Governor in Council declares otherwise. Such a discrimination is uncalled for and is likely to create problems of international magnitude. Government of Fiji is controlled by the Imperial Government from London and for any legislation passed by this Colony, the U.K. will naturally be held responsible in the Councils of Nations. The U.K. is pledged to respect the freedom of religions and to mete out equal treatment to all members of the Commonwealth in the Colonies. This Bill if enacted into law will amount to a breach of both those sacred pledges.

This is a private Bill sponsored by Mr. KS Reddy, one of the Indian nominated members, and if he was candid enough in his statement of the objects and reasons of the Bill, it would have read something like this: 'This is a private Bill, the object of which is to satisfy a private grudge which Mr. Reddy has towards Then India Sanmarga Ikya Sangam and the Ramakrishna Mission.' In order to gain the support of the unofficial European and Fijian members of the Legislative Council, a sop is thrown in the form of an exemption from control of such bodies as the Methodist Mission and the Church of England and such other bodies from U.K., Australia, Canada and New Zealand. Mr. KS Reddy, who is by birth an Indian and by religion a Hindu, ironically enough sponsors a Bill which discriminates against his own race and religion.

The reason for such surprising behaviour is notorious. He first tried to throw dust in the eyes of the South Indian community as regards the activities of the Sangam and the Ramakrishna Mission, but he could not succeed. It remains to be seen how far he will succeed in his attacks in the Legislative Council. If this Bill goes through it will create a precedent for the members of the Legislative Council to bring bills which seek to satisfy their private malice by imposing restraints and heaping indignities on persons or bodies which are not represented in the Legislative Council and against whom they have got private grudge.

103: Why Access to Books? 23 September 1955

There is a clear acknowledgement all over the world that we should not teach the people to read and then leave them without literature. For they would then certainly relapse into a dreary and ultimately dangerous state of half-education, in which they would be easily satisfied by the crude semi-pictorial approximations of the strip cartoon and by the abundant supply of degenerate literature which destroys, rather than promotes, the capacity to face the problems of the world with skill and courage.

Mr. C Harvey, Director of Agriculture, in his address at Nadi [at the Sri Vivekananda High School] the other day, warned the students about reading comics, for in the absence of any regular library service, the youths are likely to go in for such undesirable literature and get morbid satisfaction.

It is the duty of the State to provide and assist in the provision of books to inform, instruct and entertain the men, women and children of the country by running State Public Libraries with liberal grant-in-aid fellowship, and other inducements.

In the brochure, 'Access to Books,' which explains an aspect of the UNESCO programme for fundamental adult education, it is stated:

> In communities where there is no flow of appropriate reading material and no stimulus to write, literacy itself may have little significance. Experience shows that in such areas individuals who are taught to read and write frequently relapse into illiteracy unless progress in literacy is accompanied by progress in other fields, particularly in the material means of communication. The wisdom and the patient service of the school teachers must be supplemented when the students have left their schools by liberal provision of means such as public libraries for self-education of those whose ambitions and interests having been stimulated, are active forces in the development of the individual and of society. The pains of ignorance and cultural isolation are not felt until a taste for reading has been stimulated, until the desire is born to enter the world community of ideas and action for which books are a service and a symbol.

We have quoted extensively to show that the provision of public libraries is necessary both to prevent undesirable acquisitions and to foster self-improvement. All progressive countries have accepted this and are developing public library service as a means for self-education for the citizens to enable them to keep abreast of progress in all fields of knowledge and help them to be better social and political citizens of their country, to be more efficient in their day-to-day activities, to develop their creative capacities and powers of appreciation in arts and letters, to assist the advancement of knowledge and use of their leisure time to promote personal happiness and social well being.

But where are we? We had also thought of a library scheme during the war-time when we, like the people in other countries, were full of good intentions and pious resolutions. We invited a library expert from New Zealand in 1944 and he drew up a small scheme. As one of the leading thinkers of the Colony said, it was a fine report; it has not found a place even in the new educational dispensation.

The politicians, who are more for ballot boxes, may not be very much interested in any library plan for it cannot bring in more votes. And here also the government is not for it for the legislators do not demand it. The social workers and thinkers in the Colony who have been noticing the increasing larrikinism, recklessness, drink and other evils, do want some social activity, especially to attract the young and wean them away from the perils that threaten them.

'It is not enough to wait to establish libraries until a 'need' has become expressive,' says the same UNESCO brochure. Barrister AD Patel expressed the same idea when he said that one does not wait for hunger before one begins to cook.[13] And so a beginning for a public library service has to be made, although demand may not have come from the public.

'UNESCO know well enough that libraries cannot achieve their objectives without support form Governments and educational authorities,' says the same pamphlet. What is our government's policy? Says the Acting Director of Education in the course of a message sent on the Library Day of the Ramakrishna Library early last July, 'The extension of library facilities in Fiji is, from the educational point of view, most important in the furthering of culture and progress in this Colony.'

It is a clear statement, forthright and unambiguous. All we want is that this should be implemented. There should be a positive and helpful approach, a progressive policy of assisting, promoting and even floating public libraries throughout the Colony by liberal grant-in-aid, fellowships and other means. The sooner a beginning is made in this, the better it is for the future of Fiji.

104: First Things Last? 14 October 1955

'Members would make themselves look foolish if they materially added to the plan,' the Acting Colonial Secretary is said to have remarked, according to the report released through the P.R.O.[Public Relations Office], in the course of the discussion on the Education Plan in the recent session of the Legco. From the trend of discussion, it almost looks as if the members took this exhortation most seriously: they did not appear to be in the least inclined to suggest even essential addition, perhaps for fear of appearing foolish!

About 12,000 to 15,000 children of school going age are going without education, it was even officially admitted. But how is this problem to be solved? What does the debate reveal? There is the pious hope that 'to improve primary education, we must get teachers of the right quality, and we hope to get them by improving secondary education,' which the Acting Director of Education expressed at the conclusion of the debate. There was also reference to 'Pressure Cooker' courses under consideration for recognized teachers.

---

13   This he said in response to SB Patel's view, expressed on 29 July 1955, that library service may be 'premature' for Fiji. In the 1950s, Patel with Swami Rudrananda established a library at the Ramakrishna Mission in Nadi and had a mobile service, called 'Gynan Ratha' for the rural areas. A full library service for Fiji was established in the 1960s, with the Western Regional Library opened on 20 November1964, when AD Patel was Member for Social Services. Patel was appointed to the newly formed Library Enquiry Committee on 26 September 1957 whose other members were Director of Education (Chair), RA Derrick, LD McOwan, CH Miller, Semesa Sikivou, Uday Vir Singh, J Hackett, and AL Parke.

It was heartening to learn from the Acting Director of Education that there were already 22 inter-racial schools in the Colony. This certainly is a trend in the right direction. And the earlier the Department can claim that all the schools in the Colony are inter-racial schools, the better it will be for the future of the Colony, which is inter-racial and which must remain inter-racial.

When finalising a plan of education development for the next five years the case of thousands of children, who are obliged to go without even primary education, cannot be left out with impunity. Consideration must be given also to the fact that all over the civilised world, primary education is expected to be free and compulsory.

We do admit that it is not possible to set things right overnight, as by magic. But we do assert, as we have done in these columns before, that an enlightened state should recognise its primary obligations to its citizens. And the provision of free and compulsory education is the first of these. In planning and working for the discharge of this duty, the responsibilities and obligations arising out of it, must be boldly faced. It is not wise either to shut one's eyes to facts or to put first things last.

The Senior Indian Member, Pt Vishnu Deo, has, we are happy to say, boldly stated the viewpoint in this matter of all the thinking citizens of this Colony, when he told the Council 'that if needed to promote the educational plan, taxes must be levied, but they should be imposed equitably.'

This forthright statement should be considered as the undertaking given by the whole community, not merely by the Indian voters whom Pt Vishnu Deo so ably represents in the Council, but also all the Indians in the Colony who have already shown their keenness in the matter of education by their pioneering work in providing educational facilities for their children.

The state must step in at least now and see that the Colony's resources in men and material are so used that fundamental and primary obligations of the state are discharged. The provision of free primary education to all the children is the first of these, especially when responsible public opinion has expressed itself clearly to the effect that the necessary financial resources must be found by levying fresh taxes, if necessary, there is no excuse whatever for putting first things last.

105: A University College for the South Pacific,[14] 26 April 1956

'The South Pacific Commission was created some nine years ago,' said His Excellency Sir Ronald Garvey, Governor of Fiji, in his address inaugurating the conference, 'as an organ of international co-operation for the purpose of

---

14   See also CC Aikman, 'The University of the South Pacific,' *Fiji Society* vol. 13 (1974), 7-17.

promoting the economic and social welfare and advancement of the peoples of the island territories' in the South Pacific Region. What the Commission has been able to achieve during the period of its existence with the assistance of the two auxiliary bodies, the Research Council and the South Pacific Conference, speaks for itself about the success of the international co-operation in the field of economic and social development.

The place of education in any scheme of social and economic development is supreme. No scheme of economic development based on the highest expert basis can succeed if the human material is unable to work it for want of the education necessary. And rightly is the stress laid first and foremost on the primary education and on social education.

It is proper that the Commission's attention has so far been devoted to these aspects of education in the territories. A pilot library service, with the assistance and help that UNESCO has given to similar projects in India, Venezuela and other countries, may also be considered for these territories for the further self-education of the people who have left schooling. The SPC project may be a model for other insular territories like ours.

But it is time that due thought is also given to education at the secondary and post-secondary or collegiate levels. For wise and competent indigenous leadership, essential for the solution of the problems facing the territories and the general advancement of their own communities, can come only with such educational facilities. As for secondary education some provision is at present being made by the territories themselves with the initiative of the missionary bodies. But at the University level the present position is not at all satisfactory. The Commission should take the initiative in the starting of a University College for the benefit of the three million inhabitants of the territories.

An institution of this type should be a joint endeavour of the six metropolitan Governments of Australia, France, the Netherlands, New Zealand, the United Kingdom and the United States. To begin with, it may be affiliated to and associated with universities abroad—in the United Kingdom or the United States. But in course of time, it could develop into a University with different departments. And when that takes place, the different departments could work in close co-operation with or even take over the work of the Research Council of the South Pacific Commission. That no doubt can be a development only for the distant future. But a beginning can be made by the starting of a University College in the South Pacific for the benefit of all the territories here.

The problem of financing such a scheme, the details of the governing body, the subjects provided—all these and other problems can well be tackled with success once the idea is approved. Meeting as it does in Fiji, the Third South

Pacific Conference may naturally feel that the location of such an institution should be in Fiji. Many of the reasons which His Excellency gave for the Commission's choice of Fiji for the venue of this conference may well be the overriding considerations here—most of all the question of accessibility at reasonable cost. This and the educational development that has taken place in Fiji in recent years may perhaps form the overriding factors.

The South Pacific Conference, we hope, will give thought to this question of a University College for the South Pacific run by the territories for the special benefit of their people.

106: Invite the United Nations, 2 August 1956

We are amused to read an article in the June issue of the *Pacific Islands Monthly* under the heading 'U.N.O. on Indian Education in Fiji.' In his attempt to make the dark picture of Indian and Fijian education look bright, the writer has attempted to give it a glow of false colours by citing figures of expenditure on several thousand Indian and Fijian children and comparing it with the amount spent on a few hundred European boys and girls. To cut the argument short, why not let the Indian and Fijian children go to the Boys and Girls Grammar Schools in Suva, and let the European children enjoy the use of Government Indian schools at Samabula and Vatuwaqa for a change?

The writer complains that 'Any survey of educational expenditure in Fiji, particularly when considered in conjunction with taxation paid per head of population, suggests that any racial discrimination made in Fiji in connection with education is directed against the Europeans.' One has yet to find a territory where the British keep the Europeans educationally backward and give better facilities to indigenous people. Such a Colony simply does not exist on this planet.

As to the taxation, the bulk of the revenue of the Colonial Government is derived from Customs and Excise Duties, License Fees and Income Tax. The import trade, local production of excisable articles and wholesale and retail trade within the Colony, generally, are largely in the hands of a few European individuals and European-owned companies. The greater part of Customs and Excise Duties, License Fees, etc, is therefore, received by Revenue Collectors from these small number of European companies and individuals.

This does not mean that all the taxes paid into the Treasury by these Europeans fall on the European population. The real incidence of taxes falls on the consumers, the great majority of whom are Indians and Fijians. Out of a total estimated population of 345,000 in the Colony, 166,000 are Indians and 147,000

Fijians and only 17,000 Europeans and Part-Europeans. As to the Income Tax and other direct taxes, most of the Indian and Fijian taxpayers, being primary producers, pay their taxes from the new wealth which they create, while the European taxpayers pay theirs from the money which they have taken from the pockets of the Indians and Fijians by way of profits and rents.

Would it not be better to invite the United Nations to send a Commission consisting of representatives from such neutral countries as for instance, Sweden, Switzerland, Ceylon and Indonesia, to come and see for themselves whether the Europeans are racially discriminated against, as the article in the *Pacific Islands Monthly* complains of the two races, viz. Fijians and Indians, which have a permanent stake in this Colony, are deliberately and with a set purpose, kept educationally and politically backward?

107: On Sadhu Kuppuswami, 9 August 1956

The sudden demise of Sadhu Kuppuswami, President of the Then India Sanmarga Ikya Sangam, removes from our midst a yogi and silent, selfless public worker of this Colony.[15] Sadhuji was one of those few who renounced everything and dedicated their lives to accomplish something good and great for those who had chosen this Colony as the country of adoption. Sadhu Kuppuswami came to this Colony in 1912 under the indenture system but his noble spirit longed for freedom. Freedom, to him, lay in dedicating himself to the service of others.

In the dark days of indenture and the hard days that followed, the Indian community lacked facilities for educating their children. Sadhuji felt the need for an organization for the educational and cultural advancement of the backward community. More than that, he felt the urgent need for the spiritual regeneration of the Indians almost cut off from their moorings.

The service ideals of Swami Vivekananda fascinated the Sadhu. He organized the birthday celebration of Swami Vivekananda. Immediately after the celebration the Sangam was founded in 1926. Since then he had been its President except for one or two years. He had to undergo all [kinds of] troubles that generally fall to the lot of a pioneer. In those days when there was no transport, he would walk from district to district to gather support for the Sangam. No distance was too long for him to walk. No track was rough for him to tread. No door was barred against him. Going from door-to-door he brought the people message of hope, peace and good will. His meek unaffected grace brought solace to hundreds of

---

15   AD Patel called the Sadhu the greatest Indian in the history of Fiji. See also Brij V Lal, 'Swami Kuppuswami: Cultural Leader,' in Stewart Firth and Daryl Tarte (eds), *20th Century Fiji: People who shaped this nation* (Suva: University of the South Pacific, 2001), 86.

his fellowmen. His smile expressed a parent's warmth. Thus the 'Father of the Sangam' carved for himself a niche in the heart of all by his Gandhian simplicity, saintly life, and selfless, silent work in the Colony for over three decades.

Sadhu Kuppuswami was a great devotee of Sri Ramakrishna. The Sangam he founded in 1926 was not an institution for political power. Sadhuji's noble mind could never think of low material ends. He wanted this society to be a religious and cultural organization. No wonder then that he wanted the Ramakrishna Mission to be founded here, and he knew that it would be the guide and guardian to the institution he had founded. It was Sadhuji who was responsible for bringing Swami Avinasananda and Swami Rudrananda to guide the activities of the Sangam. In the course of twenty-five years, the Sangam established not only a network of schools but temples all over the Colony. Hundreds of educated men occupying positions in life today owe a debt of gratitude to the Sangam.

Sadhuji's high sense of duty was admirable. Even in his failing health he presided over the annual general meeting of the Sangam at Lovu. His exhortation to the members of the great organization which he founded has universal appeal: 'The organization was founded to establish harmony and love among all sections, and the society can survive only if it builds up moral and spiritual energy, and eschews all hatred and violence.' Thus did the great patriot teach. He lived hating none but loving all.

In the death of Sadhu Kuppuswami the Indian community has lost a spiritual guide, the Ramakrishna Mission an ardent devotee, and the Colony a great (karma yogi) selfless worker.

108: Budgeting for Educational Progress, 6 December 1956

The Colony's Budget for 1957 is now being discussed by the Legislative Council. It would, therefore, be of interest and profit to consider what the budget of a State can and should achieve. Is the budget of a State but the statement of the annual revenues and expenditures of the year, a profit and loss account and balance sheet? A State budget is much more than all these put together. For by the fiscal policies underlying the methods of raising the revenue and expending these funds, the budget can act as a lever for raising the national income.

In the hands of a wise and far-sighted administration, the budget can effectively bring about the economic, social and even political advancement of the State. By a slight change in fiscal measures, of import or export duties, new industries can be established and fostered, for which there are natural facilities. A little alteration in the fiscal system can—and in a wisely-led country will—alter the pattern of the expenditure of the public entirely. Instead of large fractions of the national income being spent on unessentials like alcoholic beverages, incentives will be provided for the saving of such funds for abiding purposes like housing and education and for the formation of capital for industries.

To take but one instance, there is urgent need for providing educational facilities for the children in the Colony. It has been admitted on all hands that provision of facilities for elementary education to ALL the children is a primary duty of the State. And in all advanced and advancing States, such education has been made *Compulsory* and *Free*.

What is the state of things in Fiji? Is primary education free? No. Is it compulsory? Certainly not. The compulsion of circumstances, on the other hand, obliges more than ten thousand children to go without any schooling whatever. And in the case of those attending schools, no one will pretend that they are getting a fair deal. Inadequate buildings, insufficient accommodation and equipment and paucity of teaching staff (in some cases, the teacher-pupil ratio is one to 80) cannot be considered by any one to be a satisfactory state of affairs. And there will be unanimity of opinion in the Legislative Council, as there is outside it, that something must be done about this.

What could be done about it? Two essential requirements are school buildings and teaching staff. Of these the former is easier to secure: with money made available, buildings can be put up. As for the latter, the cost is less—the cost of constructing a building is many times the annual cost of running a school there, but since it involves trained personnel, this takes more time and is not so easy of solution. But both these obstacles can be overcome, as we shall endeavour to show.

First, we shall take up the problem of finding adequate teaching staff. A teacher must have two essential qualifications—basic academic background and proper professional training. In an emergency, it may be necessary to be content with one of these: half a loaf is better than none. Provided the academic qualification is adequate, professional training could even wait. Thanks largely to the initiative and enthusiasm of the missionary bodies and the general public as well as the wise guidance of the Director of Education, hundreds of boys and girls are now studying in Secondary Schools. And quite a few of these are coming out successful with the Overseas School Certificate of Cambridge University or the Fiji Junior Certificate. If an attractive grading of salary is fixed for these young men and women, with an assured opportunity to complete their professional training in due course, the problem of shortage of teachers will be solved. For this will draw sufficient young men and women into the teaching profession to work in the schools in their neighbourhood.

Provision of suitable subjects in the Fiji Junior Certificate Course, the shortening of the training period from two years in the case of entrants with higher qualification, the reduction or abolition of the boarding allowance etc. to trainees are other means by which even the present financial and other provisions can be made to give a larger number of qualified teachers. Competent mission and other agencies may also be able to increase the quantum of 'teacher supply.'

Next, let us consider the question of finding means of providing the school buildings and equipment necessary for the Colony. Once it is recognized that the provision of educational facilities for the children is an elementary duty of the State, it would be easy for the Government to help missions and local committees working in the educational field. The principle should be accepted that when a community of people comes forward to provide buildings and equipment for a school which it needs, the community should be helped with half the cost of, or with an amount of money equal to, what the community itself collects. This undertaking on the part of the government will give an impetus for enthusiastic local committees to pool their resources for the common welfare.

Can the Government of Fiji honour such a general commitment? Can it find funds for meeting half the cost of all the school buildings which may be constructed by the people in different parts of the Colony? It may well run to hundreds of thousands of pounds per annum. And at first sight it may seem to be an impossible task. But it is easily practicable, provided the enthusiasm, initiative and the resources of the community are properly tapped.

The cost of building construction is an item of capital expenditure. And the current revenue incomes of a State can never meet the needs of all Its capital expenditure. Even a graduate in economics will admit that such capital expenditure may well be met from loans raised by the Government. In this case the responsibility of raising the requisite amounts by way of loans may be left to the committee concerned. Thus it comes to this: where there is recognized need for new school buildings or additional school buildings, the community, through the mission or other agency, provides the funds, half as outright donation and the other half as loan to the Government. The onus of providing educational facilities is thus cast entirely upon the community.

The most precious wealth of any country is the children there. It is the bounden duty of the Government and the people of the country to give these children the facilities necessary for the development of their personality so that they can contribute their best to the progress and prosperity of the Colony. And we earnestly trust that the Government authorities and general public, the Members, both official and unofficial, will consider the suggestions outlined in the previous paragraphs. With but a token grant from the Council and the general approval of the principles, the scheme suggested can be given a fair trial. Let the people invest all they can in their children's future. Give them a chance to do this.

109: Library Service for Fiji, 29 August 1957

It is noteworthy that the British Council is expanding its activities by introducing the 'Book Box Scheme.' We learn several institutions are taking advantage of this service. The High Commission for Government of India in Fiji, it is learnt, is also intending to start a similar 'Book Box Scheme.' This service will include books in Hindustani as well.

Our Government, which has to take up the lead in this service, seems to be satisfied with the presentation of some books to the British Council helping its Book Box Scheme. The Book Box Scheme has its limitations. There is no choice for the reader to cover different subjects. The books are limited in number. This scheme is generally intended to serve places not easily reached where a library centre with its own personnel will be uneconomic. The time is now ripe for implementing the recommendations for the establishment of Library Service made by Mr. C.R.H. Taylor as far back as 1944, when he was invited by our Government to prepare a scheme for Library Service.

The introductory remarks made by him still hold good and they deserve quotation. He says: 'I feel it incumbent upon me to stress the place of library service in the life of any modern community. The ideal of achieving literacy for a population fails of its purpose if education ceases after a few years of schooling. Unless the adolescent has some means of continuing his development, his gains become loss in as much as they engender yearnings that may not be fulfilled. And it is clearly uneconomic that an education policy costing perhaps, 100,000 pounds should be willing to let a very great proportion of its result lie sterile or become atrophied as soon as the active school years are passed. For the Fijian and the Indian, if their economic, social conditions are to improve, it must be mainly through the printed word, and directed not to child at school, but to the adult. The habit of reading, properly cultivated, will make better citizens.

Our education budget has gone up ten times the figure mentioned by Mr. Taylor. The number of and strength in primary schools has increased considerably. Many secondary schools have been established. All these mean that the responsibility of the Government is greater still to keep the growing number of literates well informed, and on right lines, by the introduction of an all comprehensive scheme of library service. Such a scheme should be introduced at the earliest possible time. There are certain ways and means for this.

The UNESCO is giving assistance in personnel and expert advice for approved library service schemes in member countries. It also offers fellowships to local men to get themselves trained to take up the responsibility of running these schemes. It recommends to member countries to help such schemes with books and other materials. Through the UNESCO, Book Exchanges have been established in almost all countries. And a national library in Fiji can very well take advantage of such facilities.

Sometime last year the Government decided to appoint a committee to study the present library facilities in Fiji. We appreciate the need for a committee to consider the present needs in the background of Mr. Taylor's report of 1944 and suggest a scheme to cover the entire Colony.

We understand the limit to which any Government can undertake this responsibility. But Government can, and in a large measure has to, take the assistance of local institutions in these matters. The Government can aid these institutions by way of grants for buildings, personnel and books; it can allot land for the buildings. It can even provide for mobile libraries.

The thirst for books in Fiji has increased considerably as can be seen by the growth in books business. It is high time, we feel, that the proposed committee is formed and further steps taken for the expansion of the Library Service in Fiji.

110: Progress & Custom, 7 November 1957

'The old order changeth, yielding place to new,' says the poet [Tennyson], 'And God fulfils Himself in many ways, lest one good custom corrupt another.' But in Fiji, the old order hardly seems to change, however great the need is for change. Hence it is refreshing to note in his report on Fijian Administration finance, Mr. RS McDougall, C.B.E., a positive recommendation for changing the customs and traditions which are now holding back Fijian progress.

Mr. McDougall has seen for himself 'how the (Fijian) system of land tenure discourages development, how some of their customs and traditions encourage shiftlessness and how personal initiative is stifled.' Naturally he feels, as other sympathetic observers of the Fiji scene have felt, that these must be changed if the Fijians are to make progress in a very competitive world, if their children are to be better educated, if they are to enjoy a higher standard of living, and above all, if they are to hold their place in a group of islands which are rapidly ceasing to be isolated from the world and in which more than one race is living.'

Mr. McDougall naturally suggests that the change from a subsistence to a cash economy is essential and should be brought about as early as possible. The present policy seems to be to keep sacrosanct any and every custom in the name of preserving local traditions, unmindful of their validity in the 20th century. Sometimes it looks as if the powers that-be are purposely following such a policy to prevent a section of the Colony's people from playing their rightful part in the Colony's progress. Anyway the results are astounding. In 1954, as Sir Geoffrey Clay, Agricultural Adviser to the Secretary of State for the Colonies, pointed out, while nearly 90 percent of the total land area of the Colony was owned by Fijians, only 10 per cent was under cultivation.

Why is the Fijian not able to play his part even in the agricultural section of the Colony's economy? Why is the Fijian not playing the part he can play in the other departments of life too? When one pauses and ponders over this, one will realise, as McDougall points out, that 'those who are leading the Fijians at this critical time have heavy responsibilities, but great opportunities.'

The earlier the realisation is made by the authorities and action taken to free the community from the shackles of unhealthy customs and traditions, the better it is for all concerned. In any case the Fijian is growing up. He is seeing what is going on in the world around him. And he can understand what is good for him. He can understand who are shedding crocodile tears.

111: The Great Irony, 2 July 1959

'Fiji is and will remain a multi-racial community and the aim of Government must be, in all its actions and policies, to strengthen the sense of unity of the people of this Colony, to avoid as far as possible anything that will entrench or increase racial differences, and to promote all measures that will help people to regard themselves not merely as Indians or as Fijians in the narrow sense of the word, or as Europeans or Chinese, but as citizens of Fiji—Fijians in the wider sense, just as for example people of European, Asiatic and American origin living in Jamaica all take a pride of being Jamaicans,' said Sir Kenneth Maddocks in his opening address to the Legislative Council. He also said, 'I would like to see the principle accepted in future development plans that new schools that may be built with Government funds or with Government assistance, should be multi-racial in character.' Sir Kenneth Maddocks should be congratulated for these very important pronouncements if they are seriously meant and if they are intended to be seriously implemented, for they herald a new era in the history of this Colony.

Hithertofore, there was a tendency on the part of Government to lay emphasis on differences of race and culture and it took measures, in utter disregard of the future, to ensure that there was as little contact as possible between the different sections of the population. The good humour and friendly relations that exist between the different sections of the community are due to the good sense of the people who ignore the nefarious propaganda of some reactionary elements to divide the people and to keep them divided.

All right-minded people will readily agree with His Excellency that the people of this Colony should not merely regard themselves as Indians or Fijians, or Europeans or Chinese, but as citizens of Fiji—Fijians. But there are people in Fiji who try to assert that even those Indians, who are born and permanently settled in Fiji, have no right to call themselves Fijians! They can only call themselves Fiji-born Indians! If Europeans settled in New Zealand and Australia can call themselves New Zealanders and Australians, if the European citizens of the U.S.A. can call themselves Americans why on earth can Indian, European and Chinese citizens of Fiji not call themselves Fijians?

One is rather amazed at the opposition of the Fijian members to the suggestion of racially mixed schools on the grounds that it will be detrimental to Fijian culture which one of them defined as 'the sum total of things which go to make up their way of life, from the bure to the meke.' The present Fijian culture begins from the time the Fijians embraced Christianity, and their present way of life is the outcome of the customs and traditions retrospectively built for them by colonial administration in conjunction with missionaries and chiefs. Most of the things which are now considered Fijian are brought from outside by Europeans or Indians. Even the flora and fauna on the main islands are largely exotic. The food they eat, the clothes they wear, the utensils and the furniture they have, is mostly of non-Fijian make and origin.

Even without multi-racial schools the bure is being replaced by iron and timber or even concrete houses under the Fijian Improvement Scheme. Even the meke is totally different in tune, dress and purport to what it was before the advent of Christianity. The present Fijian culture is not even a century old. It largely consists of things, beliefs and ideas freely borrowed from other cultures both in content and form. It owes its very existence to peoples and civilizations of other countries. It lives and grows through the Fijians' contact with Europeans, Indians and Chinese.

Racial discrimination and segregation stand universally condemned in the present world. The South African Government's policy of Apartheid has been condemned by the General Assembly of the United Nations. Even the Southern States of the U.S.A. are giving up their opposition to mixed schools for Negro and White children. It is a deplorable irony of fate that when a Colonial Government desires to take a step in the right direction, it is being opposed by people whom it is going to benefit most.

112: Address to the Fiji Teachers Union, 9 September 1964

I deem it an honour for me to open this conference this morning. I am not a stranger to you, nor are you strangers to me. I have addressed the Fiji Teachers Union's conferences many times in the past. But this time I am facing you with a great load of responsibility on my shoulders. You must not misunderstand me, but I invite you to put your shoulders to the wheel and help me as far as possible.

Your President has conveyed to me your loyal and sincere cooperation for which I am thankful. I must tell you one thing and that is this, that 'where there is a will, there is a way' if you are to fare in this all important field; if there is determination on your part to face difficulties and tackle the problems and to solve them as best and as early as you can, I am sure you can achieve a good measure of success.

I must tell you of the requirements of the Colony in the near future as far as your work and your mission is concerned. The government of this country has been committed to a policy of rapid localization of their services. That means we have got to prepare men with good academic qualifications, men of integrity and character, men of personality, and men who have practical and executive ability and we must have this in as short a time as possible. There are other needs of our services for the large and extensive programme of development which require able, well-trained and well educated workers, executive officers and artisans. Many of the industrial organizations and establishments are also reverting to this policy of localization as far as their staff is concerned. For example, the SPSM Ltd., the Gold Mines, BPs, MHs and the Banks have need of properly qualified and suitable men and women for employment. There is, therefore, a demand for properly qualified and educated men and women—a demand which has never been so great in the history of Fiji. We need hundreds of qualified people to fill these posts.

Also, there is a great shortage of teachers and unless you have good teachers you are not likely to improve the standard or the efficiency in the schools and it is not going to help in the out-turn of the numbers of qualified men and women that we want for these different purposes in the development of political, social and economic aspects of this Colony. So you can realize how great this problem is and how difficult. I am keenly aware of the shortcomings that we have. We know that a bad carpenter often finds faults with his tools. But let this not be true of you. Difficulties are there, and are there to be overcome.

Mr. Patel then quoted instances of his visits that he had once made to two schools which were devastated during hurricane blows. In one school, the headmaster and his staff laid great emphasis on the difficulties that they had to face and had closed the school and said it would remain closed for a week. In another school which he had happened to visit the same day and where the damages done were seemingly more and there was more debris in the compound, the teachers were busy teaching under trees. Mr. Patel pointed out that teachers of this school had made use of the opportunities which can be found in such a circumstances and he said that this would go to show what a sincere desire to maintain the standard does in a school.

Mr. Patel said that he was aware of the unsatisfactory and inadequate facilities that there were. He said that the President had said that text books were unsuitable to our needs in Fiji. Mr. Patel replied that the department was doing something to put this weakness right. As for the accommodation, he said, we would have to tackle the problems from all sides. We would have to use the present classrooms; have more rooms made and improvise the rooms under the trees. He said he did not need to remind Indian teachers of the great Indian institution of Shantiniketan which was started under its founder Rabindranath Tagore who had believed that a child taught inside the walls of a classroom was bound to feel imprisoned. Tagore believed that the physical and spiritual freedom came to a child by learning his lessons sitting in comfort at the feet of a guru.

Mr. Patel also went on to say that he was aware of the shortage of staff in schools. He said that teachers in some schools would have a serious handicap in basic education and knowledge and that could be set right if teachers were to equip themselves well. He said for this reason, seminars were being organized and teachers were encouraged to take advantage of the new facilities so as to raise their efficiency and the efficiency of the schools.

Referring to the President's emphasis on the need for moral instruction, Mr. Patel said that he was of the same view. He said he would go further and say there was a need for religious instruction in schools as there was no difference in the fundamentals. They all have God, prayers, taught living virtuous lives, and they all hated evil. He quoted the instance of his own son who was studying at a private school in England. He said he had once written to the headmaster saying he wondered how useful the study of Christianity was to a Hindu boy. The headmaster had replied reminding him of Mahatma Gandhi's observation that by studying Christianity he had become a wiser Hindu. There is no danger, Mr. Patel said, of your children coming into contact with the tenets of other religions. They will always be the wiser for that.

We are in the noblest profession in the world. Unity is your greatest need at present. The professions and organizations like the Law Society, the chartered accountants and others do not have separate racial organizations. They do not dream of having such things. So you who are teaching all the other professions, don't you think there is a weakness on your part to separate yourselves along racial lines—one Indian, another Fijian? The need for unity, as you all realize, was never greater as it is at present. You have got to set an example to your pupils and also to the people of the Colony. I would like, therefore, to see in the future that both these associations come together, realize their common affinity and common brotherhood, and join and amalgamate into one. We want to do away with racialism in this Colony. But if the main profession, which is the teacher of all professions—if that is going to be divided and separated along racial lines, then where is the hope of eradicating racialism from the Colony? That is why the first step to take is for the teachers to unite.

Secondly, you must make all efforts to take away the words 'Indian,' 'Fijian' 'European' from the registration of schools. In many schools that is not the correct distinction either, because now many schools take children of other races and more or less they are 'composite' schools, if I may use the word. And won't it be better if we thought less of our race and more of our nationality? We should make a beginning by talking to our school committees and persuading them to take out the word 'Indian,' 'Fijian,' and 'European and just call 'so-and-so' primary school. Whether it be a primary school or a secondary school, this racial designation should come out of all these registered names. And if you approached your committees, they would realise the usefulness of such a thing. It is such a small thing but it has got such a great effect. I would like you to pursue this with your school committees and set this defect right.[16]

We must appreciate and understand that in this period of change, if we don't come together and unite, the consequences would be very serious. We will either integrate or disintegrate. There is no third choice. You would realize how important integrating is at present in this Colony.

113: Social Security in Fiji, 26 March 1965

There is no form of overall social security provision for workers in Fiji. There is a considerable number and variety of employer/employee contributing provident fund schemes for certain classes of employees. But there is no provision for retirement or old age benefits for the bulk of the wage-earning and lower

---

16 Integration was opposed by most Fijians. According to Ravuama Vunivalu, Fijian Member of the Legislative Council, multiracial primary schools would be detrimental to Fijian culture. 'I feel that we should not be too hasty about mixing the people up.'

salaried working population of the Colony. It is scarcely open to argument that social security schemes, of the kind and range found nowadays in metropolitan countries, such as the United Kingdom, Sweden, New Zealand and elsewhere, are beyond the financial and economic capacity of relatively under-developed countries such as this. The problem has been to find some limited form of old age security which Fiji can afford. The government has concerned itself with this problem for some years. In 1957, the Secretary of State for the Colonies first put to colonial governments an outline of limited social security schemes which he thought might be within the economic potential of the territories concerned. He made it clear, however, that the charges imposed on a government budget by any social insurance or security schemes are, by their nature, charges which have to be met, no matter what future financial and economic situation may be once the scheme has been initiated.

So far as they affect they affect government budget, social security charges become a permanent feature of the expenditure estimate, and it cannot be liquidated. Charges of this nature, which of course go to employers and employees under the mutual contributing scheme, have to be calculated to take account of the level of government revenue and expenditure, and of commercial profit and loss, as the case may be. It is this important aspect, the question of timing, which countenanced fortune in the early years of the consideration of the introduction of a limited security scheme for Fiji. A good deal of preliminary material was obtained, much of it from the operation of an employers provident fund scheme in Malaya.

In 1961, preliminary discussions were opened with the Labour Advisory Board and with other employers and employees organizations. It soon became clear that while the employees representatives supported the introduction of employees providing a provident fund, the employers' representatives felt that the country as a whole could not then afford it. Further, many of them had set up their own schemes, and to this extent it could be said to be already providing a form of future security for their employees.

Nonetheless, the Governor-in-Council considered that a scheme on the lines of that in operation in Malaya should be introduced in Fiji and that preliminary planning and the preparation of the necessary legislation should proceed. By the middle of 1962, it became clear that the complexity of the problem was such that a detailed on-the-spot investigation was necessary and, at first, assistance was accordingly sought from the Secretary of State for the Colonies. In January 1963, a grant was approved from the colonial Development and Welfare fund to enable Mr. J Ashford, a senior official in the British Ministry of Pensions and National Insurance, to visit Fiji. Mr. Ashford began his work in October 1963, with the object of inquiring into the feasibility of introducing a limited extension of social security in the Colony, having regard to its economic state and paying special attention to the possibility of establishing a national provident fund. Mr. Ashford's comprehensive and valuable report was published in September 1964 and has been accepted by Government as a basis on which we should now proceed.

We cannot afford to defer the introduction of a limited scheme of social security in Fiji any longer. We owe it to the large and growing body of wage-earning workers and their families and children and to initiate action which will give them some hope of security in their old age, and in times of social difficulty. The scheme is very, very simple. It is in the nature of the compulsory saving on the part of every earner in the Colony. It starts with wage-earners, with the employees, and it is later meant to include all persons earning in the Colony. They will be called upon, as far as the workers are concerned, to contribute 5 per cent from their income which will be doubled by an equivalent contribution from the employer which will carry interest in their own separate respective account in the fund. The interest which will accumulate will naturally be like a Post Office Saving Bank Account—compound interest. When the worker reaches the age of 60, and if the accumulated amount in the fund is less than one hundred pounds, his widow stands to get the minimum amount of one hundred pounds. That is quite an amount for the class of people who do not even get a living wage. In the capital formation of the country and at the time when capital is needed most for its economic development, this Colony has to go outside, hand on knees, begging outside capitalists to come here and invest funds in this Colony. Would it not be better that the Colony itself makes an effort at providing its own capital invested in productive enterprise and thereby not only increase the total economic production of the Colony but increase the income of every wage-earner and also increase the standard of living...

I am personally gratified to have the opportunity of moving this motion. For many years, I have been deeply conscious of the need to ease the burden of old age in Fiji. The provision of adequate security for workers and their families during the sunset of the bread winner's life is a matter of special personal concern to me. I have seen enough of the poverty, the heart-burn and the worry which can afflict old age in Fiji for me to press the urgency of the need for the introduction of a scheme for cushioning the hardship which old age and insecurity can bring. It is my conviction that a national provident fund scheme is a vital part of government social welfare policy, and that there is now the prospect of being able to afford one.

114: Address to the Fijian Teachers Association, 4 May 1965

Mr. President and members of the Fijian Teachers Association, it would be remiss of me not to begin my address today without expressing to you, Mr. President, to your office-bearers and to your Executive Committee, my appreciation for your kind invitation to me to open this conference. This is the first occasion on which I have had the pleasure of attending a conference of the Fijian Teachers Association and of speaking to you all.

As you know, the ceremony today marks the opening of the 30th Annual Conference of the Association which was founded in 1935. This fact alone shows the endurance and strength of your Association; but the presence here of some 600 of your members, gathered together from near at hand and from the four corners of these islands, is persuasive evidence of the part which your Association is continuing to play in safeguarding the welfare of the Fijian teachers of this Colony. The records show that six of your office-bearers and executive committee members hold arts degrees; while the list of your past Presidents contains the names of Fijians who have been honoured by the Queen, who have come to represent your people in Legislative Council or in Local Government, and who have risen to positions of responsibility in Government administration.

I have been impressed also by the details which your President was kind enough to send to me, of the wide variety of matters which, over the years, your Association has discussed and on which it has made submissions to Government. One or two of these are, I understand, still the subject of correspondence, and, since I received the invitation to speak to you today, my office mail has contained pleas for me to make pronouncements today about these matters! You will, I know, not really expect me to be able to do this; but I have little doubt that the Association's representations will receive the same sympathetic consideration with which they have been treated in the past.

As some of you will know, I am not unfamiliar with the problems of school administration in Fiji, since I was manager of a number of schools in the Western Division, before I assumed office as Member for Social Services. I have been well-placed, therefore, to appreciate the day- by-day difficulties which confront both school committees and teachers. In addition, over the past months, I have visited many of your schools and seen your problems at first hand; and I am deeply conscious of the fact that, although the policy makers and the administrators are essential to ordered educational development, the real essence of educational success rests with the individual teacher and his relations with, and the influence he brings to bear on, the children who pass through his hands. Those of you who live in remote areas must often wonder whether your work is adequately recognized and appreciated. I can assure you that it is; but the practical problem of achieving adequate numbers of inspections and visits to remote areas is one which, I know, greatly vexes the Department of Education.

There will soon be about 100,000 children and other students receiving full-time education in Fiji. In 1963, there were 650 schools and institutions—compared with 464 in 1962—scattered over 55 different islands throughout the Colony. They were staffed by about 2,900 teachers.

Gathering such as this can do much to remedy the sense of isolation which many of you may feel; and I hope that you will take the fullest opportunity to discuss your problems with your colleagues and, where necessary, with the officers of the Department of Education who are here to help you.

There are some essential conditions for a successful professional organization. First, a combination of theory and practice. In your Training College days, you learned how to teach. You studied many topics. But this does not free you from further study of them. There is no final word on them. There is always something more to find out. Especially is this so in the field of education. There are many highly intelligent people thinking and writing about every aspect of education today, and you must try to keep up with what is written in your own field. Many people say, 'I'd never be a teacher. How dull it must be to teach the same things, over and over again, year after year.' This is a common mistake about teaching. Subjects change. Methods of teaching change. Pupils change. Pupils ask questions which lead to changes in both content and methods of teaching. There is a continuing process of development and adjustment. There is no doubt that for the successful teacher, this is the most fascinating aspect of his job. It never stands still, for society never stands still. It is changing more fundamentally and rapidly today than at any other period in history.

This common illusion about teaching arises because most of us are not in schools long enough and, of course, not at the right age, to see that schools really do change with the times. When we become parents and have to help with the homework, we think it is difficult because we are out of practice or have forgotten; but the real reason is that the subjects have changed and we do not know that they have changed. This is all right for parents as far as it goes but not for you, as teachers. You must be prepared for change. Where you can record something of interest and value from success in teaching practice as the result of theory based on study, it should be passed on. Failure should also be recorded.

Your Association might therefore hold regular meetings to present and discuss short papers on various teaching topics, both of content and method. All professional organizations realize the great value to be obtained from open discussion on matters concerning development in their special field. You might encourage your members to prepare short talks, and the reviewing, criticism and discussion of them, as part of their ordinary everyday professional responsibilities. You should not regard this as the kind of activity which belongs only to research by lectures or specialists. The professional status of your organization will grow in proportion to the increased professional knowledge and ability of your members in the eyes of the general public as well as in the classroom. You should lose no opportunity of becoming leaders in educational thinking, development, and progress in Fiji. The success of the teacher depends on the status of his profession in society. The full status of the teacher will be achieved when every teacher is immensely proud of his calling. Proud, not boastful, getting quiet satisfaction from being able to follow his calling. When every teacher is proud to teach, we won't hear so much about the status of the teacher.

I am particularly glad to know that your Association has increasing cooperation and consultation with the Fiji Teachers Union. In the matters with which you are concerned, the Fijian Teachers Association and Fiji Teachers Union have a common interest; and the development of consultative machinery between the two can do nothing but good. Many of you will know that, over recent months, a new Plan has been in the course of preparation for Education Development over the next 5 years. This Plan has yet to be considered by Government as part of the overall Colony Development Plan. At present, therefore, it cannot be said to be accepted Government policy; but it does nonetheless reflect the considered recommendations and views of the many educationalists and education bodies which have had a hand in its preparation. It has been fully discussed in the Education Advisory Council and, it has my personal support.

A copy of the draft Plan has been sent by the Director of Education to the secretary of your Association. It is a lengthy and comprehensive document and it contains some 40 recommendations for the aims and development of primary, secondary and tertiary education in Fiji; together with particular reference to technical and vocational education, teacher training and the proposal to establish 'middle schools' on practical rather than academic lines. As a corollary to this, it is proposed that the present eight year primary course should gradually be replaced by a six year course in accordance with the practice followed in many other countries.

It is not possible for me today to tell you about all the important proposals contained in the 1966/70 Education Development Plan; but I hope that many of you will take the opportunity to find out more about it from the office-bearers of your Association while you are at this Conference. Some of the proposals in this Plan are new to Fiji because new problems have arisen or are expected to arise; these require new thinking and the reappraisal of many of our accepted beliefs and attitudes of the past. It is important that all teachers should understand what is in the Plan and should lend their weight in support of its proposals when it is, as I hope, endorsed by Government and by Legislative Council in due course. I am grateful to the Director of Education and all those professional teachers, Committee members and others who have had a hand in the preparation of the new Plan or have offered advice about it.

Finally Mr. President, may I say once again, how glad I have been to have had this opportunity of talking to you all today and of expressing to you and to every teacher present at this Conference my hope that the 30th gathering of this Association will make a most useful and constructive contribution to the educational progress of all the children of Fiji.

I have the pleasure to declare this 30th Conference open.

115: Capital Punishment: Letter from Church Leaders, 12 May 1966

The Hon. AD Patel

Dear Sir

The news that proposed amendments to the Penal Code will be put to the next meeting of he Legislative Council is most welcome to us and to members of the churches we represent in Fiji.

We have already expressed our deep concern for the need to abolish capital punishment. We refer to various discussions on the subject between the Heads of Government and Churches in Fiji; our letter to unofficial members of the Legislative Council, and to the letter from the President of the Fiji Council of Churches to the Member for Social Services on the 26th March 1965, giving the following resolution passed at the first meeting the Council:

> This inaugural meeting of the Fiji Council of Churches requests the Hon. Member for Social Services to raise with the Government the abolition of capital punishment in Fiji which this Council regards as an urgent social necessity.

We believe that the Bill to amend the Penal Code has been the result of representations at home and enlightened legislations abroad.

We write to you again before the Bill is considered to assure you of our belief that the proposed amendments to the penal code will bring our legislation more into line with our concern to care for our fellow man.

We hope that the Bill to amend the Penal Code will appeal to you as reflecting the true spirit of a country that seeks to develop the highest human values. We submit the following for your consideration:

Respect for the personality of man: Capital punishment destroys a human being. It indicates lack of understanding by the society which produces the murderer. The murderer may not be wholly responsible for his actions.

Positive approach: Capital punishment defeats the purpose of restoring the murderer to society. Destroying a person for murder does not cure the problem of society which gives cause for murder.

Lost hope: Experience has shown that it is possible for a person to be executed for a crime he has not committed. We pray that this will never happen in our country. A suitable term of imprisonment can provide at least the hope that the convicted person and society will take the opportunity to deal with the real problems.

Practical assistance: The Fiji Council of Churches has appointed a sub-committee to consider ways in which the churches can contribute to the rehabilitation of prisoners.

God loves all men: We believe that God loves all men and urge that a person's hope of restoration may not be cut off completely through capital punishment.

We are aware that your own conscience will dictate your decisions. We share with you our feelings and those of the members of our churches, trusting that you will indeed appreciate the values embodied in the proposed amendments to the Penal Code and share with us our concern to adopt them here as soon as possible.

May God bless you in your deliberations.

Yours faithfully

J Clerkin

Vicar Delegate

JC Vockler

Bishop in Polynesia

M Rimoni

Minister, LMS Congregational Christian Church in Suva

JT Gardiner

Minister of St Andrews' Presbyterian Church, Suva.

SA Tuilovoni
President, Methodist Church in Fiji.

116: On the Abolition of Capital Punishment, 26 May 1966

I might claim that I am the first man to raise a voice in this House against capital sentence and that was done 20 years ago when mine was a voice in the wilderness. I did it because non-violence and non-killing is the very essence of my upbringing. As a child, I was taught to respect all forms of life including insects, and I was not allowed to kill even a fly or a mosquito. As I grew up, and as I came under the influence of Western education and Christian civilization, I modified my beliefs: I now permit the use of insecticides both in my home and in my garden. I allow my children and my wife to take meat, but still I do not believe in taking life, though law does not prohibit me from taking life of a fowl or an animal, but I would not take it, much less the life of a human being. It is not because I am influenced by this deterrent of a death sentence. It is simply because I hold life sacred and I consider that it must not be taken under any circumstances.

The first duty of any criminal legislation is to protect the life, limbs, liberties, rights and property of the people and the most primary consideration in dealing with this Bill should be the extent of protection that this Bill would give to the safety of the lives of the people of this country. I have heard both points of view. As a matter of fact, several people have approached me and asked me point blank, what is the significance of bringing this Bill when the country is on the threshold of political change. I assured them that as far as I know there was no connection between the two. There are many people who do fear that if capital sentence is abolished, there will probably be a larger amount of murder but as the European Member for the Southern Constituency pointed out, it is a sheer conjecture on everybody's part to say whether there will be an increase in the commission of murders, or that there will be a decrease.

It is agreed that capital sentence is a barbarous way of dealing with a criminal which does not befit a civilized society. It has been pointed out that we should have more compassion for the victim than for the murderer. I agree. But, is hanging or taking his life the only way of dealing with him? I hold my eyesight most precious. If a man wants to offer me the alternative of losing my eyes or my life, I would say 'Take my life, before you take my eyes.' But if he puts my eyes out he will be sentenced to imprisonment; his eyes will not be put out by the State. So it is not the question of punishment being the same in nature as the crime itself. If a man burns my house, I cannot ask the Government to burn his house. We have got to find adequate and proper punishment for the person who has committed the offence and, at the same time, will deter others from committing such a crime. That is the purport of our penal system, and our problem here is to consider whether we can find a method or system which can serve both purposes, to adequately punish the criminal and also act as a deterrent to other would-be criminals.

Death sentence appears to have been considered the highest deterrent. If it was not, capital punishment would not have been retained for what is called capital murder or repeated murder, and abolish it for ordinary murder. I consider that life imprisonment deprives the criminal of the good of which he has deprived another citizen, and also restrains him from reverting to evil, in accordance with the views of a very great Roman Catholic Saint quoted by the Member for Natural Resources. Of course I agree with him that if life imprisonment in the country like this is going to mean 7 years of bright lights at Naboro gaol, with good food, good healthy climate, beautiful view, entertainment in the evenings, probably it may not prove as a deterrent to people living in out-of-the-way islands where life is so dull and monotonous.

But that is an administrative measure. I think that if life imprisonment is made to mean what it says and if normally a man would have to spend all his life in goal and die in gaol, unless, through his conduct, through his repentance and through other mitigating factors relating to the crime he has committed, he earns an earlier release. This, in fact, which is prevalent in the minds of the people and for which there is a really good foundation should now be removed. As far as I am aware, no murderer whose death sentence was commuted to life imprisonment has served more than 20 years—that is the longest period. Some were released after serving 16 years and some have been released even after serving ten years. So the whole thing is that we can have an alternative deterrent which is more civilized, which does not inflict unnecessary worry, pain and mental agony on innocent people. Can we find a suitable alternative deterrent which will also provide adequate punishment for the criminal, which will be in conformity with the views of a civilized society? I believe that life imprisonment, in the fullest sense of the term, is an adequate and proper alternative.

So far as this Bill goes I would like to make it clear that though I am in favour of abolishing capital punishment, I go so far as to say that I will be happy to see the gallows completely banished from our penal arrangements. If the death sentence is barbarous in case of murder, death sentence is barbarous in any other case also; as far as the barbarity is concerned, there is no difference.

Coming to the question about affording special protection to policemen and differentiating between a murder committed by an ordinary man, and a murder committed by a prisoner, I would like to mention a few cases before this House. A policeman is on his way to serve a summons to a man in a settlement who is prosecuted for not taking out a dog licence, and on the way the man with whose wife this constable has a love affair attacks him and kills him. Is this policeman acting in the performance of his duty in going to that settlement to serve that summons? To my mind the answer is yes. Would the husband of his paramour therefore deserve capital punishment? Many people are taking risks; people who in public life are exposed to as much danger and risk as probably the constable. A magistrate is exposed to such risk, a judge is exposed to such risk, the counsel who is prosecuting a criminal is exposed to the same sort of risk.

Now, supposing a man who has been sent to gaol by the magistrate, after he has served his sentence, feels very annoyed against the magistrate for sending him to gaol, comes back and murders the magistrate. Is that any less serious than if he kills the policeman? The Attorney-General described the murder of a policeman as an act of anarchy. I hold the view that any murder is an act of anarchy. If there was a good government and order there would be no murder and anybody who commits murder is an anarchist from a sociological point of view and there cannot be any difference. Why should a man who, for instance, murders a Governor be liable to imprisonment for life and a man who murders a constable be hanged? Is not the man who murders a Governor a greater anarchist? Supposing a man has committed some petty offence and he has been sentenced to gaol for 6 months and he has been ordered to serve his sentence extramurally and while he is a prisoner serving his extramural sentence murders somebody with whom he has got a private grudge. Why should he be hanged just because at that time he happened to be a prisoner serving an extramural sentence? If he had committed the same murder before he was a prisoner or after he had served his imprisonment what serious difference does it make to the heinousness of his crime, to the gravity of his crime, that he should be hanged if he commits a murder while serving extramural sentence on a petty charge, but if he has served that sentence already and he is out he can have life imprisonment. There might be a recidivist, a gaol bird who always comes and goes out of gaol and who might be a real public enemy number one and if he commits murder he only gets life imprisonment.

It has been said that if capital sentence is abolished and if a murderer is convicted and sentenced to life imprisonment, and if he is serving his sentence in gaol, what deterrent is there for him to commit another murder by assaulting somebody within the Prison's precincts or outside. All that I say is that the provisions of this Bill go far beyond that argument. This sub-clause does not apply only to those prisoners who have committed murder and are serving a sentence for that crime, but this has been made far-reaching, even applying to people who were serving extramural sentence for petty offences. However that may be, I would like to ask the Government to consider one aspect involved in this. If the Government really thinks that the death sentence is the highest of deterrents and that it should not be removed to safeguard and protect the members of the Police Force and the officers of the Prisons Department or those other officers or visitors who might be visiting the gaol, then the members of the public are entitled to ask the question 'What right has the Government got to make us guinea pigs?' If life imprisonment is not a good deterrent, why do you remove capital sentence and substitute life imprisonment as far as the lives of the people of this Colony are concerned? Does not there lie a duty on the Government to safeguard the life of the meanest of the citizens in this country. I am convinced that life imprisonment, if properly inflicted, is a good substitute and a good deterrent, but if the Government is not going to accept it, then I am afraid that by keeping this clause they are putting themselves in a very embarrassing position.

I come now to the issue of repeated murder. The First Indian Nominated Member mentioned a case of a person who was found guilty but insane, who committed two murders. I remember that case very well, it happened in Lautoka some years ago. The man committed his first murder, he was found guilty but insane, and he was sentenced to be retained during the Governor's pleasure. After a few years, when the authorities considered that he had completely recovered and he was safe enough to be let loose in society, he was released, and within a few days of his release he walks into Morris Hedstrom's store at Lautoka with a cane knife and chops an Indian woman to pieces right in the middle of the store in the presence of everybody. Again he was tried, again he was found insane, and he was sentenced to be detained during the Governor's pleasure. Now, the question arises: Why do we spare the lives of insane people who are a greater danger and menace to society than of sane people in whose case at least there is a chance for repentance and reform? We are not hanging insane people for humanitarian reasons, not because the gravity of their crime is in any way less serious than that committed by a sane person. The present Bill seeks to enlarge that sphere of humanitarian treatment to sane people, and if the law considers that there is a chance for an insane man, why should the law not consider that there is also a chance for a sane man?

I would like to point out that even capital sentence has never been a complete and universal deterrent. Murders are being committed all over the world in spite of the provision of capital sentence in many countries of which our own country is one example. Merely providing for a deterrent has never kept the prisons empty or the country free of crime. If it were so, then we would not need an efficient

Police Force. All that we would have to do is to enact laws providing for these sentences, people would be simply frightened of the sentences and would desist from committing crimes. But that does not happen. Crime has its roots in so many social factors. For instance, the case quoted by the First Indian Nominated Member of that poor unfortunate woman who was hanged for stealing bread to feed her starving children, there was death sentence there, but it did not deter her from committing the crime nor did it deter many people during those days from picking pockets right in the crowd in front of a person being executed before their very eyes.

So the reduction of murder cases in Fiji will depend on many factors. One of them is effective investigation and bringing the criminal to justice. Suppose there are 10 murders and not one has been detected. Though we have capital sentence on our Statute Books, there will be an incentive for people to commit murder because they will be under the impression that it is very difficult to get caught. On the other hand, if we had a very efficient Criminal Investigation Department and all those 10 murderers were caught, prosecuted and punished, that would be a deterrent and even if people wished to commit a crime, they will think twice before committing it. The most important factor in the reduction of crime is efficient criminal investigation. But that, in itself, cannot prevent crime completely. You will find that murder has its root in maladjustment of human relationships.

I will give you an example of a case of common occurrence in Fiji; dispute over cattle theft which eventually builds up into a family feud and culminates in murder. There are no fences between the adjoining fields, a neighbour's cattle trespasses on your land, you are angry, you take the cattle to the pound, there is a row over it, exchange of abuse, and then your cattle goes on their land and revenge gradually and steadily builds up. You bring your relations and friends to help you, your neighbour brings his relations and friends to help him. And, one day, as we know in many cases, both parties know that it is going to culminate in somebody losing his life. That can be set right by improving the human relationships between the two neighbours. As the proverb goes, 'strong fences make good neighbours'. It applies in many cases in Fiji. Some murders have their root in poverty.

The case of a recent murder in Tavua, which was mentioned in this debate both by the Attorney-General and by the European Member for the Western Constituency, had its root in poverty besides mental derangement. Two companions were drinking in the hotel, they had it in their minds to visit Suva and see the Hibiscus Festival. They were in need of £4 to £5 and this man conceived the brilliant idea, while he was drinking, of getting the money from the Chinese man's shop, and it was just through a small amount of money, as the motive, to enable them to come to Suva to see the Hibiscus Festival, this

Chinese man was bludgeoned to death. There again is the question of our social condition. His life is spared because we took into consideration that he was not mentally quite all right. He had a history of being easily provoked and getting into a temper, and that he was an inmate at the leper asylum at Makogai. But, whatever it is, I would like to say that not many murders are committed in an affluent society over a loaf of bread or just a few pounds.

I will give you another example. We used to have a lot of murders and suicides in this country during the indenture system. The number has reduced considerably after the indenture system was abolished. There again it was not the death penalty which was the deterrent. In spite of the death penalty, the social condition of the time drove people to desperation and to the commission of such crimes. As soon as social conditions improved, the number of cases of suicides as well as murder decreased and if I was not convinced that life sentence was a sufficient deterrent, and that by removal of capital punishment, there is not the likelihood of increasing murder in this Colony, I would not have stood here to advocate the abolition of the sentence and expose the lives of the people of this country. But I have many reasons to believe that people's lives are quite safe. I honestly believe that the rate of murders will go down and I will tell you why. Essentially, and fundamentally, whatever people from outside may say, we are amongst the world's most civilized and well-behaved people, better than the people of the United Kingdom.

Even the criminals that we find here are a simple type of criminal you have not got those crooked, scheming minds who can commit murder in various odd ways that their detection is difficult. You do not find those sort of cases where people commit murder after murder just for the fun of it as was heard of in a case only a few months ago in England where a man just in cold blood calls a boy to his house and kills him just to show another friend how a murder can be committed. You do not find those sort of cases here in Fiji, thank God. We are, on the whole, a better behaved community. The standing example is, that in spite of the absence of police in these outlying islands in the Lau group and other areas where there are no police stations and where there is no protection, in all these years there has been only one case of murder and that was a Chinese man being murdered when the Member for Natural Resources was a young man. That does not speak for the death sentence, I say. That speaks for the natural peaceful disposition of the people of this country and good human relations prevailing here, and as long as those relations are there, as long as social relations improve, as long as the cases of maladjustment get less and less, there is every chance that the rate of Commission of crimes, including murder, will be reduced.

Humanitarianism should affect not only victims but also the prospective murderer. I have had many occasions to come into touch with murderers because I believe I am the only living lawyer in the Colony who has defended the largest number of murder cases, and I must say that I have not come across one man who did not have a human heart. There were many things that drew him to commit murder but, essentially, at the root. I found that he was not a brute and life sentence will be used I hope, in touching his humanity so that he becomes again a decent, normal human being.

117: Why I support Family Planning, 17 August 1966

Let me open by quoting poet Rabindranath Tagore: 'It is cruel crime thoughtlessly to bring more children into existence than could properly be taken care of.' I support family planning on humanitarian grounds. To have children is a natural function as well as a social and religious obligation of every man. The human race must continue to proliferate through us. Our procreative urges are in fact God's command to 'increase and multiply.' It is therefore a sacred duty to fulfill the command and have children. Children provide joy, meaning and purpose of life. According to some religions, to beget children is to carry out God's will.

I love children. I like homes full of children. I like to see humanity increase and prosper. I am not a misanthropist nor a neo-Malthusian. Man is not born with a brain only but with a pair of hands also. There is nothing wrong in having a large family if you can afford to look after the children and bring them up properly without undue strain on the mother. But only millionaires can afford to have dozens of children if they have strong and healthy wives.

Population explosion is a world-wide phenomenon of this century in spite of two destructive world wars. Even with this tremendous increase in numbers, man is comparatively better fed, better clothed and better housed than ever before even in the backward, undeveloped countries. This is brought about by the increased brain power and muscle power of mankind. The rapid increase of population has led to a still more rapid increase of knowledge, inventions and achievements. Knowledge explosion has surpassed population. Agriculture and industries are undergoing remarkable revolutions through ever-increasing discoveries of science. Fiji is an undeveloped country and increase of population is a desirable economic and political objective.

Yes, I love children. I also believe that an increase in population is necessary for the prosperity of Fiji. For those very reasons, I strongly advocate the necessity of family planning. We need children, but we want them to be healthy and well nourished. We want to give them opportunities to grow into strong, healthy, well-educated men and women, with a capacity and facilities to earn and enjoy wealth. The wealthier and healthier the parents, the more children they can afford. Ironically enough, they are the very people who make use of birth control devices in order to seriously restrict the size of their families.

On the other hand, strange as it may seem, it is the poor people in an individualistic society who need larger families in order to ensure a measure of security and provide help, comfort and happiness in the latter part of their lives. This is the case even in advanced countries of Europe and America, and it is more so in a country like Fiji.

Before the western way of life overtook Indians and Fijians, their customs were so designed as to prevent improvident maternity. It was brought about by the wife and husband remaining apart and practising continence during the suckling period. Normally there was an interval of three years between the different births. This gave the baby time to grow sufficiently so as not to need full attention and nursing from the mother. The mother got ample time to recover and recuperate from the last birth and to gain sufficient health and strength to face the new pregnancy. It also gave the father time to improve his economic condition with which feed an extra mouth.

However much we may brag and boast about clinging to our customs and traditions, this customary method of family planning has disappeared completely from Indian and Fijian societies. Indians no longer live with joint families. Fijian fathers do sleep in community bures away from their wives and children are increasingly bottle-fed.

Gandhiji was a staunch defender of birth control by celibacy and he practiced what he preached. Even his more ardent and loyal disciples found it hard and often impossible to follow his example. Family planning with medicines and devices are now substitutes for custom and discipline. I believe that it is the sacred duty of every children's nurse to persuade women of all races to teach them how to protect themselves and their offspring from the evils of improvident maternity. Family planning means happy, healthier and longer lives for both mothers and children.

I also believe that successful family campaign depends on the improvement of economic conditions and living standards of the masses. We must not overlook the fact that a poor man really stands in need of a family more than the well-to-do. Reduce poverty and you will find a number of families reduced to optimum size.

118: The University of the South Pacific, 21 March 1967

Like all other new ideas, when the idea of the establishment of a university in Fiji was first broached, there was naturally tremendous opposition and reaction. The Government also proceeded with the idea rather warily and hesitantly. The first step that was taken was the visit of a Mr. Horton from the Colonial Office. Mr. Horton made his own recommendations which took Fiji's educational system one step further but not far enough for the establishment of a regular university.

He recommended the establishment of a college which would provide education up to the intermediate standard. For the remaining two years for the degree course, it was recommended that the students should go overseas either to New Zealand or Australia and finish the course there. Later, public opinion locally, as well as in New Zealand, Australia, and some of the other territories in the region which the proposed university was to serve, turned in favour of providing higher education in this area. Some of the educationists from the Colonial Office were also keenly interested and I would like to record my appreciation to Miss G. William and Sir Christopher Cox[17] for the interest they took in the formulation of these proposals. A lot of spade work had to be done locally and I would like to record my appreciation for the time and energy that Mr. Gordon Rodger[18] put into this work. That was not enough. We needed the assistance of a Commission consisting of people who had experience of establishing and running universities, and to mount such a Mission was not an easy task. Luckily the Overseas Ministry of Development came to our help through the kind offices of Sir Christopher Cox, and it resulted in the appointment of the Morris Mission for Higher Education.[19] The offer of this Morris Report is one of the subject matters of today's debate.

A lot of work had to be done in neighbouring territories. A lot of work had to be done in New Zealand and in Australia, and I would like to put on record the work done by Mr. Ken Bain who was the Secretary for Social Services when I was the Member for Social Services. We received some encouragement and help from certain organizations and one of those organizations was UNESCO. At their Paris Conference, they evinced interest in the establishment of a university in this region. We also found a keen supporter in Dr. Henrickson, who was the Vice Chancellor of the Hawaii University. When the New Zealand Government announced its intention to vacate the Laucala Bay base, we had another problem to face locally, as there were competing claims from various Government departments and also from some outside bodies for the use of this base. That also required some manoeuvring and persuasion which resulted in the decision that the Laucala Bay base should be utilised for the establishment of this university. I would like to take this opportunity to express my sympathies to all those departments and to those concerned for their disappointment.

But this is a cause which will serve all departments and all concerned equally and will benefit the future generations of Fiji. As regards the use of our Laucala

17 Taught at New College, Oxford, after being the Director of Education in British Sudan in the 1930s, and described 'as an imperial patrician of a different kind.' He served as the Education Advisor to the Secretary of State for the Colonies in the late 1950s and early 1960s.
18 A product of Repton and Pembroke College, Cambridge, he served as an Education Officer in the Gold Coast before moving to Fiji in 1953 where he served as the Director of Education for more than a decade before retiring to New Zealand.
19 Sir Charles Morris KCMG, Vice-Chairman of the Inter-University Council for Higher Education Overseas; former Vice Chancellor of Leeds University.

Bay base I must record appreciation of Mr. Cox who recommended that this base should be utilised for the establishment of a college to train teachers who would be competent to teach up to Form IV. All this provided us with a sort of a 'jumping off' towards the proposal of the establishment of fully-fledged university. The Morris Mission visited Fiji, visited other territories in this region, and also Australia and New Zealand. The United Kingdom Government as well as this Government tried, and used their best endeavour, to get metropolitan countries interested in this region to come and join us in this venture. We were disappointed in France, because the French want to start their own university in New Caledonia. We found the support of New Zealand very, very encouraging because they came forward with this magnificent gift to start the University. We had high expectations from the Government of Australia but that Government was too much preoccupied with the establishment of a university in New Guinea[20] and we could not get the support that we expected from that Government.

After the Morris Mission wrote its report and published it, many people were converted to the idea of the establishment of a university in Fiji, people who were hostile to that proposal before. I must personally confess that when I read the Morris Report I found it very, very stimulating. Our next problem was where to get a man to take up the task of an academic planner and an administrative officer to assist him. Where would we get the funds to finance the visit of such a planner to this end. It was through the kind generosity of the Carnegie Foundation and through our good fortune in securing the services of such an able and experienced Vice Chancellor as Sir Norman Alexander who happened to have the experience of establishing universities in some other developing countries.[21]

From work carried out by Sir Norman Alexander in conjunction with Mr. Reid Cowell, we got the benefit of this other report. I would like to lay stress that this is not the work of one individual, this has not been accomplished overnight, and it would be silly and ridiculous for anybody or any person to try to take credit for that. It is a joint venture and it will have to be seen through jointly. It is no use talking about the Alliance Government supporting this proposal for the establishment of a university which will serve the South Pacific region. It is the Government of Fiji, whatever party may be in power, who will be behind this project, and let not a misimpression be created outside that this is a Party measure with Party effort, because it is not. We are all equally interested and I more so than many others because I have done some pioneering work in this.

---

20 The University of Papua New Guinea in Port Moresby opened in 1966, two years before the opening of the University of the South Pacific in Suva.
21 (1907-1997), was instrumental in establishing many universities in the Commonwealth, including Ahamdu Bello University in Nigeria, the Universities of West Indies, Botswana, Lesotho and Swaziland.

Now let me come to the appraisal of these two reports. The proposals contained in the Morris Report are described as unorthodox, and unorthodox they are in many respects. First, the choice of the subjects to be taught and the constitution of a university with a provision for associated institutes with a provision for conferring degrees as well as diplomas and certificates, following the lines of a comprehensive school, making it possible for students, who after taking degree courses, may not find themselves competent enough to finish their studies enabling them to switch off to diploma courses, students who have taken diploma courses to find that they are quite competent to tackle degree courses making it easy for them to transfer to degree courses. This is something that is new.

Another unique feature of this university is that it is a regional university. Many territorial governments and metropolitan governments are interested in that university; and the University Council which is recommended to be set up under the report has a very wide representation which, as far as I am aware, no existing university in the world enjoys. We have the territorial representatives who are members to be appointed by the Governor of Fiji after consulting the Executive Council; we have got provision for other members to be appointed from other territories which this university will serve. But the most outstanding feature is the representation of academicians from various universities, not only in the Commonwealth but universities even outside the Commonwealth. There will be one member appointed on this Council by the United Kingdom universities, one member to be appointed by the Hawaii University, one by New Zealand universities, one by Australian universities, and the University Council will be the sovereign, governing body of this institution, which means that we will have the benefit of the cooperation of outstanding universities of the world, cooperation of great powers and cooperation of emerging governments in this region. That is a unique feature in itself and as various territories in this part of the world attain full status of sovereign government, this university will become an international university. All the existing universities belong to one nation or another. This will be an enterprise of the United Nations of the South Pacific, I hope, not in the too distant future.

Again there is a provision for the court [Court of Convocation] which secures even wider representation, in which even professions, commerce, industry, teachers, groups of primary school teachers and secondary school teachers, all will find a place and they are supposed to meet at least once every two years. They will be receiving the report from the University Council and they will be passing resolutions which they can refer to the University Council for consideration.

As far as the curriculum is concerned, the syllabus, we have to bear in mind that all great institutions have a very small beginning, and by comparison with some of the great educational institutions of international renown, the beginning that the university will be making will be a fairly good one with better financial support than many of those universities had when they started. The report compares the proposals of this university with the land grant colleges and land grant universities in the United States of America, and we must remember that if a land grant university in America can reach the international status which is accepted all over the world as one of the best universities in the world, the M.I.T. (Massachusetts Institute of Technology), if our university, in the course of time, makes progress, there is no reason to doubt that this university has also got a very, very brilliant future before it. We have got one very good advantage in this part of the world to attract good staff for the university, which many other countries do not possess because most of these countries have already been covered by research workers in all fields, and there is very little scope left for new and fresh research. This area is still untapped and many professors would like to come to this new university just because they would like to carry out the research work in their own sphere in the South:Pacific region. That in itself is an attraction for a good and competent teaching staff for the University. We have also got a very encouraging assurance from the United Kingdom Government that the additional expenditure involved in the expatriate staff, will be to a certain extent met by the United Kingdom. That makes our financial burden for the current expenditure light.

Another feature is that as the university progresses both in its standards and in its activities, more help will be coming from outside areas, from other governments, or from other foundations in countries like the United States of America. The syllabus that the report recommends is of practical value and importance to this region. It is geared to the needs of developing countries in this area to help them both in social and economic development and the recommendation that a university should always keep itself a jump ahead will ensure that these territories will be able to meet the informed and trained manpower which it will require for its development without having to resort to the employment of expensive expatriate officers. It will also broaden the scope for children of poorer parents who will be able to receive their education, economically in their own country, as far as Fiji is concerned.

And what is more, if the university be expanded and other subjects are introduced later on, if the associated institutes are enlarged both in the intake of the students and in the courses of study that they provide, there is no reason why within a short time, this university should not have adequate provision for degrees in medicine, degrees in engineering, degrees in agriculture. While the Morris Mission was working here I discerned a streak of disinclination on the part of some government departments to surrender the control of the institutes which are at present in their hands, and I suspect that probably that is the reason why Sir Norman Alexander had such an extraordinary and startling recommendation to make in his report which, I must confess, came as a shock to me, and that is on page 6. After discussing the desirability of complete autonomy for the University, he went further to modify it in this respect:

> It must be kept constantly aware of changing needs, and be ready to meet them. If it is in fact fully alive it will anticipate these needs, and keep itself one jump ahead. This contact does *not* mean a loss of autonomy, in fact it is its best safeguard. If the Governments are fully aware of what the university is doing, and if the university shows that it is doing its best to meet the needs of its area, then it has the best chance of keeping its essential freedoms. Academic freedom is not a prescriptive right; it must be earned. If a university is not fully alive to its social responsibilities, and active in meeting them, it deserves a sharp reminder of its duties.

Now, even if the learned author had stopped there, it would not have mattered so much. But he went further to say:

> The mechanism by which this contact with Governments is achieved is through the membership of the University Council and its committees. These could and should include Government officers and others able to speak with authority, though to avoid giving a wrong impression overseas such members might be appointed by name and not *ex officio*.

I thought there is something [called] academic integrity. If a university does not respect truth, who will? How can we expect any university to camouflage authority in the guise of autonomy and to fool the world, and throw dirt in the eyes of other countries, to recommend that instead of these persons being appointed ex officio and describing their office as such, that they should be kept out of the knowledge of the world by just mentioning them by their names. This is rather a feature of the report which I find grating on my nerves and something that seriously detracts from the value of the recommendations which the Morris Report made; this University Council, which will be autonomous, which will be outside of political influences. Even the Member for Social Services [Vijay R Singh] mentioned the desirability of keeping this university out of political influences; even the Report mentions what harmful consequences some universities had in some African territories.

Now this paragraph defeats the very purpose. It seeks to certainly introduce political influences of the political party in power at the time, to dominate the university, and that ought not be allowed to happen. This university must have its academic freedom and academic integrity reserved. It is essential for any university and men working in any university to have open, unbiased minds, who can teach and reason objectively and who are dedicated to the discovery of truth, and imparting that truth which they and other people in this world in other universities both at present and in the past have discovered to the students who come there. That is the most important thing, and I hope that that will be borne in mind when the University Council is established.

Let me remind the Member for Social Services [Vijay R Singh] that so far, all that he had to do was to make a simultaneous announcement and to bring this motion before the Council. But let me remind this House that the real task begins now. The test is how quickly the Interim Council is appointed and how competent that council is to prepare the development plan for this university; how quickly the legislation is drafted and approved by all the territories concerned and passed in this Legislature; how quickly the Vice-Chancellor is appointed and the professor to assist him, and the Registrar to be elected to office; how quickly the present existing buildings at Laucala Bay are converted for the purpose of the university, and how quickly the teaching staff is employed and students admitted, because the aim and the recommendation of both these reports is that the university must start teaching n the year 1968, in the Secondary Teachers' College as well as some of the other Degree courses.

That will be the ordeal and the test for this Alliance Government, and I hope and trust that they will succeed in this task and commence teaching in the year 1968. When that is accomplished we will accept the boasts and bragging of the Alliance Party, and I for one will take my hat off in admiration and respect. But it is useless to prance about in borrowed feathers, feathers that really belong to other people. Before I sit down I wish to recall the great interest and trouble that our present Governor, Sir Derek Jakeway, has taken. Without his deep interest and serious support probably the Member opposite would not have been in a position to put this motion before this House. I am quite confident that circumstances are favourable. If the Government goes the right way about it, support will readily come from very many directions, and this institution will serve the economic and social needs of this area, which it so badly requires.[22]

119: A Common Name, 1 August 1967, Interpretation Bill[23]

The Fijian under this definition does not connote the original inhabitants of Fiji. It is not an ethnic description of the Fijian people. It is widened to include

---

22   Betty Aikman, wife of the founding Vice Chancellor of the University of the South Pacific wrote to Leela Patel on 8 October 1969: 'My husband always feels that Mr Patel's farsightedness has much to do with the establishment of a university in Fiji, and for this reason he is grateful.'
23   In the electoral provisions of the 1965 constitution, all the Pacific Islanders living in Fiji were put on the Fijian roll, which is what is being alluded to here.

people of other races who originally migrated from islands of the South Pacific. The Banaban is very much a Fijian under this definition as an original inhabitant of Fiji, so is a Rotuman, so is a Samoan, Tongan, Gilbertese, Ellice Islanders, New Hebridean; so it is not a question of whether the word 'Fijian' designates any particular member of a particular race. It is a political designation given to a part of the Fiji population. Now, that creates a serious complication in my mind. If merely a section of the population is to be described as Fijians, how are all inhabitants of this country, as a nation, to be described? Whatever race a person belongs to, an inhabitant of New Zealand is called a New Zealander, whatever his race an inhabitant of Australia is called an Australian; and of Great Britain, Briton. There are so many races in India but anybody belonging to India, or is an inhabitant of India, is called an Indian. How shall all the inhabitants of Fiji be described? I think it is high time now that the word 'Fijian' is kept for the inhabitants of Fiji irrespective of their race. If the original inhabitants of Fiji want to have a separate designation, I believe Fijian is not their original designation but their original designation, as they themselves described in their language, is *taukei* with pride. I would have thought that *taukei* would have been more appropriate for the Fijians as an ethnic group than calling them Fijians and including them with a number of other immigrant races who have come and settled in Fiji, debarring the Chinese, Europeans and ourselves. There is a danger in this: once people get accustomed to the use of the word 'Fijian' as applied to certain races inhabiting Fiji, it psychologically comes in the way of nation-building of this country.

NB: Jonate Mavoa's retort captured the spirit of the opposition to Patel's view: 'Although we think this is a desirable thing we cannot just do it by a stroke of a pen, by legislation, because you cannot force people to be called by a name they do not want to be called by.' 'There are many things in this world that we would like to have but we also see that there are a few things which can be put into practice.'

120: Letter to Vasantika Patel from Ocean Island,[24] 1 November 1967

I am sitting on the bed in the backroom of a bungalow on the Ocean Island. The sea is roaring in the backyard a few yards away. It makes more noise than

---

24 Letters were Patel's preferred mode of communication with his children who were receiving their schooling in England, rather than the telephone. In them, he often remarked on political developments in Fiji. In a letter to his younger son Dhimant on 22 June 1969, he wrote: 'Britain is playing up by putting forward the excuse that independence can only be considered when all parties agree. This is a clever way of denying political freedom to Fiji and blame the Indians for it.'

sugar cane trains in Fiji! It is about half past eight in the morning but there is no breeze and it is very warm and sultry. I better switch the electric fan on before going further! Yes, it is better now!

We got on board at the Suva wharf at 2 p.m. but the boat did not leave till about 5. We had three very boring hours on the boat before we could settle down in our cabin. Komaiwai is by no means a luxury liner. It is a small ship with small narrow deck with very little room to move about or play. We reached Rabi at about one o'clock in the afternoon on the following day. All the Banabans boarded the ship—about sixty strong—with loads of beddings, pawpaws, bananas, mangoes, green coconuts, pandanus, fruits and what not. We left Rabi at 3 o'clock the same afternoon. The sea was fairly calm all the way. The boat was steady but your mummy was seasick throughout the voyage. My word, wasn't she glad to set her foot on Ocean Island on Sunday the 29th at about 10 o'clock in the morning. Your mummy saw some whales a little distance away from where Komaiwai was anchored. She tried to show them to me but by that time they disappeared. Anyhow we saw a seahorse. It is a small fish with a head something like that of a horse and a little weird in shape. It seemed to like our boat and kept on swimming near it quite a long time. Soon after landing, we went sight seeing in a bus. It is a small island about seven square miles in area with nice roads. We saw the ruins of the big house of the Resident Commissioner which was bombed by the Japanese.

Ocean Island is very rich in phosphate deposit. The total population is about 1900. Most of them are the employees of the [British Phosphate] Commission and their wives and children. The employees are looked after very well. They are given nice quarters free of rent, free electricity, free water, free medical treatment, free food and more than what they can eat(!), free education for the children, free bus service, and even taxes are paid by the Commission. On top of all these they are paid handsomely! There is no fresh water supply on this tiny island—there being no fresh water springs or rivers. The soil is very porous and the rainwater unless collected in tanks disappear quickly in the ground. You know, fresh water is imported from Australia. They maintain a regular supply. Every house is well equipped with large concrete tanks holding several thousand gallons of water and they replenish from the main tank which holds a million gallons of water. Just imagine. We are using Australian water on Ocean Island! Everything comes from Australia, including vegetables and fruits.

People are very sociable and cheerful, which is quite natural when they are so well looked after. Suva City Councillors should come and see this little Island and learn from the Commission how to pay and look after their labourers! Though grossly unfair to the Banabans who are the owners of the Island, the British Phosphate Commission is more than fair to its employees. It is this inequity that Daddy is called upon to help and advise the Banabans to get redress.

Today is Diwali. Your mummy had made some basudi for lunch. I had a very strenuous walk in the hot sun inspecting some areas of land. So when I returned for lunch I was feeling more thirsty than hungry, and even after lunch and couple of bottles of water, I still fell thirsty. I feel I can drink gallons of water. It just shows how hot this Island is.

We shall stay here till next Monday. Then we go to Nauru. We intend to leave Nauru on Wednesday and hope to reach Fiji by following Tuesday. I wonder which of us will reach Fiji first—we or this letter? Hope you are having a happy Diwali. Best wishes for a happy and successful new year. I hope you are writing to Amita every few days so that she doesn't feel lonely.

Goodbye my dearest, with love

Yours Daddy.

121: Out of Many Races — One Nation, Nadi Jaycees, 1968

Mr National President, Ladies and Gentlemen, You will hardly realise how satisfied and happy I am with your official designation, that is, National President, because this implies at least that your organization accepts us all in Fiji as one nation, and our task therefore becomes so much the easier. I am wholeheartedly in agreement with your creed. But there is one thing which I am sorry to say that I can't see eye to eye with you: that is, you believe a man after forty becomes an exhausted rooster. I believe that life begins at forty. That is the only difference in outlook that we have got and I hope that you will excuse me for it.

The subject of today's address in any other country would appear as a sort of a platitude. For instance, if I was to take up this subject in a country such as the United States of America, or even the U.S.S.R., they would simply say, 'of course, all nations right throughout the world are made up of many races. Show me one country in the world where there is one pure race which exists today as a nation.'

But as far as Fiji goes, we are today standing at the cross-roads of history, and a subject which might happen to be a dead issue in other countries has become a very lively and burning topic of the day. If you look at history, man in his present image has existed for nearly a million years on this planet, and in the last few thousand years of his existence on this planet, he has created God in his own image. Now, man has come to believe that God has created all of us; that we are all his children; and therefore there is no difference between man and man. Mankind is but one family. All important religions of the world [teach this], and the very name given to our species on this globe, exemplifies it. For instance, those who believe in Semitic religions call man Aadmi—descendant of Aadam, now anglicised to Adam. Those who believe in the Aryan religion call him Manushya, Manu and Manav, sons or the descendant of Manu who is the first man according to Aryan beliefs, in the same way as Adam is the very first man according to Semitic beliefs.

It therefore becomes a very interesting question: how on earth we, who have been created by the same God, and we who have come from the same parents (because both Adam and Manu are said to have created a woman out of their body) have so much differences? One would have thought that if there is a common parentage there would not have been so much of difference, so much of trouble in human history in the name of race. Now when we talk of race, let's first make sure of what we believe in our own mind when we use the word 'Race'.

Mankind has been divided into what they call three large groups: Caucasoid, Mongoloid, and Negroid, and then all different types of men are made to fit into one compartment or the other according to the shape of the nose and their lips, the colour of their skin, the texture of their hair and its colour, according to what they call the cephalic index, and the shape and size of the skull. These are matters all related to the physiology of man and therefore when we talk of race we are dividing mankind into different groups, and different entities physiologically—it has nothing to do with the mind of man; it has nothing to do with the spirit of man.

Let's take the instance of what modern science has to say about it. Darwin first propounded this doctrine or theory of evolution, and, according to that, we at some stage came into existence on this globe due to some sort of mutation. We at present to do not know how many mutations took place, where they took place, when they took place. We do not know today whether mankind first originated in one particular place on this planet or simultaneously, or on different occasions in different centres in various continents of this world. Science is yet obscure because we do not have sufficient evidence.

But, whatever it is [whether human beings first evolved in Africa or Asia], the patent fact remains that through ages of interaction of climate and natural environment on human beings, we started evolving in different colours, and acquiring different features. In some places we have sharp pointed noses, in other places, we have broad and flat noses. In some places we have blond hair probably because of the lack of sunshine, in other places we have black hair because we have enough of sunshine and probably more than enough of it. In some places, we had coppery skin, and in other places yellow skin (there is no such thing as really white skin) and black or brownish. Somehow or the other, man who got so much enamoured of his own image, and gave the same image to his Creator, naturally was an egocentric being, and being an egocentric being, he first thought that his own image was the best in creation, and there all this trouble started.

We know differences between animals; we know that a black cow or a brown cow or a white cow will all mix together, and graze together, but the white cow will not think she is superior because her skin is white nor the black cow feel inferior because her skin is black. However, because of our egotism, we started making this distinction at a very early stage of our history and you find cases of what we call colour prejudice in the Vedas, and in Vedic times, where 'varuna' is a very important word. Varuna means colour. Even in those days, colour was so important especially to the Aryan conquerors that those who lived in India before them were looked upon as people of inferior stock because the colour of their skin was black. They called them un-Aryans, and if it was left at just that, nobody would have anything to complain of, because they were Aryans, and the others Un-Aryans, but they went to the extent of calling them Dasyus: those who we consider inferior to us in appearance are also believed to be inferior to us in morality. Colour somehow got mixed up with morality and one thought that one's own colour, if it was the best in the world, one's own morals or way of life must also be the best, and that is how the divisions started.

Probably these divisions would have remained confined to various areas where differences and the distinctions in the features took place, but by nature man is a migratory animal. He cannot stay still. He must wander not only in spirit but even physically. He is an eternal wanderer and he can never feel happy by staying at one place; he must go on moving; he must go on exploring, he must go on discovering. Now, we have reached the stage where we feel we have discovered everything worth discovering on this planet, and we have now started wandering into space.

Now that wanderer: naturally, when he moved into another wanderer's territory, created what we call in modern political terminology 'problems.' As an outsider, first, he was disliked and mistrusted, and there was resistance. In many cases he asserted his authority by conquering, and overpowering the people of the territory to which he went; in other countries he tried probably to insinuate his way and settle down there by pleasing them, by being friendly with them, by serving them. But that is how all these interminglings right throughout the world took place, and that is why when we talk of these three groups, we all have to agree that there is no such thing as pure Caucasian, or pure Mongolian, or pure Negro.

That is why we have to say caucasoid, mongoloid, and negroid, but, essentially it is all now a mixture, an intermingling of all races and features. In one man you might say that he has got a Caucasian nose, but if he comes from Assam, you might say the nose is Caucasian, but the eyes are Mongoloid—you might say of another man that he has a Caucasian chin or a Caucasian nose, but his lips are definitely Negroid. You might say of a man that all his features, except his hair, are Caucasoid, but his hair is definitely Negroid. So it is very difficult now to distinguish which human being belongs to which race. As a matter of fact, you might find various features in the same family—one brother might have a thick nose while another brother might have an aquiline nose like a Jew, a third brother might have thick or what we call sensuous lips, or a fourth brother might have a strong jawbone such as we associate with the Melanesians and the Polynesians. So in these days when we talk of race, it becomes more of a myth than a reality and in these days myths are more formidable and dangerous than realities can be.

And let us see what havoc these myths have created in history, but how, with all that havoc, it has nevertheless led to unity in many parts of the world. If we talk of the United Kingdom as a hotch-potch of races, probably people who call themselves English will raise their hands in protest, and say: what nonsense! But if they look at their own interesting history, they will find there have been waves of invasion. They now call themselves Britons but we ask where are those Britons? They were overpowered by their conquerors one after the other. Where are the Celts, the Gaels, the Angles and the Saxons? And in our own time, if you go to London, you will find that in a day's walk, every race on this planet is represented in London. You meet an Arab, you meet an Indian, you meet a Chinese, you meet all the various races of Europe, and still, if you tell them you are a multi-racial society, they raise their hands in horror and say 'no, we are not.'

Why? They have not confused the intellectual political concepts with physical features. Though there have been waves of invasion, one after the other, they were conquered even by the Romans, and later on, Germans came and ruled over them. Still, they all feel they are one people. They speak different languages. If you go to Wales, even on the railway stations, you will not be able to read the names of the place because they are written in the Welsh language. Sometimes the letters are so long that you start wondering what an effort it would be to pronounce the word, and then they say it and you simply stand surprised that all the length could not surely stand for such a short pronunciation.

They have realised what we call a common nation; in spite of all their differences they consider themselves inhabitants, and citizens of one country, with one problem, one cause. The most recent example of what they call multi-racial society, and the most outstanding example, is the United States of America, where all the races of the world are represented, where even the territories are far-flung, as far north to include the Eskimo, as far East to include the Polynesian. They all, in spite of all their racial differences, call themselves Americans. They say that they are a united nation of all races, or as President Kennedy said—a nation of immigrants. [In Australia, a man could not] speak a word of English, and the Customs people were having difficulty in finding someone who could speak Greek. Yet, he was an Australian. He became an Australian as soon as he set his foot on the continent. It wasn't the language; it wasn't even his domicile; it wasn't even his culture, but one thing: his consciousness, and the consciousness of the people amongst whom he came and decided to reside.

Let's come nearer home now: Fiji. What has happened? How did we all happen to come here? Those whom we call Fijians they also did not come here in one wave. Nor are we sure that they all came from one place. Nor can we definitely say that they all belong to one racial stock. There were waves of invasion; they came and settled here and these waves took place as has happened in other parts of the world, through so many causes: some through the outside pressures in their original homes; they were pressed out by an invading race; some because they drifted on the high seas of the Pacific; some because they were going out through a spirit of adventure looking for new lands, and a new home and over the centuries these people settled down and now they all believe they are one people, one race.

Later on, the Europeans came here. First, men who had drifted here from shipwrecks, men who deserted and came here, later followed by other people who came here to live and settle down—so much so, that by 1874 (the time of the Deed of Cession) there was quite a large European community settled in Fiji, large enough to give enough trouble and enough headache to King Cakobau and Cakobau felt that the safest and the best way to get out of this trouble was to hand over this country to the British Crown. Those of you who have read the history of Fiji would know his memorable utterances at the time when he ceded Fiji to Great Britain where he describes the local Europeans of the day as 'cormorants on the beach.'[25] That is how the Europeans' first settlement took place in Fiji. After this, the Government came here, then the administration, members of the administration, capital came and with it came the managerial staff, and the question of labour arose.

Before the Deed of Cession, those Europeans who came to Fiji resorted to what is called the practice of black birding, and the Governor of Fiji, Sir Arthur Gordon, in order to save the Fijians from the European settlers of those days, decided that indentured labourers should be brought from India. That is how the Indians came to Fiji, with the result that we had a stratification of Fijians already in Fiji, some of whom may have originally passed through India in course

---

25 Cakobau said, justifying cession, 'If matters remain as they are, Fiji will become a driftwood in the sea, and be picked up by the first passer-by...Of one thing I am assured, that if we do not cede Fiji, the white stalkers on the beach , the cormorants, will open their maws and swallow us.'

of their migration after generations. It is not a novel matter of theory: there are many anthropologists who hold that view that many of the Polynesians and Melanesians at some stage in their migrations may have passed through India, through Malaya and all these territories north of Australia and the East Indian islands to reach the South Pacific.

So it is a question of the time of migration: some came to Fiji early, while others came late, but let us face the hard fact: we are a nation of immigrants, in the words of President Kennedy. And the question now is that if we are a nation of immigrants—all of us—why is it that we do not recognise this fact and behave as a nation? History is responsible. Imperialism everywhere has been the greatest enemy and antagonist of nationalism. In every country which was under imperial rule, people were never described even as people, they were always described as peoples (in the plural). You go through the official documents of Fiji in the past, and you will find that officially we are referred to as peoples of Fiji communities, peoples, communities, never as people, never!

The same thing you find in other countries. In India, it was always peoples of India—even the British historians when they wrote India's history, it was always the peoples of India. Now we say people. So just now, there is a cross-current going one against the other. People who have awakened nationally and have national consciousness now realise that religion is immaterial, race is immaterial, even your way of life is immaterial. What is most important is a sense of political solidarity, a sense of unity, a sense of oneness. How can that come? Some people say that it is a very difficult process, that it is a time-consuming process, that you can't achieve it in a day, you can't achieve it in a decade, it must take a very long time, and you must start with your schools. Unless children of all races and religion attend the same school, you can't, they say, build a nation.

I agree to a certain extent that it [common background] helps in building a nation but it is not a sine qua non that children of all races and groups should go to the same schools to develop that sense, that consciousness of a nation because, in England if that was so, students who receive their education in public schools and the Universities of Oxford and Cambridge would be a class apart from the rest of the English people, an exclusive group, a snobbish group, who never even socially mix with others. I remember when I was at school there and I wanted to find out to what class an English girl who a friend of mine wanted to marry belonged, and my friends of whom I enquired said to me: 'Look, to be frank with you we would not shake hands with her, we would speak to her across the counter.' Now, did that prevent our friend who said that he would not shake hands with her but speak to her across the counter and this lady who served her across the counter from feeling that they are both one people, both are English and both are members of the one nation. No, it is a question, as I said, of consciousness, it is one of mental consciousness—it has nothing to do with the physical features. Mentally, it is a question of attitude, and it is a question of outlook.

We can go on attending the same school, the same university, but quarelling all the while, fighting all the while, calling each other all sorts of names—you are an Indian, you are an European, you are a Fijian, you are a Chinese. In spite of studying in one place, we can't even then achieve unity. So after all is said and done, it is a question of the mind, not a question of the colour. There is one sentence of the Bhagvad Gita which is very appropriate. The sentence says: 'All creatures are bewildered because knowledge is covered with ignorance. Remove the cover of ignorance, and knowledge shines.' It is the same thing with our nation, covered with the ignorance of racialism and sectarianism. Remove the cover, and the nation is there.

122: Bau—Renovation,[26] 13 December 1968

In view of the historical importance of the chiefly island of Bau, this Council suggests that the Government provide ways and means to start the renovation of the island and to preserve its historical relics and monuments. It is needless to say that every country cherishes and attaches a great deal of importance to its history, and Fiji is no exception. Unfortunately, the recorded history of Fiji is very, very short, in fact it is hardly more than two hundred years old. Before we lose the landmarks it is high time that the Government took some steps to preserve them.

Ratu Popi [Seniloli] was a friend of mine and at his invitation I visited Bau and spent three days with him as his guest, and I must say I have very happy memories of that island. The First Council of Chiefs member [Ratu George Cakobau] was a student at Waganui then, the Minister for Commerce and Industry [Ratu Edward Cakobau] was working in the Magistrate's Court in Suva. Ratu Popi showed me some very important relics and I am quite sure some of those would pass on as heirlooms of the family and, as far as they are concerned, I am quite confident that members of the House of Cakobau will be quite capable of looking after them. But, it would be, in my opinion, unfair to place the entire burden on the people of Bau to preserve the monuments and historical landmarks on that island, as well as undergo considerable expenditure to conserve the island from serious erosion.

---

26   This motion came after a highly charged by-election in 1968, when race riots were threatened. Sir Vijay R Singh told me that the Alliance Party was completely taken by surprise, 'flattened,' by Patel's motion, and how it helped in healing frayed relations in the Legislative Council.

I was reading a paper by Sir Ronald Garvey[27] which was read before the 'Fiji Society' on the chiefly island of Bau. After going through the very interesting history of that island, he came to the present state of that island, and when I read that part I personally was deeply moved. This is what the report says: 'His Excellency said that he had chosen his subject to emphasise the importance of Bau in the history of Fiji. Since he had been here as Governor, Bau had not been maintained in a satisfactory state of repair. The comparison of photographs taken in 1947 with those taken in 1952 were very depressing. In 1947 it was a spick and span island—and I can testify to that myself, it was so in the year 1933—the docks were well maintained but somehow since the 1950's the island had not been kept in a good state of repair. His Excellency said that he had been looking for suggestions on how to maintain it as he had got the impression that the island was going to slip back and become a mangrove swamp.'

If that is [not] the state of affairs, a responsible person like Governor Garvey would not have stated it in a very responsible paper read before a very responsible Society of eminent scholars of this country. If that is so, then I emphasise that it is not only the duty of the people of Bau but of the Government of this country to see that that island does not get into that state and, as I have mentioned before, it is the duty of this country to see that the historical relics and monuments on that island are preserved and passed on from generation to generation.

Those who have gone to Britain must have seen with what loving care and attachment the Government and people of Britain look upon and preserve such ancient relics of the days of heathenism—like the stone henge. It is not too late even now to preserve and protect the platform and site of the famous temples of this historic island, to take steps to preserve and protect places and buildings which are associated with King Cakobau and his ancestors.

According to Sir Ronald Garvey, the amount required does not appear to be very much. His Excellency said that he had thought of an idea which was probably a new one for Fiji, 'A Society of Friends of Bau'. The members of such a society would subscribe each year and provided the Society was large, the annual subscription would be small. The money would be used to maintain the island. When he had been thinking about this idea, His Excellency said that he had not quite realised that something new was happening at Bau. The present Vunivalu, Ratu George Cakobau, had been applying his mind and energies to the very problem that His Excellency had been concerned about for many years. Ratu George hoped to raise £2,000 to start the renovation of Bau. The most recent estimate that His Excellency had had was slightly over £5,000. However the Vunivalu had come home and he hoped to raise the money but there was still quite a large gap. His Excellency suggested that there might be some value in exploring his ideas. He did not himself wish to take the initiative.

---

27   Governor of Fiji, 1952–1958.

Now I say that the time has now come when the Government can take the initiative and serve posterity in keeping up, maintaining and preserving links with the past.

123: New Year's Greetings, 1969

As the Leader of the Opposition and President of the National Federation Party, I extend to each and all my best wishes for a very happy, peaceful and prosperous New Year. In many ways, the year 1969 is a year of great promise for mankind, Man has already circled around the moon at a close range, and it will not be long before man sets his foot on another world. It will be the greatest achievement in mankind's history.

This most wonderful achievement in science and technology remains sadly unmatched by wisdom in man's relations with his fellow men. The people of Vietnam, Nigeria, and the Middle East are subjected to destruction and privation before which the year's natural disasters, grave and tragic as they were, pale into insignificance. Let us all hope and pray that those who occupy seats of power will be blessed with wisdom and strive to bring about peace and brotherhood among men.

All men are brothers and all brothers should enjoy equal status, equal rights, equal responsibilities and equal opportunities to live and serve one another with equal dignity to promote wealth and prosperity for all. This is what the United Nations Charter of Fundamental Human Rights stands for. Let us hope that the words of the Charter will be translated into deed everywhere to the greater glory of man and his Creator.

On the domestic scene, the year 1969 is a year of great promise. This year, Fiji most likely will see most important political changes. If the people of Fiji are to live in unity and peace and prosper, it is most important that the political changes should, as clearly as possible, translate the fundamental human rights into a reality for all the people of this country regardless of race, religion, sex or origin. To bring about such a political change requires good will, courage and dedication on the part of all concerned. With the existing fund of good will and harmony, we can build a grand edifice fit for free men and women to live with dignity, peace and prosperity.

The economic amelioration of the people of this country, especially the cane farmers, will largely depend upon the contract they will be able to negotiate with the [Colonial Sugar Refining] Company. Let us hope and pray that the parties succeed in negotiating a contract which ensures a fair and just return to the farmers who are the economic back bone of this country. Let us hope that the structure of wages will also improve considerably, ensuring a higher standard of living to all concerned. Let us hope that the new year will bring increased health and wealth to each and all, here and everywhere.

Mere good wishes and hopes do not take us very far. We have to strive and work hard to realize our aspirations. We cannot improve our standard of living unless we share what we produce equitably. Even with the most equitable distribution, unless we produce more, we cannot have much to share. Our prosperity largely depends upon purposeful and tireless endeavour on the part of all. It is hard intelligent work accompanied by thrift which makes individuals as well nations prosperous. Let us not forget that our destiny is largely in our own hands. Let us bend to the task and direct our energies in the channels which will make Fiji a prosperous, strong and peaceful nation of free, happy and prosperous men and women.

124: Hail Deliverer[28]

There is already so much written and said about Gandhiji, and there will be so much more written and said in this hundredth year of his birth, that it appears naïve and presumptuous to add to this already existing plethora. It would be impossible to find another man in the history of mankind who has spoken, written and done as much as Gandhiji has done, dealing with all subjects and matters touching human life. It would be more appropriate to read what he has written and said (which is preserved for us by faithful devotees like Mahadev Desai and Pyrelal) and remind ourselves of the great message he has left for each and all of us rather than make a foolish attempt to show the sun with a candle.

And yet, I cannot resist the urge to pay my humble tribute to the Great Father who has guided my footsteps and saved me from many pitfalls in life. In spite of great strides which a portion of mankind has made in science and technology, in spite of man becoming a visitor of moons, in spite of some countries possessing the power to wipe out life from the planet, we are living essentially in the age of great pollution. The atmosphere is polluted by nuclear fallouts and poisonous discharges which engines and machines are emitting ceaselessly day and night on the land, on the seas and in the skies. Our air is polluted, our waters are polluted and so is our land and what grows on it. The machine has become the master and man its slave. Though that champion unscrupulous master of psychological warfare, Dr Goebbels, perished towards the end of the Second World War, his spiritual children have sprung up all over the world, thicker and more prolific than nut grass, who are polluting all media of mass communication

---

28   Written very shortly before his death on 1 October 1969.

with half truths and downright lies, vitiating the minds of the trusting and the gullible, so much so that trust which was a commendable virtue once upon a time, has now become a dangerous weakness. We drink and wash in polluted water, we breathe polluted air, we eat polluted food, our minds, our emotions and our spiritual life are polluted daily in the name of news, information, knowledge and religion. In this age of physical, mental, moral and spiritual pollution, Gandhiji lived as an embodiment of physical, mental, moral and spiritual purity. He was the greatest purifier the world has known.

Apart form the Punjab, Bengal and Maharashtra which were led by Lal, Pal and Bal,[29] politics in the rest of India had more or less fallen in the hands of self-seeking, educated sycophants who called themselves moderates and who led their existence completely isolated from India's masses and whose political activity consisted mainly in holding meetings, passing resolutions, sending petitions and leading deputations. Gandhiji was already enshrined in the hearts of the teeming millions of Indians as a true friend of the poor and the downtrodden and as a man of God. He was a saint before he entered politics and his very presence, and the moral and spiritual means he employed to overthrow the biggest empire in history, sanctified politics which was, and still is, a dirty word in many parts of the world. He exhorted people to spin and weave their own cloth, and hand spun and hand woven khaddar which even a man like Jawaharlal Nehru initially described as a 'livery' of freedom, became a symbol of moral purity, sacrifice and selfless service. It was the passing of the odious and oppressive Rowlett Act[30] which brought Gandhiji into Indian politics. His first step was to declare a India-wide hartal (strike). He urged that the day should be a day of fasting and prayer. This was to be followed by a Satyagraha Campaign but the mob violence in Chauri Chaura, which had nothing to do with Gandhiji, or his Satyagraha Campaign, made him change his mind at the last minute because he thought the people of

India were not ready for it.

Gandhiji called Satyagraha pledge an attempt to introduce the religious spirit into politics. We may no longer believe in the doctrine of 'tit for tat', we may not meet hatred with hatred, violence with violence, evil with evil; but we have to make a continuous and persistent effort to return good for evil. The Satyagraha Campaign constituted an attempt to revolutionise politics and restore moral force to its original station. By resorting to non-cooperation, the spinning wheel and the salt Satyagraha, he made India free in 1930. Not all the King-emperor's horses nor all the King-emperor's men could bring unarmed Indians to their

29   The reference here is to Indian nationalist leaders Lala Lajpat Rai, Bal Gangadhar Tilak and Bipin Chandra Pal.
30   An act passed on the recommendation of the Rowlatt Commission in March 1919 indefinitely extending emergency powers during World War I to control public unrest and conspiracy.

knees. The pure weapon of non-cooperation and Satyagraha made the British raj powerless and India invincible. He purified politics by non-cooperation and Satyagraha, he purified religion by wiping out untouchability and breaking down barriers of caste. He purified individuals by placing before them his own example of simple living and high thinking and selfless service. There was no aspect of life which Gandhiji did not touch and by his very touch purified and sanctified it.

Gandhiji began his political career as the leader of the opposition to the British Raj though he never sat as a member of any legislature or parliament, and he continued as the leader of the opposition even after India became free and his own disciples became the rulers of India. He criticized the extravagance of the Nehru government and kept on reminding him that a poor country like India could ill-afford the pomp and ceremony which was continued after India's independence. He even criticized the expensive quality of stationery used by ministers. It is one of the great ironies of life that a few weeks before his assassination, he had to resort to fasting against his own followers including Nehru and Sardar Patel.[31] It is equally an irony of life that a man who was revered and worshipped by millions as an incarnation of God was killed by a Hindu. He lived and worked and sacrificed his life to bring about unity and peace. Partition of India made both communities mad and savage and both of them in the hour of savage madness turned on him. While Gandhiji was killed in New Delhi, his statue was being destroyed in Karachi.

Since his death Gandhiji has become an instrument of exploitation in the corridors of power, but he lives in the hearts of the oppressed and the downtrodden, giving them hope, inspiration and courage to face arrogant oppressive power with their knees unbended and their heads held high.

British Raj was destroyed in the early morning of April 1930 when Gandhiji bathed in the sea and picked a pinch of salt on the shore at Dandi. No wonder Mrs Sarojni Naidu, the great poetess, who was standing by his side cried out, 'Hail Deliverer!' The echo of these words will always reverberate through the corridors of history. Mankind will always remember him as the Great Purifier— the Great Deliverer.

Of all the lawyers who appeared before me, AD Patel was outstanding; intellectually the most brilliant, as a character the most honourable, and as an advocate the most persuasive. Quick in mind, fluent in speech, he stood out above all. He even outshone Mr. Brennan [former Chief Justice of Australia]. It was his persuasive advocacy that led me to my report which was in favour of the growers and against the millers.

---

31   Sirdar Patel, India's Deputy Prime Minister and Home Minister, whose hardline tactics brought the Indian princely states into the Indian Union.

www.ingramcontent.com/pod-product-compliance
Lightning Source LLC
Chambersburg PA
CBHW061237270326

41928CB00030B/3351